THE ENTITY LETTERS:

A Sociologist on the Trail of a Supernatural Mystery

James McClenon, Ph. D.

ANOMALIST BOOKS
*San Antonio * Charlottesville*

An Original Publication of ANOMALIST BOOKS

The Entity Letters: A Sociologist on the Trail of a Supernatural Mystery

Copyright © 2018 by James McClenon

ISBN: 978-1-938398-79-7

Cover images:
Floating pen by Honig/iStockphoto; Trees by Valeriy Andrushko/Unsplash

Book design by Seale Studios

For information about the publisher, go to AnomalistBooks.com, or write to:
Anomalist Books, 5150 Broadway #108, San Antonio, TX 78209

TABLE OF CONTENTS

PREFACE

The Entity Letters is a sociological study of the Society for Research on Rapport and Psychokinesis (SORRAT), a group that met regularly for over 50 years (1961-2015). SORRAT practiced table tipping, a type of séance in which participants sit around a table, place their hands on the table top, and believe that the table moves paranormally. SORRAT members reported witnessing anomalous table movement and levitations, spirit rapping, unexplained lights, psychokinesis within locked and sealed containers, and other paranormal phenomena including messages, called entity letters, allegedly written by discarnate spirits.

This book consists of three parts. Part 1 is the original manuscript, completed around 1988, describing SORRAT events that occurred between 1981 and 1983. The text includes my introduction to SORRAT, reports of paranormal claims, personal observations, and skeptic/believer controversies. Part 2 presents a history of SORRAT and an update of my interactions from 1983 to 2017, including additional paranormal claims and accusations of fraud. Part 3 contains a review of psychical research theories pertaining to SORRAT, a comparison of equivalent psychical research cases, and an evolutionary theory explaining anomalous experiences and shamanism. Appendix A provides comments from people familiar with SORRAT. Appendix B offers advice to those who wish to form a PK group. Appendix C provides a list of videos pertaining to this research project, available through *YouTube*.

A brief definition of key concepts and theories will help you interpret *The Entity Letters*. The parapsychological term psi refers to psychic phenomena, defined as events that cannot be explained by established scientific principles. Psi includes extrasensory perception (ESP) and psychokinesis (PK). ESP is defined as communication that occurs independently of known sensory processes. PK refers to the movement of physical objects without use of known physical means. Because SORRATs used group processes to generate PK experiences, I refer to SORRAT as a PK group.

CAST OF CHARACTERS

Society of Research on Rapport and Telekinesis (SORRAT)
John Thomas Richards
Elaine Richards
Ivan Richards
Steve Calvin
John Hunt
Vern Mottert
Alice Thompson
Joe
Lisa (seeking healing)

Researchers
William Edward Cox (magician, also in the SORRAT group)
James McClenon (also in the SORRAT group)
Peter Phillips
Mark Shafer
Michael McBeath
George Hansen
Marian Nester
John Beloff
Dennis Stillings

Psychokinetic Performers
The Entities (John King, John G. Neihardt, Black Elk, Three-Times-Three, Imperator Group, Jay, and others)
Steve Shaw
Mike Edwards
Masuaki Kiyota

Magician and Skeptic
James Randi

PART 1: THE ENTITY LETTERS
(ORIGINAL MANUSCRIPT: 1970-1983)

CHAPTER 1
BEGINNING AT THE EDGE

I had a bad year in Vietnam. America sent us to fight a war we didn't understand. In 1970 and 1971, I was in the U.S. Army, an advisor to various South Vietnamese combat engineer battalions. We built dirt roads.

Soldiers on both sides were shot and blown up. The Viet Cong wanted to stop us. They buried land mines in the roads. Peasants stepped on the land mines and their feet were blown off. Children were crippled and killed by shells. For me, the war had little meaning. The Viet Cong could not stop us from building the roads, but the monsoon rains could. The roads turned to mud. I tried to reason it out as I watched the rain fall. Why did America send us? Why did we go?[1]

After I got out of the army, I spoke with a history professor. "Do you think America learned anything from fighting in Vietnam?" I asked.

He thought awhile. "Americans periodically get involved in wars," he told me. "The outcome of a war is not certain at its beginning. History demonstrates that we tend to forget the lessons learned in war. Then we get involved in another war. It happens every generation."

His answer disturbed me. He suggested that the Vietnam War was meaningless, and I couldn't argue with his conclusion. I decided to travel slowly east to Katmandu, Nepal. I can't explain why I chose to go there. I heard that it was a good place to meditate, and I needed inner peace. Veterans may understand why I went.

As I traveled, I talked with people in the countries I visited. I spoke with Brits, Germans, French, Swiss, Italians, Croatians, Serbs, Greeks, Bulgarians, Turks, Iranians, Afghanis, Pakistanis, and Indians. I learned that people everywhere fight with their neighbors rather than care about them. Normal people kill about a million of their fellow men each year. Normal people may blow up the world.

I learned about different religions. All religions tell people to get along with one another, but peace and harmony do not follow. Some religions emphasize mental quietness and deep relaxation. Hindus and Buddhists meditate. Muslims bow rhythmically as they chant their prayers. Christians and Jews close their eyes and bend their heads while praying. They use a kind of self-hypnosis to reach stillness of mind.

I could not wipe out my memories of Vietnam, but I wanted to learn how to achieve a mental calmness. I began meditating daily as I traveled overland toward Katmandu.

In India, I spoke to fellow travelers during the long evenings. We discussed life, travel, religion, meditation, love, everything. A man in India suggested, "You should seek out a guru and surrender your will to him."

"I'm a very independent person," I replied. "What could I learn from a guru that I couldn't learn from a book?"

"A great deal," he said. "You would learn without the words. Words are not necessary. Your reasoning is not getting you anywhere. Your thoughts are merely the dreams of the Lord Shiva, the god of heaven and earth."

I knew nothing of Shiva in those days. It seemed like a strange thing to believe. I thought about what a person might learn from a guru without words. Maybe my Indian friend was talking about *extrasensory perception* (ESP). I did not believe in ESP. I spoke with other Indians. Their religion included belief in phenomena they called *siddhis*. Siddhis are paranormal or magical powers.

In India, I was surrounded by a vast sea of belief, but it was not tangible for me. As a scientifically trained American, I required evidence. The stories I heard were folklore and mythology, not scientific evidence.

In Katmandu, I listened to the rain at night. In its steady patter, it seemed to have a voice of its own. I thought about Vietnam.

"This is the voice of Shiva, a voice that does not use words," I told myself. "I might be learning something without knowing it."

My odyssey was not over. I left Nepal, returned to India and continued traveling east. I had not thought about it when I left, but my constant trek eastward eventually took me back to where I started. In the fall of 1976, I enrolled in graduate school at the University of Maryland. My travels had helped me come to terms with Vietnam.

My sociological studies were not concerned with peace or religion. Sociologists talk about income inequality and social status. There was no talk about inner peace. One wintry afternoon, I sat at a desk in the library and daydreamed about Asia. It was a cold, wet day, and the rain was beating against a window. I remembered the sound of the rain falling during the Nepali monsoon and what my Indian friend had told me. I thought about ESP. I wondered why anyone would accept such a foolish notion, although I knew that millions of people around the world believed in stuff like that.

I pushed the article I was reading aside. "I must stop being normal for one afternoon," I told myself. I looked up the words "extrasensory perception" in the subject index of the library's card catalogue. There were many books on the topic. There was even a journal, the *Journal of Parapsychology*. I spent that afternoon, and the next day, reading recent volumes of the journal. I learned that certain altered states of consciousness, such as meditative states, seemed to facilitate ESP.

The idea seemed preposterous. If it were true, legitimate scientists should have verified it long ago, I thought. Did meditation enhance ESP? I decided to test this hypothesis scientifically.

I ran an advertisement in the student newspaper asking students who were interested in meditation and psychic phenomena to contact me. Five responded and, at our first meeting, I led the group through a deep relaxation exercise. I asked them to imagine that they could see into the future. I asked them to imagine my tossing a coin three times and told them to note each time whether it came up heads or tails. Then I had them open their eyes and write down their predictions on cards that I collected. Before looking at their guesses, I tossed a coin three times.

We performed this experiment once a week, and I statistically evaluated their ability to accurately predict the outcome of the coin tosses. After six weeks, there was less than a one out of twenty chance that they could have guessed all the coin tosses accurately through luck. One physics student had been correct in 15 out of 18 guesses.

She was afraid. "I don't want to continue with this experiment," she told me. "I don't believe in ESP. If it were real, they would have told me about it in my classes."

I wondered what had happened. I had tested only five students, yet one had achieved a remarkable score that should occur fewer than four times in 1000 (p<0.0038). I should have had to test hundreds of students before a score like 15 out of 18 would occur by chance. Perhaps I had not conducted the experiment correctly? There had to be an explanation.[2]

I described my experiment to one of my sociology professors. He had written many books and was internationally renowned.

"I have no opinion," he said firmly. "Only a true believer could accept this type of outcome." He seemed irritated. Was he afraid that ESP might be real? Why should such an eminent scholar be afraid of an ESP study?

A week later, I drove to the Foundation for Research on the Nature of Man (FRNM) at Duke University in Durham, North Carolina. This institute, founded by Dr. J. B. Rhine, [and later renamed the Rhine Research Center] was devoted to studying ESP, the ability to perceive information without using the five senses, and psychokinesis (PK), the ability to affect outer reality with one's mind. I described my experiment to one of the researchers and asked him if I had conducted it correctly.

"Not completely," he said. "You need to set a number of trials before you begin collecting data. You also need a better system for generating random targets. You can't be sure your coin tossing was truly random. Since all your subjects guessed at the same target, you may have what we call the 'stacking effect.' The subjects might have given responses that were biased in the same direction as the target series. You would have to conduct a far more carefully designed experiment for it to be considered valid."

He was far more cautious than I had expected. Rather than finding a true believer, glad to accept any evidence as valid, I found a scientist who observed that my experiment required better controls.

I looked at books in the FRNM library and found articles that concluded that psi (the term for ESP and PK) had been demonstrated scientifically but that it was difficult to repeat the effect consistently. I saw books critical of the field. They said that the successful parapsychological experiments were flawed. I decided to continue my research into psi and the conflicting opinions surrounding it. I ended up writing my dissertation on this topic.

In the summer of 1979, I traveled around the country interviewing parapsychologists. My doctoral dissertation was based on my sociological investigation into the interactions between parapsychologists and mainstream scientists. Because of these interactions, the parapsychologists had developed special methods for precluding fraud and error. One method seemed particularly valid. Researchers electronically recorded all ESP guesses, using machines that randomly selected targets. This technique prevented both recording errors and subjects' cheating. The machines statistically calculated subjects' guesses to determine the probability that psi occurred.

I decided to keep a careful record of my own score whenever I tested myself on such a machine. This way, I could determine whether psi was real for me. After a few months of testing, I calculated that the chance of achieving my score through luck was less than 1 in 20. That was almost as improbable as tossing a coin four times and getting all heads; unlikely, but not impossible.

In August 1979, I attended the Parapsychological Association meeting at

Moraga, California. I had just completed a week of intensive hiking and meditation, and my mind felt clear. At a workshop on parapsychological computer applications, a computer terminal had been set up with a psi game program. The idea was to get the little racing car pictured on the screen to win its race with the other cars. A random number generator, built into the machine, determined the speed of my car. The goal was to affect the random number generator through PK to make my car go faster than the others, all of which would move based on random numbers. The computer would statistically evaluate the performance of the car after the race was complete.

I pushed a button to begin the race. My car traveled very slowly. Finally, it finished, losing the race, and the computer evaluated my psychokinetic performance. I scored very badly. I tried again. This time my car was even slower! I tried to focus my energy on speeding it up. During the third race, my car just crept along. I laughed to myself. Maybe it has a flat tire! Maybe the engine has thrown a rod! The computer finally evaluated my finish. My result was terrible! I tried again. Still, no luck. The car came in last again.

"I need a new car," I remarked, and left the room.

When I returned, a parapsychologist was holding a computer printout and calling, "Who produced this result? Who was playing at this terminal?"

At first, I did not understand what the commotion was all about. Then I became nervous. Did I break the terminal?

"Who was using this terminal?" the parapsychologist asked again, more sharply.

"He did it," someone said, pointing at me.

"I was playing with it for a while," I said meekly.

"Look at this," the parapsychologist said. "The probability of producing this result by chance is less than one in a million! It's in the negative direction, though. You were psi-missing."

"Is there something wrong with the machine?" another parapsychologist asked. "This result is astonishing. It seems impossible!"

The first parapsychologist looked at the computer printout closely. "All the other results are in order." He then ran an experiment on himself. "The system is working properly," he said. He ran another experiment; the program was functioning normally. "There's no reason to disbelieve the previous results. Your results were negative, so strongly negative that it is unlikely to have occurred by chance. It's an example of psi missing. You produced a result that deviates negatively from the normal random effect."

I was astonished. What did this mean? If I were to include these results with my previous trials, I would have to tell people that my personal belief, based on my experimentation, was that the probability of psi existing was better than a million to one. Who would believe me? I did not believe it myself. Even if I never produced another example of psi, I would have to tell people that my personal psi score could not have occurred by chance, that its unlikelihood was greater than a thousand to one. My research had taken a bizarre turn.

"How does it feel to be a psychic?" someone asked me.

"I don't know," I replied. "I'm not sure that I believe in it."

"That explains your result," he stated. "Perhaps subconsciously you wished to show that psi doesn't occur, and you psychically overdid it."

"I still don't believe," I laughed.

Later I spoke with a skeptical parapsychologist. "Sometimes machines fail temporarily," he explained. "They develop electronic glitches—unexplained equipment failures. Then they recover without explanation. A result like yours could be explained in this manner. It isn't at all certain that you produced the result through psychic ability. Of course, your PK could have caused the glitch. Some people argue along those lines, but no one can say for sure."

My hope of basing my belief on a logical process had been thwarted. It seemed more rational to believe that an electronic glitch had produced my result than to believe that I was a powerful psychic. My plan of recording each experimental result was ruined. I could not throw out the results of a trial just because I did not like the conclusions.[3] Believers tend to accept results that prove psi, while skeptics regard experiments valid only if no psi is found.[4]

I noted that laboratory experiments lacked meaning. Even if I believed that I had psychically slowed my racing car's progress, the event had no significance. It was only a statistical effect. It had nothing to do with real life. But, in real life, decisions about validity are also difficult. We have no way to determine, with certainty, which experiences are valid and which should be ignored.

In September 1979, the Psychical Research Foundation requested that I investigate some "disturbances" happening to a family in Baltimore. The trouble included unexplained lights, noises, shaking beds, and strange sensations on the face and ankles of family members. I was intrigued. I telephoned the family and arranged an interview. They seemed normal enough people, but their experiences were anything but normal. They told me story after story about apparitions, peculiar lights, nightmares, and a strange kind of paralysis. They had heard unexplained moans, music, chanting, drums, and banging sounds. Sometimes beds would shake in an inexplicable manner. On occasion, two family members had simultaneous experiences, confirming each other's perceptions. Even the skeptic in the family could not explain what was happening.

"You can't imagine how terrifying all this has been," one daughter said. "We didn't know where to turn. My father had two ministers here to pray, but it didn't help. I never thought things like this happened. I thought they only happened in haunted castles in medieval times."

The family seemed quite sane. They opened their house to me. I spent one night in the room that was considered most haunted. A son and daughter, both in their thirties, stayed up with me until we all fell asleep. At around 3 a.m., I woke to see an unusual light on the wall. It flickered slightly and coincided with a rapping sound. I could not determine the origin of the light. The son called out in his sleep. He got up and the light disappeared.

"I was having a nightmare," he later explained. "In my dream, the entity was talking to me. It said that it wanted you out of that bed. It wants you to leave the house."

I went back to sleep, but early in the morning, the bed I was sleeping on began shaking mysteriously. I felt a sensation in my chest and my heart was pounding. I checked my pulse because I wanted to determine if my heartbeat might be causing the bed to shake, although that seemed implausible. I found that the bed was vibrating at a different rate from my heartbeat. After a while, perhaps 30 seconds, the bed stopped shaking. I could not explain it.

The Baltimore case became a turning point in my parapsychological research. I began to focus on hauntings and poltergeists. I monitored the frequency of phenomena in each case and kept investigating as long as the case was active. I visited the Baltimore family periodically for three years without finding an explanation for their experiences. I could never be certain that my experiences were not the result of fraud, but unlike laboratory experiments, these episodes affected my belief. My experience made me curious—but I can't say that I became an actual believer. I was a skeptic who began doubting my own skepticism.[5]

I read about other haunting investigations and was surprised to find that hauntings were not as unusual as I had assumed. There were records of appearances of the dead down through the ages (Finucane, 1984). A British survey in 1890 found that 10 percent of those responding had sighted an apparition (Sidgwick and Committee, 1894). Parapsychologist John Palmer (1979) reported that seven percent of a random sample of Charlottesville, Virginia, residents felt that they had lived in a haunted house. Pollster George Gallup (1979) reported that 10 percent of a random sample of the American public believed in ghosts in 1978. One study, published in 1975, surveying a randomly selected national sample of Americans, found that 27 percent felt that at one time or other they had "actually been in touch with someone who had died." In a follow-up study, published in 1987, 42 percent of the American sample claimed this experience (McCready and Greeley, 1976; Greeley, 1975; 1987).

Later, other cases came to my attention. I interviewed military policemen who had seen apparitions and had paranormal experiences while serving at their station. They saw a female ghost on the second floor of their headquarters, heard pounding sounds, and found the water faucets had mysterious turned on. I spoke with people in Virginia who reported visitations from a poltergeist (the word *poltergeist* can be translated from the German as *noisy spirit*.) Mirrors and glassware had cracked and broken inexplicably. In North Carolina, similar poltergeist problems were coupled with activity of a haunting. Strange backward writing appeared on their windows, and objects were transported about the house in an inexplicable manner.

Many of my observations fit the patterns that parapsychologists have noted in other cases. Hauntings include apparitional visits from the dead; poltergeists often involve objects moving inexplicably, with unexplained noises. Hauntings occur in a specific location or building, while poltergeists usually center about a person known as the agent (Gauld and Cornell, 1979; Roll, 1976, 1977). Some researchers theorize that poltergeists result from psychological tensions in an individual or group. The agents are unable to express their emotions in a normal way, causing the energy to express itself as a poltergeist. I found that it was unclear whether a case was a haunting or a poltergeist since the elements were often intermixed. In many cases, people assumed that the phenomena were caused by a spirit, but they had no information regarding the identity of that spirit. Information gained from a medium or psychic rarely agreed with information provided by another medium or psychic.

Although my investigations did not *prove* the existence of the paranormal, I came to understand why some people accepted occult phenomena as authentic. Certain people have a propensity for anomalous experience, and these people have many experiences. Such people develop an inner certainty and often acquire a reputation for having unusual experiences. Those around them also have had experiences.

I was at a party with Gary, Eppy, and Mark, who had invited me to visit them because they believed that their house was haunted.

"Tell Jim about what happened in the kitchen last week," Gary suggested to Mark.

Mark hesitated. "I'm not sure exactly what happened."

"We heard a loud explosion from inside the coffee can in the kitchen," said Gary. "Mark checked everywhere but couldn't explain it. That's what happened, didn't it, Mark?"

"Yeah, that's what happened," Mark agreed. "But I don't see that it proves anything. The unexplained is just unexplained."

"What about the misty images we saw?" Eppy interjected. "Don't you think it had something to do with Mary?" Mary, wife of the former owner of the house, had hanged herself in the house a few years before.

"It could be our imagination," Mark said.

"Did we imagine all those glasses breaking?" Gary said. "That's not something we imagined. It's a fact. You can't deny it."

"No, I can't deny it," Mark replied. "But I can't accept its significance as readily as you do."

I enjoyed talking with Gary, Eppy, and Mark, but I shared Mark's dilemma. I had considered the possibility they might be lying, but why would my new-found friends lie to me?[6]

I wrote a paper describing my Baltimore investigations and presented it at the Southeast Regional Parapsychological Association conference at Rollins College, Winter Park, Florida, in February 1980. The parapsychologists listened politely and seemed interested in my case. I carefully worded my description, using the words *alleged, ostensibly*, and *reportedly* with great frequency. Parapsychologists were very cautious and appreciated the guarded approach. They trusted laboratory methods, but tended to be suspicious of reports of spontaneous experiences.[7]

I recognized W. Edward Cox at the conference from the summer before when I had interviewed the FRNM parapsychologists. He had been involved with psychical research since 1933 and had written 48 articles on the subject. Cox met Dr. J. B. Rhine in 1935 and knew all the people who had worked at Rhine's center. Unlike most of those working with Dr. Rhine, Cox did field research. In 1950, he investigated a Missouri farmer's claims. The farmer's water barrel kept mysteriously filling with water. No matter how much water was taken out, the barrel would gradually fill back up. Cox spent nights watching it, hoping to find out what caused the effect but was not successful. Even though he maintained continuous observation, the water kept entering the barrel without human intervention—a paranormal phenomenon.

I had heard others talk about Cox. Some were concerned that his outspoken and abrupt manner harmed the professional image that parapsychologists desired. Cox was abrasive and irritable at times. It seemed to me that he had been affected by his personal experiences. He was absolutely convinced that PK was real, a conviction that gave him an air of certainty that others lacked.

I had watched Cox give a presentation at FRNM. He described constructing a "bubble machine" that produced random data by counting air bubbles rising to the surface of a water tank. He felt he had found a psychokinetic effect within the data that the bubble machine generated. Not only was the idea too far-fetched for me to accept, but the statistical analysis was unclear. Other parapsychologists laughed about Ed Cox and his bubble machine.

Cox approached me after I completed my haunting case presentation. He was wearing a plaid jacket and striped tie. He addressed me in his usual abrupt manner: "Do you know any other parapsychologists who are interested in macro-psychokinesis?"

I did not know what he meant by macro-psychokinesis and was concerned that he considered me a parapsychologist. I was a sociologist, a graduate student presenting a paper. I hadn't thought of myself as a parapsychologist. Because of my Baltimore case presentation, I wondered if people would label me a crackpot as they did Cox.

"I'm not sure what you mean by macro-psychokinesis," I replied.

As Cox smoked his pipe, I watched the smoke drift over his strong chin, wire-rimmed spectacles, and silver hair.

"Your haunting case is an example of macro PK. Things physically moved. Beds moved." He puffed his pipe, keeping his eyes on mine. "Raps were heard that required physical energy. That's macro-psychokinesis."

I looked uncomfortably at Cox. He expressed no doubts, no face-saving qualifications. I guess doubt is a luxury, I thought to myself. Doubt seems to function as a kind of protection, but with enough personal experience, we give it up. If I continued my field investigations, would I lose my doubt and become like Cox? I didn't know how to respond to Cox's question.

"Let me show you something," Cox said. His manner changed. Now he was my friend, a co-conspirator. "I can't show this to everyone. They wouldn't believe it. Come with me for a moment."

He led me away from the crowd. I looked around the room, hoping that no one saw me leaving with Cox.

"This is highly confidential," he warned me. "Please don't talk about this.

I'm still gathering evidence."

He flipped open a notebook full of Xeroxed pages. "This is a copy of an eight-millimeter film. Look, you can see each frame of the film. Here is an inverted aquarium that has been secured with a lock and seal onto a board with metal bands. We call it a mini-lab."

Cox puffed on his pipe and watched my eyes, observing my reaction. He seemed more visually oriented than most people. He placed a schematic diagram in front of me. Then he directed my attention to a set of frame-by-frame film images.

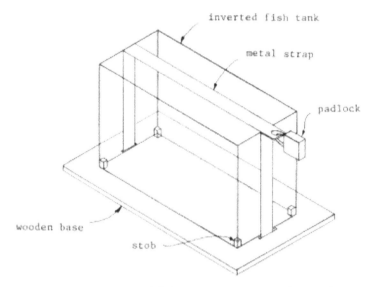

Figure 1: Typical Cox mini-lab (exact construction varied among boxes; Hansen, 1985: 18)

"See the pencil standing up in this first frame?" he asked. "It triggered a micro-switch that started the camera. Now in the next frame, you can see that it's writing. See, it's writing 'Rethink time.' And, now it falls back down to the bottom of the mini-lab in these final frames. Look at this one." He continued to flip through the pages.

I was bewildered. "What caused the pencil to write *rethink time?*" I asked.

He shook his head. "I don't know. I guess the powers on high, or whatever, want us to rethink time," he replied sarcastically. It was clear that he had doubts about the "powers on high." He was unconcerned with the message.

He pointed to the next page. "Now look at this. It should be impossible to link two leather rings without cutting one of them. Such a cut could be detected easily. Here you see two leather rings. They are rising in front of the mini-lab. Look! Here they link. They remain linked. And look, here they break apart; one falls to the table on the outside, and the other hangs on the edge of the aquarium. I have carefully examined these rings. They have not been cut. How can you explain this? Isn't this the best case of matter passing through matter that you have even seen?" he asked proudly.

I was puzzled; it seemed very complex. "Well, for one thing, I have never seen a case of matter passing through matter; this is the *only* case I have ever seen. I am afraid that this is a bit beyond my depth. My haunting case is baffling enough."

Cox became indignant. "How do you explain this? You can see the untampered lock and seal in every frame."

"I don't know, Ed," I said lamely. "Maybe there is trick photography involved with this."

He became even more indignant. "I have scrutinized these films carefully. In some frames ectoplasmic threads are visible, and they are *certainly* paranormal. In previous cases, investigators detected similar ectoplasmic threads, so it is not uncommon.[8] By using a locked and sealed mini-lab, we preclude the possibility of fraud."

As he grew more emphatic, I became more skeptical. I don't enjoy emotional arguments. I prefer calm scientific inquiry. Cox's research was outside normal science.

Cox let loose with a short tirade. "Fraud is not a logical explanation," he said. "I have prevented the possibility of fraud." As he talked, I tried to figure out the psychological dynamics of what was going on between us. I had been exposed to "secret knowledge." He had granted me entrance to a private aspect of his work, and I had rejected him. I had a hard time accepting the elements in my haunting case. I did not wish to stretch the edges of my beliefs any farther.

Cox seemed determined to convert me to his point of view. He went over the history of his case. The mini-lab was in the basement of a house owned by a medium in Missouri, he said. Most honest mediums demonstrate only extrasensory ability. Some mediums claim to produce macro-psychokinesis. This is known as *physical* mediumship. Because the man in Missouri was a physical medium, the pen could stand up and write, the leather rings could link, and matter could pass through the glass front of the mini- lab. The events in Cox's film occurred before the eye of a camera that was activated by micro-switches whenever a *target object* moved. Cox believed the medium, Dr. John Thomas Richards,[9] had a good reputation. Dr. Richards was a member of a group known as the Society for Research on Rapport and Telekinesis (SORRAT) that had been meeting for 20 years. Spirits allegedly caused paranormal events to occur before the camera when no one was watching.

Cox was by no means a scientific derelict. He wished to adhere to all scientific norms. He used theories to make hypotheses, tested his hypotheses, and revised his theories as a result. He made it clear that he did not really believe in spirits.

"Scientifically, belief in spirits or entities is not required," he said. "There are many different theories as to how these phenomena are possible. I can only speculate as to which theory may eventually prove valid. That is why I refer to the power that creates these effects as an *agency*. That is a value-free term. I am just gathering evidence using the knowledge that I've acquired by being in this field for 48 years."

I wondered who was fooling Ed Cox. I certainly couldn't say since I had not met the people in Missouri. The whole thing was obviously foolish.

Cox was adamant and too aggressive for a conversation between new acquaintances. Why was he attempting to force me to accept his secret experiment? Confronted by his extremism, I pondered the credibility of my own research. Believing in ESP could lead to believing in ghosts. This could lead to believing in all kinds of ridiculous things. I would become a fool if I accepted things like this film as evidence. Cox was already considered a fool.

He wanted me to take a Xerox copy of one of his film segments. I tried to refuse politely but found that I could not be firm enough. Cox was adamant. He had begun this investigation in 1969. He had retired and moved to Rolla in 1977 to devote his life to this case. He was burning with missionary zeal. It would be rude for me to refuse his Xerox copy.

By the end of the conference, I noticed that no one wished to talk to Cox. Perhaps he was too far off the deep end, I thought. I had progressed to the very edge of respectability with my haunting investigation, and he was trying to lead me over that edge. Or maybe I had already fallen off from seeing the ghost light, hearing the rap, being on the shaking bed! I couldn't forget those things. Maybe it was too late.

I looked closely at my Xerox copy. I was ambivalent but felt honored in a strange way. Cox trusted me not to ridicule him. Could psi manifest itself in such a vigorous manner? The pen wrote, "Rethink time." Maybe that was good advice.

I took Cox's Xerox paper home and taped it on the wall in my hallway where I fastened newspaper articles concerning strange and controversial topics. I had articles about hauntings, miracles, healings, pictures of Indian gurus, and a picture of the shroud of Turin. It was a kind of game that I played, not just a means of decorating a blank wall. The tape would eventually give way, and a picture or article would fall off the wall. When this happened, I would laugh and say, "Aha! That's a sign! That case is fake!" Periodically I would find some new article to put up. It would require a miracle for a paper to remain on the wall forever, but after all, "exceptional claims require exceptional proof!"

Cox's paper stayed on the wall for a long time. Once there was a thunderstorm and I forgot to close a window. The wind blew all the papers off the wall except for Cox's magic pencil writing, "Rethink time."

"Maybe there really is something to the mini-lab business," I thought with amusement. I inspected the tape holding it up. How had it remained on the wall when all the other papers had blown off? I put a thumbtack in the wall to hold the paper in place. "That tape can't hold up forever," I told myself. "Maybe I should *rethink time*!" It was a symbolic gesture, an act of belief in the absurd.

I continued my haunting investigations. The military police station case was particularly interesting. At least a dozen men, all of whom were entrusted by the government to carry weapons, witnessed events that they considered paranormal. Experiences included seeing an apparition of a young female on numerous occasions, hearing footsteps on an upstairs floor, lights and water coming on without explanation, and inexplicable movement of furniture (even under close observation). Doors and windows opened even after being secured by the MPs. The MPs spent a great deal of time and energy attempting to find an explanation for their experiences. They even brought a trained German Shepherd to the station to locate the "intruder." The dog's handler was amazed when the dog refused to go into the station's basement, where the spirit had been seen. No intruder was found.

My investigation of cases of this type supported my opinion that hauntings, although perhaps not *physically* real, should be considered *sociologically* real. The experiences produced real results – changes in belief. I presented a second paper on my haunting investigations at the Southeast Regional Parapsychological Association conference in Durham, North Carolina, in 1981. I spoke as cautiously as I had the previous year, stating that I could not preclude the possibility of fraud in these cases but had come to accept their sociological reality (McClenon, 1981).

Ed Cox's presentation of filmed psychokinesis followed. He showed his film of the pen inside his sealed and locked aquarium, writing "rethink time." Leather rings could be seen to link and unlink. ESP cards emerged from a sealed box and jerked themselves into order. They then popped back into their sealed box. Cox described each weird and unnatural motion like a carnival barker accentuating the bizarre and disconcerting nature of these events. One film showed a balloon inflating and deflating inside the mini-lab while its securely tied neck was visible. Objects moved in and out through the solid glass aquarium wall.

A toy car rolled around inside the mini-lab. Back and forth, back and forth, it moved as if pushed by an invisible child. A pinwheel turned as if blown by the wind, while a sheet of paper waved back and forth in the windless, sealed mini-lab. Pens lifted themselves up and wrote brief messages. Objects disappeared from one point and reappeared instantaneously at another. The images on the film were of poor quality, and the camera work was amateurish. This gave the presentation a surrealistic quality. Cox seemed to ignore or misunderstand questions that were addressed to him while he projected his film. He abbreviated his comments to keep pace with the onrush of images revealed on the films.

Cox had difficulty operating the eight-millimeter projector. He kept shifting it about, constantly changing the position of the film's image on the screen. He talked more rapidly and excitedly as the presentation progressed. More than anything, he demonstrated how not to give a scientific paper. Scientific presentations are generally carefully prepared, emotionless, and boring. This presentation violated every norm.

The films looked as if they had been produced like a Gumby show from the 1950s. The person creating the hoax probably shot a frame of film, moved an object slightly, and then shot another frame, so that objects would appear to move without being touched. Sometimes the object moved a few inches or even a few feet. This made the object appear to "jump" from one point to another. The locks and seals must have been carefully replaced, since Cox solemnly affirmed that they had not been opened. No skilled trickster would wish to be associated with such a clumsy piece of filming. The quality of films suggested that whoever fabricated them was delusional. A normal person would not produce something so outlandish.

Cox was part of the strange situation. His choice of target objects portrayed a strange sense of humor and childishness. His mini-lab was cluttered with toys: crayons, balloons, toy cars, pinwheels, and plastic rings. One film segment showed a metallic knight sliding back and forth in a strange dance. Another showed a pen writing a message on a piece of paper that suddenly flew inside an envelope and vanished (it was subsequently found to have been delivered by mail to a parapsychologist in Edinburgh, Scotland). Another showed a typewriter with unusual ribbons tied to its keys. Why were ribbons tied on the keys? Cox did not explain. The effects sometimes involved two movements at the same time. Balloons blew up while pinwheels turned. The knight slid around doing his weird dance and pushed a pen. Even without the ostensible paranormal effects, one could see that Cox's staging was for a theater of the absurd.

How could solid objects pass through solid objects? How could objects dematerialize and then rematerialize? The answer was clear. The films were fake.[10]

I felt embarrassed for having entertained the slightest notion that Cox's evidence might be valid. I was certain that very few people in the room accepted the authenticity of the films. I felt relieved when Cox's movies ended.

The chairperson refused to allow Cox to continue with his presentation. "Time has run out," she said. He was allowed time only for a few brief questions from the audience.

"Could you go over the precautions that you took to prevent fraud?" someone asked.

Cox was unable to answer effectively. "My precautions against fraud are too numerous to describe," he stammered. "I had a large lock on the mini-lab to which only I had the key. I sealed it with special thread that can only be obtained in Europe. The lab was also sealed with my notary public stamp. Other precautions were taken that are too numerous to mention." Cox's manner was abrupt and tactless. He seemed threatened by the question. It was apparent the parapsychologists considered his precautions insufficient.

"How was the mini-lab constructed, and how was the camera arranged so that it would start filming an alleged paranormal event?" someone asked.

I felt a tinge of sorrow for Cox. These elementary questions indicated that in the brief time allotted, he had been unable to convey even the basics of his research. He had carefully constructed a device, his mini-lab, with the idea of precluding the possibility of fraud. He had spent years working on this device and was being asked to describe it in 45 seconds.

Cox briefly described his mini-lab aquarium and the metal bands that held it secure. The film and light were activated by micro-switches under each target object in the mini-lab. Whenever an object moved, the camera and light activated, and the events were filmed. "No one has even seen movement in the mini-lab in person," he said. "Apparently the agency is unwilling to be observed by a human viewer but allows itself to be captured by the camera." The chairperson rose to signify that Cox's time was up.

"Why is it that the *agency* causes the clock's face to turn away so that we can never see it while the camera is filming?" a woman in the audience asked sarcastically. She emphasized the word *agency* as if to imply that the *agency* was a person using frame-by-frame photography.

"I don't know," Cox answered.

"I'm sorry, but no more time remains," the chairperson stated emphatically. "We must move on with the program." Cox was dismissed. His presentation was over. The strangest scientific session I'd ever witnessed had ended (Cox, 1981).

People seemed to shun Cox afterward. He approached me and spoke. "We certainly are involved with unusual and dynamic cases," he remarked. He seemed unconcerned about how abruptly the chairperson had ended his discussion. I felt uneasy. My own presentation would be considered unscientific by many of the parapsychologists. I was afraid that they would connect me with Cox. I backed away from him but was blocked by a cluster of people standing in the aisle. I felt desperate.

"Today was an important event in the history of parapsychology," he said. "This is the first time that these films have been shown publicly." I did not want to hear him out, but I could think of no way to exit politely.

"You or any other member of the Parapsychological Association can visit Rolla any time you wish," he said. "You will see the most astonishing display of psychokinetic phenomena in this century. You will not believe your eyes. I didn't at first, but I stayed to investigate it."

I looked around the room. There was no escape. "It certainly looks as if someone shot one frame of the film at a time," I said to him. "They shot one frame, moved those ESP cards, then shot another frame. Then they moved the cards. Then shot another frame. That is why the cards jerked so rapidly."

"How could they have gotten into the locked box?" Cox demanded.

"They picked the lock," I answered.

"How did they get my notary public seal?" he replied. "How did they get my special thread? Did they go to Europe? And I suppose you think that Dr. Richards, a busy English professor, has time to shoot each frame, then move the object, then shoot another frame, opening and closing the lock and replacing the seals each time, 16 times for every second, for all the hours of film that have been shot?" His angry voice grew louder.

"Well, I don't know," I said. "I need to talk to some other people."

"You don't know," Cox echoed mockingly. "How did he get the notary public seal? You don't know. Where does he get the time to do all this photographic trickery night after night? You don't know."

"That's right, Ed, I don't know," I stated in conclusion.

The problem was that I liked Ed Cox, perhaps because he burned with a sincere enthusiasm. He was confident and I felt ambivalent. I had struggled to shape my presentation so that it would be acceptable to the parapsychologists. I had not been able to describe what it felt like to see the anomalous light or to be on the bed when it was shaking. Cox understood those things, it seemed. He had been bluntly honest with me.

I still wanted to get away. Perhaps I should have been more direct with him. Perhaps I should have said, "Ed, I just want to walk away from you, and forget that we ever met." I pondered my attitude. To fake the films might require more expertise than I had, but it certainly seemed absurd for an "entity," "agency," or whatever to become involved with something as fishy as this. Who, alive or dead, would support this nonsense? What purpose was there?[11]

That evening the younger parapsychologists and I went out for pizza and beer. We laughed about the strangeness of the field of parapsychology. It seemed like a huge joke. We kidded about the various types of people interested in parapsychology and accused each other of fitting into the humorous categories we devised.

First, there were those involved with laboratory research. We called them *anal retentives*. They clung to the same type of experimental method for 50 years with only minor variations. Sometimes they found that psi occurs, sometimes they didn't. They used sophisticated statistical techniques that no one could understand. They were boring.

Then, there were the *new age theorists*. They pondered the philosophical implications of psi and expected a new era to arrive in which psychic phenomena would be scientifically accepted. But the New Age never came. They thought up "far out" theories to explain psi, but their ideas were not testable.

Then there were *field investigators* who never proved anything. This was my category. "Look, there's a ghost!" someone cried out. "Whooooo," he moaned, imitating a haunted groan. "There goes McClenon after it!" he said. Everyone laughed.

Then there was Ed Cox. Cox was unique. We laughed about Cox.

"Is it possible for anything, ever, to top Cox's films for silliness?" I asked.

"Michael's been out there to Rolla, Missouri," someone said. "Ask him." Michael McBeath worked at the McDonnell Laboratory for Psychical Research in St. Louis.

"Tell us about the Rolla case, Michael," someone asked.

Michael was shy. I had not heard him speak while we were eating.

"I've only been out there once," he stated. "I was with Peter Phillips and Mark Shafer. It's kind of hard to say exactly what was going on out there. It seemed as if there was a kind of tension between Ed Cox and Dr. Richards. The mini-lab is in Dr. Richards' basement." Michael spoke slowly and reflectively. Everyone at the table fell silent. We were astonished that Michael was serious about what had just seemed so humorous.

"Cox and Richards argue a lot," he continued. "Maybe that is why they get the phenomena that they do. Maybe it's like a poltergeist or something. Richards is an interesting fellow. He seems like a methodical, plodding type of person, quite overweight, but he is very intelligent. He makes a lot of puns. Maybe his personality somehow clashes with Cox's in a manner that contributes to psi. Dr. Richards is an English instructor with Columbia College in Missouri and apparently quite knowledgeable in his field. If this is a kind of poltergeist, I would say that he is the agent." Michael hesitated. He seemed to be unsure whether people were interested. Everyone was listening very closely.

"What happened while you were there?" someone asked.

"Raps came out of the floor," he said. "They are knocking sounds that communicate messages. They spell out letters to form words and sometimes sentences."

"What makes the raps?" a woman asked.

"It's hard to say. Richards claims that there are entities that make the raps. There's a long tradition associated with it. The group was started by a famous poet, John G. Neihardt who wrote a book, *Black Elk Speaks*. Dr. Neihardt developed a friendship with the Native American medicine man Black Elk in the 1930s, and both he and Black Elk are some of the spirits thought to make the raps. When they rap, Cox gets excited and puts his ear on the floor at the point where they seem to be originating. He tries to get them to answer his questions. He had concealed some random digits that he wanted them to guess paranormally, but they seemed to have a mind of their own. They spelled out the word 'ring.' Then we all went down to the basement and there was my ring inside the mini-lab."

"How did it get inside?"

"I don't know. Maybe someone has Cox's key. I had taken my ring off to wash my hands a few hours earlier and hadn't kept close track of it. I can't swear to the validity of Cox's security measures. I've only been out there once. But my ring was inside, and the lab as all locked up and sealed and everything."

"Then what happened?" I asked, finding myself leaning forward to hear his answer.

"That evening, Richards wanted to do what they call an ESP/PK experiment. He made a big thing about how we should not demand anything from the entities but that we should let whatever happens, happen. He got out one of those folding metal TV tray tables, and we sat around it with our hands on its top. Then they turned out the lights, and the table started vibrating and jumping around. It wasn't completely dark but was a funny situation. It's hard to tell if someone is cheating with the lights dimmed like that. The table vibrated in a funny manner. Then Tom Richards took his hands off the table for some reason and his wife did also. We three parapsychologists were the only ones with our hands on the table, and it still vibrated. Richards wasn't using his feet either. I can't explain it. So, I really don't know what to make of what is going on out there."

Michael sat quietly. He was finished. Everyone was silent. Michael's sincerity was disturbing. We stopped laughing about Cox and talked about something else.

"Spirits do this?" someone asked.

"Black Elk, John G. Neihardt, and other spirits—some are Tom and Elaine's deceased relatives," Michael noted. "There's a Spiritualist element in this but there are alternate theories."

"Like what?" I asked.

"A British researcher, Kenneth Batcheldor, argued that fear of psi prevents it from occurring," Michael said. "Like SORRAT, he did table-tipping experiments. He found that people, sitting in the dark, tend to push the table slightly due to unconscious muscular movements. Because they are not aware of this, they think the table is moving due to psychokinesis. That helps them get over their fears, and over time authentic PK can occur as a result. Other researchers argue that the same results could be achieved through fraud. People who think they are experiencing PK get over their fear of it and authentic PK can then occur."

"A sitter group in Toronto extended this theory," Michael continued. "They sat together during weekly séances and devised a story about a fictitious spirit, Philip. According to their story, Philip lived during the 1500s in England. He killed himself after he failed to prevent his mistress from being burnt at the stake for witchcraft. Although Philip never existed, the group got their table to move about, and they communicated with paranormal raps produced by Philip. The Batcheldor and Philip experiments demonstrated that you don't need spirits for these phenomena to occur. The group mind can make it happen."

I drove home after the conference and tried not to think about Cox. My haunting cases were still active; I resolved to focus my attention on them. They were baffling enough. Cox was associated with something that was too strange for me to consider.

When I arrived home, I looked at my special wall in the hallway with its taped-up articles and pictures. There was Cox's Xerox of the film. "Rethink time," it stated. It wasn't funny anymore. Maybe there were strings attached. I was not sure of anything at this point. But there was a tremor in my stomach that would not go away. I picked up the telephone to call Ed Cox and then put it down. I could not think of anything to say to him.

CHAPTER 2
DRAMA IN ROLLA

In April 1981, I drove to Louisville, Kentucky, to present a paper at the meeting of the Southern Sociological Society. Michael McBeath had previously invited me to come to the McDonnell Laboratory for Psychical Research in St. Louis. It seemed like a good time to visit him, as St. Louis is not far from Louisville. I needed to interview the parapsychologists at the McDonnell Laboratory to complete my goal of visiting all the major parapsychological research centers in the USA. I decided to visit Ed Cox in Rolla, Missouri, since he was close to St. Louis.

I regarded the SORRAT claims as too far-fetched to accept, and I hoped to devise a way to reveal SORRAT as fraudulent. I contacted the professional parapsychologists at the Foundation for Research on the Nature of Man (FRNM) in North Carolina. They suggested that I design an experiment to evaluate the SORRAT entities' ESP ability. I would take some special envelopes, with the ESP targets inside, to Rolla. If the SORRAT people tried to break into the envelopes, I could reveal them as frauds.

George Hansen, a FRNM researcher at the time, prepared three sealed envelopes containing random digit ESP targets. I asked that the envelopes be sealed in a way that would make it look easy to break into them. I suggested taking special precautions such as secret hairs, threads, or seals—methods that would reveal fraudulent opening. I mentioned exposing undeveloped film to light with a special, secret pattern. A person fraudulently opening the envelope would encounter the film and might attempt to replace it with unexposed film before resealing the envelope. The new film would not have the secret pattern, and this would reveal the fraud.

I requested that I not be informed of the security precautions so that I could not subconsciously tip off the trickster. George sent me the three envelopes in the mail. I planned to leave the envelopes in Rolla so that the trickster could steam them open and be caught cheating.

I wrote to Ed Cox asking if I were still welcome to come to Rolla. He responded enthusiastically. He told me that he had placed a postcard addressed to me in his locked and sealed mini-lab. A few days later a postcard arrived in the mail. (In reporting on these communications, I will follow the convention of placing a "Q" for *question* before all written requests to the entities and an "A" before their *answer*.)

Q: *Dear "3 X 3' and all;*
Would "you" be willing to perform for a friend of mine, Jim McClenon, when he visits here? If so, transport this postcard out of the locked and sealed mini-lab and place it in the mail. Write a message on it if "you" wish.

W. Edward Cox

Under Cox's typing was a hand-lettered answer:

A: *Welcome, Jim,*
If "you" don't believe in "us" why should "we" believe in "you?" Belief is two-way street, W.E.C.

I taped the card on my wall beside the paper advising me to "rethink time." Someone is playing a bizarre game, I thought.

At the Southern Sociological Society conference, I found that my colleagues regarded me as unusual for studying parapsychologists. I was unlike the other graduate students in that I had served in Vietnam, traveled around the world, and was older than everyone else.

"How's your psychotic—I mean—psychic research going?" one girl asked. They laughed at her joke. I tried to explain that I was doing sociological research—a study of deviant behavior. "Psychic, psychotic, same thing," she stated and they laughed again.

I began to understand Ed Cox's personality. His bluster was a reaction to ridicule. No matter how careful he might be regarding fraud, he was stigmatized.

I met a woman at the conference who was a sociology instructor at a major university. I enjoyed talking with her. She was intelligent and charming, and she seemed attracted to me. I asked her about her research interests, and she described a study of the structure of economic and social relationships between labor and management. She had recently gotten her Ph.D. and was excited with her career possibilities. She was co-writing a paper with a well-known researcher, and they planned to publish their results in a highly respected journal. I encouraged her to continue talking. I like dynamic women who enjoy their success. She was a winner!

Then she asked me what kind of research I did. I hesitated to answer. I was close to completing my Ph.D. dissertation regarding the deviant science of parapsychology. I told her that I was on my way to interview some parapsychologists in St. Louis and then to Rolla, Missouri, to investigate a psychic phenomenon case. She looked at me strangely.

"Where can you publish that?" she asked derisively.

"I don't know," I said. "I'm doing a kind of sociology of science or perhaps sociology of religion."

I could see by her reaction that her opinion of me had changed. I was not headed for academic success. That was the end of our love at first sight. She promised to attend my presentation the next day but did not show up.[1] Very few people came. I was disappointed and was glad when it came time to leave for Missouri.

When I arrived in St. Louis, I interviewed Michael McBeath. He was curious about my planned study of SORRAT. "You will be surprised," he told me.

I drove to Rolla and found Ed Cox's house. He answered my knock but did not invite me into his home. He wanted to leave immediately for the Richards.

"Ed, can I use your toilet?" I asked. I wanted to see the inside of his house. I was thinking that the most likely explanation for Cox's films was that he produced them himself. He might be the trickster. If I got inside his house, I might see equipment suitable for producing the mini-lab films—perhaps a duplicate camera and mini-lab. Later, when I mentioned this idea to some professional parapsychologists who had known him for years, they laughed. "Cox would never engage in fraud," they said. "That's not possible."

"The plumbing is broken," Cox told me. "Let's go over to the Richards' house. It's very close."

My strategy had failed. At the time, I thought it was funny that he wouldn't let me inside. Later, Tom Richards told me that Cox tried to keep anyone from entering his house. It was part of his mini-lab security precautions. A person would have greater difficulty stealing Cox's key, his special thread, and his notary public seal if that person had no opportunity to enter his residence. But the possibility remained open; Cox might be the trickster I sought to catch.

Cox introduced me to Dr. John Thomas Richards and his wife, Elaine. As Michael had described him, Dr. Richards was very much overweight, looking close to 400 lbs. At the time, he was 44 years old (I was 34 years old). He was dressed casually in huge blue jeans and a freshly laundered white shirt. His wire-rimmed glasses, brown hair, and mustache gave him the appearance of a jolly, middle-aged intellectual, yet his first words to me were reserved, almost formal.

"Pleased to meet you, Mr. McClenon," he stated evenly as we shook hands. He said he would help me with my research in any way that he could. I tried to figure out my reaction to him. Was he the trickster? Was he concerned that I might catch him cheating? My impression was that he was not concerned. He was ordinary, methodical, friendly, down-to-earth, even-tempered, and intelligent. He had a good sense of humor. He did not seem like a trickster.

His wife, Elaine, also radiated a straightforward, Midwestern friendliness. She wore a loosely fitting pink flowered smock. Like her husband, her graying hair revealed she was in her forties.

Tom and Elaine did not appear to be particularly sophisticated people. They were not becoming wealthy living on Dr. Richards' modest instructor's salary. They were normal people, living in an average house. The furniture looked slightly worn. An easy chair, a davenport, a piano, a television, and assorted chairs filled their living room. I noted a picture of their only son, Ivan, on the wall. He was a frail seven-year-old with a charming smile.

The Richards seemed to fit in well with the small town where they lived. The University of Missouri at Rolla, known for producing engineers, was only a few blocks from their house. A Methodist church, which the Richards attended weekly, was across the street. One would never guess that these two people were primary suspects in a case that almost all parapsychologists considered to be fraudulent.

I felt somewhat uncomfortable as I sat in their living room. I did not know Cox well, and I certainly did not know these suspected tricksters.

"Mr. Cox, are you going to work on the mini-lab this afternoon?" Elaine asked, impatiently. Cox had warned me by letter that Elaine was not always tolerant of his scientific attitude.

"That's right. I'm going to show young Jim McClenon here, my security precautions," he replied. "Jim, I hope you brought some experiments of your own so that the agency might be tested to your satisfaction during your visit." The tone in his voice indicated that he did not doubt the authenticity of his *agency*. He expected it to pass any test that I devised and that I would then join him in his certainty about the phenomena. The prospect was disquieting.

"I brought some sealed envelopes with me," I said. "I was hoping that the agency might guess the target digits inside."

Cox looked at the envelopes carefully. He inspected the seams. My plan was to keep the envelopes under my control, at first, then relax my control, giving the trickster a chance to open them.

"Do you think that the agency can guess the target information?" I asked.

"It is certainly worth trying," Cox said with enthusiasm. "I have done similar tests, and the agency has proved highly successful in demonstrating its extrasensory ability."

"I can't say whether they will or won't do your test," Tom interjected. "We don't really know what factors contribute to their success, although rapport within the group seems very important. It also might depend on which entity you ask. They have different personalities just as people do on this side. And sometimes they don't seem to be able to do much of anything. We have gone for months at a time without any phenomena occurring. I certainly hope they will attempt your test, though. It seems like a valid and interesting experiment."

"Rapport within the group?" I asked.

"Yes, when Dr. Neihardt founded this group in 1961, he named it the Society for Research on Rapport and Telekinesis. He had had various psychic experiences himself and was familiar with the literature regarding psychical research. He believed that rapport was very important in producing these types of phenomena. I think we have found that group harmony *does* contribute to success."

I felt disconcerted. I was searching for a trickster, and he was talking about group harmony. Cox stated that he had an errand to run and abruptly departed. I was left holding my envelopes and wondering how I had come to place myself in such an absurd position. I was not really a psychic investigator. I was a sociologist. What was I doing with these three envelopes?

I tried to make polite conversation. The Richards seemed sincere and friendly people. They were concerned about me as a person, not just as an investigator, and invited me to stay in Ivan's room since he would be sleeping at Tom's parents' home. I accepted their invitation but worried about accepting the hospitality of people whom I hoped to reveal as frauds.

Cheating is wrong, I rationalized. Tricksters should be unmasked. If I refused their hospitality, I would be revealing my distrust to them.

Then we heard some raps. "Rap, rap, rap. Rap, rap, rap. Rap, rap, rap." They came out of the floor in the center of the living room. They came in patterns of three. "Rap, rap, rap. Rap, rap, rap. Rap, rap, rap."

Elaine had gone into the kitchen to begin supper. "There's Three-Times-Three," she called. "Ed Cox must be coming back soon."

"Three-Times-Three?" I asked. "What's that?'

"Three-Times-Three seems to be an entity totally derived from Mr. Cox's subconscious," Tom told me. "The story we have gathered from talking to the raps is that Mr. Cox's subconscious refuses to accept the fact that some psychokinetic phenomena come from disembodied entities. As a result, a part of his subconscious has created Three-Times-Three, whose sole purpose is to help Ed Cox do this research. Three-Times-Three got his name from the signature he used to identify himself."

Three-Times-Three rapped out his signature again, "Rap, rap, rap. Rap, rap, rap. Rap, rap, rap." I looked at the floor where the raps seemed to originate. Tom did not move his body in any fashion while the raps sounded. I could see nothing that would indicate he was responsible for producing them. "Rap, rap, rap. Rap, rap, rap. Rap, rap, rap." I felt faint vibrations coming out of the floor. Elaine was correct. Glancing out the window, I saw Cox arriving. Three-Times-Three's rapping grew louder, as if happy that Ed was returning. "Rap, rap, rap! Rap, rap, rap! Rap, rap, rap!" Maybe it was a coincidence that Cox arrived soon after Three-Times-Three began rapping. We knew that Cox had gone on a short errand. Perhaps some kind of rapping device was hidden in the floor.

As soon as Cox walked in the door, Elaine called out from the kitchen, "Mr. Cox, Three-Times-Three is here to talk to you."

"Oh, good," he exclaimed. "I have some questions for him I've been meaning to ask. Three-Times-Three, are you there?"

"Rap, rap, rap. Rap, rap, rap. Rap, rap, rap," came the signature.

"Hello," Cox called happily. "Would you try to demonstrate your paranormal abilities to this gentleman here, Mr. Jim McClenon?"

"Rap." The raps followed a special code. One rap signified *yes*. Two raps signified *no*. Three raps meant *maybe*. The raps had indicated "yes"—they would try to demonstrate their paranormal abilities.

"Why don't you ask Three-Times-Three a question?" Cox asked me.

I was struck speechless. I had never talked to an entity before. I turned on my tape recorder and self-consciously fiddled with the microphone.

"I don't know. What can I say?" I asked. I tried to think of a question. "Three-Times-Three, how are you?"

The raps began spelling out letters. For this they had a second code system. One rap stood for "A." Two raps stood for "B." Three raps signified "C," and so on.

"F-I-N-E," the raps laboriously spelled out. My tape recorder documented this message. I laughed nervously. [I have listened to my recording of this original conversation many times. The raps have an unusual acoustic quality in that they sound as if they originated within the floor. I sent a copy of this recording to the American Society for Psychical Research (ASPR) for analysis but did not receive a reply.]

"Three-Times-Three, will you tell us the names of the two cousins who are responsible for that mail theft that occurred last week?" Cox asked. He was attempting to use the agency's paranormal ability to solve a local robbery. The entities had previously revealed that the two robbers were cousins and that they lived in a town close to Rolla.

"Rap, rap, rap." Maybe.

"OK," Cox responded. "You said you might tell us the names. Do you know the names of the two robbers?"

"Rap, rap, rap." Maybe.

"When are you going to attempt this?"

The floor was silent. Cox waited. He wanted to prove to me that the raps were authentic.

"He might be able to rap directly on your microphone while you watch it. I cannot imagine how that could be replicated fraudulently," Cox said. "Three-Times-Three, will you rap right on Jim's microphone?"

The raps were becoming fainter. "Rap, rap, rap." Maybe.

"Will you please try?" Cox requested.

The raps did not respond.

"Maybe he can demonstrate his ability to rap wherever I direct him. I have had astonishing results within some of my field experiments. At times, they are capable of rapping at the exact point to which I direct them."

Cox made another request. "Three-Times-Three, will you please rap on the wall over there?" He vaguely indicated the far wall.

The raps faintly began spelling out letters. Cox lay down on the floor and pressed his ear to where the faint raps seemed to be coming.

Tom Richards labored to keep track of the letters as they were spelled out "O-N-T-H-E-W…"

"He's saying 'on the wall over there,'" Elaine blurted out.

"Rap." Yes.

I was quietly amused. Cox was irritated. "Three-Times-Three, this is an important scientific test. Will you please make it seem as if your raps are coming from the far wall? This is very important. I am attempting to convince my colleague of your authenticity."

There was no sound of rapping from anywhere.

"Please, Three-Times-Three," Cox begged. "Demonstrate your ability to rap at a different location besides this point on the floor. My colleague might think that you don't really exist, or that you are created by a hammer concealed in the floor." The raps were virtually inaudible.

"I guess the energy's down," Tom remarked.

"You want him to prove that he is real. Do *you* believe that he is real, Mr. Cox?" Elaine asked sharply.

"I believe that vibrations occur paranormally," Cox said. "Although I must admit that I cannot prove this in a manner acceptable to my scientific colleagues."

"But do you accept the entities as real? You're asking Three-Times-Three to prove that he is real, but I don't think that you really accept the entities yourself, Mr. Cox."

"Scientifically, there is no proof of the survival after death hypothesis, if that is what you are getting at, Elaine," Cox stated. "As a scientist, I suspend my judgment."

"I suppose everyone forms their opinions based on their own experiences," Tom said diplomatically. "I think that Three-Times-Three would make every attempt to help Ed since he is supposedly a derivation of Ed's mind."

It was a strange drama, a kind of allegory. Cox symbolized the essence of soulless science. He wanted to verify what seemed to be a magical force, a force that ironically was thought to come directly from him, but it would not, or perhaps could not, obey him. He was reduced to lying on the floor with his ear pressed against the point where the raps had come from as he argued about survival after death. His silly physical position weakened the force of his argument.

I was curious, baffled, and slightly sad. I no longer was certain that I would be able to catch the trickster. The situation seemed too complex to figure out. I was not certain I could discover the secret.

"I have made many attempts to explain these raps normally," Cox informed me, his ear still pressed against the floor. "When the parapsychologists from the Mind Science Foundation were here, one was in the basement while the raps sounded on the floor upstairs. She could hear them above her, while we heard them below our feet. It isn't a matter of Tom cracking his toes or anything like that."

"Do they always come from the same points?" I asked. "I should think that skeptics would suggest that there are hammer devices hidden in the floor."

"No, I have heard and felt them outdoors. I have put my hand on the exact source of the energy. It is as if someone is under the ground with a hammer trying to get out. I've heard and felt them coming out of solid concrete floors. Once, Tom and Elaine directed the agency to make raps in my car while I was driving alone. I heard them and thought there was something wrong with my car. My phone rang as I arrived home, and Elaine asked, 'Have you been hearing raps?' The raps indicated to the Richards that they had tried to make raps in my car."

"What?" I exclaimed, "You heard the raps while you were by yourself?"

"That is what happened," Cox said. I was beginning to understand the nature of his certainty regarding the authenticity of the phenomena he investigated.

"There isn't any way that some secret device might have been hidden in your car? You're sure that the sound wasn't made by a thermal expansion or contraction?" I asked.

Cox looked at me seriously. He lifted his ear off the floor. "I've been interested in parapsychology since 1932. I never have had experiences like these before I met the Richards. I have made every attempt to preclude the possibility of fraud, and you should realize that I am a knowledgeable magician. That car incident did not occur under controlled laboratory conditions, and parapsychologists do not consider these anecdotal stories to constitute valid evidence regarding claims of the paranormal. You can be certain that I thoroughly checked over my automobile, but this is not something that should be considered as particularly evidential. Tom and Elaine were just trying to convince me personally. These mini-lab experiments are an entirely different matter, though. There is no normal explanation for the filmed effects that I have documented."[3]

I was startled by his attitude. "Why do parapsychologists refuse to accept the authenticity of the raps?"

"I'm afraid the history of the Spiritualist era was filled with trickery," Cox told me. "It began in 1848 with the rapping sounds that occurred around the young Fox sisters in Hydesville, New York.[4] Even though many different investigators were unable to find a normal explanation for the phenomena, the whole case was surrounded by controversy. The publicity launched the Spiritualist movement. In later life, two of the sisters confessed to fraud and reportedly demonstrated the toe-snapping method they used to produce the raps. Most skeptics don't realize that many researchers witnessed phenomena they could not explain—people who were aware of toe-snapping. They took particular pains to preclude that as a possible explanation. I'm afraid that the sisters had fallen into destitution and had hoped that, by their confessions, they might make some money. They later retracted their disclosures, but this fact is generally ignored by skeptics. Their escapade gave raps a bad name. Actually, raps are not uncommon in physical mediumship and poltergeist cases. I'll bring over a paper I have written about investigations of individuals who purportedly have macro-psychokinetic abilities. I think you would benefit from reading it."

Cox directed me down to the basement room where his mini-lab was set up. His apparatus appeared to be a Rube Goldberg-like contraption with clothespins holding together electrical connections, an old eight-millimeter spring-wound movie camera, and many wires and micro-switches, all connected to an inverted aquarium attached to a heavy wooden board by metal bands padlocked together.

"This is the mini-lab," Cox exclaimed with pride. I puzzled at the contraption.

"Steve Calvin's here," Elaine called from the top of the stairs. "Just go on down, Steve. They're in the basement fooling around with the mini-lab."

Steve was a tall, thin, scholarly-looking individual in his mid-thirties. He had a receding hairline and wore old blue jeans. Computer cards protruded from his front shirt pocket. I felt a kinship with him from the beginning. He was a graduate student like me, struggling to live on a modest stipend.

"Steve is working on his Ph.D. in chemical engineering at the university here," Cox told me. "He helped put together much of the circuitry for this mini-lab."

"How did this mini-lab business get started?' I asked.

"Dr. J. B. Rhine, at the Institute of Parapsychology, suggested attempting to get PK effects within sealed containers during field investigations," Cox replied. "Dr. J. G. Neihardt, the founder of SORRAT, contracted Rhine after his group observed some paranormal effects. Rhine suggested the mini-lab concept in 1966. He advised building a locked, sealed container to preclude fraud. Neihardt was quite open to scientific exploration of psychic phenomena, and under his supervision, the first mini-labs were constructed. Tom Richards was a graduate student working on his dissertation under Neihardt's direction in those days, and I was aware of Rhine's idea. The SORRATs had some success with their first mini-labs in 1967. Objects moved inside in a manner that indicated that psychokinetic effects occurred."

"What about the first films?" I asked. "How did that get started?"

"The entities had shown the ability to write messages, even within the sealed containers that Ed constructed, so we were curious about what would happen if we tried to film it," Steve continued. "Our first attempts in 1978 were very primitive. We took no security precautions. We set up a pen sitting on a micro-switch so that if the pen moved, the camera would switch on. On the very first night, the camera was activated, and the film showed the pen making some scribbles. That first day, we did not know what triggered the camera. We thought that the Richards' cat must have done it. They had a cat in those days and that seemed the most likely explanation. But after we got the film developed, we saw that there was no cat. The pen appeared to rise and write by itself. Then we started building in more and more security precautions. Ed keeps making his mini-lab more fraud-proof all the time."

"It takes me about 20 minutes to lock and seal it each time to get it ready for the camera," Ed remarked.

I looked at the locked and sealed mini-lab. It was filled with all manner of junk: leather rings, crayons, paper, balloons (one of which was blown up,) toys, aluminum foil, pinwheels, plastic rings, sealed containers, ESP cards.

"You have a golden opportunity to keep track of this mini-lab since you will be staying here at the Richards' house," Cox said to me gleefully. "I hope you will call me immediately the minute that something happens within the lab."

He was trying to draw me into his research. I did not want to become associated with Cox, his mini-lab, or these strange people. I remembered the ridicule that his films had elicited among the parapsychologists. Cox spent much time insuring that the mini-lab was properly sealed. He locked it with a padlock and then threaded the clasp with special thread that he tied and melted at the ends with a lit match. "No one can enter this mini-lab without me being able to detect it," he said.

In the evening, the Richards wanted to do what they called an "ESP/PK experiment." They brought out a metal TV tray, and everyone sat around it with their hands touching the top surface.

"Jim, try to vibrate this table as fast as you can," Steve requested. I was not sure what he was getting at, but I tried vibrating it, nonetheless. My shaking of the table was clumsy and not very fast. I felt as if I was being set up for a trick.

They turned off the lights and I thought, "There goes the possibility of scientific observation." Actually, the street lamps and moonlight outside enabled a high degree of visibility. The table began vibrating in such a rapid manner that it seemed impossible for a person to duplicate it using muscular effort. I could clearly see that everyone's hands were on top of the table. Cox got down on the floor under the table. He wanted to maintain a position of complete vigilance and to locate the point of origin of the raps that had begun sounding.

"Rap, rap; rap, rap, rap. Rap, rap; rap, rap, rap."

That's Black Elk," Elaine exclaimed. "That's Black Elk's signature,"

"Rap, rap; rap, rap, rap." It sounded like the beat of an Indian drum.

"Hello, Black Elk. Welcome," Tom said.

Black Elk began spelling a word, and we all began keeping track of the letters. "H-I," he laboriously spelled out. Black Elk had been an Oglala Sioux medicine man, the subject of J.G. Neihardt's 1932 book, *Black Elk Speaks*.

Black Elk was visiting that night to heal a friend of the Richards. "H-E-A-L" he rapped out at various times. Cox scrambled around the floor to locate the exact point where the raps seemed to be coming. I noticed that they came from a different place than those earlier in the afternoon.

Then the table began jumping around. It would push up against various people within the circle. It seemed to have a life of its own. I was trying to act relaxed as I carefully watched each one of the participants. Elaine took her hands off the table. Only Steve's, Tom's, and my hands were left while the table continued to jump and vibrate. I noticed that Steve and I were allowing the table to slide under our hands. This meant that Tom was the only one who might be causing it to shake, since his fingers seemed to be glued to it. It was hard to believe that he could vibrate the table so rapidly, but why wasn't he allowing the table to slide under his fingers, as we were? I didn't say anything because I didn't want to appear too skeptical. Otherwise, I would never catch him cheating. It seemed best not to mention it. I would just go along with the "show" and let things happen naturally. I would accumulate evidence and allow the drama to unfold. I tried to suspend judgment.

All of a sudden, the table hopped into the air. Everyone cried, "Aah!" in surprise. It jumped about two feet up and seemed to hang for a few seconds; then it fell to one side and dropped to the floor. How did that happen? Was it sleight of hand? Then, while I watched everyone's hands, it leaped up in the air again but dropped almost immediately. Did someone lift it with their foot? "Rap, rap; rap, rap, rap, Rap, rap; rap, rap, rap." The table was jumping about, pounding out Black Elk's rhythm.

Cox hoped that Black Elk would demonstrate a capacity for clairvoyance. "Black Elk, can you tell us the names of the two mail thieves?' he asked.

"Rap, rap." No.

"Would you attempt to tell us the digits that Jim McClenon has in his sealed envelopes?' Cox asked.

"Rap, rap." No.

"Will you try to do another levitation?" Tom asked. He kept his camera close by with the hope of taking the table's picture while it was up in the air.

"Rap." Yes.

Minutes passed. The vibrations continued. Again and again, the table made small leaps into the air. I could not figure out how these occurred, but I knew that I was watching from only a single vantage point. A sleight-of-hand magician can perform amazing feats.

Eventually, the raps grew fainter. They spelled out the words, "H-E-A-L, L-O-V-E," and finally "E—N—D." The raps finished and the "experiment" was over.

Tom took careful notes regarding each experiment. He summarized each table-tipping event in a standardized fashion. A table levitation was counted a "success" only when the table remained in the air after everyone removed his or her hands from it. Anything else was a failure. He recorded the evening's experiment as a failure.

The SORRATs were aware that table-tipping phenomena could be produced by fraud or by unconscious muscular movement. They were interested in events that could not be explained by these processes. They believed that hands-off levitations could not be explained by fraud or unconscious muscular movements.

Elaine brought out photographs that they had taken during past ESP/PK experiments. Apparently, the goal was to get the table up into the air and snap its picture. It was obvious that the still photographs could have been faked, but fraud seemed somewhat pointless. Tom did not consider his photographs of levitating tables as evidence, but as personal mementos of evenings during which he felt convinced that psychokinesis had occurred. He knew that on those occasions, neither his nor anyone else's unconscious muscular efforts were holding up the table.

As I lay in bed at the Richards' house, I reviewed the events I had witnessed. I had heard raps that I could not explain. I had seen a table jump around during a group session, which I also could not explain. Both phenomena could be produced by a magician. I had seen Tom engage in suspicious movements when his fingers were tightly fixed on the table. I began to feel more secure in my skepticism.[5] My envelope experiment could prove very important, I thought. It might reveal fraud. All was not lost.

In the morning, I went with Cox down the stairs into the Richards' base-ment. Cox wanted to check his mini-lab. "Here's the paper I promised to bring you," he said. "My paper describes the evidence regarding macro-psy-chokinesis, events like what we see in this house."

We inspected the mini-lab. "It looks like there's been activity," Cox noted.

I tried to remember exactly how the mini-lab had looked the day before. The balloon that had been fully inflated, was now only half-full. Some plastic rings were now resting on top of a sealed container. A message had been writ-ten in crayon on a paper. It read "Hi, Jim." I looked at the locks, thread, and seals. All seemed intact. I wished I had photographed the seals the night be-fore. I could not remember the exact position of the thread but it seemed that it was pointing in exactly the same direction as the day before. I was glad, in a way, that I had not photographed it. I did not want to become responsible for Cox's experiment. All the seals looked exactly as they did the day before, and I had no explanation for how things had changed inside the mini-lab.

This event was an emotional turning point in my investigation. I had en-countered something anomalous, and I realized that I did not want to become closely involved in it. Very few people accepted the mini-lab phenomena as valid. I remember saying to myself, "I'm only a sociological observer. I should not be required to explain this. If I stay detached, I won't be involved in this. I'll just suspend judgment." This attitude might be classified as a *willing sus-pension of disbelief*—a stage that allows progress toward belief—but I was not thinking about stages of belief at the time. People have told me, over the years, about their inability to believe certain claims. "I can't believe in psychokine-sis," a man told me. "I can't believe that the mini-lab phenomena are valid," another said. That was my stage at the time. Everyone sets a level after which they refuse to believe. Someone told me, "I believe in psychokinesis but I can't believe that the spirits can write a message. That seems too far-fetched to me." I understand these positions because, while standing in front of the mini-lab, I faced the same dilemma. I was open to the idea that psychokinesis occurred because my haunting cases supported that belief. But, in front of the mini-lab, I was disturbed because I knew that the parapsychologists did not accept the mini-lab evidence. If I accepted it, I would be part of a very small minority, like a cult-member. I noted that the position of the thread and lock were *exactly* the same as the day before. The trickster must have some alternate method for getting into the mini-lab, I thought. I looked at the glass panels and noted the dust along the seams was not disturbed. There was no evidence that someone had tampered with the mini-lab.

"Do you think that the balloon deflated paranormally?" I asked.

"I tied the end of it very tightly last week. It inflated inside the mini-lab on Tuesday. I hope that the event was captured on film. In all likelihood, whatever agency created these other paranormal effects also deflated the balloon."

Cox looked closely at the camera. "Darn," he said. "The camera doesn't seem to have functioned. I wonder why that is?"

I viewed the scene critically. Perhaps the trickster disconnected the camera and then slid the paper with "Hi, Jim" written on it under the edge of the mini-lab, I tried to lift it off its wooden base to create a slight space. My activity disturbed the mini-lab's contents, and it would have been detected by future observers. Did someone shake the mini-lab to rearrange the rings? The balloon might have deflated on its own.

"Are you sure that someone couldn't get your key, thread, and notary public seal away from you and get into this lab?" I asked Cox.

"That's impossible," he stated with certainty. "Even if they did, I have various other secret methods to determine whether anyone has opened it. I have secret hairs and hidden booby traps placed in strategic places. No one opened this lab last night."

I could not be as certain as Cox. I have seen magicians put on stage shows in which spectators are asked to tie up the magician with a long rope. After the task is complete, the spectators find that their wallets and watches have been taken by the magician's quick fingers. Something similar could be happening to Cox.

"You know, to me all this seems like a magic trick," I said. "The raps, the table-tipping, things moving around in the mini-lab—although I can't explain it, I can't be certain that anything paranormal happened. I have seen a magician pull a rabbit out of what seemed to be an empty hat, but I didn't conclude that psi occurred."

"What you don't realize is that the magician requires props," Ed replied. "He has control over what occurs. With these mini-lab experiments, I maintain a specific area over which I have control. The magician would be unable to pull a rabbit out of his hat if I inspected it and placed it in a locked and sealed mini-lab. I know what magicians can and can't do; I am one."

"Do you think the agency will be able to correctly guess the digits in my sealed envelopes?"

"Why don't you let me put one of your envelopes inside the mini-lab? That way you can be certain that your envelope is secure, and the agency might be able to predict the digits."

"That sounds like a good idea." I was secretly thrilled. I had carried one envelope with me to the basement and left the other two upstairs while I was talking with Cox. Perhaps someone was attempting to unseal them at this very moment. If I later found that the envelopes upstairs had been opened, I could be sure that Cox didn't do it.

"Ed, what do you expect to prove with this mini-lab research?" I asked. "No one accepts your films as authentic." I was irritated by the careful way that he was inspecting each object in the mini-lab. I could not forget the ridicule that people had heaped upon him at the parapsychology conference.

He looked at me cautiously. "What do you mean? This is a scientific investigation. I can't promise that I will ever be able to explain the phenomena that I observe, but I know that careful documentation of anomalous events will eventually lead to a greater understanding of them. We can come closer and closer to knowing the truth by scientific methods. The people at the Institute for Parapsychology have particularly rigid requirements regarding claims of the paranormal, and I am making every effort to meet those requirements."

"Don't you see that people are laughing at you?"

He was not flustered by my remark. "Anyone who engages in innovative research risks ridicule," he replied. "You should have heard all the hostile remarks directed at J. B. Rhine. He proved that ESP was real, and what happened? Established scientists ignored him, but it's still real. The truth doesn't change. They can laugh all they want, but that will not change anything. What is real is real. Look at Galileo. Look at what happened to him. They threatened him. They laughed at him. But the Earth goes around just the same."

"Well, I can't become deeply involved with this stuff. I'm trying to get a job as a sociology instructor. My haunting investigations have already tarnished my credentials, and I'm afraid this is really too much. I just can't risk it."

"You do what you want," Cox said with resignation. "But while you are here, you have a good opportunity to observe what is going on. As a sociologist, perhaps you can explain this thing. It certainly has me baffled." His candor was disarming. I felt troubled by his remarks.

I inspected the mini-lab closely. Cox was adding a dandelion to his array of target objects. "I want to observe what effect teleportation might have on this organic material," he explained.

I promised myself that I would become more observant, but I still didn't want to be connected to Cox's bizarre experiments.

Cox had something more to add. He seemed disturbed by my attitude. "A scientist can't ignore evidence just because it doesn't fit his preconceived notion of what is real. Scientists seek to uncover the truth. Doing experiments, making observations, even daring to try new methods; that is what science is all about."

I was disgruntled. Cox irritated me because I had no answer for him. He was a crackpot posing as Galileo. I was experiencing cognitive dissonance in a drama I had hoped to just observe. I had supposed that Cox was playing the role of the fool in this drama, and he was attempting to seize the role of a hero. I had to admit he had courage. I thought back to the evening in India when I had been advised to seek a guru. Perhaps Cox was my guru, I thought. The irony was discomforting. I was not going to follow him, I decided.

After breakfast, I spoke with Tom and Elaine in their kitchen. They were genuinely warm and friendly people.

"Was Mr. Cox over here this morning?" Elaine asked.

"Yes, he was concerned because his camera didn't seem to be working," Tom answered.

"Elaine, does Ed Cox irritate you?" I asked, "I catch a tone of resignation in your voice when you talk about him."

"Well, it's not that he irritates me exactly," Elaine replied. "It's just that he refuses to accept all these things that happen around here for what they really mean. The entities try to help him, but he ignores the message and meaning behind it. They're trying to show us that there is life after death, that there is a world beyond and that we should really try to help each other as much as we can to raise our spiritual levels. Without understanding that, all these psychic phenomena are meaningless."

"Elaine, I think Ed acts that way because he hopes to convince his scientific colleagues," Tom said, "He certainly has seen enough phenomena to know that different personalities are involved."

The raps began sounding from the kitchen floor. They came from a point close to my left foot. I switched on my tape recorder and placed the microphone directly over the point from which the raps seemed to be coming.

"Who's there?" Elaine asked the raps. We counted as a letter was rapped out.

"J," the raps answered.

"Oh, it's Jay," Elaine exclaimed.

"Who's he?" I asked.

"Jay is Elaine's brother who died when he was only three days old," Tom explained. "The story is that he has grown up on the other side and is supposed to be equivalent to twenty years old in relation to our time frame. I know it seems farfetched. Dr. Neihardt was always skeptical of this explanation, but I tend just to accept these entities as they wish us to. I mean to say that I really have no way of proving or disproving Jay's story, so I just accept him as he wishes to be accepted."

"Jay, is there any reason you came by?" she asked.

"Rap, rap." No.

"You just wanted to say hello?" she asked.

"Rap." Yes.

"Jim, maybe he would like to guess at your digits," Tom suggested. I looked at the envelope I held in my hand. The second one was locked "safely" in the mini-lab. The third was hidden "safely" in the guest room.

"Jay, would you guess at the digits inside this sealed envelope?" I asked.

He hesitated, then started rapping. At first, we thought he was spelling out a word. Then, we realized he was giving us the numbers. He rapped out 10 numbers before his power seemed to fade. My tape recorder had captured the audio portion of this event.

"Well, I guess I've accomplished my mission," I said gleefully.

"Are you going to open the envelope?" Elaine asked.

"Oh, no! These envelopes can only be opened at the Institute for Parapsychology in North Carolina. They're the ones who prepared the digits, and they must evaluate this experiment."

Tom seemed happy that a carefully controlled experiment had been conducted. I wondered if someone had unsealed the envelope while I had been talking to Cox in the basement the day before. It seemed undisturbed. Now I would have to wait until George Hansen at the Institute of Parapsychology evaluated the internal security devices. Who knows? Perhaps Jay had successfully guessed the digits.

During the afternoon, I read the paper that Cox had loaned me. I was astonished at the farfetched claims he seemed to accept. Cases like the one surrounding Dr. Richards occurred sporadically in the past. Raps, table levitations, spirit writing, and other unusual phenomena had been demonstrated by numerous psychically gifted individuals. The Scotsman Daniel Dunglas Home (1833-1886) was carefully investigated by the most famous scientist of the time, William Crookes. Home demonstrated an astonishing array of psychic feats, from raps to full levitations of his own body, often under controlled conditions with good lighting. Like Cox, Crookes devised special equipment that seemed to authenticate the amazing abilities of Home (and as with the mini-lab films, the scientists of his day ignored Crookes' findings).

Eusapia Palladino (1854-1918) was an illiterate Italian peasant who was recognized as a great medium during her era. She was closely investigated by various researchers, many of whom believed she had authentic paranormal ability. Professor Cesare Lombroso, considered "the father of modern criminology," found that Palladino could produce paranormal effects during experiments conducted in 1909. Other researchers, such as Pierre and Marie Curie, and Hereward Carrington, reached similar conclusions. Like the events surrounding Dr. Richards, some of the psychic phenomena that occurred around Palladino were photographed by researchers. She admitted to cheating whenever given the opportunity, and some investigators who conducted loosely controlled tests caught her engaging in fraud.

The Austrian Rudi Schneider also displayed an astonishing array of paranormal abilities. He apparently could interrupt an infrared beam paranormally while being tested under controlled conditions (Nicol, 1977; Rogo, 1975; Gregory, 1985).

Other more modern groups have also demonstrated phenomena like those claimed by SORRAT (Batcheldor, 1979; Owen and Sparrow, 1976). Batcheldor theorized that unconscious muscular movements generate PK-like effects that help people get over their fear of psi. The Philip Group in Toronto devised an imaginary spirit who seemed able to produce PK. In both cases, the energy required for psychokinesis seemingly came from the people present.

Cox's mini-lab experiments could be considered an extension of previous lines of research. SORRAT phenomena were no more extraordinary than those verified by researchers in the past. Cox's innovation was to construct a mini-lab and to document results with a film camera. His level of documentation seemed to exceed all previous studies.

SORRAT spirits' writing ability was not unique. In the psychical research literature, this phenomenon was known as "direct writing." Ancient Chinese writing evolved from divination; spirits were thought to generate symbols predicting the future. The Bible describes the origin of the Ten Commandments, a process involving direct writing (Deuteronomy 4:13, Exodus 32: 16). The Old Testament book of Daniel (5: 1-30) describes a spirit hand writing on a wall. With the emergence of Spiritualism in the 1850s, some mediums included direct writing as part of their séance performance. Baron Ludwig von Guldenstubbe (1820-1873) investigated the phenomenon in 1856. He placed paper and pencil in a small locked box, keeping the key on his person, and distinguished witnesses, upon opening the box, found messages in Latin, Greek, Russian, French, German, and English. The most famous of the direct writing mediums was Henry Slade (1825-1905). Although various psychical researchers verified that Slade's demonstrations of direct writing were authentic, he was caught cheating on occasion, like most Spiritualist mediums. Direct writing was only one of many trance performance skills that involved fraud, although some events were "proven" authentic. Famous mediums demonstrating direct writing included Eusapia Palladino, Helena Petrovna Blavatsky, and Indridi Indridason. Investigators who verified the phenomenon included William Stainton Moses, William Crookes, Horace Greeley, and Arthur Conan Doyle. The practice was sufficiently common that advertisements for séances sometimes mentioned direct writing as part of the performance, and specific mediums were thought particularly skillful in producing the effect. Cox's films of direct writing and other PK phenomena should be viewed as an extension of Spiritualist research. Many of those critical of Cox's films believed that PK was possible and some accepted the possibility of direct writing. Their concern was that his methodology was not sufficiently rigid.

In the evening, Tom, Elaine, Ed, Steve, and I conducted another ESP/PK experiment. I tried to be especially vigilant. I wanted to discover what caused the table to leap into the air. After the lights were dimmed, the table began vibrating in its rapid manner.

"Who's there?" Elaine asked.

"J," the raps spelled.

"Hello, Jay," Tom called.

"H-I," Jay rapped. I was amused at the difficulty of this minor exchange. Each letter had been laboriously rapped out.

I watched everyone's hands very closely. I could see that Ed and Steve were not producing the table vibrations. I noticed that the vibrations continued when either Tom or Elaine took their hands off the table, but they never took their hands away at the same time. Perhaps the vibrations were the result of a conspiracy between them.

"Jay, will you guess at the digits in Jim's envelope that is in the mini-lab?" Ed asked.

"Rap, rap, rap." Maybe.

"Could you rap directly on the microphone of Jim's tape recorder?" Ed asked.

"Rap, rap, rap." Maybe.

"Can you make something appear inside the mini-lab while our experiment is in progress?" Steve asked.

"Rap." Yes.

"Will you make something disappear off the table top and appear inside the mini-lab?"

"Rap." Yes.

"What can we use?" Steve asked, "What should we put on the table?"

"A-I-R." Then the table began jumping about rhythmically in merriment. It was not spelling out a message.

"Is this a song?" Elaine asked.

"Rap." Yes. It was a game that the entities played with the SORRATs. The table would beat out a rhythm, and the group would try to guess the song. Sometimes the SORRATs would give up and ask the raps to spell out the song's name. Then they sang the song together, and the table jumped in time with the music. It was a method for developing rapport. One song we sang was a parody the entities had written to the tune "Aquarius" in honor of Cox's mini-lab:

> It is the dinning of the ancient aquariums,
> Ancient aquariums
> Aquariums
> Aquariums.
>
> Harmony and understanding,
> Peace and love will now abound.
> Aquariums, aquariums!
>
> Mystic PK revelations,
> Rap sessions in all the nations.
> Mini-labs and levitations
> Fill the blokes with consternations
> Aquariums!
> Aquariums!

I could not keep from laughing at the absurdity of it. Then the table made a calypso beat. I thought of the "Banana Song" made popular by Harry

Belafonte but was too shy to mention it. No one else could guess the name of the song.

"We give up," Elaine told the entities. "What song is it?"

"B-A-N-A-N-A-S."

"What does that mean?" Tom asked.

The raps were silent. "You mean 'The Banana Song?'" I asked.

"Rap." Yes.

I sang "The Banana Song," and the table rapped along, but no one else seemed to know the words. They tried to hum along. Did I, alone, subconsciously influence the table?

The session eventually came to an end without any conclusive results. I decided that I would make a special effort to catch the trickster.[6] As I went to bed, I tried to program my subconscious mind so that I would awaken at the slightest noise. The Richards' house is small, and, in the quiet of the night, I thought I could hear any movement. I felt mentally prepared to solve the mystery.

In the morning, I awoke with a jolt. Something was happening. I crept out into the hallway. Everything was perfectly quiet. I felt my way down the basement stairs. No one else was there. I checked the mini-lab. The balloon that had been partially deflated was now totally empty, outside the mini-lab. Cox's dandelion, previously outside, was now inside the lab. Somehow these two objects had been transposed during the night. I was irritated with myself. The trickster had struck again—or perhaps the entities really existed. I looked closely at the dandelion stem. It was strangely charred. It seemed to be burnt at the end; the inside of the stem was damaged, but not the outside. Either this thing is authentic, or the trickster is a very imaginative individual, I thought.

I looked closely at the lock, string, and seal. They were intact. Cox's string is unique in that he seals it with a match and it melts slightly. I noticed that it had exactly the same length and configuration as when Cox charred it with his match. The trickster would have had to be astonishingly careful to duplicate the original shape of the melted thread. The dust on all four sides of the aquarium frame was undisturbed. There was plenty of dust. If a glass pane had been removed, this dust would be disturbed. I felt unsettled. I was too closely involved with this case.[7]

During the day, Tom showed me his collection of tape recordings of past ESP/PK experiments. He had over a hundred cassettes. He wanted me to listen to a lecture by John Neihardt, his advisor. Neihardt had been the poet laureate of Nebraska and the Plains States and a poet-in-residence at the University of Missouri at Columbia. He was the author of many widely read books including *Black Elk Speaks,* a book describing the teachings of an Oglala Sioux medicine man. I was shaken by the mini-lab events and listened to the tape recordings to avoid discussing my early morning experience with Tom.

The quality of the recording was poor, but Neihardt's voice was captivating. He sounded like a dynamic, creative, and wise man. The message was simple. Neihardt stated that he felt without doubt that raps, table tipping, and all the various other phenomena experienced by the group were real. He presented an image of a new consciousness associated with these phenomena. It was a holistic vision of a world in which psi was merely one aspect of the interconnected reality. The gentleness, strength, and wisdom within his voice made him doubly convincing.[8]

I knew that I had to get away. The world of Tom and Elaine Richards was filled with spirits, raps, levitations, matter passing through matter, and too many other unexplained events. It was a world that to me seemed insane and one that most scientists rejected. Elaine believed in the entities. Tom believed in the entities but encouraged Ed, and Ed believed in science. Neihardt's orientation supported them all.

Later in the day, I talked with Tom and Elaine. They were as normal as apple pie. No raps occurred. Cox came over and marveled at the events that occurred around his mini-lab. The camera had malfunctioned again. The trickster could work quickly when he or she did not have to fake the filming.

The next day, I prepared to leave. "You're coming back next weekend, aren't you?" Tom asked.

"I don't know yet," I answered. "I doubt that I can come back. I need to interview more researchers at the McDonnell Lab and then leave for Maryland."

I didn't want to return to Rolla. I did not want to ruin my career as a sociologist by becoming associated with a situation that was destined to draw criticism from the scientific community and that I could not begin to explain. I had accomplished my mission with the envelopes.

"May I loan you some of these tapes?' Tom asked, offering me cassettes from about 25 SORRAT sessions. I had listened to two the day before. They were as strange as the ones I had experienced in person.

"No, I don't think I'll really have time to listen to them. I have a lot of work to do."

Tom seemed hurt. "You can borrow them and mail them back whenever you're finished. There's no rush." I got the impression that he wished more people would show a scientific interest in the phenomena he experienced. Few people had stayed at his house as long as I had. He sincerely wanted me to understand what had occurred and why he believed as he did.

I accepted his tapes. It was the only polite thing to do. I wanted to get away and forget this craziness. I had the door open and was walking out when the raps began spelling out a message.

"I don't think I'll tape record any more raps," I said. "I have enough recordings. They can rap away all they want, but I need to be on my way."

Tom was not listening to me. He was counting the raps to figure out the message.

"J-N," it spelled out. John Neihardt.

"Dr. Neihardt!" Elaine exclaimed. "What an honor this is for us."

Enough is enough. This insanity must end! I stood waiting for this last act of the drama to conclude. It would be impolite to walk away from this distinguished guest.

"What is it that you want, Dr. Neihardt?" Elaine asked. The raps began spelling a word.

"You want Jim to come to Skyrim?' Elaine asked. Skyrim was Neihardt's home, now owned by his daughter Alice.

"Rap," Neihardt signified. Yes.

"We'll have to set it up with Alice for next weekend," Tom stated. "You are coming back, aren't you?"

I was at a loss for an excuse. Maybe Neihardt really was aware of what I was thinking! The idea was distressing. I could hardly make up a false excuse if he could read my mind! "OK, OK," I said with resignation. I decided I could call them up from St. Louis with an excuse to cancel this event.

I would have said anything to get away. I did not want to hear any more raps! Maybe Neihardt would be unable to read my mind and discover my deceitful excuse when I distanced myself from Rolla. The irony of my supposition troubled me, but I wanted to get away without offending my hosts.

"It was nice meeting you, Dr. Neihardt," I said as I left. "I'll talk to you later."

"Rap." Yes.

CHAPTER 3
SKYRIM

In St. Louis, I listened to more of Tom's cassette tapes. He began each session by announcing the date, location, time, and full name of each person present. The audiotapes recorded their conversation as they sat around the table. I listened to the sounds of the table moving about and the raps coming from the floor. The sessions were like the ones I had experienced. People communicated with the raps, and sometimes Tom described the table's movements so that his audiotape would capture the drama. When a levitation occurred, some participants grabbed their cameras and took pictures.

I grew familiar with the SORRAT members' voices. There were Tom, Elaine, Joe, Vern, and several others. John G. Neihardt was present at the earlier meetings. (Neihardt died in 1973.) Not all the sessions produced paranormal events. Much group time was spent sitting around the table, engaging in mundane conversation. The group often discussed personal psychic experiences. Sometimes they repeated a poem:

Two, four, six, eight,
Come on, table, levitate:
One, three, five, seven,
Come on, table, up to Heaven.

Some sessions were particularly startling. Tom, the record keeper, tried to document the group's experiences accurately. His voice had an incredulous tone when ostensibly paranormal events were taking place. For example, during a session labeled "The Night the Table Climbed the Tree," he told about the table jumping all around the room. It then led the group out a side door. It levitated up into the air, and Tom noted that it was caught in the branches of a tree, beyond the reach of the participants. During the action, the top of the table had flown off into the darkness. Someone was searching for it with a flashlight.

Certain props (test devices) were part of the drama. Cox moved to Rolla in 1977. He constructed what was termed a "coffee box." This was a sealed, shallow box with a glass top and a bed of coffee grounds on the floor. A light wooden cube, a medium- weight clay cube, and a heavy lead cube were sealed inside the box among the coffee grounds. The entities were encouraged to move the clay cube psychokinetically and thereby produce a pattern in the coffee grounds. If the pattern showed that the cube had lifted off the floor of the box, then levitation had apparently occurred. Fraudulent shaking of the box would be obvious since all three cubes would slide in relation to their individual weights. During some of the SORRAT sessions, the coffee box would be placed on a high shelf. Later, the entities would rap out "B-O-X" and the participants would gather around the box to marvel at the pattern that had apparently been produced psychokinetically by different movements of the cubes.

Another prop consisted of a paper sealed inside a transparent container. The entities could write a message on the paper during the group experiment. A skeptic pointed out that a cheater might use laser beams to mark the paper. I listened to a taped session that occurred after new containers made of plastic (that would be damaged by lasers) had been fashioned with aluminum foil as the medium for the entity writing. The entities were provided a stylus for writing. At the beginning of the session the participants observed that the foil was unmarked. Later they observed that a message had been transcribed on the aluminum foil. The epoxy seals on the box were observed to be undisturbed.

Cox was present during some of the taped sessions but not all these tapes were available to me. Cox coaxed the agency (as he called it) to guess correctly at concealed random digits he had prepared previously. He also rolled a die and covered it with his hand. The agency correctly guessed the die number. Cox repeated this die experiment again and again.

Dr. Neihardt attempted various tests of the entities' capabilities and seemed convinced of their paranormal nature. The tapes indicated that one SORRAT member, Joe, was especially skillful at going into trance. At times, Joe delivered messages to Neihardt from deceased acquaintances who had known the poet many years before. One tape documented Joe speaking to "three Indians" who wanted to give Neihardt a message. It seemed to me that the dialogue was typical of Spiritualist séances. Although the message was somewhat ambiguous, Neihardt interpreted it as coming from Black Elk. It seemed that Neihardt himself had gone through a process of increasing belief by his contact with Black Elk. Early in his relationship, he had recognized Black Elk's ability as a healer and later witnessed other feats, including clairvoyance and rain-making. Neihardt believed in life after death and, after his death in 1973, he convinced the group of his survival by rapping messages to them.

On some tapes, Elaine spoke with the entity named Jay, who spoke through Tom in trance. They carried on long, pleasant conversations during which Jay referred to Tom in the third person. These private sessions seemed like a clever way to maintain marital communications. Most couples have no means of talking over their problems in this unique manner. The tapes indicated that Tom can go into trance and suggested that he would not remember what he did while in trance.

During some sessions, objects *apported* (appeared out of nowhere). On occasion, Neihardt mentally requested a particular book to apport, and it had done so; a kind of paranormal magic trick that proved to Neihardt that the phenomena were real. Tom Richard's book, *SORRAT: A History of the Neihardt Psychokinesis Experiments, 1961-1981*, provides a more complete discussion of these phenomena.

Entity messages, communicated by raps and trance utterances, frequently had a moral theme. The spirits counseled the group to love wisely and to show altruism. The theme differed from the Christian message since the advice was to focus on those who seemed worthy of altruism. Although universal love was a goal, the entities stated that this was beyond the ability of the average individual. They advocated loving good friends and relatives as fully and completely as possible as a realistic goal.

The entity messages also explained that existence on the "other side" (after death) was very pleasant. Each entity could create whatever setting he or she desired, in a way that was "better" than reality. Once a participant asked if they had trees on the other side; the entities replied that they had the "essence" of trees, or trees with a quality that surpassed anything that we might experience on earth.

I was beginning to see the futility of conducting a parapsychological investigation of the table-tipping phenomena. My situation seemed equivalent to that of Spiritualist séance researchers. Séances conducted by the early Society for Psychical Research revealed that magicians could not only fool people but that afterward, eyewitness testimony varied considerably as to what had occurred.[1]

Listening to the tapes sparked my curiosity as a sociologist. Sociologists investigate *deviant behavior* (behavior that brings sanctions from others), and table-tipping falls in this category. SORRAT participants often concealed their activity from others, since non-believers, after learning about the table-tipping, tended to treat them unfavorably. Some people argued that the SORRATs were deceiving themselves or that they were frauds. Others thought table-tipping was demonic. Because of this stigma, the group, which had met regularly since 1961, developed an intense cohesiveness. Table-tipping was an aspect of their backstage selves that they shared only with those who were sympathetic.

Listening to the tapes weakened my hypothesis that Tom and Elaine produced all SORRAT phenomena fraudulently. Levitations occurred at group meetings when they were not present. They sometimes conducted table-tipping sessions with only themselves as participants. Why would they do this if they were both cheating? Why would Tom keep such complete records of all sessions if they were faked? Of course, movement of the table might result from unconscious muscular movements, but this could not account for all the reported phenomena.[2] Something highly unusual was occurring, at least from a social-psychological standpoint.

I decided that it would be better to conduct a sociological investigation rather than a parapsychological one. As a sociologist, I could publish my findings in an academic press. Table-tipping was a form of deviant behavior associated with an unusual system of beliefs. I would focus on the ways that the SORRATs explained their ostensibly paranormal experiences. In doing this, I would not need to worry so much about being fooled by faked paranormal events. I would just be a participant-observer in the drama. Changes in my own belief system would be as relevant to my investigation as would changes in others, since I would be focusing on belief rather than proving that observed events actually occurred. The questions I needed to answer were: "How did the actors in this drama come to believe as they did" and "how do they cope with the cognitive dissonance created by conflicting viewpoints?"[3]

On Wednesday, I called the Richards, and Tom answered the phone. Elaine called out, "That's Jim calling!"

"Okay if I come back?" I asked.

"Yes, of course!" Tom said. I had forgotten how much they wanted to make me feel welcome.

Tom gave me a friendly greeting when I arrived. "You know that I'm not a magician like Cox," I told him. "I'm a sociologist and I think I would be better off trying to learn as much as I can about the sociological aspects of what is going on around here rather than trying to prove that these paranormal things are real. Is it okay if I tape record an interview with you?"

"Oh sure!" Tom said. "I've been hoping that more people would take at least some interest in what's been going on here. Let's sit in the living room. You can leave your tape recorder on, and then if any raps come you'll be all set!" He was kidding me, I think, since I had been so eager to record raps on my previous visit. I decided that I would treat the raps as offstage actors in the SORRAT drama. We sat down, and I began my interview.

"Could you tell me about the early history of the SORRAT group?" I asked.

"Well, it really began with John G. Neihardt, who had been interested in psychic phenomena from a very early age. In 1882, at the age of 11, he had a severe fever and what we now call an out-of-body experience. Later, around 1902, he worked as a troubleshooter for J.J. Elkin, who ran a big trading post on the Omaha Reservation. He came to realize that there was a great deal of meaning within the Sioux religion, and he eventually was adopted into the Oglala Sioux tribe as Black Elk's spiritual son in the early 1930s. The Indians would shut themselves inside a tent and summon the spirits to answer their questions. Then the sides of the tent would shake paranormally as a means of answering. I suppose it was not unlike the rapping that we have here in that it was a means of spirit communication. Neihardt's wife, Mona, was somewhat of a psychic herself and had a precognitive dream about their eventual home at Skyrim, near Columbia, Missouri."

"So, you see," Tom continued, "John Neihardt was quite knowledgeable about psychic phenomena and knew that it was real from his own personal experience. He had come to believe that rapport within the group was a primary factor in eliciting psi and, consequently, he decided to organize a group in Columbia, where he taught at the University of Missouri. Although I knew nothing about psychic phenomena, he was my advisor for my Ph. D. dissertation, and I very much enjoyed talking with him. I was instrumental, in a way, in helping the SORRAT group meet in those early days, since I was the only student with a car. I would round everyone up and drive them over to Skyrim for the weekly meetings."

"Who came to the meetings?" I asked.

"We were mostly students at the University of Missouri. I was the oldest of the group. I think most of them were attracted to Dr. Neihardt more than anything else. That certainly was my reason for coming. He was a person whom people liked to be around."

"What happened at the meetings?"

"At first, nothing. We would sit around and talk. He had a 40-pound wooden table, and we would put our hands on it and try to get it to levitate. Although nothing happened week after week, it was still fun. Dr. Neihardt was a very wise and warm man, and the group was building rapport, so people enjoyed themselves. I guess it was after about three months that we got the first raps."

"You mean raps like the raps here?"

"Yes. Only in the beginning they were not as clear. I think it was Black Elk. As time passed, the raps got stronger, and Dr. Neihardt put a great deal of effort into investigating them. Once the raps came from the arm of a chair, and he had the chair disassembled to look for rapping devices. Another time he pulled up the floorboards, looking for an explanation for the raps. Once he had everyone place their feet on pillows to prevent anyone from making rapping noises with their feet."

"Dr. Neihardt knew Black Elk very well and asked the raps many questions to which only he and Black Elk knew the answers. He eventually became satisfied that it really was Black Elk."

"He also began to get vibrations from the extremely heavy table and later we even got levitations with it. Dr. Neihardt borrowed an infrared scope so that an observer could see in the dark and attempt to spot fraud. After a great deal of effort in precluding the possibility of fraud, he corresponded with Dr. J.B. Rhine at Duke University. That is how they came to devise the concept of the mini-lab. In 1966, Rhine gave a lecture in Missouri, and Dr. Neihardt gave him some photographs of levitating tables. That attracted Mr. Cox's attention, since he was an associate of Rhine's at the Institute for Parapsychology in North Carolina. Mr. Cox first came out here in 1969. If you want a more detailed explanation of the history of the SORRATs, you should read my book."[5]

Tom went on to tell story after story of paranormal events that the group had experienced. In the early days, the sessions attracted huge crowds. Officials at the University of Missouri learned of the sessions and harassed the SORRATs, since they were engaging in what many considered to be occult activities right in the heart of the Bible belt. One woman was temporarily committed for psychiatric examination by her parents (they attempted to force her to deny that she had seen tables levitate). A German student had to return to her country because a dean at the university prevented the renewal of her visa. Other members lost scholarships because of the university's disapproval of the group. One was disowned by his family after the university informed his parents of his SORRAT activities. Eventually, Dr. Neihardt and the core group decided that small, private meetings would be more suitable.

In the morning, Tom, Elaine, and I sat at the kitchen table. The raps began spelling a message.

"B-A-R"

"What does that mean?" Tom asked.

"Maybe they're thirsty—do you have a bar here?" I joked.

"Is someone at a bar?" Elaine asked the entities.

"Rap, rap" No.

"Ok, so what does it mean?" Tom asked.

"B-A-R-B-E-N-D."

"Is there a bar in the mini-lab?" Tom asked.

"Rap." Yes.

"OK, let's go down and check it out!" I exclaimed. We rushed down to the basement and saw that a heavy aluminum bar inside the mini-lab had been bent. But we discovered that Cox had not locked or sealed his lab. He hadn't been able to fix the camera and was not planning to document any evidence. Anyone could have bent the bar during the night. In fact, the markings on the bar seemed to indicate that it had been bent by pressing it against the edge of a table.

"Why did they bend the bar when it doesn't prove anything?" I asked Tom.

"I really don't know," he answered. "Maybe they didn't realize that the lab wasn't set up to collect data."

"Maybe they just felt like doing it," Elaine said, smiling. "Doesn't bending a bar seem like fun?"

Later in the day, I bought a postcard and wrote a question on it for the entities: "How can we conduct our research with you in a better manner?" I placed a stamp on the card and addressed it to myself. When Ed Cox came over I had him place the card in the mini-lab before he locked and sealed it. As a sociologist, I was free to address questions to anyone, even to "offstage" actors. I knew the trickster could retrieve my card. I wanted to encourage him or her to write, so that I could get more handwriting specimens. I carefully checked Cox's lock and seals after he left.

The next morning, my postcard was gone, and a message had been written inside the lab. The message was "Easter Cheer" and was signed "J." It was the day before Easter and the day we were to meet at Skyrim. I inspected Cox's lock and seal. They were in the exact same condition as he had left them. The melted thread still had its slight twist and was bent in the manner I had observed after Ed had melted it with his match.

"Happy Easter, Jay," I said to the mini-lab. There was no reply.

Alice Thompson, Dr. Neihardt's daughter, supported herself by running a horse stable at Skyrim Farm. The property was on a high point in the area, looking out in all directions at the rolling Missouri landscape, hence its name, Skyrim. After we arrived, Tom and I walked to the side of the aging wood-frame farmhouse and talked with the people standing there. I was surprised at the warmth with which the SORRAT members greeted each other. It was obvious that they were old friends. The raps were excited by the interaction, also. Someone was rapping from out of the ground from a point in front, and slightly to the right, of Tom's foot.

"Who's there?" Tom asked.

"S," the raps began.

"Is it Sig?" Tom asked.

"Thump." Yes. The raps were not really raps. The sound they made coming out of the earth was more like a "thump." I had heard Sigurd, nicknamed Sig or Siggie, communicate by raps on the tapes that I had listened to in St. Louis. Sig was Dr. Neihardt's son. He had died in 1972, a year before Neihardt's death.

Tom was excited and pleased to talk with Sig again. "We had some really good times together," he told me. "I really am quite fond of the man. We used to ride together on his motorcycle. He was not only an incredibly talented concert pianist, but a real daredevil on the bike."

"Thump," Sig agreed.

I told the group about an event that occurred on a tape-recorded session to which I had listened. Sig had been asked what had happened to a recording of one of his concerts. "L-O-S-T," he replied.

"Oh, that's a real shame," a group member exclaimed.

"D-A-M-N-R-I-G-H-T," Sig responded.

People laughed at the story. I asked Sig if he felt that he still had the same personality. He rapped out, "Thump; thump, thump, thump," which is generally translated by the SORRATs as "yes, in a way."

Tom and I went inside the farmhouse where the energy seemed to be even more intense. The raps came from three different places at the same time. The group members seemed more interested in talking to one another than in communicating with the raps. "We are very used to it," Alice explained. I viewed the scene with skepticism. How difficult it must be to create the raps fraudulently while engaging in active conversation! Perhaps it was like a ventriloquist's act. It was quite a show! Why were they going to so much trouble to convince me? I was just a visitor, an observer.

I sat down at one end of a table and Tom sat at the side. Some raps were coming from the floor behind me. "Rap, rap; rap, rap, rap. Rap, rap; rap, rap, rap."

"Hey, Black Elk!" I said with surprise. I recognized his tom-tom beat. "That's you, isn't it?"

"Rap." Yes.

A woman named Jackie whom I had just met was sitting to my right. She had never associated with SORRAT before, and this was her first encounter with the raps. I was amused by the role I now played. I was the individual who counted and interpreted the raps' message. Tom had always done this for me before.[6]

"What's that?" Jackie asked.

"That's Black Elk," I told her. "He's an Indian medicine man, and old friend of Neihardt."

"Oh!" she said, her eyes widening.

"Black Elk, do you have a particular message of us?" I asked.

"Rap, rap." No.

"Are you coming back tonight for the main part of the experiment?" Tom asked.

"Rap." Yes. He then launched back into his signature or "power beat." "Rap, rap; rap, rap, rap! Rap, rap; rap, rap, rap! Rap, rap; rap, rap, rap!"

Later in the afternoon, other raps began sounding, often simultaneously from different places in the room. Elaine walked to where I was sitting with Steve Calvino.

"Who is there?" I asked the raps. Elaine and I counted out the letters.

"P.W."

"Who's that?" I asked. Elaine didn't seem to know.

"Maybe we made a mistake in counting," I said. "Could you rap that out again?"

"P.W."

"Is this someone we know?" Elaine asked.

"Rap." Yes.

It was like a game of charades. "Okay, give us a hint. First letter is P. First word, sounds like?" I laughed, trying to coax a response.

But Elaine had a flash of insight. "Is it Patience Worth?" she asked.

"Rap." Yes.

"Who's Patience Worth?" I asked.

"She was a famous spirit during the early part of this century," Elaine said. "In about the 1920s, a woman in St. Louis, Mrs. Curran, would go into trance, and Patience Worth would write through her. It was really a remarkable case, since Mrs. Curran was almost completely uneducated and yet the books that she produced with Patience Worth writing for her were judged by many to be of high literary quality."

"Rap," Patience responded. Yes.

"Patience was a highly religious lady who lived in England in the seventeenth century. Later, she came to America and was killed by Indians."

"Rap." Yes.

Patience Worth began spelling. "C-A-R-D."

"Does this have to do with Jim's card that got out of the mini-lab?" Steve asked.

"Rap." Yes.

"Were you the one who mailed it?" he asked.

"Rap." Yes.

Apparently, the person or thing that made the raps knew what happened last night with the mini-lab.

"H-O-L-Y- M- E-A- L."

"Holy meal," Steve interpreted. "Is this the message on Jim's card?"

"Rap." Yes.

"Are we supposed to have a special meal for Jim before he leaves?" Elaine asked.

"Rap, rap." No.

I would have to wait until I returned to Maryland to find out the meaning of this message. How very strange!

Later in the afternoon, Black Elk's power beat became very dynamic. Some people were sitting around a metal TV table with their hands on it in broad daylight. For a while the raps seemed to be coming directly out of the center of the table.

"Black Elk, could you make raps on the microphone of Jim's tape recorder?" Tom asked.

"Rap, rap, rap." Maybe, he answered, and continued with his power beat.

"Black Elk, could you guess the digits inside my sealed envelope?" I asked. I had brought one envelope with me.

"Rap, rap." No. Then he continued his power beat. "Rap, rap; rap, rap, rap. Rap, rap; rap, rap, rap. Black Elk seemed to be busy with a personal ceremony.

The people in the group continued talking with one another. Alice told me that because of her interactions with Sigurd and her father while they were on the other side, she was certain that there was life after death. For her, the evidence was irrefutable. They had convinced her of their authenticity many times over. This was a pattern that I had observed during my haunting investigations; people who had many anomalous experiences acquired powerful beliefs regarding spirits, souls, life after death, and magical abilities.

Black Elk ended his power beat and began a message. "B-O-X," he spelled out. A SORRAT member had previously shaken the coffee box to smooth out the grounds and placed it on a tall cabinet. The box was visible to all, but the movement of the cubes could not be observed. Alice took the coffee box down from its place. An Indian design with a tepee had been formed. It looked as if the clay cube had levitated in places as it had moved about creating the design. The wooden cube had remained stationary.[7] Black Elk continued his power beat. The whole table shook with his rapping. Later, when I played back my tape recording of the afternoon's events, I found that at one point it sounded as if the raps were coming directly on my microphone. I later found that this evidence had disappeared. It seemed as if the raps had been erased from the audiotape.

Later that evening, Steve Calvin showed mini-lab films to the group. What had seemed ridiculous to the parapsychologists was accepted as normal by this group. Could objects pass through the aquarium glass? Of course, they could! The films were merely a documentation of what the entities had been doing all along. The SORRAT group was entertained and thrilled by the films just as they had been by the coffee box "trick." The raps sounded in the room in three different places as the films were shown. They rapped "yes" as Calvin explained each segment. They seemed to enjoy the show, too!

After the arrival of an original member, Joe, the group formed a large circle of 17 people. The raps requested that various people switch places. Apparently, they wanted a special arrangement of those present. Again and again, they requested changes. "This is going to take all evening," Joe joked. "By the time they finish rearranging us, it will be time to go home!" Everyone laughed.

Finally, the experiment began. Some of the group put their hands on the metal TV table. I had both my hands on the table, but I also had my camera ready to record any levitation that might occur. The lights were dimmed, but the moon was bright enough so that everything in the room was visible. The table started vibrating vigorously, leaping from side to side. I watched people's hands. Black Elk was rapping his power beat. Finally, the table rose about four feet into the air. I reached down with one hand for my camera. The table was vibrating and bobbing around. I leaned back, taking my other hand away from the table and shot a picture. I could not aim, only shoot. The flash blinded everyone. I shot another picture although I couldn't see anything. Then I reached into the circle to locate the table. It was bobbing around at waist level. I snapped another picture and the table fell. It seemed to be hung up on a chair but eventually began vibrating and freed itself.

Then the raps began giving messages. Several relatives of people in the group signified their presence. They rapped out initials and were identified. Joe began groaning. He seemed to be going into a trance.[8] I kept my hands on the table as did Jane, the young woman who sat beside me. The table began sliding into the next room, taking me and half the group with it. The rest of the group remained behind to listen to Joe talk while in trance.

The table began leaping around violently and pounding out Black Elk's rhythm: BEAT, BEAT . . . BEAT, BEAT, BEAT. Suddenly, a pine cone appeared with a thud on the table. No one had taken their hands off the table, so I could not figure out where it came from. Who threw it? It seemed to have appeared rather than to have been thrown. As the table jumped around, the pine cone rolled vigorously back and forth on the tabletop. It seemed impossible that it could stay on a table that was jumping about so violently. I could not explain the effect.

"Did you bring the pine cone, Black Elk?" someone asked. Someone remarked that it was astonishing that the cone remained on the table while it jerked up and down.

"Rap," Black Elk sounded. Yes.

The room had many artifacts that had belonged to Neihardt and his wife. The objects began vibrating. The effect lasted for perhaps a minute. I focused my attention on a ceramic turtle that had rocked on its legs. I touched it and it rocked for about ten seconds due to my touch. The legs were not even, apparently. A moment later, it began rocking on its own. I carefully timed the rocking with my watch. It rocked for 60 seconds. I wondered what caused the effect.

Then the whole room seemed to shake. It felt like an earthquake, except that the vibrations came in waves. All the objects were shaking. I felt a deep rapport with everyone there. We were smiling and laughing. I held hands with

Jane beside me. Was she part of a conspiracy to divert my attention? I felt foolish for being so skeptical. Everyone else was relaxed and enjoying the effect.

How was the earthquake effect possible? Perhaps the beams under the floor were not particularly strong. Would it be possible to cause the room to shake by jumping up and down? I tried flexing my knees and shaking followed. It lasted for a while after I stopped. Did my flexing cause the shaking or did it begin on its own? I flexed my knees again. Once more, the earthquake effect occurred. I waited until the shaking stopped and watched the people in the room. Apparently, it was possible to make the room vibrate by jumping up and down. Had someone else created the earlier effects?[9]

Another earthquake wave began. I did not see anyone flexing their knees to cause the effect. I watched everyone very closely. Could it be that all the people in the room were subconsciously flexing their knees in an undetectable manner? I saw no one causing the shaking. I tried to view everyone's legs and feet. Then I felt another wave of rapport.[10] It was something different from the earthquake, but it was a kind of wave that swept over me and over everyone else, I think. I realized my skepticism was out of place. I could not verify anything by just watching. I was a sociological observer. I had the impression, at the time, that as I jumped up and down the room shook very slightly and that this activated authentic phenomena. It was certainly a strange experience! The earthquake seemed to come in waves and exceeded the effect I had produced on my own. I also had the impression that the phenomenon acted in a way that allowed it to conceal itself from me. I could not be certain that it was paranormal. It was acting in a way that allowed me to think that it might not be paranormal.

The entities began rapping out a message, "E-M-B-R-A-C-E." Everyone put their arms around one another in a large circle.

Like Joe, Alice had gone into trance. She had become Black Elk and was waving Black Elk's staff. She ceremonially blessed each one of us. The tension built as Black Elk, using Alice's body, struggled to speak. We became silent, but Alice was unable to talk. Someone asked the raps, "What should we do?"

"R-E-L-A-X," they spelled out. We sat down. Black Elk continued his ceremonial movements through Alice.

Joe was led into the room. He was deep in trance. He spoke very slowly and deliberately. "I am Many Voices. I have come to tell you that we are all one. I am the collective voice of many high levels. In spirit, I join with you. We are one. You may now come to me and ask questions."

One by one the SORRAT group members sat before Joe. First, they embraced him, and then spoke with him. He talked at length with each. The raps spelled out my surname correctly. I guess this proves that something paranormal is occurring, I thought to myself with amusement. Rapping out "McClenon" correctly is no easy task.

Then the raps spelled out, "B-E H-E-R-E!" Jane pushed me toward Joe.

"It's your turn now," she whispered.

I went forward and embraced Joe. He held me for a long time.

"You are very strong," he said, in trance. "It is good. I am Many Voices. All life, all entities, all the universe, are one. No matter how lonely you feel, you should know that we are one with you. We are always with you. We will help you. Even in death, you are not alone. All life is one. If you have any questions, ask."

"I am wondering what will become of me," I asked. "Soon I will receive my Ph.D., and I am looking for a job as a college instructor. I wonder where I will get one."

"Do you wish to work in the city or in the country?" Many Voices asked.

"That doesn't matter," I answered. "I just want to serve. I wish to work in my profession."

"You have answered correctly." Joe pulled me away from him and looked into my eyes. "Tomorrow is Easter. It is a day of peace. One day you will know where your job will be. When that day comes, you will know. We will always be with you, helping you. You will serve well. Believe in us and trust in the Other Side. We will help you to do good."

I was overwhelmed. It was not the content of the message that touched me, but the energy that passed beyond words, striking a note deep within my soul. I could not stop crying. Something beyond science was occurring here. I remembered the monsoon rain in Vietnam. I remembered the voice of the rain in India. I was learning without words.

It was late in the evening. Jane brushed away my tears with her fingers. "What did he say?" she asked.

"He said we are all one."

The raps had everyone come together. Joe and Alice came out of their trances. "P-E-A-C-E," the entities rapped. "L-O-V-E, H-A-P-P-Y E-A-S-T-E-R. E-N-D." The experiment was over. We bid each other goodbye.

During the long drive back to Rolla with Tom and Elaine, I came back down to earth. As my thoughts became more logical, the "skeptical" part of me made a joke to see how they would react. "That was really something," I said. "You had all those people hiding under the floor, making raps, but I can't figure out how the coffee box trick was done. How did you do it?"

They seemed hurt. "Do you really think we all were cheating?" Elaine asked.

"No," I answered. I waited for a response, but they didn't say anything. "I was just kidding. I can't figure any of it out."

"It's like that for many people," Elaine said. "You'll get used to it. It takes time. It's surprising at first, but you will get used to it."

I didn't know what to believe. Experiences that occur under uncontrolled conditions do not constitute scientific evidence. I knew that I had gathered no evidence that would convince a parapsychologist.

The next morning, I tried to sleep while Tom and Elaine were at church. Ed Cox was in the basement, working on the mini-lab. I was irritated because we had gotten in late, and Cox was making noise early in the morning.

I heard him knock at the door of my room. "Did you throw my aluminum bar into the corner?" Cox demanded.

"Ed, why would I do something like that?" I said. He irritated me. I was trying to sleep.

"I brought it up from the mini-lab and carefully put it on the table," Cox stated. "Now it's lying in the corner as if thrown. I hope that this hasn't damaged any fingerprints that might have been on it. I'm taking it over to the police station this afternoon for fingerprinting."

"Ed, I'm trying to sleep. I didn't touch your aluminum bar. Maybe Tom and Elaine snuck back from church and tossed it in the corner."

"No, that's impossible," he said, looking at me strangely. "I would have heard them come in the door. Maybe there's a poltergeist loose here."

"Yeah, maybe there's spirits here or something."

"You joke, but I am trying to gather important evidence. This aluminum bar appears to have been bent in a normal manner. I want to get to the bottom of this."

"Good luck," I replied. The memory of Skyrim was fresh in my mind. Perhaps these spirits really existed. If none of this was paranormal, then Cox must be part of the huge conspiracy. If the spirits were real, why would they throw his bar in the corner? Why did they bother to bend it in the first place?

Tom, Elaine, Ed, and I went to a restaurant for dinner. Even though it was Easter Sunday, it was not a peaceful meal—because Ed was with us. Ed had me describe my experiences at Skyrim. I told him that I had communicated with spirits, raps, the table had moved around, a pine cone had appeared, and the room had shaken as if there was an earthquake.

"There is no reason to assume that discarnate entities (beings without physical bodies) produced any of the effects that you described," Ed told me. "A scientist would not make that assumption."

"I told you what I experienced, Ed," I replied.

"But as a scientist, you must realize that it is quite possible for humans with psychokinetic abilities to produce effects that seem to be related to spirits and entities. A scientist tends to lean toward the simplest explanation for a phenomenon, and in this case, it is that living humans are responsible for the effects."

Elaine grew angry. "Someday you will open your mind, Mr. Cox," she said. "Someday you will have to stop playing scientific games. Someday you will be on the other side. Then you will stop quibbling about these things."

A heated argument ensued.[11] What happened to Easter, the day of peace? I reviewed my experiences at Skyrim. I knew that in emotional situations, people's perceptive ability sometimes becomes inaccurate. Perhaps I had been fooled. Parapsychologists have uncovered many cases that at first seemed astonishing but later turned out to be fraudulent. As I was not a magician, how could I know for sure what actually occurred?

But for a while, at Skyrim, I did not doubt. My life had been changed. I had come to Missouri to find fraud but had instead found an unknown aspect of myself. I had undergone a deep emotional catharsis at Skyrim. I had hoped to catch a trickster, but instead the entities had caught me.[12]

As we walked out of the restaurant, Elaine winked at me and smiled. "Do you know why we brought you to this restaurant?" she asked.

"No, why?" I answered.

"Because sometimes we're able to hear raps here!"

"Really! You mean with all these other people here?"

"Just act normally," she said. "Don't look down. Don't cause a scene. I think there's some raps here right now." Ed and Tom were still carrying on a heated discussion. It was hard to hear anything above the noise of people talking in the restaurant.

I was standing close to the door. I felt some raps under my feet. It felt as if someone were underneath the floor tapping lightly and quickly with a hammer. "Who is it?" I asked. I tried to count the first letter.

"It's nobody we know," Elaine said and pushed me out the door. "We can't stand there and count the raps with everyone looking at us." I had felt the raps very clearly under my feet. They were spelling out a letter. Who was making the raps? This was not something that I had expected or imagined. There had been many raps; maybe a "P" for Patience Worth?

The next day I left to return to my home in Maryland. I was puzzled. What had I fallen into by visiting the SORRATs?

CHAPTER 4
LETTERS FROM THE SPIRITS

The postcard that I had addressed to myself in Rolla arrived at my home in Hyattsville, Maryland. The message was written in a strange and seemingly archaic form of English. It was signed "Patience Worth." The text read:

THINKEST THOU THAT THE VITILIERS WERT DULCITTE YER?
THOU SHALT SAVOR THE SMACKE OF HOLINESS FAR MORE IF YE COMME INTO THE KINGDOMME FEAST!

I was not certain about the exact letters in some words. I went to the library to get information about Patience Worth. I found that she was a spirit who came through a St. Louis medium, Pearl Curran, in 1913. Patience said that she had been born in England in 1649 and immigrated to America as an adult. She explained in her messages that she had been killed by Native Americans in 1694. Patience Worth, through Mrs. Curran, wrote numerous historical novels, the most famous of which was set during the time of Christ. This was considered quite remarkable, since Mrs. Curran had a limited education and had traveled little. Skeptics argue that Patience Worth was a trance creation of Pearl Curran, and there is not sufficient evidence to refute that argument. A major psychical investigator during this era, Dr. Walter Franklin Prince, believed that Mrs. Curran's writing revealed information (confirmed by historians) that her mind could not have obtained by normal means. Although Dr. Prince considered this case as supporting the existence of the paranormal, modern skeptics disagree and provide evidence indicating that Patience Worth was a fictitious creation of Mrs. Curran.

Other psychical research cases revealed parallel features: the phenomena's weirdness implied an extraordinary quality even if the evidence regarding its authenticity is lacking. There seemed to be a link between creativity and distortion of consciousness—psychotic, schizotypal, unusual, anomalous, mystical, and shamanic experience.

I interpreted the text as saying: "Do you think the food was sweet here? You'll like the feast in heaven even more!" I could not determine if the text represented Patience Worth's era. During the 1600s, British people spoke English as in Shakespeare's plays or in the King James Bible, but I did not know if the words *dulcitte, vitiliers*, or *smacke* were used.

I had my film of the table levitation developed. The first picture showed the table at head level. The people behind it had astonished looks on their faces. The person beside me was reaching in and touching the top of the table, but his thumb was slightly under the edge. It seemed impossible to hold the table up in this manner, but it could be that his arm had lifted the table up and he was in the process of releasing it. I looked at the photograph closely. The arm and hand were Tom's. Why was he cheating?

The second picture showed people's faces, nothing more. The table had fallen out of view. Blinded by the first flash, I had not aimed properly for the second shot.

The third picture showed the table slightly above waist level. Again, a hand was holding it. The fingers were clearly grabbing the table with the thumb under the rim. I had documented cheating, but it was not Tom's arm. He was getting his camera ready at that time. I was furious. There was a conspiracy. Someone else was cheating. I looked closely at the ring on the finger of the cheater's hand. It was mine! I had reached in to locate the bobbing table!

How was the table staying up? Was I subconsciously supporting it? At the time, I did not believe I was lifting the table. I was trying to locate the table so that I could aim my camera. It seemed that my photographs did not prove anything. I had documented an ambiguous situation.

Perhaps the postcard would shed light on the problem. I sought advice from an expert in Elizabethan English at the Folger Shakespeare Library in Washington, D.C. I showed her my postcard. She rubbed at the pen marks with her finger suspiciously.

"How did this script get on the card?" she asked.

"I'm a member of the Society for Psychical Research. Patience Worth is a disembodied entity who claims the ability to write."

"I don't believe in ghosts, but I suppose the people during Ms. Worth's era believed," she said.

"What era is that?" I asked.

"Actually, the text can't be said to fit in with any particular era. It has Elizabethan qualities, but it is a mixture of archaic styles."

We went over each word, but she was uncertain about some words because the letters were not clear. We discussed the word *dulcitte*, for example.

"I can't make that out," she said. "It may be dulcitte, meaning sweet, but it might be fulcitte, meaning false or deceiving. It could mean, 'Thinkest thou that the food providers (vitiliers) were deceiving you? You'll get better tasting food if you go to a righteous place!' Were you in a place associated with fraud?"

"Perhaps," I said. "Patience Worth may not be an actual person."

"It could mean something completely different. 'Thinkest thou that the food (vitiliers) were sweet (dulcitte) here (yer). Thou shalt savor the taste (smacke) of holiness far more if you come into the Kingdom Feast!'"

"What is the Kingdom Feast?" I asked.

"I don't know," she answered. "Could it mean death?"

I felt a shiver go up my spine.

When I returned to my house, I looked at my photographs of the table levitation. Was the food sweet? Was I being deceived? Dr. Richards, an English professor with knowledge of the Elizabethan period, could have written the message. I was no closer to resolving this issue than before I received the postcard.

I sent George Hansen, at the Institute for Parapsychology, the sealed envelope with the spirit Jay's guesses of its contents. George informed me that there had been one correct guess in ten attempts, a result exactly equal to what could be predicted by chance. The seals had remained intact. No one had tried to break in, he said.

I reviewed my evidence. I had photographs, archaic writing, and the results of a controlled test. Nothing had been resolved. Was the "holy meal" sweet or false?[1]

I decided to conduct another test of the entities' ESP ability. I had previously told myself that I would do a sociological study of SORRAT, but I figured that SORRAT had been founded with the goal of doing scientific research. As a SORRAT member, I was supposed to conduct scientific studies. I set a time and date when I planned to send a mental image to the SORRAT entities. I sent Tom a self-addressed envelope with instructions that he place it in his basement by the mini-lab. Inside the unsealed envelope was my message requesting that the entities describe or draw the target image. I also requested that they teleport the envelope to the post office when the task was completed.

"This shouldn't be too difficult for them," I thought. "After all, I'm not even asking them to get the envelope out of the sealed mini-lab!"

After mailing the package, I prepared a set of ten pictures and used a random process to select which picture would be considered the "target." The selected picture was of St. George sitting on his horse, spearing a serpent-like dragon. When the appointed date and time arrived, I focused my mind on the picture.

Not long afterwards, my self-addressed envelope arrived in the mail. It was marked with an unusual return address: a drawing of a clock without hands above the symbol for infinity (the number "8" on its side). I carefully opened the envelope. It contained papers and ashes. The entities had guessed at my ESP target image by drawing a picture, but their artistry had been burnt into thirds. The drawing that they created was of a horse positioned in the same way as the one in the target picture. Their artwork contained two small birds in the place of the dragon. (Later Sammy, the entity who sent the drawing, explained that he did not like reptiles, so he replaced the dragon with birds.) Their response seemed remarkably similar to the picture of Saint George, but the burning of the sketch was certainly odd! Also enclosed in the envelope was a letter from the entities responding to test questions from Dr. John Beloff, a parapsychologist in Scotland. He hoped that they would answer his questions, which were sealed inside an envelope he had sent them. The envelope had been burned open, destroying the evidential quality of the entities' responses. The envelope also contained some small gold-plated squares and two unlinked and burnt leather rings. I carefully mailed Beloff's envelope along with the gold-plated squares and charred rings to him in Scotland.

Although the entities' guess was fairly accurate, this trial was just the first of a planned ten-part series. I wrote to Tom and Elaine and enclosed another self-addressed envelope with more questions for the entities. I hoped to establish a dialogue with them. Among my questions, I asked about some leather rings that had been provided to the spirits for linking. SORRAT hoped to create a permanent example of a paranormal event.

The response to my questions came back in less than two weeks.

Q: Dear Spirit Friends, I enjoy communicating with you. Could you answer some questions for me?

A: Yes.

Q: Could you cause this letter to disappear from the mini-lab and not go directly to the post office? Does it require extra effort for you to hold on to it for a few days?

A: Yes and yes. It requires incredible effort to do any physical act across the barrier.

Q: Did human beings evolve from apes?

A: No, both humanoids and apes physically evolved from an (extinct) common ancestor. Spiritually, the evolution was vastly different and not to the disadvantage of the apes.

Q: How can we help mankind to lose the fear of psi?

A: Durned if I know, if you don't! Seriously, Jim, people tend to fear what they don't comprehend. It upsets their zeitgeist to think that zeit might also contain some geists. So, keep running tests, publish, let the world know, but be brave for the fearful.

Q: Why can't you link the leather rings? Is it because of this fear of psi? Why were Beloff's envelopes burned?

A: Folk don't operate by the rules of Hoyle. We try, but they reject because nature abhors an anomaly. They require constant energy to maintain an "impossible" state. Fear of psi is a lot of it, too. Belief has much to do with how the universe appears and thus, objectively/subjectively, it "is." Really, you know it is in flux, but try telling that to the "doubters" (who do not doubt they know their view, materialism, is the only possible way the universe can ever be). It would make a dog laugh! What fools these mortals be! Most do not want an uncomfortable verity.

Sorry about the envelopes. Paper ignites easily if we do not control its passage just so. The molecular friction during a botched apport is a real bitch.

Love,

Ellis, J., John K., Rector

I wrote to Tom asking him to tell me about the entities who had signed this message. He informed me that Ellis is Elaine's deceased older brother. "J" referred to Elaine's infant brother, Jay (now apparently a young man). John K. was John King, a seventeenth century buccaneer who had served under Sir Henry Morgan. Rector was a member of the Imperator Group, a collection of "high level" entities, active during the Spiritualist era. The Imperator had been a "control" (a kind of spiritual moderator) for Mrs. Leonore E. Piper (1857-1950), known for her authenticity. John King had been connected with many mediums caught cheating.

I decided that I would attempt to form a psi group of my own with the hope of replicating the SORRAT phenomena or at least getting raps. I did not think I could prove much without adequate controls, and the SORRATs led me to believe their phenomena could be replicated. I continued my dialogue with them.

Q: Spirit Friends: Do you have any advice that you might give me concerning the levitation group that I am trying to get together? Where is the best place to meet? Will you help me to get proper people?

A: Meet where all are most comfortable together. Dim lights help. Trust and selfless affection help more.

Q: Is there anything we, on this side, should know in order to develop better practical applications of psi?

A: Know that you can do it yourselves. Direct your lives to doing good, and like Padre Pio,[2] you can levitate in ecstasy unawares. Know your own natures.

Q: Is there something that we, on this side, can do to help the people on your side? Is there any specific favor that I personally might do?

A: Be kind to one another on your side of the Barrier. Altruism, tempered with wisdom, helps far more than you can see. Live to raise the spiritual level of others and thereby of your individual self, too.

Q: What tasks are most difficult for you to do and what tasks are least difficult? Why is this so?

A: Our most difficult task is to prevent evil, power-perverted men from destroying and enslaving and hatefulling the goodly planet God entrusted to your stewardship. This is so because freedom of choice lets man choose wrongly.

Q: Are there any activities that we might engage in that would optimize your ability to perform psi tasks?

A: Love wisely. Do not squabble among yourselves. (Hate only evil, but love the person within wise limits; the world needs no more bleeding victims!) Treat each in your circle, and all humanity, as part of the All. Let your minds achieve at-one-ment. Let the vibes of unity flow. Do not get hung up on trivia. Believe psi can and it will occur. Know it will.

The burnt pictures, the failure to link leather rings, the failure of the Beloff experiment, and the tone of the messages suggested that there were basic difficulties within the parapsychological paradigm. Meanwhile, my psi group in Maryland was unable to generate any anomalous events. Although we met regularly, we heard no raps and our table would not tip. We wrote the entities for advice.

Q: Dear Spirit Friends: Why didn't you make raps for us here in Hyattsville, Maryland?

A: Dear "flesh" friends: It takes "time" (as you think of duration) to build a psi-circle. You may not get any PK activity for a long while. Persevere!

By the way, what difference does it make to you whether your friends, or acquaintances, or any "body" else, for that turn, have their skins on or not?

You are "spirits" too, you know.

We realize that you do not really share the pervasive anti-dead prejudice common to large groups of humans on your side, but others whom you will contact may misunderstand and mistake your attitude. If you knew a black man named John, would you try to prove your unbiased liberality by addressing him as "Dear Black Friend"? Think about it, especially as you are in no danger of changing your pigmentation, but you will live outside a body eventually, as yourself.

Love,
All of Us

During this time, John King, the seventeenth century buccaneer, left a special message by the mini-lab. I had asked him to guess at the digits inside the sealed envelope FRNM had prepared for me.

A: Your guess is as good as mine.

It is vital to love and to be kind to one another. If I had known and followed that great rule of life, my level would be much higher now, and I would not have to do this nonsense.

John King

I continued my correspondence. In June 1981, I noted that the Rolla letters were postmarked from distant places: Bethlehem, Connecticut; Columbus, Ohio; Atlanta, Georgia; and Middlesex-Essex, Massachusetts. The entities also placed un-canceled foreign stamps on the envelopes (in addition to the US stamps that we had already applied). These stamps were from such countries as Portugal, Honduras, Brazil, French Guinea, Chile, Hungary, Yugoslavia, United Kingdom, Mexico and Germany.

Q: Dear Friends: Could you take this letter, transport it to Australia (or some faraway place), and get it postmarked, all on the same day? This would demonstrate your paranormal quality, especially if Dr. Tom Richards saw that the letter had vanished on a certain day and it was later found to be postmarked in Australia on the same day!

A: Yes; but it would not prove a thing. You could have had a friend in Australia do it.

Q: Does it require more energy on your part to transport an object, such as this letter, a long distance than it does for you to transport an object a short distance?

A: Not really, just awkward.

Q: Can you give us any hints on how you do this teleportation?

A: Yes. We see your dimensions of existence as at-one. It is like a two-dimension, to use the flatland analogy. "Nowhere" is also "now-here"; "here" is "there" to us. It makes teleportation easier but plays hell with controlled communication, as it is like looking through running, rippling water, or "through a glass, darkly" instead of "face to face." Comprehend?

Q: John King: You wrote that "It is vital to love and to be kind to one another. If I had known and followed that great rule of life, my life would be much easier now, and I would not have to do this nonsense." What do you mean by this? Is it nonsense for you to do psi tasks for us?

A: I would rather learn and grow, in more blessed, pleasant pleasances; however, because I was often selfish and cruel, I must learn patiently to help others. I am under no compulsion, but I know these chores are a task I should do.

Q: You tell us to love wisely, to be kind to each other, to try to raise our levels. All the religions say similar things, but doing it seems like a different story. Love doesn't seem to be something that a person can get just by telling him or herself to have it. Do you have any further advice about this?

A: Where do you think the genuine (not fake) religions come from? Primeval ooze?

Like yourself. Realize others are pretty much the same as you. Then, like the ones you can like. Don't confuse liking with love. Put yourself in a secure position from which you can do good, and then lose your petty self in the All. It is infinite gain to "lose" the petty aspects of "your" self that prevent union with the All.

Do good. Don't tell yourself—do it. Give food to a hungry person. You have not solved the problem of world starvation en totalle, but you have solved one fraction of it. Often, remember, "for talking about it, it never gets done." So, act.

Q: What about pain, heartbreak, suffering, misery, and depression? Do you have advice that you might give us on how we can handle these things? Life certainly doesn't seem very meaningful at times.

A: Help others!

Of necessity, if you live in a body and are subject to the chances, frailties, and wearing out of the carcass you must lug about, you will often suffer. So long as you care deeply, you will experience joy and grief. That goes with being human.

If you concentrate on helping others, you will be too busy for the petty concerns of the self to whine down your finer self.

Realize that we, on our side of the change you consider death, are also human, sentient and often feel just as you do, morally and psychologically. Pity abides. Try to do all you can, and then you feel no guilt for omissive harms.

Rector/J.K.

Other SORRAT members heard about my success in communicating with the entities by mail and began sending in their own self-addressed envelopes and questions. The entities seemed to enjoy this. John King acted as the scribe, providing messages apparently dictated by other entities. The speaker/transcriber was signified by the names following the message. For example, Rector was the "speaker" of the first message and John King was the "writer." This is signified by the signature, "Rector/J.K."

The entities generally switched everyone's envelopes so that each SOR-RAT member received another person's message. We were forced to interact with each other just as much as we interacted with the entities. This furthered one of the entities' goals: to increase rapport among group members by forcing them to communicate. Often, they would send a message to one member telling him or her to contact another member. For example:

A: Let John know that C.D. says alternating bilocative nodal (EEG) oscillations of quanta (packets of mass/matter energy) can be controlled by the mind in a state of awareness. Sharp attention to stimuli inhibits psi effects such as apports, PK, and, ultimately, deliberate quantum teleportation from one area to another on your side or from one reality to another of the many worlds/dimensions or even directly at right angles to them all to our side.

For the early SORRAT letter writers, message writing was an exploratory game and the entities responded playfully. The entities enclosed plastic restaurant "medium" markers (used to denote steak that is cooked *medium* rather than *well done* or *rare*) within their envelopes. They also enclosed small items from the mini-lab, such as leather rings, pieces of yarn, and the small gold-plated squares that Cox used in some of his tests (the squares were highly visible for his camera). The entities seemingly teleported letters to distant post offices so that the stamp would receive an unusual postmark. At times, the envelopes were overweight because of mini-lab objects inside. Sometimes the foreign stamps that the entities had affixed to the letters allowed them to arrive without the postal service charging extra money. In some letters, the entities enclosed fortune cookie messages such as:

Loosen up and enjoy life.
You will soon gain a valuable lesson from a new friendship.
Tomorrow is too long to wait for happiness.
The obvious is that which is least understood and the most difficult to answer.
Courage is the master of fear. Foolishness is the absence of fear.
Distance makes everything look better.
Build new acquaintances close to friendship.
Cope with differences of philosophy and opinion.
Reaffirm belief in yourself.
Know your own feelings and do as you want.
When the heart is bitter, sugar won't help.

SORRATs discussed the meaning of the objects enclosed in the entity letters. Some felt that the "gifts" were very significant, while others found no meaning to them. I was seeking a job after graduating with my Ph.D. I received a photograph of a sculpture of a buffalo, a country and western record, a brochure about the Association for Research and Enlightenment (a group founded by the famous American clairvoyant, Edgar Cayce), and extensive advertising for Japanese plates. Tom and Elaine acknowledged receiving information about Edgar Cayce's association, but said they knew nothing about the other items. Why did the entities mail me so much information about plates with Japanese art designs on them?

In one message, the entities listed various people they wanted me to contact. They said we each had a part of the puzzle.

A: Each part, not by our choice, but due to the nature of psi and our limits, is part of the answer. How one thinks of reality helps to create as well as to define reality and what we can get through to you.

Do return to Skyrim. It is on a major ley line crossing, thus the power we can use is more concentrated there, if we have a medium we can use and if all conditions are in correct balance. There is much more to it, of course.

Eternity may be in love with the productions of time, as W.B. [William Blake], that very high level, once wrote, but it is very hard to tell you about our side without sounding trite. Can you imagine complete harmony, liberty, absence of limits, yet equally absolute adherence to a universal pattern? Call it Brahma or whatever you will. It is the perspective that is the problem in telling you what we wish and what you wish to learn.

J.K. and all

Tom explained that the term ley line crossing pertained to ley lines mentioned in previous SORRAT messages. These are earth grid lines (hypothetically) created by magnetic forces and the rotation of the earth about its axis. Concentrations of psi energy, which coincide with ley line crossings, facilitate psi.

I attempted another ESP experiment with the entities. This time, their target was a picture of George Washington. They sent back a drawing of a man's head with hair that look like George Washington's wig. Ed Cox and I were hopeful that they would succeed in the last eight trials since they seemed to have been very successful on the first two. The experimental design required ten trials with judges evaluating the results after all trials were completed.

I planned another visit to Rolla. I felt I had come to understand the different personalities of the entities and had developed a kind of personal relationship with them. They were pen pals. I hoped to prove, at least for myself, the authenticity of SORRAT phenomena.

I began reading about the history of psychical research during the Spiritualist Era so that I might gain a deeper understanding of the SORRAT entities. John King had a history of working with mediums who had been caught cheating. Was I skillful enough to catch whatever cheating might be occurring at Rolla?

John King claimed to have helped a medium named Henry Slade in the 1860s to do *direct writing* (writing without a human hand). Slade placed two boards together with a piece of chalk in between and held them under a table. The sitters at his séances were allowed to hold the board while the session occurred. They usually heard a scratching sound, like someone writing, and later found that a message had been recorded on the chalkboard. A famous scientific commission during this era repeatedly caught Slade cheating and concluded that he was a charlatan.

The Davenport brothers were famous mediums in 1850. John King claimed to communicate through them using the spiritualist trumpet, a device he invented as a means of addressing séance participants. The brothers allowed audience members to tie them up, and after the lights were extinguished, musical instruments played, bells rang, and spirit hands appeared. John King addressed the audience though a levitating trumpet in a voice distinctly different from that of either of the mediums. After the séance, the Davenports were found to be tied as firmly as before with their hands still full of the salt placed there as a test before the séances began. The brothers challenged magicians to duplicate their act. Like most phenomena produced by mediums, magicians found that, after practicing, they could duplicate the Davenports' show. Escape artistry, darkness, and confederates were important factors in the magicians' successful performance. Although the brothers' reputations were damaged, people who knew them well were certain that their performances were authentic. The brothers seemed firm in their belief in the validity of John King, their spirit assistant, but modern parapsychologists regard the evidence surrounding Henry Slade and the Davenport brothers as weak.[3]

John King and his daughter Katie communicated through many other mediums, most of whom were surrounded by controversy. Some claims exceeded what might have been accomplished by a magician but invalid witness testimony was not uncommon. On one occasion, John King was said to have completely materialized in full daylight.

Perhaps the most famous medium with whom King was associated was Eusapia Palladino. John King claimed to help her levitate tables and produce various other paranormal feats, much to the astonishment of psychical investigators. Eusapia developed the ability to switch her hands so that those attempting to "control" her movements (preventing her from engaging in fraud in the darkness) were often fooled. Two researchers would be holding the same hand while thinking that they had both her hands under control. Because she was known to engage in fraud, skeptics dismissed reports of events that investigators were unable to explain. There were times when she seemed under the control of a spiritual force that compelled her to cheat. On one occasion, she called out "Hold me tight or I'll cheat!"[4]

As noted earlier, some of the messages that originated in Rolla were signed by members of the "Imperator Group" (most frequently, Rector and Imperator). This was a famous group of entities who were associated with various mediums during the Spiritualist Era. The Reverend Stainton Moses (1839-1892) wrote the book *Spirit Teachings* under the guidance of the Imperator Group. The book had an important impact on the Spiritualist movement because it advocated a relativistic orientation toward religion, establishing an ideological foundation for Spiritualist belief. The SORRAT entities viewed themselves as part of a continually evolving ideological process. They stated that religious ideas change to fit their era, and that fixed, codified doctrines require modification. The *Spirit Teachings* message was consistent with the SORRAT Imperator Group texts. The physical phenomena associated with Reverend Moses' mediumship had characteristics similar to the SORRAT phenomena. Only a private circle of believers reported compelling events.

The trance medium L. E. Piper (1859-1950) was also associated with the Imperator Group. Her messages assumed a dignified and lofty character whenever these "high-level" entities spoke through her. Mrs. Piper was investigated closely and convinced many researchers of her authenticity. Neither Reverend Moses nor Mrs. Piper were ever associated with any form of fraud.[6]

Table-tipping was a favorite method for common people to communicate with the "Other Side" during the Spiritualist Era (1848 through the early 1900s). In 1852, the English scientist Michael Faraday (1791-1867) devised and conducted an experiment that indicated that table-tipping effects could be explained by conscious or subconscious pressure of the sitters' fingers on the table's edge. This finding could not explain levitation that occurred without touching the table. Only by miss-observation or conjuring could "hands-off" levitations be interpreted as normal events.

It is difficult for us, today, to evaluate the many alleged paranormal events reported in the past. The evidence supporting Spiritualist medium authenticity is ignored by most modern parapsychologists. Could it be that the Rolla phenomena are a continuation of some subconscious aspect within mankind expressed by this movement?[7]

I decided to learn more about the modern manifestation of this movement by attending Spiritualist Church services. During the services, a person in trance delivered the sermon. At the end of the service, the medium gave individual messages. The medium's statements were generally vague, yet useful. Mediumistic statements included:

(1) You are having problems with someone at your work place. Try to be patient. This will work itself out. Pray for help. He who asks, receives.

(2) You need to find a way of using your talents as an artist. You have great artistic ability that has not been developed. You should be using your hands in some creative way. Perhaps this means a new job, but more likely you should think about a new hobby. This capability of yours could be very beneficial to others.

(3) You are engaging in very creative and intellectual work at the moment and earlier I saw angels hovering above you, hoping to help. Perhaps you should go to the mountains or the seashore. You will receive help during your meditation.

Sometimes the messages seemed highly appropriate to me but other times they were not. It is difficult to evaluate this type of information scientifically. Although the form and philosophy of the services were derived from the Spiritualist movement, the mediums did not demonstrate any of the physical phenomena that allegedly occurred during that time. "You need to go to a Spiritualist camp to find that kind of thing," a church member told me. "Physical mediumship has become somewhat rare."

I attended a week-long spiritual development course at Camp Silver Belle, a Spiritualist camp in Ephrata, Pennsylvania. This Spiritualist camp met in hotel rooms rather than tents and cost over a hundred dollars to attend. The lessons delved into the occult lore that pervades Spiritualism. One belief was that a medium can use ectoplasm to produce physical phenomena. Ectoplasm is a substance that flows from the medium's body, causes objects to move about magically, and forms the "voice box" by which a spirit can speak through a levitating Spiritual "trumpet." (The spirit John King claimed to have devised this system.) Sometimes the spirits make objects apport, or appear out of nowhere. My fellow participants in the course showed me their collections of small objects that had appeared during séances. The apported objects had rolled out of the levitated trumpet into their outstretched hands. Sometimes the objects felt warm. Complete darkness was required since the ectoplasm was highly sensitive to light. Sometimes the ectoplasm made spirit shapes, or apparitions, appear.

I had a plan to test the authenticity of these mediums. Before his death in 1979, the parapsychologist J. Giather Pratt had set a combination lock that could be opened with a secret five-word message that only he knew. If I could get a medium to relay a message from Pratt, this would constitute evidence for Pratt's survival after death. Pratt, who had worked alongside the famous parapsychologist J. B. Rhine, was highly trusted within the parapsychological community. He had conducted a variety of experiments indicating that ESP was real. If I could determine this message, it would create quite a stir within the field.

During my first séance, I tried to remain especially alert. The participants were seated in a circle, and the medium sat in a special "medium's cabinet," a kind of curtained enclosure. The medium had an assistant who seemed in charge of maintaining order and turning out the lights. The assistant is certainly a person to watch, I thought. This turned out to be a futile notion.

When the lights were turned off, the darkness was absolute. I could not see my own hand when I held it in front of my face. The medium made heavy breathing sounds, apparently going into trance. I saw the phosphorescent marking on Spiritualist trumpets, and the trumpets began swinging around in wide arcs. It was absurd! They moved in exactly the way that would be expected if the medium's assistant had left her chair, picked them up, and waved them around. Surely the spirits were not causing this movement! Why should the spirits imitate fraudulent motions so exactly?

The medium's spirit guide began speaking through one of the "levitated" trumpets. It sounded as if someone was speaking in a high falsetto voice. The spirit guide requested each member of the circle to tell the name of a "doctor guide" whom the participant wished to contact. I asked to speak to Dr. J. Gaither Pratt. Then each person's "doctor guide" began speaking in turn. I was surprised when Dr. Pratt identified himself and began addressing me in a Cambridge accent. He began rambling on about developing one's musical talents. To me, this seemed absurd. J. Gaither Pratt was an American parapsychologist who had lived in North Carolina and Virginia all his life. Why did he have a British accent?

"Dr. Pratt?" I asked. "Don't you have a particular short message you wish to give us?"

"No," he sputtered, apparently surprised by my request. "Do you have a particular message you wish to give to me?"

I was disgusted. The true J. Gaither Pratt would be aware of his secret message. I was not talking to Dr. Pratt. I had paid $12.00 to listen to twaddle.

I was curious about the social dynamics of the Spiritualist séances. Why did people believe in them? I interviewed many of the mediums and the participants afterward. The mediums presented themselves as sincere and religious people. The participants were satisfied that the séance had been genuine. They felt that they had been helped by information they had obtained. Some described periods of emotional crisis in which their relatives spoke to them during a séance, giving comfort and aid. The mediums seemed to provide a form of counseling for the participants.

I attended more séances. It was disheartening to watch them reciting the Lord's Prayer and sing a hymn, and then engage in what seemed to be fraud. I found that any information that I revealed about myself to one medium would be brought forth by another medium at a later séance. The mediums probably kept a shared file on each séance participant.

I also observed the mediums doing what I regarded as standard magic tricks. For example, the participants wrote questions on pieces of paper and passed them to the stage, where a blindfolded medium answered each one in turn. This is what is known as the "one ahead" trick. The blindfolded medium picks up a folded paper and addresses a member in the audience, who is actually the medium's confederate. After the confederate acknowledges that the medium has correctly addressed his question, the medium innocently unfolds the first paper, and puts it aside. The medium peeks down the side of his nose through the blindfold and reads the first question. Flexing the nose creates a peek-hole, even with the tightest blindfold. The medium then picks up a second paper and pretends to read it mentally while vaguely answering the question on the first paper. The medium seems to demonstrate ESP by addressing each person's question.[8]

The tricks that I saw were fairly simple. Apparently, it is common practice for many mediums to maintain a filing system of information about potential sitters, to buy or steal objects that are later "apported" during séances, and to create phony levitations and materializations.

Evening after evening, Dr. Pratt spoke to me through the trumpet during the séances. Never did he show any knowledge of the test he created before his death. He did not appear aware that he had been a skillful, competent parapsychologist while alive. What a terrible case of amnesia!

After my Spiritualist lessons, I decided to visit the arch-skeptic and magician, James (the Amazing) Randi. Randi had offered $10,000 to anyone who could demonstrate an authentic paranormal event to his satisfaction. Many have attempted to win this prize money, but no one has succeeded.

Randi was happy to talk with me. Even when he was young, he had been interested in magic, he told me. He had attended a Spiritualist meeting and observed tricks similar to the ones I saw. Unlike me, he had exposed the fraudulent medium. A spiritualist called the police, and Randi was arrested for disrupting a religious meeting. He could not understand why the church members would not acknowledge the medium's performance as fraudulent. As he grew older, Randi became a skilled and famous magician. He was concerned that people were being ripped off by individuals who claimed to be psychics. He had never, after years of searching, uncovered a single case that he considers authentically paranormal.

"How does table-tipping occur?" I asked. "How do people get a table to jump around with just their fingertips on it?"

"It's generally a matter of unconscious muscular movements on the part of the sitters," he replied. "They frequently are very sincere in claiming that they're not consciously pushing the table, but that's often how it's done. Sometimes they get upset when they can't perform under my test conditions. If you require them to place their hands on pieces of paper, then the friction between their fingers and the table top is reduced and they can't unconsciously push the table. If they're required to place their hands inside from the edge of the table, they can't unconsciously tip it when they push down. Of course, you should be careful that someone doesn't lift the table with a foot, knee, leg, hook, coat sleeve, or thread. I find that if you take proper precautions, the table will not move."

"You have tested table-tipping groups?"

"Oh, yes! I tested one in Italy not long ago. I placed a tape on the tabletop marking the inner area where they were allowed to place their hands. They didn't like it very much because they couldn't get the table to move. One even said that I must be associated with the Devil! But that's the way it goes—many people don't want to acknowledge that there is more evidence for the existence of Santa Claus than there is for the existence of extrasensory perception and psychokinesis."

Randi showed me a videotape in which he duplicated many of the metal-bending feats of famed Israeli illusionist Uri Geller. By sleight of hand, Randi made forks and spoons bend before the camera's eye. Randi was providing this videotape to be shown at the Parapsychological Association meeting later that summer.[9]

I now felt ready to return to Rolla. My experience with the mediums had taught me that no matter how honest or innocent a person might seem, he or she can still be a cheater. Randi showed me ways of testing metal-benders and table-tippers. I hoped that if I showed extreme alertness and common sense, I would be able to resolve the Rolla controversy.

Not long before I was to leave for Rolla, Tom Richards wrote suggesting that I visit a young PK metal-bender named Steve Shaw. He lived in Washington, Pennsylvania, which would be on my way. Tom and Steve had met while subjects in experiments at the McDonnell Laboratory for Psychical Research in St. Louis.

I telephoned Steve and he invited me to visit him. He said that he was willing to try to bend spoons or forks before any legitimate investigator. I invited him to the small group laboratory at the University of Maryland where we had three video cameras to record his metal-bending feats. The lab also had a one-way mirror where observers could see into the room without being seen by the subject. I knew that James Randi was willing to participate secretly in this experiment. I felt it was important to attempt parapsychological experiments in order for me, as a sociologist, to understand the problems of this type of research. I hoped that either Steve Shaw would be caught cheating or Randi would be forced to give him $10,000. I felt that I should aggressively attempt to discover the truth, if only to satisfy my own curiosity.

When I visited Steve at his apartment, he allowed me to tape record our interview. He told me that his parents had divorced when he was young and then his mother had left his stepfather. He had lived in England, South Africa, and the United States, and was still in his early twenties. He described poltergeists and personal psychic events that he had experienced. When he was about 15, he saw Uri Geller do psychic metal-bending on TV and realized that he could do it, also. There was intensity about Shaw that reminded me of Geller.

When the McDonnell Laboratory for Psychical Research sought people who had metal-bending ability, Steve Shaw wrote them a letter and later became involved in their research. On various weekends, Steve was given airfare to fly to St. Louis where investigators videotaped his spoon-bending feats. Although Steve's bends had been recorded on tape, the researchers had not been totally satisfied. They had been unable, so far, to capture an event that could not be duplicated by a magician. During his visits to the lab, Steve met Mike Edwards, another metal-bender, and they became friends.

Steve Shaw had a flair for the dramatic and could do well as an actor. He was very poor and regarded money as important, even though he told me that he didn't care about material things. His poverty was restricting him, and he hoped his psychokinetic ability might be his ticket to fame and fortune.

Steve expressed dislike for Mark Shafer, one of the researchers at the McDonnell Laboratory. He felt that Shafer's methods of investigation were sloppy and his beliefs regarding psychokinesis were unscientific. This seemed strange. Most parapsychologists believe that psi occurs more frequently in harmonious situations. Were the researchers at the McDonnell Lab aware of Shaw's feelings toward Shafer?

"Have you ever had any interaction with anyone from the Committee for the Scientific Investigation of the Claims of the Paranormal?" I asked. This was CSICOP, a group of scientists who were debunkers of psychic claims. James Randi was an important member.

"Once I did an interview for a radio station in Pittsburgh, and I met a man who was with the committee," Steve said. "I found that out later. He completely concealed the fact that he was a skeptical debunker or that he was testing me. I couldn't believe how he distorted everything that happened! He wrote an article that hinted that I tried to set up a situation where I could cheat. All I did was share some hamburgers with him before the interview. I even paid for his! I can't say that I'm impressed with the way he operated. It wasn't a scientifically controlled situation. It was a radio interview!"

"Have you even had any contact with James Randi?"

"I wouldn't mind meeting him, but so far I haven't. I'm curious about how he does his metal-bending tricks.'

"You don't know?"

"No, I'm not a magician."

"Then what are all those posters in your hallway out there? It looks as if you advertised for a magic show." I had noticed his posters when I entered.

"That was for one show I put on a while back as a benefit. I'm not a magician. I can't promise anything when I perform. I really can't control this ability that well."

"And you have never cheated?"

"Never!"

Shaw was an intense young man. I felt friendly toward him but was put off by a vague sense of ambiguity in the way he answered questions. Some things did not fit. I couldn't believe that a hardnosed CSICOP investigator would allow a young guy like Steve Shaw to pay for his hamburger.

Later in the afternoon, his girlfriend and best friend came over. She was an attractive, open person. She claimed to have seen Steve perform many "impossible" feats, such as psychically opening locks by just holding them in his hands. Later, some of his other friends came over. All of us, Steve, his friends, and I seemed caught in a web created by our environments. By helping each other, we could increase our probability of gaining what we wanted. I think we all had this feeling as we talked to each other and listened to rock and roll music that afternoon.

Later, my talk with Steve took a bizarre turn. "You're investigating Tom Richards?" he asked.

"In a manner of speaking, yes. I'm on my way out to Missouri after I leave here."

"Do you think that he's authentic?"

"I don't know. I've seen some awfully strange things, and I've had some strange experiences."

"I met him two weeks ago at the McDonnell lab," said Steve. "He was there with his wife and a guy named Steve. Mark Shafer was conducting the research but Tom Richards had a sealed bottle with a pencil, a paper, and a pipe cleaner inside. It seemed like a silly experiment to me, but they wanted me to focus my attention on it. I stared at that bottle for five minutes and nothing happened.

"Then Richards took the bottle from me and put it on a table," Steve continued. "He turned it so you couldn't see the stuff inside. The label on the bottle hid everything. Later they got all excited. The words Love, Faith, and Hope were written on the paper and the pipe cleaner was bent into the shape of a man. They said that I must have done it with psychokinesis. It was strange. Let me make this clear: I'm not saying that Richards faked this. I don't know. I know attacking him is kind of like throwing stones at Santa Claus. I mean, who can argue with love, faith, and hope? But when I was concentrating on the bottle, the end of the pencil was gold. Afterward, when they discovered the supposed PK effect, I saw that it was blue. I suppose you could say that the color changed psychokinetically, but I think that Richards switched the bottles!"[10]

I was speechless. I had been searching for fraud in the Rolla case, and now I had a witness to it. I was glad that I had switched on my tape recorder.

"There were raps that afternoon, also," Steve continued. "Have you heard the Richards' raps?"

"I sure have," I said.

"Well, the next chance you get, watch him real close. I think he has some sort of device in his right shoe. I noticed that each time before the raps would begin, he would take a slight step forward on his right foot and then flex slightly. I think that's how he makes the raps."

"It's hard for me to believe that this could explain all the rapping phenomena," I replied. "I've looked at his legs and shoes very closely while the raps occurred. I didn't detect anything."

"Listen, I'm just trying to help you out," Steve said. "My name and reputation are associated with the McDonnell Lab, and if they allow themselves to be fooled by Richards, it might reflect badly on me, since I'm a subject there too."

"Well, I'll have to talk to Peter Phillips. He's the director of the lab."

"No, don't mention any of this to Peter Phillips. Don't tell him how you found this out. I can't be certain of any of this, but I just wanted to warn you. Be careful around Richards. Check it out. Then, if you find something, you can warn Phillips about what you find. There's more to this, though. If I tell you the rest of this, will you promise not to say anything to the people at the McDonnell Lab?"

"Okay, go ahead," I said.

Steve was talking forcefully and quickly. I adjusted the microphone of my recorder so that I was certain that his voice would come in clearly.

"Later in the afternoon, the raps spelled out 'spoon bent,' so we checked

84

the spoons in the next room, and one of them that was set up before a video camera had bent. Then the raps spelled out that 'M.E.' had done it. We figured that Mike Edwards did it with his PK ability. But when we played back the videotape, it showed that Tom Richards came into the room, checked out the camera angle really carefully and then blocked the view of the spoon with his body with his hand behind his back. When he moved his body, you could see that the spoon was bent. Mike told me later that he was out in the hallway when this occurred. The door was slightly ajar, and he saw Tom Richards bend the spoon with his hand."

"Do you think I could get Mike to verify your story?" I asked. I hoped to collect testimony from these two witnesses and confront Tom with the evidence.

"I don't know. He might deny the whole story. He doesn't want to be associated with fraud in any form. He's planning a career as a lawyer and doesn't want the metal-bending stuff to get in his way."

I was disturbed by Shaw's response. If Mike Edwards would not confirm Steve's story, I did not know whether I could believe it myself. The whole thing seemed so contrived!

"There's more," Steve continued. "In the evening, they attempted a table levitation. They put their hands on top of a TV tray table and got it to jump around. It was a joke. I saw Tom Richards and that guy Steve put their thumbs under the edge of the table and lifted it up. Mike saw it also. That's when Mike and I stopped taking this thing seriously. They're fakes! Then they wanted to do another table levitation and asked the raps if we should turn down the lights. I rapped out an answer with my foot: two raps for 'no.' You should have seen the look on Tom's face! He was angry! He knew I faked it, but what could he do? We sat around the table again, and I caught Mike's eye. They started moving the table around again so Mike and I hooked it with our fingers and lifted it up."

"Did the video camera record the two levitations?"

"Sure."

"Where was Mark Shafer? Didn't he see you two cheating?"

"No, he was looking through the camera, and I don't think he figured it out."

"I can't believe he would ignore fraud when it occurred right in his own lab!" I exclaimed. "Where was Peter Phillips?"

"Phillips wasn't there."

"I'll have to tell Peter Phillips," I said.

"You promised not to tell! This isn't really that important. It was just a joke. We didn't mean any harm. I can help you in the future if you keep cool and don't spoil things for me. Just check Tom Richards closely. I'm warning you. That's all. But don't tell Peter Phillips how you found out." He was playing the role of a pleading friend. I didn't know how to evaluate his performance. The pieces to this puzzle were not fitting together.

"One thing is for sure," Steve concluded. "And I know that I'm doing you a big favor by telling you this. The raps are fake. After Mike and I lifted up the table, the raps started up again; they spelled out, 'Mike is forgiven,' then later, 'Steve is forgiven.' So you see, Richards knew we faked it! He was mad at first, but I guess he thinks we're fakes too. We're not, or at least I know that I'm not. And I might be able to help you in the future because Richards trusts me now."

Later in the afternoon, Steve wanted to show me his metal-bending ability. "I can't really evaluate it since I'm not a magician," I told him.

"It's okay. Let me try to show you what I can do," he replied. I remembered what Randi had advised me about testing metal-benders: if the researcher checks the spoon or fork before the bender is allowed to touch it and then keeps his eyes riveted on the metal, the bender will not be able to use his conjuring skills without being detected.

Steve got a spoon from his kitchen. I checked it to be certain that no one had tampered with it, and then gave it back to him. I kept my eyes glued to the spoon. Minute after minute passed. Steve tried to focus his mind. Nothing happened. This is getting boring, I thought. Maybe if I look away he can do a sleight-of-hand trick. I started talking to his girlfriend and took my eyes off the spoon.

After about five minutes, Steve let out an exclamation. "There it goes!" he said, holding the spoon in one hand. The handle seemed to be drooping before my eyes. He gently stroked the handle on its top part, and I placed my finger underneath the handle. It appeared to continue its downward bend.

"Well, that's really something!" I said with a laugh.

"Are you convinced that it's real?" Steve asked.

"No, I took my eyes away and the bend occurred within your hands. A skilled magician might be able to duplicate what I saw. I would be very interested in attempting to get videotapes of what you do, though. The camera would be a better observer than I am. It wouldn't become distracted and look away."

"Sure!" Steve said with enthusiasm. "I want to be investigated scientifically. I want to show people that this is real. I know it may be hard to prove, but we have to try, right?"

"Right!" I replied, trying to hide my lack of confidence. I didn't know if I would be able to authenticate Steve's effects. First, I would need the help and advice of the researchers at the McDonnell Laboratory in St. Louis. If it were easy to verify macro PK, they would have done it by now. Second, I needed to see their videotapes. Was Shaw telling the truth about Richards? Third, Randi would have to help me. To bring Randi and Shaw together secretly would create a dramatic and interesting situation.

CHAPTER 5

ENTITY GAMES

In 1982, as I drove toward the Richards' house, I reviewed my evidence for fraud. I had a tape recording of Steve Shaw's story about the experiment at the McDonnell Laboratory. Steve said that Tom had faked a spoon bending and made raps fraudulently. He said that he and Mike had faked a table levitation. He said that the McDonnell Laboratory had a videotape that showed these things. I hoped to view the McDonnell Lab video and ask the researchers what they knew about this.

I also planned a special research project at the Richards' house. I would sleep on a cot next to the mini-lab and check on it every hour of the day. I decided that the only way to be certain that the mini-lab evidence was authentic would be to see objects move inside the lab while the camera was documenting the phenomena.

After I arrived at Tom's house, I asked him about his experience at the McDonnell Laboratory. He was completely open with me. He answered all my questions carefully and fully. He showed me the notes he had taken the day he was there. His notes stated that his body had blocked the video camera's view of a spoon that had been found to be bent after he moved away. He said that he and the people at the lab had watched the videotape together. The tape showed him coming into the room and blocking the view of the spoon. Then, when he moved away, the video showed that the spoon was bent.

"It must have bent while I was standing there," Tom said. "I didn't touch it. Some other things happened before that. We did some half-levitations of tables but that can't be considered evidential because we had our hands on the table." Tom showed me his notes, indicating that the experiment had been a "failure." This was consistent with his method of labeling table-tipping results: for an experiment to be a "success," the table had to remain in the air after everyone took their hands away from it.

"Someone could have lifted the table up," he said. "We had our hands on it."

89

"Did you see Steve and Mike lift the table?" I asked.

"I did not see that, but the light was not good and I was busy listening to the raps," he said. "I was counting the raps so that I could understand the message." His notes indicated that the raps had signified that Steve and Mike were "forgiven."

"Why were they forgiven?" I asked.

"I don't know," he said.

Tom showed me the bottle with "Love, Faith, Hope" written inside. I looked at it closely. It was still sealed. The glass was tinted, making it impossible to determine the color of the pencil inside. How could Steve Shaw say that it had at first been gold and now was blue? It didn't make sense. Why would he lie about the color of the pencil? I would have to talk to the other metal-bender, Mike Edwards, and view the videotapes.

Cox asked me to write some questions for the entities to answer. He wanted to film the entities writing a message. His basement camera was ready to record any penmanship that might occur. I wrote three brief questions, and we set them up on a clipboard before the camera. I felt a tinge of embarrassment. I did not believe that the entities could write a message under these conditions. I thought that they could write only in situations where Tom would be regarded as the author.

I'm in Rolla again, participating in this absurdity, I thought. When I began removing things from my backpack, I noticed that one of my books was missing. I had planned to be extremely vigilant, but it seemed that I had already failed. How could I have misplaced a book? Where could it be? I searched through my pack again. It was gone. I wondered how much the library would charge me for losing one of their books.

Elaine called out from the kitchen. "I hear the mini-lab. It's filming something," she called out. "Something caused the camera to begin filming!"

Steve Calvin, Tom, and I rushed down to the basement. My questions had been answered briefly. A large lock that had previously been on the work table was now missing its key. It had been moved to the front of the mini-lab, and it had three leather rings linked to it. Cox's second, older mini-lab, on a side shelf, contained my library book. I thought about this. I had left my pack in the bedroom while I spoke with Tom and Elaine. I had gone down to the basement with Steve and Ed. We had returned to talk with Tom. Now the book was locked in the spare mini-lab, but this mini-lab was not sealed with the thread and notary public stamp. The trickster could have picked Cox's lock and inserted the book. Had Tom or Elaine done that?

I looked at my questions and the recently written answers:

Q: Dear Friends: Why do some people seem to have more ability to act as mediums than others? Are personality factors related to mediumship? Is the ability inherited?

A: They are more open. Yes. No.

Q: Will you call me on the telephone at my house in Hyattsville, Maryland? Will you call on Monday, August 17, 1981 around 10 P.M.? You can call collect.

A: Maybe.

Q: I am going to put particular effort into getting psi group results in September. Do you have any new advice?

A: Be patient.

I looked at my book, now locked inside the second mini-lab. It was entitled *You Will Survive After Death* by Sherwood Eddy (1950). This book coincided with the entities' message for us. They wanted us to believe in life after death. The book told about mediums who contacted people on the other side and brought back messages. These mediums were not like the ones I met at the Spiritualist camp. The book told about people who had learned about their deceased loved ones by attending séances. They received information that the medium could not have known. The book told of haunting cases in which apparitions provided information unavailable to any living person. It described dying people appearing to others at the moment of their death. The witnesses were surprised because they had been unaware that the person was dying. The psychical research literature has hundreds of stories like that.

Near death experience researchers have gathered evidence supporting belief in life after death. Some people, judged to be clinically dead before being revived, tell about leaving their bodies. Some describe complex medical procedures that their doctors performed on them during the experience, things they should not have been able to see. How could they be aware of these procedures when they were under sedation? Near death experiencers often tell of seeing a "white light," a religious figure, deceased friends and relatives, and other heavenly beings.

Sherwood Eddy's book reviewed evidence gathered by careful researchers, but it did not go over the skeptical positions regarding life after death. Most parapsychologists regard the life-after-death evidence as incomplete. The events "proving" life after death can be explained by other theories, such as the hypothesis that people generate the life-after-death phenomena using their

ESP and PK abilities. Also, witnesses are often mistaken or deceived. The evidence could be fabricated.

I felt conflicted. I wanted to do valid sociological research, but I also wanted to get to the bottom of what was going on. I planned to check the mini-lab hourly during the day and to sleep beside it at night. I wanted to keep track of everyone in the house so no one could tamper with Cox's experiment in the basement. I would accompany anyone who went down to the basement, and I would inspect the mini-lab carefully afterward. I wanted to preclude the possibility of fraud.

At first, I felt vaguely spooked sleeping in the basement. The basement room containing the mini-lab was completely dark. Supposedly, the spirits came here and did things before the camera. Was my anxiety preventing the phenomena? As time passed, I became more accustomed to the strange environment. I meditated in the basement, beside the mini-lab.

I took careful notes regarding events at the Richards' house. My notes began on August 4, 1981. I described the first PK phenomenon. My book had vanished and I found it later in the spare mini-lab. Cox's lock had been moved, its key was gone, and three leather rings were now locked to it.

My notes indicate that nothing happened on August 5.

On August 6, Elaine, Tom, Steve Calvin, Ed, and I spent the evening watching films of past mini-lab events. I had seen these films before and I felt irritated. Normal people did not accept these films as authentic. The images were absurd. The objects jumped from one place to another, disappeared at one place and then appeared at another place. The filming looked like stop action photography, unless you believed the entities or agency or whatever could make objects appear and disappear. Objects sometimes passed out through the glass front. Sometimes paper burst into flames, balloons inflated and deflated, and objects moved around.

Tom, Ed, and Steve became excited when they saw each ostensibly paranormal event. They exclaimed that the phenomena could not have been fabricated. Paper bursts into flames! How could that be done by stop action photography? I was angry because I knew no one was going to accept this case as valid. I was investigating something that no one would accept.

The whole thing was a contradiction. No sane person would fabricate these films this way. The work was too clumsy! Whoever made these films created effects that were too absurd to accept. With a little effort, the trickster could have created effects that would have been more believable. Even a halfway competent trickster could have done a better job. I wondered what was actually going on. Maybe the trickster was suffering from some type of mental disorder. No sane person would be involved in something like this.

I tried to figure out the psychology of it. Perhaps the trickster made the films look absurd so that logical people would reject them. A logical person would assume that the films were fake. Were the entities making the films appear so absurd that people would ignore them?

I considered another angle. The films were a kind of art. They provided a hidden message. We generally do not think about reality. The films say to us, "It is possible to break the rules governing reality."

There was another factor involved. It seemed as if the trickster was purposely revealing fraud. That worried me. I was caught up in some type of psychological trick. Was the trickster actually cheating or was he pretending to be cheating? The films looked fraudulent, but certain scenes seemed extremely difficult to duplicate in one's basement, like the paper bursting into flames while a balloon expanded and deflated.

The appearance of fraud within the mini-lab films was parallel to Tom blocking the view while the spoon bent at the McDonnell Lab. It looked like Tom did it, but how and why would he do it that way? The films, the table-tipping, the McDonnell Lab accusations; things looked like fraud until something happened that could not be explained. Tom and Elaine pushed the table around, but then it would vibrate in a bizarre way. It was as if the phenomena wanted someone to create fraud to allow future authentic events. It was as if the phenomena were concerned about the skepticism of future observers, so it engaged in behavior that would cause them to turn their attention to something else. Kenneth Batcheldor, a British parapsychologist, hypothesized that fraud could enhance belief that allowed future phenomena, but it seemed as if the phenomena itself was using his idea.

What about the letter writing? The letters seemed like an extension of the mini-lab hoax. Were the entities making the letters seem fake so that they could slip things past the skeptics? It was a silly theory, but the whole damn thing was silly.

After Steve left for his home, Three-Times-Three began rapping.

"Three-Times-Three, do you know where the key to my lock is?" Cox asked the raps.

"Rap, rap." No.

"Will you write a message tonight with the red pen while Jim is watching?" Cox asked.

"Rap, rap, rap," Maybe.

"Will you cause the lock to enter the mini-lab?" he asked.

Who cares about this? I thought to myself. Those damn entities can't make the lock go into the secure mini-lab unless Cox and I let our guard down. The locksmith sealed the damn thing up so tight that it didn't seem likely that anything could get in or out at this stage, particularly while I hang around. Maybe if his filming system breaks down, the lock can get in, I thought. Without the camera, it might be able to do something before my eyes because few people would believe me.

"Will you make the lock enter the mini-lab?" Cox asked again.

"Rap, rap, rap." Maybe.

I tape recorded this momentous conversation (note irony) and took notes, documenting each event. Science lurches forward, I thought. The festival of absurdity continues. The trickster has Cox's key.

Later, I went downstairs to the basement to inspect the mini-lab. I checked Cox's new security procedures. Since my April visit, Cox had brought in a locksmith to supervise his security procedures. Cox was continually enhancing his strategies to preclude fraud. He had asked a locksmith to design a fraud-proof system. The locksmith had placed larger metal bands around the new mini-lab and had poured epoxy glue into the two huge locks that secured the metal bands in place. The locksmith had sworn before a notary public that he had carefully undertaken these security precautions. Despite these measures, Cox's camera had recorded two occasions when coins had levitated and flown through the solid glass front of the lab. George Hansen later suggested that the trickster could have cut off the lock, fabricated the films, and then replaced the lock. Cox says that theory is impossible because of his security precautions.

That day in Rolla, Cox wanted the entities to get the heavy lock to go inside the sealed mini-lab. His camera was in place and everything seemed in order. I looked around the basement. Nothing was unusual.

I went upstairs to get a tee shirt from my pack. Tom and Elaine were in the living room, but I am not sure where Ed was. I remember feeling kind of foggy and thinking, this is strange. I'm trying to be particularly alert but I my brain feels foggy. Then I heard Cox shout excitedly in the basement. I rushed down the stairs to see what was happening. I was concerned because I thought I was keeping track of everyone in the house, but apparently I had failed. Cox must have been in the living room and gone down to the basement right after I walked into the side room.

I rushed down the basement stairs and saw Cox inspecting his mini-lab. The large lock was inside, and the glass was shattered. The lock appeared to have crashed through the glass. How had this breakage occurred without anyone hearing it? It seemed very strange. I spoke with Cox for a while, then Tom came downstairs to see what the commotion was about. I watched him come down the stairs. He can't move very fast, due to his weight. He stood beside Cox and me. I noticed a pool of water on the floor. Then I noticed water dripping from the ceiling. I looked up to see an ice cube resting on a beam. The ice was just beginning to melt, and the drops were falling on the floor. I began tape recording my impressions.

The situation was astonishing and slightly frightening because of the violence of the breakage. There were glass shards on the floor, table, and bottom of the mini-lab, as if the lock had been hurled violently. The ice cube began dripping more rapidly, indicating that someone had placed it on the beam recently. Who had hurled the lock through the mini-lab glass and placed the ice cube up on the beam?

Cox was excited and angry. I didn't ask him if he had broken into his own mini-lab because it was clear that he was just as surprised as I was.

Raps began sounding from the concrete floor. I could feel their vibrations through my shoes. I watched Tom's legs and feet very closely. His feet and legs did not move. I had secretly inspected all his shoes the day before and had found nothing unusual. I also had inspected all the visible basement ceiling beams of the house. I found no device that might be used to make raps, but I did not rip out floor boards or ceiling panels. The raps were a puzzle. They came out of the solid concrete floor.

The raps spelled out "C-A-R-D-S." We looked at a deck of ESP cards on a shelf in the basement. I had looked at the same deck earlier in the evening. They contained the symbols: plus (+), circle (o), wavy lines (~), square (□), and star (*). When I inspected the deck, the cards had been unordered. Now they were sorted with two cards out of place, both bearing wavy lines. What did this mean?

"Is there a connection between the wavy lines and the ice?" I asked the raps.

"Rap, rap." No.

The wavy line symbol had been used by the entities in a previous message to SORRAT member John Hunt. It had something to do with brain states and teleportation. I planned to talk to John Hunt about it. Could Tom or Elaine have gone down to the basement, placed the ice cube on the beam, broken the mini-lab, and sorted the deck? This would have required either a secret passageway or lightning speed. The thought of Tom or Elaine rushing down the stairs at lightning speed was amusing. Tom was too heavy and Elaine was not very athletic. Sorting the cards would have required too much time: could that have been done previously? How had the glass been smashed soundlessly? Did Cox do it? The idea of Ed Cox destroying his own mini-lab seemed absurd. He would have to pay the locksmith for a new one.

We stood looking at the damage. Everyone was shocked. The entities had never engaged in violence before, but it was logical to assume that they had done this. Had my increased observation and the locksmith's high security caused the entities to do this?

"I would never destroy my own mini-lab," Cox said. "This research is extremely important to me." Cox had spent years attempting to get the parapsychologists to accept his SORRAT research. He had recently learned that another of his papers regarding SORRAT had been rejected. The reviewers said that his precautions did not meet their criteria. If Cox were the trickster, he would have written a paper that the parapsychologists would accept. Was this the end of Cox's research program? His security conditions were not rigid enough to meet the parapsychologists' standards but they were so rigid that they thwarted the phenomena.

Could I have been so stupid as not to have seen the damaged mini-lab when I was in the basement minutes before? That was hard for me to accept. I had been trying to be especially vigilant but the "foggy mind" memory raised my own suspicions.

The melting ice cube signified that someone or something had just placed it on the beam. I watched as Elaine checked the ice cube trays in the refrigerator. She found no ice cubes missing. How long had the ice cube been on the beam? It was hard to say. There had been a series of events: I had checked the mini-lab. There was no water dripping from the beam. Cox found that the glass mini-lab was broken. I came down to the basemen and spoke with him. He was anxious, angry, alarmed. Tom came down the stairs. I looked at the glass on the floor and the dripping ice cube: all within five minutes, I think. My notes do not indicate exact times.

The next evening, Ed, Steve, Elaine, Tom, and I sat around the kitchen table. We were playing with the ESP cards, informally testing our ESP ability. Tom seemed to be doing fairly well, but I was not keeping score. At about 9:30 p.m., the raps spelled out a word.

"C-A-N."

"Can what?" Elaine asked.

"C-A-N."

"We don't understand." Elaine said.

"C-A-N," they rapped again.

"What does this mean?" I asked.

"C-A-N," they rapped.

I went down to the basement and checked the mini-lab, set up to film spirit writing. Everything was in order. Suddenly, the micro-switch under the pen activated. I felt a surge of excitement throughout my body. This was what I had been waiting for: the pen was about to write! The pen remained motionless. I heard music playing loudly above me. I returned upstairs.

"Ed, you'd better reset your camera. It activated, but nothing happened," I told him.

"Did you put that record on?" Elaine asked me. I thought she had been in the kitchen, but she had been in the bathroom.

"No, I was in the basement," I answered.

"Who put it on?" Elaine wondered aloud. She was the likely suspect, I thought. Everyone denied doing it. Ed, Steve, and Tom had been in the kitchen while I was in the basement.

The raps were beating time to the music. It was Offenbach's *Can Can*! Now we understood the meaning of the rap's message.

"Who put the record on the record player?" Elaine asked the raps.

The raps spelled out, "J."

"Hello, Jay!" Elaine called. "Why did you put on Offenbach's *Can Can*?"

The raps were silent.

"That's from Orpheus in the Underworld," Tom commented. "Maybe there is symbolic meaning to the underworld concept." The raps were still silent.

"Is it just because you like it?" Elaine asked.

"Rap." Yes.

"Jay, did you activate the micro-switch downstairs?" I asked.

"Rap." Yes.

"Did you try to write?" I asked.

"Rap." Yes.

"What was the problem?" I asked.

The raps did not answer.

This was silly! Elaine could have put the record on the record player. Each event I experienced could have been done fraudulently. Perhaps she had a remote control means of triggering the micro-switch down in the basement. Why should she do that, though? It was remarkable how each event could have been done by trickery, but it would have required incredible skill and dexterity. It would seem that the trickster would be caught, eventually.

The entities played with Ed Cox even more vigorously than with me. Two more leather rings became attached to the lock. Cox had the locksmith prepare a new mini-lab, and he set it up in the basement.

Cox told me that he had secretly placed a hair inside the lock after the first three rings had been attached. He wanted to determine if the key was used to open the lock afterward. He found that the key had been used. It was logical the think that the trickster had opened the lock and re-locked it with the rings attached. The lock had been opened and closed normally. Now, lock and five leather rings were all affixed to the mini-lab. Cox was attempting to maintain extremely secure conditions but the locksmith's mini-lab, Cox's most secure so far, appeared silly. Nothing had entered or exited from this min-lab.

It seemed futile to try to conduct controlled tests of the entities' abilities since they seemed to like to play games. They produced PK-like phenomena, but anyone with the key could have done it. Before, the entities had made coins fly around inside the locksmith's mini-lab. The parapsychologists had rejected this experiment. Although a film showed coins coming out through the glass front, the entities seemed unable to perform that feat again.

Two evenings later, Tom, Elaine, and I conducted an ESP/PK experiment. I didn't attempt the tests that Randi had suggested for table-tippers. Testing seemed pointless. It had been my experience that the table would not move unless the experimental conditions were relaxed. It was more fun just to socialize. Our hands were on the table and it was vibrating. Black Elk was rapping his power beat. I noticed, cynically, that Tom and Elaine's fingers were firmly fixed to the table top. The energy was low and the table motions were gentle. Sometimes the table would tip toward Tom and sometimes toward Elaine. I decided that as long as I did not subconsciously push down on my side of the table and as long as Tom did not lift his side, it could not tip toward me. I grew more and more certain of this as time passed.

The table tipped toward Elaine for a long time, then again toward Tom. Elaine took her hands off the table and she seemed to be resting with eyes closed. Maybe she was in a kind of trance. Tom's hands were clearly on the table top. The table vibrated under his fingers, perhaps the result of unconscious muscle movement. Then I saw that his fingers were not in full contact with the table. The table was resonating on its own. His fingers were not producing the effect. The table was tipping toward me. Was I subconsciously pushing on it? I lifted my hands and the table continued to push against me. I looked under the table and saw Tom's feet firmly on the floor. He was clearly only touching the tabletop lightly with his fingers. I put my fingers on the table top. The table top was sliding, resonating, under his fingers. I withdrew my hands and moved them around the table. I searched for secret wires or strings with my hands. How was the table staying up? I put my hands on the table again. It continued to vibrate, sliding back and forth, rapidly now, beneath Tom's and my fingers. The table remained in its impossible state, on two legs, for minute after minute, while I puzzled over how this could be.

"Can you explain this?" Tom asked me. He knew that I could not. "Maybe I have magnets embedded in my fingers," he said.

"But how does it vibrate?" I asked.

"You got me," he said, smiling. People would tell me later that the effect was done using some type of electromagnetic device. What type of device? I have not heard of a hidden device that can make a metal table vibrate. I can't explain what I witnessed.

Elaine put her hands on the table. It continued to dance around. Tom held his hands above the table and tried to get it to rise up to his hands. It would not raise all four legs off the floor but it would tip toward me while it vibrated under Elaine's fingers and while I looked underneath the table for signs of fraud.

I remembered my visit to the magician James Randi. He had described how he tested table-tippers. That evening, I had witnessed events that could not be explained by typical methods for making a table move with one's hands.

Perhaps there were electromagnets in the floor? I did not think this explanation was valid, but I did not wish to become a full believer. I found it impossible to believe that a table could move on its own.[1]

Later, I spoke with John Hunt. He told me a long and complex story. He said that he had not been interested in psychic phenomena while he was a college student majoring in physics and mathematics at the University of Missouri at Rolla. One night, some of his friends were playing with a Ouija board. John wanted to demonstrate to them that the motions of the planchette were derived from their own unconscious muscular movements.[2]

"I decided to conduct a test," John told me. "While they touched the planchette, I asked questions to which only I knew the answers. I couldn't believe it! The board gave the correct information. I asked a question about Israel's defense capabilities, about the quantity of various types of weapons possessed by Israel. The board always came up with a reasonable answer. I must admit, I became curious.

"I continued with the same group at other sessions," he told me. "I was informed that my *spirit guide* was 'C.' The board had a message for me that had to do with *quantum teleportation*. The message was 'ABNO.' The board predicted that I would become involved with another group in Rolla. I didn't really understand these messages, and I wasn't completely convinced that the Ouija board was authentic. It could have just been a matter of autosuggestion.

"Then in 1978, I heard raps in my apartment wall. The raps came three at a time. 'Rap, rap, rap; rap, rap, rap.' I demanded that if they were being made by 'C' that they come from the other wall in order to prove themselves. Then they rapped out two sets of three on the other wall!

"It was about this time that I ran into Steve Calvin," John continued. "Steve invited Tom and Elaine over to my apartment and they did the standard table-tipping experiment there. 'C' made raps! I didn't know what to make of it. It was hard to accept, but I'm into science fiction, so this was like a game for me.

"I decided to devise a test of the raps during an ESP/PK experiment with Tom and Elaine. I asked that the raps tell me what I was thinking at that moment. I thought of the Rolling Stones album, *Goat's Head Soup*. The raps spelled out 'goat.' How can you explain that?"

John laughed nervously at the absurdity. Although he could not completely accept the authenticity of the raps, he wondered how they could read his mind.

In my notes, that evening, I noted my impressions of John. He had an engineer's personality, more at home in the realm of numbers and things than among people. He enjoyed talking, laughing, joking. He seemed logical, sane, perhaps naïve. A magician might find him easy to fool, but how could a magician have set up the *Goat's Head Soup* trick?[3]

During later ESP/PK experiments, the raps revealed further information to John. The raps said that "C" stood for "Charles" who lived in fourteenth century Wales. Charles had been John's son in a previous life. One night at 2 a.m., John was walking down a street when he heard raps coming from the hood of a car. The raps spelled out "D-A-I." He checked the car and determined that the engine block was cold and could not have produced the raps. Later, during a table-tipping experiment at Tom's house, the raps informed John that Charles Dai was the name of his son in a past life.

The raps said that "ABNO" stood for "alternating bilocative nodal oscillations," words that the entities said explained how PK occurred. The meaning of this phrase was not clear, but it seemed to refer to brain function.

"It sounds like something you would put on an undergraduate exam for a question that you had no idea about the answer," John noted.

Tom, Elaine, Ed, and Steve must have considered John to be conducive to psi, since the original mini-lab and camera were set up in his apartment. They hoped that the entities in his apartment could affect the mini-lab. During this period, John pondered the possibility that Tom and Elaine were frauds.

"They thought I was nervous, but actually I was suspicious," John told me. Later, Cox's first set of leather rings linked at the Richards' house. John examined the rings and found that they had not been cut, even after linking. "I found it difficult to accept," he told me.

These linked uncut leather rings constituted permanent evidence of the paranormal, something that psychical researchers have sought to create for many decades. Later the linked rings were mysteriously destroyed; seemingly by poltergeist activity. Other SORRATs told me that they had seen similar evidence, but each time the artifacts were destroyed, ostensibly by paranormal processes like spontaneous fires.

Although the supernatural still seems strange to him, John adjusted to his life as a believer. He had not told his co-workers about his paranormal experiences.

"I'm suspicious of deluding myself, but I'm totally convinced that Tom and Elaine are not frauds," he said. "The recent messages that I get have a lot to say about ABNO: alternating bilocative nodal oscillations. That is probably what the wavy lines meant that were out of place in your ESP card deck. It means being in a state of flux between alpha and beta/delta brain waves. The entities say that is the state of mind needed before you can do teleportation."

"It's hard for me to accept all this as real," I told John.

"It's hard for me, too. Maybe it's all a hoax. Maybe someone is tricking us."

"But how did they do the Goats Head Soup trick?" I asked.

"Maybe this is all the work of the Devil!"

"Is that the way a skeptical engineer talks?"

"We don't seem to be dealing with your average run-of-the-mill entities," he noted.

"I think that the Devil would do a more competent job of proving himself!" I said.

John introduced me to Vern, another SORRAT member. Vern had been a student at Southeast Missouri State University in Cape Girardeau when he met Tom Richards. Although originally skeptical, Vern became convinced in the authenticity of the SORRAT phenomena by taking part in ESP/PK experiments. He showed me pictures he had taken of tables floating freely, after everyone had removed their hands.

"I was there," he said. "It isn't as if it happened only once or twice. It isn't as if it happened in only one place. There were no hidden strings. I know it isn't fake. I'm certain that this type of thing happens because I saw it. I don't know whether it is caused by entities, PK, living people, or whatever, but I know it is real."

Vern told me about a time that the table led the group around a SORRAT member's front yard. He described watching people lightly touch only the center of the table by themselves and seeing it vibrate vigorously. Vern constructed other plastic boxes containing aluminum foil that were sealed with epoxy. The entities (or PK power or whatever) put some marks on the foil sheet during one session. Vern inspected the box and verified that no one had tampered with it.

"How certain are you that no one tampered with your box?" I asked.

"I'm one hundred percent certain," Vern said. "Alice has one of my boxes at Skyrim. As far as I know, it is still glued shut. There's no way a person could tamper with one of my boxes during a session without it being detected afterward."

I told Vern about the cassette tapes Tom loaned me and the sessions during which messages appeared in boxes. I had heard his voice during some of the sessions. "Some of the messages written inside the sealed boxes were complex," I told him. "One message said, 'conduct research, but realize that the PK we use requires a spiritual power greater than all the universe.'"

"Then you know that it can happen," Vern said. "There's another thing about this—all the people who have seen these things are not raving believers. They're not weirdos. One time the whole house shook while we were doing an experiment. It was incredible! It doesn't happen in just in one place; it has happened in many places."

I showed Vern a list of SORRAT members that Tom had given me. He looked it over.

"You should get hold of these people," he advised me. "They'll verify that what I've told you is true. I'm not the only one who can affirm that this stuff is real. They will tell you the same thing. The phenomena are too vigorous to be explained away by fraud."

"Do you still go to SORRAT experiments?"

"I live too far away to go to Rolla meetings," he told me. "I would go to

meetings in St. Louis, but there aren't many SORRATs here so I don't participate that much anymore. There are only a limited number of questions you
can ask and their answers are fairly consistent. There's a repetitive quality to it.
I can't say whether they are discarnate entities or not. All I can say is that the
effects are real."

Vern was a successful salesman who had no reason to lie about SORRAT.
He seemed honest, but I had no standards to evaluate what he said. Within the
field of parapsychology, anecdotal stories have only limited evidential quality,
and the history of Spiritualist research is filled with examples of observational
errors.

I stopped by the McDonnell Laboratory to view the film segments that
Steve Shaw had described. To my surprise, Mark Shafer would not let me view
them.

"Why not?" I asked.

"It's an ethical matter. We need to protect the identity of our experimental
subjects. I can't let you view any of the videotapes until after we present our
paper at the Parapsychological Association meetings in August."

"But I'm only here in St. Louis for a few days,"

"That's unfortunate, but it's the lab policy."

"How can guarding the identity of your subjects be a factor?" I asked. "I
was at Steve Shaw's apartment just over a week ago, and I visited Tom Richards
last week. It isn't as if I don't know who your subjects are. I have questions
regarding fraud."

"I'm sorry. It's the lab policy," he repeated.

"I'm planning to bring Steve Shaw to the University of Maryland to do
some experiments with him there. He's agreed to come. I need to know about
the evidence you have. That's how science works. Scientists share their findings
with each other. They work together."

"We would rather that you didn't do research with him," he said.

"Yeah? Why not?" I was getting slightly angry.

"We're at a very delicate stage of our research. It's very important that we
have no publicity at this stage. If you bring Steve to your university, I'm sure
that people there will get excited. Macro PK is a very controversial thing. How
did you get Steve Shaw's address?"

"Tom Richards gave it to me."

Mark appeared disturbed. "We would rather that Tom had not done that.
We're at a crucial stage. We're trying to produce a film segment of a macro PK

event that would be impossible for a magician to duplicate using sleight-of-hand. This is an important, prestigious place. The McDonnell Laboratory is associated with Washington University here in St. Louis. Peter Phillips is a distinguished physicist. If we are successful, this would be a momentous event in the history of parapsychological research. Everyone expects this achievement to occur here. Give us some time. Hold off your research with Steve for a year or so. Then you can replicate our work."

"I guess it all boils down to the fact that you don't want me to test Steve Shaw."

"Have you ever tried videotaping macro PK?" he asked.

"No, that's why I need to see your tapes. I need to see how you're doing it, and I also want to see the funny business that went on when Tom Richards was there."

"It's not easy to film macro PK. We haven't been completely successful yet but we're getting close. We can't let you see the films."

Mark was a suave, cultured individual, younger than I was, with handsome, finely chiseled features. He wore a blue sports jacket and a shirt open at the neck. He appeared to be completely relaxed as he sat behind his desk. Did he know that some of his subjects had cheated right in front of his video camera? I decided to press him more fully.

"Why won't you let me see the films? Is it because they show someone cheating?" I asked.

He didn't even blink. "That's not it at all," he stated, unruffled. "We have absolutely no reason to believe that any of the subjects who have been here have ever cheated in any way. It's totally a matter of lab policy. After the conference in August, you can view the films."

He seemed ignorant of what had occurred in his lab. Did his films show Tom Richards entering the room, bending the spoon fraudulently, yet blocking this action with his body?

"I hope you're being cautious. You don't want to be fooled," I warned. "I hear rumors that some of these people cheat."

He was unconcerned. "We're being cautious. We are continuously tightening our test conditions. After we produce a film segment of a bend that we feel cannot be duplicated by a magician, then you can replicate our work."

It seemed to be an ego thing. He did not want anyone else to be successful before him. I would have to postpone testing Steve Shaw. I did not want to offend the researchers at the McDonnell Laboratory. It seemed puzzling to me that the McDonnell Lab was not more supportive of my research. I believed that rapport was an important factor in getting PK results. It appeared that the metal benders did not have high rapport with Mark or they would have told him about their concerns.

I planned a strategy for continuing my investigation. Steve Shaw had told me that Mike Edwards had seen Tom cheating. He told me that Mike had told Jan, the McDonnell Lab manager, about it. He said that she had shrugged it off. Perhaps Jan could verify what Mike had told her.

I wrote Jan a letter. "Did Mike Edwards tell you that he saw Tom Richards cheat?" I asked.

She wrote back, "I cannot answer your question. It is lab policy not to comment on rumors. We must confine our statements to what we publish in scientific journals or present before scientific meetings."

I found this a strange response. Doesn't a scientific laboratory have an obligation to tell other researchers about possible fraud? I speculated that Mike had probably told her about his observations or else she would have denied the rumor. I wrote Mike a letter asking if he would be willing to share his observations on being tested at the McDonnell Lab. He did not respond. My research into what had occurred at the McDonnell Lab had come to a dead end.

Cox and I looked forward to the Parapsychological Association meeting in Syracuse, New York, in August 1981. Although Cox's formal paper had been rejected, Peter Phillips allowed him time during an evening workshop to show some of his films. We were interested in the reception these films would receive.

I attended the meetings in August. Dr. Phillips's evening workshop was not part of the formal Parapsychological Association program. His presentation, in an informal setting, included his films showing possible psychokinesis. His work had not been accepted for presentation at the meeting, but he was allowed to conduct a "workshop." Dr. Phillip's workshop consisted of three parts. First, he showed a video of the metal-bending of Steve Shaw and Mike Edwards. The consensus of the attending parapsychologists was that the controls regarding fraud had not been adequate. Dr. Phillips was aware of this problem and did not claim that his videotapes were authentic cases of psi.

Afterward, Dr. Phillips showed a videotape in which the magician James Randi duplicated many of Israeli illusionist Uri Geller's metal-bending feats. Randi explained the tricks that he believed Geller used and urged parapsychologists to consult magicians before testing metal-benders.

Ed Cox showed his films during the third workshop segment. The audience burst into laughter when they saw the film of the sorted ESP cards suddenly jumping back into their sealed packet.[4] Cox was unable to describe all his precautions against fraud within the time allocated to him. Some parapsychologists expressed the opinion that Cox was being fooled.

I spoke with a parapsychologist afterward, who asked to remain anonymous. "I've known Ed Cox for many years," he told me. "I cannot believe he would ever do fraudulent research. I assume he has run into a trickster whose skill as a magician is greater than his."

Another parapsychologist was even more blunt. "Those films are fake," he said. "They can't be authentic."

Later, I ate lunch with a group of parapsychologists. They discussed the Rolla case.

"Someone is going to have to go out there to Missouri and catch whoever is fooling poor old Ed," one stated.[5]

"You've been out there, Jim. What do you think?" a younger parapsychologist asked me. I felt a sense of role shift. I had been an observer, and now I was required to participate in the discussion. I was caught off guard.

"I hate to say this, because I know everyone is skeptical about the Rolla case, but I watched Cox's experiments while I was there. If a person believes that all the effects can be explained by fraud, they must hypothesize that Cox is part of it. There are many SORRAT members and they support each other's stories. There would need to be several skilled magicians working together, but the SORRAT members describe things that happened when the main members were not present. It's like a poltergeist case—recurrent spontaneous PK. It might be that some of the SORRAT members, including Cox, are core figures in a poltergeist case."

An elderly parapsychologist coughed in surprise. "There's fraud involved, but it's hard for me to believe that Cox could be connected to fraud. I've known Ed Cox for over 20 years!"

I briefly described the incident in which Cox claimed that someone had thrown his metal bar into the corner. "Cox was the only one present. From his vantage point, it's like a poltergeist case, but the phenomena seem capable of extremely complex behavior—even written messages. I've read that that happens sometimes in poltergeist cases."

"And the SORRAT explanation for the phenomena is that they are caused by spiritual entities, right?" the younger parapsychologist asked.

"That's right," I answered. "Ed Cox has a very scientific attitude, but entities making the raps say they are discarnate spirits."

"Why do these entities act so strangely on camera?" he asked. "Don't they have any consideration for us poor doubting parapsychologists?"

"I don't know. I guess I'll have to ask," I stated. "Sometimes, it seems to me that they lack empathy for our failure to accept them at face value."

When I returned to Maryland, I received an answer to a question I had left for the entities:

Q: Dear Friends: Apparently, it is difficult for you to do psi tasks before the camera while I am watching. Am I correct in assuming that it is more difficult for you to perform psi tasks while I am watching than when I am not present? If so, why is this the case?

A: Dear Jim: Psi is curious; there is a whole melding of constructs when physical and nonphysical factors are mixed like tripe in a pail. It does seem hard for us to use psi when the alpha state or the beta state predominate in your mind. The energy is inhibited, but exactly how, I am uncertain. I will ask someone at a higher level about what precisely happens and then try to tell you.

My ten series ESP test, which I was conducting with the entities, had been very successful in its first two trials, but the entities were unsuccessful in later trials. Overall, the experiment failed to demonstrate ESP. I decided to make another attempt. Using a random number table and a dictionary, I selected a noun to be used as the target in the next ESP test. My selection system randomly selected the word "river." I sent another entity letter request through the Richards.

Q: Dear Friends: I just got back from the Parapsychological Association Convention in Syracuse, New York. I showed various people (as many as were interested) the written messages that you have sent me. Many people laughed at the research work that we have done. In the letters I received from you, I failed to produce any proof of your paranormal ability. I know that in the past you have done things to prove your psi abilities for people. For example, John Hunt once asked you to rap out the words that he was thinking in his head. He thought of the Rolling Stones album Goat's Head Soup *and someone rapped out "Goat." I need you to do a task like this for me in order that people might become more interested in your other writings. Would you please write the word that I have selected in the space below? If you cannot do this task, could you devise some other task that would verify your authenticity?*

A: *Jim - The Randis of the world will never be convinced; it is not in their interest. Even telepathy could as easily be from those who still wear their skins as proof we exist. Do not be concerned. "Some who come to scoff, remain to pray," and to think. If you enjoy telepathy, good. Do not confuse proof of telepathy with proof that we are real.*

In September 1981, I designed a five-page questionnaire to mail to my list of SORRAT members. I asked them to furnish their name (optional), age, gender, marital status, and occupation. I also asked questions about their experiences both within the group and by themselves, and how these events affected their beliefs.

Of the 38 questionnaires mailed, 21 were returned (55%). I interviewed two other SORRAT members face-to-face, so that I had an overall 60% response rate. Many described events that exceeded what magicians might do by standard trickery. For example, people described paranormal experiences that happened when no one else was present. Others wrote about situations in which they spontaneously devised tests of psychic phenomena during group sessions (like John Hunt's *Goat's Head Soup* test). The entities passed the various tests. The respondents were unanimous in their belief in the authenticity of the phenomena they described. They reported that the entire room shook during table-tipping sessions in various people's homes. A few respondents saw apparitions or received messages from deceased relatives. Several observed the table vibrate without anyone touching it. One woman remarked that table-tipping experiments seemed to "energize" the room where the experiment was conducted. She saw her children successfully communicate with raps in the same room the next night. She noted that, as the days passed, the children were less successful in hearing the raps.

The respondents also described apports (objects materializing during a séance) and complete table levitations under conditions that seemed to preclude fraud. They conducted experiments with sealed boxes, like Vern's, and felt certain that the writing inside was paranormal since they had kept the boxes under supervision during the experiment. Many respondents stated that their initial skepticism had changed to belief. For example, one wrote:

Originally, the group consisted only of other faculty members who were essentially non-religious, intellectually curious people. All of us looked at the evening meetings with great skepticism. We attended for scientific reasons but also for entertainment.

After many such meetings (about which I took notes), I modified my personal generalizations about the nature of the world to <u>include</u> psi phenomena. I arrived at several hypotheses as to what psi might be and why it could not be predicted, and why it only occurred in the presence of certain people. This ability to precipitate psi activity is an inexplicable talent in some people. It is like musical or artistic ability, that is equally inexplicable. This talent cannot be controlled or turned on and off at will. The idea of a sporadic talent explains why, after one year, all the phenomena stopped. Tom continued to have gatherings but nothing paranormal happened. I believe that the phenomena were subconsciously directed by Tom's mind.

Here are some of things I experienced:

1. I witnessed a TV tray "climb" the front of a fireplace.

2. I felt a whole room shake violently.

3. One Sunday, raps, with whom we engaged in conversation, followed us from a graveyard, to buildings in Cape Girardeau. Raps came from the floor of our car, in the corner of the living room, when we came in the front door of our home, from the kitchen floor and from a table as we had lunch. All of this was during daylight hours.

4. One evening, we broke up into groups and, among other things, levitated an ordinary small sofa pillow. There was cold air underneath the pillow, which was suspended above the floor several inches.

5. Another time, the center of a TV tray began to pop rhythmically up and down. You could put the palms of your hands above and below the center and the metal would still pop back and forth.

6. One evening a large group of people gathered. Most were students and all were novices to the phenomena, which was like a poltergeist. There were many, many raps from all over the room; ceiling, floor, and walls. A large heavy wooden table levitated despite a man who stood on it trying to keep it on the ground."[6]

About half the people who responded to my questionnaire said that they had few or no paranormal experiences outside of the SORRAT meetings. Many said that they had no experiences except when Tom Richards was present. Some people reported experiences outside the group and also when Tom Richards was not present. Three variables were well correlated:

(1) belief in spirits and life after death,

(2) experiencing SORRAT phenomena when Tom Richards was not present,

(3) paranormal experiences outside of SORRAT sessions.

Although many respondents said that they no longer participated in

SORRAT meetings, all said they had witnessed paranormal phenomena. One reported fraud—but within the context of belief:

> *During that year we met in many different houses, with personal friends that I knew very well. We were skeptical, yet the phenomena still occurred. There was no way that the houses or furniture could have been rigged. Later, when the group degenerated into an association of social misfits, I lost interest in participating. When no real phenomena occurred, which was often, there were obvious fraudulent efforts to generate noises and table movement; to keep the party going, so to speak. Although I did not continue my participation once this happened, it did not negate my conclusions regarding my previous experiences.*

One respondent, who had been part of the original SORRAT group with Dr. Neihardt, said that she "realized that there were many things about the world I do not understand" but expressed concern that the SORRAT members had "closed themselves off from the rest of the world" in order to experiment with the phenomena. She hoped future studies would involve a more scientific environment.

One respondent, who reported powerful SORRAT experiences, had taken part in a Philip group session (the artificially created spirit used by a group in Toronto) and found the phenomena equivalent. During the Philip group experiment, the table stood on two legs and the respondent attempted to force it back to the floor. It resisted his entire weight. He checked for and detected no wires attached to the table or other normal means of support for it.

Reading the questionnaires helped me evaluate my personal SORRAT experiences within the context of SORRAT's history. Early SORRAT members, in Columbia, reported extremely robust phenomena, as did Richards' Cape Girardeau group: rapping, levitations, earthquakes, and apports. Twenty-three respondents, a diverse collection of people, were certain that they had experienced psychokinesis. Their experiences were like mine, but their reports implied that the phenomena they witnessed had been more robust than what I had witnessed. I had not seen a table levitate with no hands touching it.

I sent one questionnaire to Tom Richards to be placed in his basement. I wanted to give the entities a chance to respond to my questionnaire. The completed questionnaire was returned to me by mail:

PSYCHIC EXPERIENCE QUESTIONNAIRE
Name (optional): John A. King

Age:347
Sex: Masculine
Marital Status: Merrie Widower
Occupation: freebooter, govt. clerk (no real difference)
This questionnaire has been designed for individuals who have participated in psi groups. Respondents are invited to disregard questions that seem inappropriate. Short or incomplete answers are acceptable. Feel free to express any additional opinions on the blank sheet that follows this questionnaire or to write me if you have additional questions, attitudes, or opinions.

Q: How and when did you first begin participating in a psi group? When did this participation terminate?

A: I started rapping for Mr. Winters circle in November of 1848, although I soon rapped for Kate and Maggie Fox and many others.

Generally, participation terminated as soon as I gave them what they thought they wanted, or else when their group would get bored and break up, or when the other participants all were on our side and knew by experience what I tried to tell them. I still do participate, as you ken.

Q: How did your system of beliefs regarding psi change by participation in the group?

A: I grew to understand what those who met me in 1698 meant when they said I would get the hell I expected when I was assigned/volunteered to help those on the meat level.

I used to think only the dogs of Spain were thoroughly vile. I soon learn'd better.

Most members of most séance groups are complete asses, although those who make fun of them are far worse.

Q: What would you regard as some of your most important or significant experiences obtained within the group?

A: When I materialized in a cabinet in Philadelphia, I scared the "urine" out of some old women. Y'see, I forgot to do my eyes!

Q: What would you regard as some of your most important or significant experiences (if any) obtained outside of the group?

A: Here you mean everything I have kenned on both sides. Meeting God would probably be the most important.

Q: Feel free to express any attitudes or opinions regarding the nature of the psi phenomena that you have experienced or the social interaction that surrounded it.

A: I think much of it is flapdoodle, but I like writing to people like you, Jim.

I decided to ask John King questions about his life. I hoped to gain insight into the nature of this entity. This began a series of five letters in which he wrote an autobiography.

A: Dear Jim - My life story is hardly a good example. I was birthed in Bristol on July 25, 1637.[7] I was of poor but honest parentage; well, usually honest and always poor. The Anglican Shopboys School, a free society, pounded some book learning into my stubborn skull, so I could read and write better than most of my fellows. (I have improved through the years, as I had no love of slothful ignorance.)

At age 13, I was a stout, strong lummox, so I betook me to a merchantman and went slops, then sailed before the mast as a man. We were taken and I was sold in Barbados to work the treads for grinding cane for rum. I will not try to tell you the evils of that brief part of my life, for it was hell. We were blessed to have bugs to eat. I didst bide my time, and was chosen to wield the whip, which I did with a strong arm, and little pity for the poor devils who were my mates. I outdid my masters in cruel brutality until they laughed with me and let me lie unshackled on the husks. I learnt enough, and even converted to papistry, kissing the crux.

One night, I slew my masters in their linen, lacy sheets and set out with their blackamoors in a prowl sloop. Of our hardships I will not tell, but after I sold the sloop and crew in Jamaica, I sign'd on with Captain John Morris. I was with Morris when he and Jackemann took Vildemos and Trujillyo. Then, for greater booty, I joyned my old Bristol mate Captain Henry Morgan and did myself proud at the fight at Grenada.

I stayed with Morgan. He backed Captain Edward Mansefield and took Santa Catalina. The whole isle was ours ripe for the taking, and we took it cannon and cutlass. We free booters chose Henry Morgan our admiral. This was in the summer of 1666.

Sir Thomas Modyeford was royal governor of Jamaica. He sent us out to take Spaniards prisoner and make them tell how they planned to attack Jamaica. We took a galliant ship and made the capitaine sing a merrie note with warm, cherry-red swabrods in his arse. We took Puerto Principe, Puerto Bello (on the mainland) and seized much of Panama. In Cuba, we did bravely. We sacked Maracaibo in 1669, and made a bold pass at Gibraltar itself, showing it as invincible as a wench's stocking. On our return, three galliants, right, left and middle, surrounded us. Morgan peppered port and starbord, and rammed ahold. We slew all day in the sun, and most of the night, with no quarter hand in hand. They were very brave, and thrice our numbers. We sent most on to Davie Jones, captured the two survivors, and got much gold for our sport, then took Maracaibo yet again. The soldiers, who spied the Sea-fight, had no stomach to try us. We got much booty there.

Henry Morgan was made King's commander of all ships of war in Jamaica. In 1670, we took Santa Catalina again at Christmastide and made the bells ring; we melted them to silver ingots. We took all of Panama by August 1671. Yet—-perfidious politicians! They made peace with Spain in July of 1670, and did not let us know it. They carried Morgan to London in irons. Vile! Yet the king saw him fair, I heard. In 1674, he returned, Sir Henry Morgan, as Gov-Lieutenant of Jamaica. He made me Clerk-Sec'ty for I could write as well as fight.

Those were good days. I wed Belle Harper of Leeds, she who was old Jake Harper's gal, with plantation money laid by. I had of her my bonnie Katie, a fair and winning lass, for all her troubles and later sorrows.

The grand life, and a reward, I thought, for our early troubles! I grew no slower at sport, you may be sure, though I missed the days when loot and taking were there for the grabs, and even pick'd fights with cockscombes out fresh-faced from England when they came buzzing round my Kate to cozen her and do her shame. But enough for now, friend Jim.

——John King

Q: Dear John King: Would you please continue telling us about your life in Jamaica?

A: Friend Jim—'Twas merrie 'til Morgan over-reached himself and dallied with Ladie Von. She let slippe to her husband that Henry had tupped her, and from then on, Von was down upon Sir Henry and all his men. He called free booterie mere piracy and Sir H.M. the Prince of the Pirates. Hypocrisy most foul!

I well remember that fair October, the twelfth, it was, when Lord Von publickly strippt Sir Henry Morgan of his publick office and turned him out. Not to rot; we saw to that! We'd buried the bell plate ingotts; no point in sharing all our bootie with the crown, who'd not swinked blood for it, so we lived out of the Main Eye. Sir Henry died of a phrensie in his blood at his greathouse in mid-dogge-days 1688.

Afterward, I lived quietlie in the King's Towne until the trouble with my bonnie Katie's wee babe.

Later,
John King

Q: Dear John King: Would you continue telling us about your life?
A: Dear Jim,
'Tis sadnesse and sorrows of which I now write. In 1667, my bonnie Katie,

mainstay of my life, took uppe with a carpetknight named Sydnie Marrow. Aye, he look't brave, and made much of me and honor'd me with his tongue. Had my poor wife lived, she would've seen thro that skouncell, but by then she lay in the Alders Kirkyard on the hill above the Kings Towne, and poor Katie was forced to rely on me for a proper upbringing. I was not able to keep her from harm. She had small help from me.

In brief, she bore a bastard babe.

I slew young Marrow and left his bones to lie in unhallowed ground, and his wife to wail her moan to that darned Lord Von who'd driven Sir Henry out to die of phrensie.

The bonnie babe, my Katie slew with her own white hands, for all of it were her own, to wipe away the shame. Now I know it was hellish wrong. Yet, in your time, Master Jim, you let abhornsons murder many wee babes, and let the rascals go unhanged.

Yet the vile villains put my bonnie lass away, and there she was strangled in a string—not so much for infanticide but because I was her old Da, and I spoke aloud, and they laught me to scorne. Von did it because I was Sir Henry Morgan's own right hand, I do believe.

It was not long before my house was gone. In the fall of 1698, on my way to Mamaloi Lil's from the Grouper's Head, full to the gills with grog, as was common to me then, I was thumped dead and came to this side; 'twas two or three of Von's lickbootes as did me in most likely. The best was to comme, tho.

John King

Q: Dear John King;

Would you tell us about your death?

A: Dear Friend Jim: When I camme to the other side, as you ken it, I was very confussulated. My headache was there, then gonne. I look't and saw the wretches clubbing a man on the ground. I set upon them with my blade, but lo! it went thro their bodies without touching them! They paid me no minde, but fled a ligher's lathorn. By itte's glister, I sawe that the corpse wore my clothes and had my face, or what was left of it. Then the hue broke out, "John King has gone to hell at last." None, I ken, was muchly sorry!

I was then pull'd thro the gap, which is indeed within your own mindes, like a shot thro a cannon's bore. My old Mam mette me and shed teares, and I claspt my wife againe. But best, best of all, my darlin Katie came to me, holding a glowinge balle of pure light which was her owne sweet babe.

With these camme others, no least Sir Henry.

At first, I was sore afeered, for once I knew I was dead as salt pork, I knew that I must frye for my sins. But then I saw the light; God, and knew myself fullie.

Instead of being onlie old John King, I was part of every living spirit, of all, of God.

Then I knew I must return and help others on your side. That is only faire I ken, as I had helped many get to the other side from the meat level, by spiling their meat. I made this known; I was told I would finde the frustrations of this effort far worse thanne the hell I'd feared.

This has largely been true, as you ken.

At first I rapp't, but in 1850 I first spoke directly, and a few yeares later, when cabinet séances came into vogue, I was able to materialize for Slade (who was much like my worse self). I oftime scribbled on slates. Altho when I could not, he soon learn'd to write messages himselfe for a showe (to bee sure he got all the facts straite, I'd ween). Many others I help't, some with my Katie, who was photograft with Lodge. She did enjoy that!

Now, I did not always tell the truth about myself, for somme are helpt or impresst by a clever twiste. Somme ken me by other names, even that of Morgan himselfe.

The power waynes.

Later,
John King

Q: Dear John King;
Would you continue telling of your life on the other side?
A: Thisse information is of no evidentialle value, and can be read in bookes such as Roman *by Lodge, who knew my daughter Katie. To be fine, we can learn from those wiser than we, and from ye all.*

Dwellinges we can have, and all that the fancy can conceive (I favor a home like that I hadde on Tower Street, but with more dulcet aire).

Beyond this simple levelle of houses or harpes-and-haloes is the larger world of pure mind and pure sensation. Encompassing all this is complete freedome, empathy, light.

Those are the first stages.

John King

John King's autobiography contained many pseudo-archaic phrases and spellings, a clumsy imitation of a 17th century Englishman's writing. Scholars would argue that his autobiography was fraudulent; that it was not written by a 17th century buccaneer. Tom Richards suggested that John King acquired a mixture of writing styles from his existence on the other side, outside of time and space.

I made a list of ideas about my SORRAT research:

(1) I could not distinguish artifact from authentic psychokinesis, but I felt I had experienced a continuum of events that were becoming increasingly implausible.

(2) I had no method for determining the source of the phenomena. It might be produced by fraud, by the minds of living people, or by disembodied spirits. I suspected that all three processes came into play, but had no way to prove it.

(3) The phenomena seemed to be thwarted by close monitoring and tightened security.

(4) Providing the phenomena with the ability to write allowed them to seem more human. At least they were not smashing mini-labs.

(5) Although a group seemed to facilitate the phenomena, the presence of Tom and Elaine Richards was a more important factor during the time of my observation.

(6) The phenomena seemed to be testing the boundaries of what I considered possible. The phenomena were implausible, but it was possible, in most cases, to devise normal explanations for them.

(7) People who participated in the group experience came to believe in the phenomena, even though some witnessed ambiguous situations and fraud.

(8) The phenomena could not be produced on command.

CHAPTER 6
SEEKING PROOF

The entity letters attracted the attention of other SORRATs, and I urged them to send questions with self-addressed envelopes for Tom to place beside the mini-lab. Tom asked that anyone receiving answers mail both him and me a copy of the entities' response.

Many people assumed that the entities had psychic abilities and submitted extrasensory tests. For example, Donna McCormick, editor of the *American Society for Psychical Research Newsletter,* provided clairvoyance and precognition test questions. The entities responded:

A: You assume that we "see all, know all, and tell all," merely because we are no longer limited by (generally) living in the meat. This is obviously absurd from a typical viewpoint. If you lived in China, would that mean that you were personally acquainted with every Chinese citizen? Of course, you would be more likely by propinquity to know any <u>given</u> Chinese; I almost said "Chinaman," but some in your day think that a racial slur, than would a Londoner who never saw China.

I do not mind helping but, even were I able, the Amazingly Raunchy Prestidigitators[1] would still scoff and count coins for their poor shows, and the psi-materialists would cry "<u>mere</u> telepathy from the living," and those who "know" I cannot exist will still know what they did before. Tis fools-game to try to convince a materialist that spiritual realities are the realest reals of all. They will not read Plato with sympathy; even Aristotle had his doubts! Each should find his own truth (small and grotesque that it may be).

This idea that the entities had ESP was not implausible. They had previously answered mentally framed questions during group PK sessions. John Hunt had told me about one such event; the Goat's Head Soup incident. Tom described similar experimental results in his book, *SORRAT: A History of the Neihardt Psychokinesis Experiments, 1961—1981.*

Because of these successes, letter writers continued to seek paranormal proof. Lisa wrote:

> *Q: Dear John King and friends,*
> *I have a rather pressing problem that requires a decision (very soon) on my part. What will happen if I do nothing, or what will the consequences be if I do take action? What are your feelings about my problem?*
>
> > *Thanks,*
> > *Lisa*
>
> *A: Dear Lisa,*
> *It would certainly help if you let us know what the problem is. Your statement of question is somewhat vague. Please be just a wee mite more specific, and perhaps we can help you.*
> *Never depend on us to solve problems, however. We cannot allow you to fall into the trap of using things of our side of the change to serve as a crutch. That would hurt your own independent development into a very high level while you are still cased in mortality.*
>
> > *Love –*
> > *Infinity*

The letter-writing entities seemed to have less perceptual ability (or willingness to comply with requests for proof) than they did during table-tipping sessions. Cox sent a request to his helper, Three-Times-Three.

> *Q: Dear "111 x 111": Can you please stamp and mail this letter to me? The stamp is under the "genius at work" label on Tom's desk. Use that one please.*
> *A: I can't find it.*

When asked about specific deceased relatives, the entities sometimes provided vague answers or no information at all:

> *Q: Grandma, please leave me a message. If you cannot write me now, perhaps someone else "on the other side" could tell me what you are doing now. Are you incarnated now, and in what "carne"/meat/physical manifestation?*
>
> > *Love,*
> > *Lisa*
>
> *A: Not yet, if ever.*

Although not a paranormal proof, the entities letters had strange imaginative qualities. Typically, the entity letters arrived with strange postmarks from places such as Tombstone, Arizona, or Deadwood, North Dakota. Postmarks sometimes suggested that the letter had traveled backward or forward in time since the date of the postmark did not fit with the time the letter left the Richards' house or with its time of arrival at the recipient's house. The volume of letters, the strangeness of the postmarks, the variation in times and dates of the postmark with when the letters were sent or received had an anomalous quality. A normal explanation involved fraud; perhaps someone had the capacity to create counterfeit postmarks.

Entity letters also had extra stamps, sometimes foreign, affixed to them as well as childish or humorous stickers on the outside of the envelope. The message conveyed was somewhat obscure beyond reflecting the poltergeist quality of the phenomena.

The method by which the postmark feats were accomplished remained unknown for many months until an address label, affixed by the entities, fell off a large envelope containing a set of entity letters. As a result, the envelope was returned to Ed Cox. Inside the envelope was a request, written in the entities handwriting, asking the postmaster at the distant city to postmark the letters so that a "postmark collector," named in the letter, might obtain new specimens. The letter provided the name and address of a person in Rolla who was allegedly making the request. Cox was unable to locate any such individual in Rolla. When confronted by Ed, the entities quickly admitted to "artifact induction." They said their fraud was a "psi energy" conservation measure; by using regular mail to send the envelope they hoped to stimulate belief in their existence.

The entities claimed to use artifacts to generate enough belief so that authentic phenomena could follow. Their response to Ed Cox's question illustrates their attitude:

Q: Why do some of the very significant effects, both in and outside of the ML (mini-lab) take so long?
A: The effects depend upon availability of psi energy. The psi energy, which is a natural force, is frequently unstable from the standpoint of being used to accomplish tasks on your side. It can better be used to learn and grow, but it <u>does</u> work for PK, with the same efficiency as a spanner [wrench] can be used to drive a nail, if you do not have access to a hammer. There are bands of energy extending universally, but these flux and change as your planet moves through space.
Q: I have analyzed the varied and seemingly capricious mistakes and other

deviations you have made with what is known in psi as the "psi missing" effect. Am I correct here in suggesting that entity mistakes are similar to psi missing?

A: There are also psychological factors, as psi is a mind-related force. Often you are correct. However, what you think of as a capricious mistake is often not an error but an effort to impose our pattern on your test. As an instance, a letter may be sent to someone who can be influenced or helped; it is rarely by transfer of energy along with the target object. More frequently, it is the psychological effect of getting the letter, and the harmony involved in making contact with the intended recipient that helps, with spinoff domino effects on both. Sometimes, of necessity, it is a genuine error. We do err. Faith plays a role, too. Those who are more impressed by foreign stamps and letters from distant cities will get these, either by psi-mailing or indirectly through postal remailings.

Rector/J. K.

The entities acknowledged "postal remailings" as a way of conserving psi energy. The mini-lab films, tampered experimental envelopes, and postal re-mailings indicated a pattern of entity fraud.[2] The entities seemed to admit that psi phenomena are rare. They admitted to cheating by pretending to "teleport" letters to distant post offices when, in reality, they sent letters through the mail in a regular manner. I found it strange that the entities would fail to adequately glue on their address label. I believe that they purposely revealed their fraud.

I formed this opinion by talking with Ed Cox. He told me that he had found segments of his films with trickster qualities. He gave me a paper describing these qualities. The films showed objects disappearing in one frame and then reappearing in the next frame. When played at normal speed, this phenomenon was not apparent. This did not "prove" fraud (believers label this as an apport), but skeptics would assume the effect occurred due to stop-action photography. The trickster seemed to be leaving a hidden clue—evidence for fraud. Cox detected this only after careful frame-by-frame analysis of his films. In one case, a large object disappeared and appeared for no reason. The trickster had not made an error; the effect had been purposely created.

I believe the "label falling off" phenomenon to be a parallel situation. The entities had carefully glued on address labels during previous mailings. They were skilled at this. Their failure to properly attach an address label on a package that clearly revealed their fraud suggested that they wished to be caught cheating. This motif (the "label falling off" trick) was later repeated in a way that revealed further fraud.

Tom Richards engaged in similar behavior (revealing his own fraud) when he wrote his article supporting the use of artifact induction, published in the *Archaeus Newsletter* in 1984. The article implied that he was familiar with inducing psi through artifact. I took part in many PK experiments where the table would move only after Tom put his hands on it. Although he did not appear to be pushing it, I assumed that he was. The table began moving as if pushed, but after a while it acquired a strange vibrating characteristic that seemed anomalous. Tom could remove his hands and the vibration would continue.

When I asked the entities about artifact induction, they suggested that I contact Mrs. Marian Nester and gave me her address. Mrs. Nester's father had been an important figure in the psychical investigation of the Margery case of the 1920s and 1930s. The entities indicated that Mrs. Nester had a piece to a puzzle that, when put together with my information, would be valuable.

The Margery case presented many contradictions and attracted a great deal of publicity during its era.[3] Mina (Margery) Crandon [Margery was a pseudonym] and her husband, Leroy, a surgeon, discovered that she had apparent mediumistic ability. They conducted lively table-tipping sessions in which her deceased brother Walter spoke, even when Mrs. Crandon's mouth and nose were completely covered. The table moved about, seemingly controlled by a spirit. Although some early investigators found a carpet thread that they assumed was used to make the table move, many other witnesses reported events they considered inexplicable by normal means. They took photographs of something that looked like hands coming out of Mrs. Crandon's mouth and, at other times, her vagina. Supporters claimed these hands were made of ectoplasm; anatomy experts said the hands were cut out of the lung tissue of some animal.

The famous magician Harry Houdini conducted some controversial tests on Mina Crandon, and the spirit Walter angrily accused him of attempting to frame the medium. Houdini, who felt certain that Mrs. Crandon was a fraud, swore he was innocent. Years later, one of Houdini's assistants, familiar with this incident, stated that Houdini was dishonest; he made false claims to frame individuals he felt were frauds.

Walter left his thumb prints in wax during some of the séances to prove his authenticity. This impressed the sitters since none of their own thumb prints matched those found in the wax. Later (after much investigation) a researcher discovered that Walter's thumb prints belonged to Mrs. Crandon's dentist, who had previously given her some dental wax.

With the revelation that spirit fingerprints were not authentic, most investigators decided that the case was not worth their attention. Mina Crandon continued to hold séances and her small circle reported remarkable experiences. She died of alcoholism not long after the death of her husband.

Parapsychologist D. Scott Rogo (1976) referred to this case as almost impossible to evaluate, but noted that one investigator, Hereward Carrington, accepted the genuineness of some of the phenomena. The Margery case was like SORRAT; most rejected it as fraudulent, but insiders believed some aspects were authentic.

I spoke with Mrs. Nester at the Parapsychological Association Conference in 1981. She was excited by the prospect of looking into the Margery case. She believed that some of the events that occurred around Margery were paranormal and planned to look over her father's detailed notes regarding the Margery séances. We hoped that the entities might supply information that could be verified by these unpublished notes, many of which she had not read. The entities claimed to be in contact with Walter, and since Walter claimed to have been present during the Margery séances, he should be able to describe events written in the séance notes.

Mrs. Nester asked the entities a series of questions regarding the Margery case. They wrote that Walter was "*damn* sorry about that fingerprint—dentist touched it and that spoilt all our efforts." Their answer infers that Walter believed himself to be authentic, but that the dentist had ruined the result. His statement does not explain why Walter claimed that the dentist's thumb prints were his own. The evidence indicating Margery's fraud was overwhelming, and the SORRAT entities did not shed light on the Margery case beyond seeming to support belief in Walter. This situation was consistent with previous cases discussed; although Walter should have been able to provide information about the Margery séances, he seemed unable to do so. The information the entities provided was available in previously published accounts. The spirits consistently failed when pressed for good evidence.

The entities' writing contained a word misspelled in the same way that Tom Richards misspelled it, evidence that suggests Tom wrote the message. Ed Cox and I found other examples of correlations between the entity letters and Tom's letters to me: misspelled words and similar phrases. Tom was very irritated when Cox pointed this out to him. He denied writing the messages.

The evidence linking Tom to the letters was not extensive, but it was suggestive. Tom referred to Mina Crandon as Myra and the entities also made this error. Ed Cox and I had detected perhaps a handful of similarly misspelled words. On two occasions, Tom used exact phrases from the entity messages in his letters to me, which arrived almost simultaneously in the mail. The phrases were sufficiently complex that the similarities could not be considered coincidental. A label on one of Tom's tool bins in his basement had lettering similar to the entities' writing. Major explanations included: (1) The entities drew their inspiration from Tom's mind; they were connected to him; (2) Tom wrote the entity letters in trance; (3) Tom purposefully used the same misspellings, phrases, and handwriting to reveal that he wrote the letters, but he denied that he wrote them anyway; this constitutes an alternate form of pathology. Most people would select explanation #2, except that Tom, Elaine, and their son Ivan said that this was impossible. The letter writing required thousands of hours of labor, and those living with Tom would have detected him doing it. Of course, it is possible that someone in trance might write extremely rapidly (there are cases of this in the psychical research literature). I would like to see Tom writing rapidly because that would be amazing! He was not known for rapid movement.

Ivan's behavior indicated that he fully accepted the authenticity of the entity messages; he submitted many questions over the years, and his behavior, in every respect, indicated that he accepted the answers as of central importance in his life. I was curious about Ivan's involvement because, if Tom were perpetuating a hoax, it seemed particularly cruel for him to deceive his own son. Ivan was deeply involved in a story about a time-travel ship upon which he would be a crew member in a future life. It was a far-fetched story that the entities had created for him through their letters.

I asked the entities to provide information that would verify their authenticity.

Q: Dear John King: Would you tell the names of some of the ships upon which you sailed? This information would be valuable in convincing people that you are real. If you could give us any other information that would be difficult for people in Missouri to obtain yet might be verified by a historian, that would be appreciated.

A: Friend Jim: My favorite was the old <u>Walsy</u>, that is, the Lady Alicia Walsingham. She was a fine craft, with headroom, yet she was nimble in a frey and with a brisky in her sheets, she could chase down the fastest merchant-men or flee from any dogship. Sir Henry was a proud man when he took her, you can well ken! Yet he did not use her as his flagship, as some have said, preferring larger, heavier-gunned ships. He gave her over to Cap. Jeremy Logarth, who did her proud, ringing in seventeen fat galliants and five hump-barges before shelving her in a blow off Puerto Rica. (Yet, the doubters still will disbelieve.)

John King

I was not able to verify this information, and I came to agree with John King that "doubters still will disbelieve." Perhaps some unpublished document connects the ship with Captain Jeremy Logarth, but I have not located this information.

George Hansen at the Foundation for Research on the Nature of Man (FRNM) visited the Richards in 1981. While there, he prepared two sealed decks of ESP cards and asked the entities to sort them, while leaving the seals intact. Later, he wrote me, describing his motivation: "When I prepared these two, I had no intention of trying to adequately seal and document them in order to obtain evidence of paranormal effects. The only reason I prepared the decks was to see if there would be an effect (under loose conditions). It was commonly felt that anything prepared by someone at the FRNM would not be acted upon successfully by the 'entities.'"

When the two decks were successfully sorted, SORRAT members thought this proved the phenomena authentic, as the entities had passed a test designed by a parapsychologist. George did not regard this to be the case.

Several months later, while in Durham, NC, George prepared and sealed three decks and randomly selected one to be sent to Rolla. If the Rolla deck was successfully sorted with the seals intact, he planned to randomly select a second deck and give it to a skeptic who could attempt to duplicate the result (Hansen and Broughton, 1991).

George sent the test deck to Rolla in the autumn of 1981. It was placed in the Richards' basement, among letters for the entities. It disappeared and was received by a SORRAT member, Ann, in Oregon. Ann took it from her daughter, who had brought the package in from the mailbox, and returned it to George. Because it would require a great deal of effort to prepare a new test deck, George forwarded it to Ed Cox without opening it.

Cox placed the deck back in the Richards' basement. The entities claimed that they then attempted to mail it to Susan (an individual with mental disorders who they were trying to help). The deck was delivered by the post office to FRNM. Apparently, an address label had been glued over the FRNM address but this label had fallen off (the entities had a habit of blundering in ways that revealed their fraud). When the researchers at FRNM carefully opened the deck, they found that it had been tampered with in a manner that implied fraud (they detected solvent near some of the glue). There was "spirit writing" in pencil on the heat-sensitive paper inside the package, suggesting the entities were guilty of the tampering. George considered the "re-addressing" to be an attempt to cover up the botched tampering job.

FRNM circulated a report to researchers interested in SORRAT. They demanded that this report be kept secret from Tom and Elaine since it implied fraud. At the insistence of Ed Cox, a researcher at FRNM prepared a new deck, even though FRNM had no real expectation that the entities would sort it without disturbing the seals. FRNM sent the new deck to Ed Cox, and he placed it beside the mini-lab at the Richards' house.

Cox sent letters to interested researchers stating that a thief at the post office could have opened the package. Apparently, he did not know about the entity writing inside the package. The FRNM researchers sent out letters ridiculing Cox's idea. They considered the fraud hypothesis more logical.

The entities did not return the new deck to FRNM. It remained beside the mini-lab until it disappeared. When FRNM revealed their secret report, Tom and Elaine felt they had been treated as guinea pigs. They regarded FRNM's accusations as inaccurate and abusive. The FRNM parapsychologists discontinued their SORRAT research.

This event marked a kind of turning point in SORRAT history. Dr. J. G. Neihardt and Dr. J. Thomas Richards had solid reputations. Their groups had demonstrated psychokinesis for decades, and they had consistently advocated scientific investigation of the phenomena. Dr. Richards took meticulous notes following each experimental session. Although the FRNM report did not specifically claim that the Richards had engaged in fraud, most people assumed this was the case. I found myself in a difficult social situation. I regarded both George and the Richards to be my friends, but I could not explain to the Richards why they had been treated in such callous manner. The Richards seemed fundamentally puzzled by the situation. Elaine was angry. Tom was deeply troubled that anyone might think he had engaged in unethical behavior.

A strange drama unfolded around Cox and the vanished FRNM deck. The entities rapped that the deck had been sent to a man named Samuel Csar in New Preston, Connecticut. Cox frantically attempted to locate this man. He searched through numerous telephone books for Samuel Csar's name to no avail. Later, the raps informed us that Sam Csar had moved from Connecticut because his wife had left him. They said that he had fallen into despair, was now in a transient hotel in San Diego, and that the deck may have been forwarded to him.

In March 1982, Cox wrote a pleading letter to the entities, asking that they locate the deck. Cox stated that FRNM was on the entities' side and that FRNM would certainly accept the entities' existence if only an ordered and sealed deck could be produced. The entities answered:

A: Dear W.E.C., I do not feel that they really believe we exist. We believe that they exist, so we are sad that they do not return the compliment, although they will in a brief time, give or take a few decades. It would now upset them to affirm that we are.

During the summer of 1982, John Hunt also asked about the tampered deck:

Q: Dear Rector, John King, Charles Dai and All: There has been much controversy lately over what happened to the deck of cards that FRNM claimed had been tampered with by someone. What really happened?
A: We will try to find out. iii x iii did the sorting. Grady had me add a note to Ann. We mailed it to Ann to help her. Then to Susan. Some low level on your side or ours messed up the packet and kept Susan from being helped.

The FRNM researchers presented their findings at the Parapsychological Association meetings in Cambridge, England, in August 1982 (Hansen and Broughton, 1983, 1991). As a result, most parapsychologists came to believe that the Rolla case was fraudulent. Science works like a court of law, with the same strengths and weaknesses as the legal system. Cox, as the entities' representative, was unable to present his case effectively, and his evidence was not accepted. As in a court of law, only certain evidence was admissible before the parapsychological community.[4]

I was not surprised at Hansen's failure to achieve a "proof of psi" while distant from Rolla. None of the letter writers had gained proof. Only those closely connected to SORRAT had witnessed events that compelled them to believe. Hansen did not fall into that category.

The parapsychological community did not realize that Tom was surrounded by poltergeists that sometimes engaged in fraud. To me, the situation seemed like the Margery case. Parapsychologists uncovered fraud, stopped investigating, and regular participants continued interacting with the spirits.

John Hunt speculated that Susan's parents opened the envelope and attempted to conceal their break-in. This seemed logical to him because he knew that Susan's parents were hostile to SORRAT. The parents wanted to stop her from interacting with SORRAT and could have opened to package, then tried to conceal what they did. Hansen doubted this explanation, as it did not explain the spirit writing inside the package.[5]

The entities succeeded in accomplishing one of their goals. They considered their interaction with Susan as a form of therapy. When she first contacted SORRAT, she suffered from a delusion. She believed that she was destined to marry Mick Jagger of the Rolling Stones. Tom Richards and John Hunt helped her evaluate this idea and, after attending a Rolling Stones concert, her delusion dissolved. Although the FRNM deck experiment was a failure, the entities regarded their intervention as a success.

I suggested to some parapsychologists that the entities had "framed" Tom and Elaine. Psychical researchers have encountered this in the past. In his book *Spirit Teachings*, Reverend William Stainton Moses described situations in which spirits seem to frame mediums. The book was ostensibly dictated by Imperator Group, the same entities who sometimes wrote SORRAT letters. In a similar vein, poltergeists sometimes attempted to frame the poltergeist "agent" (the individual about whom the events centered). This is not to say that these agents never engaged in fraud, as many have been caught cheating. Gauld and Cornell (1979: 109) reviewed a case where investigators saw stones fly about the room and afterwards, the nine-year-old agent's pockets were found full of rocks. Investigators repeatedly emptied the nine-year-old's pockets while watching him closely. His pockets kept refilling with stones.

Some parapsychologists suggested that Tom went into trance before engaging in fraud. A similar theory was presented to explain Mina Crandon's cheating in the Margery case. I listened to audiotapes of Tom slipping into trance without any warning, after which the entity Jay spoke. One version of the trance theory suggested that Tom or Elaine subconsciously wished to be caught cheating, which explained why the tampered deck fell into FRNM's hands. A psychical researcher wrote to me arguing that "There are many reports of somnambulistic people carrying out the most intricate tasks while going about in a profound trance." Studies indicate that people in trance can act in a fashion that thwarts detection.

Ed Cox and I discussed our data regarding the relationship between Tom's mind and the entity messages: (1) similarities in misspelled words, (2) similar phrases and puns in Tom's speech as in the letters, (3) Tom and the entities having similar interest in correcting other's grammatical errors (see entity comments in Appendix A for an example), (4) one example of similar lettering on Tom's tool bin, and (5) correspondences in narrative focus—the entities used story lines that Richards had developed previously.

A conscious fraudster would have taken precautions to avoid generating this type of evidence. It is logical to believe that Tom wrote many, perhaps all, of the letters, but like the mini-lab phenomena, the mechanics of the endeavor are uncertain.

FRNM's experimental results apparently affected the entities' attitude. They decided to reduce their focus on scientific experiments. In a response to a question by Ed Cox, they wrote:

A: Dear W.E.C.: No one will accept a sealed deck, not even the person who sealed it, unless he can overcome his perceptions about the nature of the "real" world. We have played with cards, boxes, and other trivia. Now it is best that we go on to more vital tasks. Perhaps we will do more of these stunts to amuse you one day, but not now.

I sought entity advice regarding design of our experiments. In October 1981, I asked the deceased Dr. Neihardt, using the telekinetic mail system in Richards' basement, how we could "better conduct our psychical research." In response, I received an autographed Xeroxed copy of a poem he had written while on "this side."

A:ENVOI
Seek not for me within a tomb;
You shall not find me in the clay!
I pierce a little wall of gloom
to mingle with the Day!

I brothered with the things that pass,
Poor giddy Joy and puckered Grief;
I go to brother with the Grass
and with the sunning Leaf.

Not Death can sheathe me in a shroud;
A joy sword whetted keen with pain.
I join the armies of the Cloud.
The Lightning and the Rain.

O subtle in the sap athrill
Athletic in the glad uplift.
A portion of the Cosmic Will

I pierce the planet-drift.

My God and I shall interknit
As rain and ocean, breath and air;
And O, the luring thought of it
Is prayer!

With all kind thought for Jim McClenon
from his friend, John Neihardt

A few months later, Dr. Neihardt composed an original poem, apparently from the other side, and again signed it.

  A: Dear Jim McClenon,
I thought you might enjoy this poem. I make no windy claims about its quality.

  FIRST PRAYER
Life blinded me, and I was prone to stray
Down the dim ways of old philosophies.
Although I loved the scintillating day
And caught the wordless hymning of the trees
Still went I seeking 'mid weird mysteries
That cling about the ruined piles of Eld -
The Brahmin's mystic writ, and the Parsee's
Seer-visioned tomes; wide-eyed with wonder spelled
Their jargon old to learn what caused all I beheld.

In old pagodas with the mystic dread
My spirit knelt in contemplation deep;
Lisping the words the might Manou said,
Craving the boon of everlasting sleep.
Out of the snarl and tangle and the sweep
Of pangful being, my soul sought to see.
Nirvana's calm and awful dawning creep.
In vain I cried unto the tranquil Three.
I found my altars cold. The spell was not for me.

I read, I dreamed, I all but prayed, until
My brain was shaken with its warring dreams.

I saw the Evening flush the western hill
With burning footstep; heard the cry of streams
Like music in my pulse; the Morning's beams
Went through my blood like Soma's golden brew:
And my soul swelled with sudden joy, as streams
Swell with the spring-thaw! And 'twas then I knew,
O God, tho' lips were dumb, my heart had prayed to You!

Sincerely,
John Neihardt

Dr. Neihardt had had previously provided his signature, following his death, to other SORRAT members. One sent me a copy of Neihardt's signature that she found in one of his books that had been published posthumously. The woman said the signature had appeared in the book while in her possession while living in a state distant from the Richards. I have known this woman for many years and regard her as extremely honest. She wished to remain anonymous as she did not wish to jeopardize her professional government job.

I brought the three Neihardt signatures, along with some authenticated ones, to a certified handwriting authority, David Mayer, who served as an expert witness in many court cases.

"How old was the man who allegedly wrote these signatures?" Mayer asked.

I did not know how to answer. Neihardt had died many years before these signatures were created. "I'm afraid that information is unavailable," I answered, not wishing to bias Mr. Mayer in any way.

"What was the state of health of the person who allegedly wrote these signatures?"

Again, the irony was amusing. I could not answer. Is a dead person in good or poor health? I explained that I did not wish to bias his evaluation.

"These specimens look authentic at first glance, but I must compare them with examples of signatures from different time periods in the man's life," he stated. "The specimens seem as if written by a man who is very old or perhaps ill."

I obtained authenticated specimens of Neihardt's signature from museums. After carefully comparing all the samples, Mayer made a formal report: the first of the three test signatures was probably fraudulent. The authenticity of the second and third signature could not be determined. "If fake, they had been produced with a great deal of care and skill," he said.

Either Neihardt was unable to reproduce his signature exactly (without his body) or a skilled forger duplicated it. Lisa attempted to elicit other signatures, but the entities did not furnish any.

In 1981, Cox had his mini-lab sealed by an independent locksmith, and afterward his equipment filmed coins leaving the sealed lab. This occurred on two occasions (Edwards, 1993). He planned further experiments but the McDonnell Laboratory wished to replace his mini-lab with their own. They had a $500,000 grant and were a prestigious organization. Cox graciously allowed them to put their mini-lab in place of his. Tom Richards felt pressure to perform PK to show that he was not a fraud.

The McDonnell mini-lab was constructed by Michael McBeath, under the supervision of Dr. Peter Phillips, lab director. McBeath's mini-lab included built-in mirrors and clocks to prevent speculation that single frame photography had occurred. The lab could be opened only by a special lock and key that could not be duplicated. Phillips, who supervised the experiment, decided that the lab would remain at the Richards' house for six months, after which the experiment would be considered complete.

After Peter Phillips installed the new mini-lab, nothing happened for many weeks. It was my impression that there was tension in the relationship between the McDonnell Lab researchers and the Richards. The McDonnell Lab had no representative in Rolla and did not maintain frequent contact with Tom and Elaine. Cox felt shut out of the McDonnell Lab experiment. Tom had a dream in which Three-Times-Three prevented the other entities from producing paranormal effects. Later, objects moved around the lab, but nothing passed in or out of it.

Tom wrote me that he looked forward to the day when the lab would be taken away. He said that Phillips had told him that some *slight* effects had been captured on film and that this was best since the skeptical parapsychological community would not believe *dynamic* effects. Phillips said that his camera had filmed a paper and box moving inside the lab. It seemed that these phenomena had been verified under highly controlled conditions. Tom hoped that these experimental results would cause people to realize that the SOR-RAT phenomena were authentic. He hoped this success would help restore his reputation.

I was surprised to learn about this experimental success. I thought the McDonnell Lab had failed to generate the rapport required for PK to be verified.

The McDonnell Lab researchers had just installed their experimental mini-lab and left it. Had the entities somehow overcome their need for a sympathetic relationship?

In the end, Phillips' report, presented before the Parapsychological Association (PA), was worded ambiguously. It did not support belief in SORRAT phenomena. Dr. Phillips left open the question of whether the filmed phenomena could be produced by normal means. At the 1982 PA Conference, the Phillips paper was grouped together with the FRNM paper and listed under the heading "Macro PK: Failures to Replicate" (Phillips and McBeath, 1983; Hansen and Broughton, 1983).

SORRAT members were puzzled. Had Phillips not stated that he had gotten unexplained movement within the lab? Why would his paper be regarded as a failure to replicate? When I spoke with Dr. Phillips, he explained that he thought all the filmed effects could be duplicated by normal means. If the wooden box had some metal inside, a magnet could have made it move. The movement of paper might be explained by powerful charges of static electricity.[6] This seemed strange to me. Why had they put things in the lab that could have been moved using a magnet or static electricity?

I questioned parapsychologists who had attended the Hansen, Phillips, and Cox presentations. They said that further SORRAT research would be fruitless. Cox had not presented his evidence clearly. His film projector broke down at a crucial moment, and he spilled a glass of water on himself in front of the audience. Phillips's paper advocated skepticism. The British parapsychologist Tony Cornell showed a film created using frame-by-frame photography that mocked Cox's mini-lab films. His students had produced the film by taking out a glass panel from the mini-lab they had constructed. They had produced a humorous, animated movie with jerky images that resembled Cox's films. This film brought howls of laughter from the audience. "I couldn't keep from laughing," one woman told me. "It was funny how things jumped around."

The results of my participant study indicated that people who took part in SORRAT meetings came to believe in the phenomena. Those who conducted experiments from afar did not become believers. I think that SORRAT members had expected to be able to change outsiders' minds because the SORRAT phenomena had been so robust. When that didn't happen, they were disappointed and demoralized.

I wrote the entities to see what they had to say about this.

Q: Dear Friends: Why is it that in our world we can never really "prove" life after death or even ESP? It seems somewhat strange that we must always depend on "faith"—what do you think?

Your friend,
Jim

A: Friend Jim - There are a vast number of things that are not "provable," such as love, goodness, the nature of black holes, many aspects of non-Euclidean geometry, or God Himself. What is wrong with Faith or Love, or Hope, or Charity, for that matter?

You have lots of proof *of ESP, PK, and* our existential reality.

Shanti,
Imperator/Rector/J.K.

CHAPTER 7
TEACHING AND HEALING

When I asked the entities to write answers to my questions, I opened a new line of research. Letter writing phenomena allowed SORRATs, distant from Rolla, to take part in experiments. I regarded the spirit letter writing as a sociological experiment. I wondered what would happen if I facilitated better communication between entities and SORRATs.

At first, only a few people wrote messages to the spirits. Then, a few more SORRATs began submitting questions. Tom asked the participants to mail copies of the entities' responses to both him and me.

Between April 1981 and August 1982, about 20 people received entity messages. Five stopped writing when they realized that the entities could not pass the paranormal tests they had designed. Four were satisfied with their responses and saw no need for further interaction. Four wrote relatively regularly. These people recruited five new letter writers.

The number of letter writers was about a dozen during any year. The entities mailed out letters, on average, about once every two weeks. Each letter might involve three pages of entity hand-written text, but letters were most frequently about a page long. I received more than 20 pages of hand-written text every week or two.

Commonly asked questions by early letter writers were: "What is it like after death?" or "Do you have advice for us?" The answers were standard: "It is great here. We are outside of space and time. Do good; be kind to others."

I became very familiar with the style and answers that the entities provided to people. Their answers reflected a central ideology, with variations governed by the specific entity providing the answer. After a while, I felt that I could predict how the entities would answer any specific question addressed to them.

At times, the volume of messages was so high that it seemed hard to believe that Tom Richards was spending that much time writing these letters. The psychical research literature has cases where people engage in extremely rapid writing while in trance, but the Rolla output seemed to be setting a record for word volume. Most messages were not of general interest and had no evidential quality regarding paranormal phenomena.

I stopped telling anyone that I was involved with SORRAT because of the stigma. From the beginning, skeptics were highly critical of the idea that spirits could write.[1]

The main categories of entity letter correspondence were:

(1) *seeking proof*: people submitted parapsychological tests, hoping to verify psi;

(2) *spiritual information*: writers sought information about past lives, morality, or spiritual quests;

(3) *metaphysical knowledge*: the entities provided a kind of cosmic ideology regarding time, derived from quantum mysticism;

(4) *healing*: people sought help for their ailments and I monitored the results.

Seeking proof

None of the parapsychological experiments conducted by mail generated evidence verifying paranormal phenomena. Most writers seeking proof stopped writing after their experiments failed. The entities stated that they were no better than anyone else when confronted with ESP experiments.

Spiritual Information about past lives, morality, and spiritual quests

Questions about past lives were answered with a list of incarnations. Many were informed that they shared past lives with other SORRAT members and that they had been involved in a specific quest during that life. Past life information seemed like a form of therapy, as writers were encouraged to think about their present self-concept regarding past life activities. The letter writer's problems, attitudes, and skills might be explained as a result of past life events. Some quests involved present-life actions, and SORRAT members were encouraged to work together on these activities.

During the early phase of this study, I hoped the entities would reveal information that implied they had anomalous abilities. Answers to past life questions might include verifiable, yet obscure, information, difficult to obtain in Rolla. Instead, the entities provided unusual, sometimes inaccurate, information. For example, one questioner was given the following list of past lives:

20000 BC	*Early horse. Eaten within one year.*
2000 BC	*Larva*
1126 - 1121 BC	*Tortoise*
8201 - 8174 BC	*Indo-European*
6573 - 6539 BC	*Mede Laborer*
4921 - 4897 BC	*Nubian warrior*
3657 - 3612 BC	*Chaldean Magus/astrologer*
1917 - 1859 BC	*Boadacian herdsman*
121 -184 AD	*Turius Gaullus, tribune, Murcia*
198 -199 AD	*Ranu, a dog of mixed breed, eaten by a wolf in Matania*
291 - 297 AD	*Esther, died of a fever in rural Palestine*
561 - 595 AD	*Horg-Bogrn, helped Osorik fight off Huns of the Danube*
790 - 794 AD	*A Hohokam boy, lived near the site of present-day Elroy, Arizona*
1263 - 1321 AD	*Abduhl Au Ksoraghan, scribe and money changer, Kermanshaw [Iran]*
1691- 1730 AD	*Sees-Bear-Sitting, Kuna tribesman (and warrior, of course)*
1837- 1842 AD	*John Jacob Seltzmann, died of typhoid*

The man who received this information noted that this list did not coincide with information he had previously received from a psychic. The entities were apparently mixed up about Horg Bogrn's life. The "Huns" or Hungarians (Magyars) did not live in the Danube Basin during the 6th century. Since they were slowly migrating south, they could hardly be called "Huns of the Danube."

The entities wrote to John Hunt that, in a past life, John had been Marshal Michel Ney, a military commander who had served under Napoleon. After Napoleon was defeated in 1815, Marshal Ney was arrested, court-martialed, and executed by firing squad. During another life, John had been Daniel Flaumel, a wandering merchant born about 1320. Flaumel had a son, Charles Dai, whose mother he abandoned before the child was born. Charles Dai had been previously introduced to John as his spirit guide "C" via raps. Dai helped John by providing information during SORRAT experimental sessions.

According to the entity messages, SORRAT member Lisa, in a former life, had assisted Flaumel in attempting to swindle a nobleman by using a magic crystal. They also met with SORRAT member Kathy who, the entities told them, had taken part in magical gatherings in medieval Ireland. The entities revealed, in segments, a saga tying together ancient Celtic lore, alchemy, King Arthur's magician Merlin, and Daniel Flaumel's life. Part of the story involved a magic harp that attracted spiritual energy. The story included specifications that allowed another SORRAT member to construct a symbolic harp thought to be useful for rituals.

At the conclusion of the story, SORRAT members were called upon to wake Merlin, who was actually a time traveler from the 25th century. The entities stated that Merlin (or Medwin) was sleeping in a vivitorium beneath Cadbury Tor in England. He could only be awakened by special magical incantations that the entities revealed to certain SORRAT members. Awakening Merlin was required to avert a global catastrophe.

Although John Hunt doubted the scenario's authenticity, other participants took the story seriously and tried to fulfill the entities' request. One member, Bill, traveled to England to join English participants in trying to wake Merlin. Bill sent back reports of miraculous experiences and stories of astonishing coincidences. Later experiences turned negative. He reported that some type of demonic force was opposing him. There was friction among the SORRATs taking part in this quest; they had major disagreements and accused each other of being at fault.

I interviewed Bill in 1987 and he said that he did not want any further communication with SORRAT. He told me that a curse surrounded the vivitorium. When he visited Cadbury Tor, he saw his female companion break her leg while walking. She had not fallen or slipped, and the situation seemed extremely anomalous to him. The woman's fractured bone was verified by her physician's x-ray. This incident was just one of a series of extremely anomalous events that led him to believe that he might come to both spiritual and physical harm. Although the woman's leg healed extremely rapidly (to the surprise of her doctor), Bill decided to flee Britain, hoping to get away from the negative paranormal force.

The SORRAT Merlin story was one of various narratives provided by the entities that wove SORRAT lives into supernatural narratives. It seemed to me that these entertaining but fantastic narratives were something that Tom Richards might write. In 1992, he told me that, during his teens, he wrote a fantasy story about Merlin and a vivitorium. He said he was surprised when the entity letter saga presented a variation of his account. He said that he was uncertain how these events should be interpreted since he did not feel he had any physical connection with the actual writing of the entity letters. He revealed this information to me in an off-hand manner. He was aware that some people assumed that he was writing the letters but was busy teaching classes and working on other writing projects, including a series of fictional books about early SORRAT experiences.

I spoke with Tom about the parallel features within some of his fictional writing and the entity messages. He showed irritation when anyone suggested that he was the author of the entity letters, particularly when Ed Cox pointed out to him that misspellings in his letters coincided with misspelling in the entity messages. Tom supposed that the entities sometimes used themes within his mind as the basis for some story themes in the entity letters, but the entity letters took innovative directions, divergent from Tom's original ideas.

Another SORRAT quest involved a search for treasure buried on Cocos Island, an Ecuadorian possession off the coast of Costa Rica. Lisa and I were assigned this quest. From the information I gathered, there may be three different pirate treasures there.[2] The entity John King provided me a map marked with the treasure's exact position.

The first treasure was buried by Captain Edward Davis, who sacked the city of Leon in Nicaragua in 1685. Davis accepted the amnesty offered to pirates by King James II but later returned to pirating and disappeared mysteriously before he could return to Cocos Island.

A second treasure was hidden by Captain Benito Bonito (Bonito of the Bloody Sword), a pirate who operated along the Central American coast between 1818 and 1820. In 1821, Bonito was murdered in a mutiny in the West Indies.

In 1820, the Spanish Viceroy of Lima, Peru, loaded a storehouse of gold and silver on board a British merchantman, *Mary Dear*, hoping to prevent an army under Jose de San Martin from capturing the treasure. The British crew murdered the Viceroy's representatives and took the treasure to Cocos Island. The silver they carried was worth at least twenty million dollars (according to Fodor writing in the 1960s) and is almost certainly still there. The *Mary Dear* was later captured by the Spanish, who hanged all the crew except the captain and first mate. The two were taken to Cocos Island so that they could show the Spaniards where the treasure was buried. While taking their captors to the treasure, they escaped, hid on the island, and were eventually rescued, only to perish elsewhere. Legend has it that the Scottish captain drew a deathbed map in 1844. Those using this map were unsuccessful in finding the treasure, perhaps due to a curse placed on it. Although some 450 expeditions have searched for treasure on Cocos Island, none have been successful. The treasure is thought to be protected by spirits who prevent people from retrieving it.

Q: Dear John King: Do you have any further information that you would like to tell us about the Cocos Island treasure?

A: Dear Friend Jim: There is scant harboring on this isle. Sail cautiously inne from the East and send a skiff inne with implementes and geare. You will need tackle and blockage to lift the bootie out.

Proceed westward across the isle, a foote. The vegetation is very thick and the lows are boggie. You will not need heavie digging equipment, but to bag all the remainders, you wille need a powerfulle treasure-beeper with a 20' range. (Use two of these for triangulation, perhaps.)

John King

Q: You suggest we search for the treasure of Cocos Island. Many articles and books have been written about the treasure. Professional treasure hunters have searched the island with expensive, highly technological equipment and not so experienced people have sought the treasure, all to no avail. Why do we stand a chance of finding this treasure? What could we find?

Love,
Lisa

A: Sweet Lisa: You would use it for the good of others, not merely for your own wants. Consequently, we would not befuddle you or drive you away from the isle in terror.

You could find enough silver bars to load your craft to the plimsol. Does twenty plus million dollars on the market in Geneva seem reasonable? Good hunting.

Q: Dear John King,
We really need more information from you if we are to look for the treasure on Cocos Island and succeed. Any suggestions?

Love,
Lisa

A: Dig where John King drew the cross on the map. Use two metal detectors. That will make the task far easier. Take along provisions and a good medical kit. Make sure that you enter and leave the island privately. Be certain that someone stands sentry; someone with the intestinal fortitude to do his duty and repel boarders. And I do not mean "to disgust people renting rooms in a boarding house." The scent of great, tax-free treasure still draws pirates like a dead hog draws flies in July.

There is no reason to think that John King, if he existed, had anything to do with burying this treasure. I suspect that the real treasure we would find would be the friendship developed among the adventurers joining the quest. The Costa Rican government no longer allows visitors to stay on the island overnight because they wish to prevent damage to island's ecology. Although the entities have provided treasure maps locating buried wealth in Jamaica and close to my home in North Carolina, I have made no effort to locate these treasures. The North Carolina treasure is buried under what is now a housing development. My experience as a psychical researcher causes me to be skeptical of such claims.

Metaphysical Knowledge

The entities claim their vantage point is outside of space and time, a position that allows them to see all time at once. They visualize time as consisting of a series of "branches" that signify decisions made by individuals or societies. The image is not static, like a tree, but in a state of flux, like vibrating strings. The branching image leads to concepts such as "spiritual levels," "multiple personalities," and the "unification of the self after death." People are not unique personalities but multiple with each branch, giving them the opportunity to raise their spiritual levels. At death, they perceive the branches in a way that helps them learn, which can raise one's spiritual level.

John Hunt attempted to understand the entities' "decision tree" concept (associated with quantum mechanics theory). The entities drew a diagram of part of his decision trees. In one life (branch of the tree), he became an engineer, rather than his current decision to become a mathematician. In another life, he was institutionalized as delusional. Some pathways involved military careers (parallel to his previous life as Marshal Ney). The entities enclosed a train ticket and a German souvenir pin that they claimed he had used in an alternative pathway. The ticket was for transit to Berlin and had "Lt. Col. Hunt" written on it. Tom told me that he knew no one in Germany who might have mailed him this pin and ticket.

I asked the entities to clarify this explanation. They replied:

A: Imagine that you stand outside of the ordinary flux and flow of duration, which you call "time." Look about and see the currents of durational energy, from the sargasso doldrums of the giant black holes to the extreme condensation of megapoints that exist/do not exist too quickly to be measured, yet which "internally" exist for eons per second. Imagine all of these lines of force as branching lines of probability. Causation is influenced on the personal level of cause-and-effect events "in time" by choices; whether conscious or on the random particle level makes little difference. Causal lines are only one type of "time-line," albeit the type which you can most easily affect, of course.

Imagine seeing yourself from out of time, at right angles, as it were, to "your" timelines/dimensions of reality. You might appear as a blurred pink worm writhing from birth to all possible deaths, at which "you" would join "you" outside of time, to learn or observe as part of a unified self.

Observe further. What appeared at first to be "many Jims" on many different lifelines, are but different aspects of the "total Jim" that is you.

Then look further — to "Jim writ large in the Sky." The lifelines of many total individuals merge to form a larger Self, yet each self and each time line is a unique cell or thought-being, with access to all the memories of all the other monads of being.

Shanti
Rector/J.K.

Lisa asked about the concept of "spiritual levels."

A: "Level" refers to the stage of spiritual development. Obviously, this is as true of those still in the meat as of those who are free of it. A "high level" is one who is highly developed. An example would be St. Teresa of Avila, or, in your era, Mother Teresa. Some high levels are recognized as such on your side, but most are not.

The higher level may be simple or complex. Usually there is conflict and the frustration of not being able to help as much as one would desire. On the whole, high levels are happier than are low or average levels, although happiness is not important because it is only personal, in the common sense. If by "pleasure" you mean satisfaction of the sense of workmanship, of creativity, of benevolence, of selfless affection; then yes, high levels experience great pleasure. To a low level there might be pleasure in the hollow gauds [showy gaieties], for whatever one can imagine, that is what our side is.

A misdeed or wrongdoing hurts until it is expiated: this moral law is internal, not imposed.

Many do not desire to be high levels; one seeks one's own level. An analogy, if a rock musician insisted on playing acid rock in a garden where Brahms was conducting a concert, he would soon feel out of place and would leave to practice with Heavy Metal.

Q: How do animals rank within this level "system"? How do cats, dogs, birds, turtles, fish raise their levels? Do plants have souls?

A: Of course, all living beings raise (or sometimes lower) their levels. There is an old saying that "man is the noblest of the animals." Now, I wonder who thought that one up? Don't underestimate plants. A good tree is better than most of the books into which it might be made.

The Imperator Group perceived themselves as partaking in an evolutionary, spiritual process:

A: Humanity is now moving into an age of increasing emancipation from many of its past limitations. Technical achievements and medical advances confer growing freedom from various oppressions and ills. Man's greatest problem is still himself and his orientation to his fellow beings. To understand himself fully, he should become aware that he does not consist only of a temporary form that is doomed to age and die. He has an immortal soul that is housed in an immortal multi-personality and is endowed with a mind that is independent of the physical brain. That is the great fact of life.

An organized group of high levels, most of whom have departed from "life" on your planet, are now attempting to establish a precept for mankind: physical death is a transition from one state of consciousness to another, wherein one retains one's individuality but has access to the cosmic consciousness of the All. The realization of this truth should assist man to greater insight into his own nature and potential super-terrestrial activities. The knowledge that incarnation in your world is but one chosen stage of man's external life should foster policies that are more far-reaching than those usually adopted at present on your side, and encourage a more balanced outlook regarding all matters. Thus, we strive for love, peace, freedom, cooperative helping, altruism, faith, harmony, and wisdom, but the choices are up to you on your side of the Life/Death barrier, an illusory barrier that is misperception.

Imperator/J.K.[3]

The entities periodically refer to "alternating bilocative nodal oscillations" (ABNO) and define this as "mind in a state of balance between alpha and beta delta wave levels of awareness." The triple wavy lines symbol, mentioned in a previous incident involving an ice cube, stands for ABNO or "varying in flux back and forth; becoming first one and then the other." They stated that telekinesis occurs when the mind fluctuates rapidly between alpha and delta wave lengths (EEG). On various occasions, they provided more specific information about ABNO:

A: Biofeedback helps set up the ability to repeat positive psi acts.
A secretion given off by the pineal gland (each person differs) helps by acting as a catalytic agent to allow us to slide between synapses as psi "messages" are flashed

(cortex). Ergo, you can get in harmony to use psi.

Have faith and help others. Lose all common thought for the petty self and look outward to All, which is the same as the All one touches in deep meditation, within.

Yes, it is possible for you to utilize ABNO for direct teleportation, but it will take much emptying of trivia from the selves that comprise the group self.

Suppose you sit in a séance circle and start to get results. You start to feel the table vibrate and there are a few raps. Do not respond with excitement or psychological discomfort. Go with the flow and float eternally in solution. A pleasurable sensation should permeate your self as it loses its entrapment in the little self and starts to feel unity with the other selves in the psi circle, and all of you feel the oneness with the universal self (Bucke calls it Cosmic Consciousness).[4]

The pleasurable sensations will crest and fade as each wave occurs. At the same time, other psi events may occur. Accept them, PK, quantum teleportation, as natural. Then, it will be psychologically easier next time. Recollect, it is a holistic unity. Subconsciousness loves contrast, too.

The philosophy expressed by the entities was compatible with some of the ideas expressed by modern physicists.[5] This philosophy is a branch of Aldous Huxley's "perennial philosophy," the idea that the human soul exists as part of a divine Reality.[6]

Healing

The entities attempted many spiritual healings. In all cases, individuals sought licensed, traditional medical treatment before requesting the entities' aid and considered their advice as an adjunct to professional medical care.

My attention was first directed to healing when Leah, who had been diagnosed with bone cancer, sought healing from the spirits. Her eyesight and overall health were failing rapidly. The cancer had spread through her body, and her doctor said she would die within a few months. The entities stated that they would help. They provided her with the address of a woman named Apantha, who had a reputation as an amateur psychic. Apantha told her that she would pray for healing but that "only God can heal." Leah was highly concerned about witchcraft and learned that John King was a pirate. As a result, Leah ended her involvement with SORRAT. The entities seemed unconcerned with this development and considered that Leah's contact with Apantha had been beneficial and successful.

Later I learned from Leah's friend that her cancer had gone into remission.

Leah's health then continued to improve, to the amazement of her doctors. Although this "cure" was not attributed to the entities, no one had an alternate explanation. Leah had been told she would die, yet she recovered completely. Because Apantha had a history of successful spiritual healing, it seemed possible that the SORRAT intervention had helped Leah. I had no previous experience with this type of thing and had not expected that Leah would survive. This case was the first to demonstrate a recurring motif: SORRAT healing had a favorable outcome, but the patient did not directly connect SORRAT with the outcome.

I wrote to psychiatrist Dr. Berthold Schwarz who was interested in the Rolla phenomena with the idea of monitoring an entity healing treatment more closely. "Could you suggest someone for a healing experiment?' I asked.

He was delighted to suggest his 24-year-old daughter, Lisa, who was going blind from diabetes. I wrote Lisa asking for a letter of permission and for a description of her medical problems. Lisa granted permission and described her condition. She wrote that she had been diagnosed with diabetes in November 1969. In September 1979, she suddenly developed proliferative retinopathy and required laser surgery for her left eye. She was treated at the Bascom Palmer Eye Institute by a world-famous ophthalmologist who specialized in diabetic retinopathy. Her right eye hemorrhaged in June 1980, for which she also had laser surgery. In August 1980, a Mayo Clinic ophthalmologist stated that her worsening eye problems were the worst case of proliferative retinopathy she had seen. At the suggestion of the famous ophthalmologist, she went for consultation at Duke University Hospital, Johns Hopkins Hospital, and Retina Associates (Massachusetts General Hospital in Boston). All gave her a poor prognosis. The doctor at Johns Hopkins told her in December 1980 that "Your condition is extremely grave. People with your condition typically go completely blind." She was declared legally blind in November 1980. Lisa had another operation on December 18, 1980, and then second and third operations on her right eye. Just before her third operation, her left eye hemorrhaged. She was forced to give up her job. She went to the Division for Blind Services, got a white cane, received special transportation services, and took mobility lessons.

Although Lisa's condition seemed hopeless, we wrote the entities for help. They replied quickly.

A: Lisa, We are trying very hard to help your vision to be healed. Please be patient and always strive to help others as you do. *We are proud of you and very pleased that you are so strong for the good.*

Love, Peace, Faith,
Rector, J.K.

Not long afterward, Lisa informed me that her eyesight was improving. The doctors told her that although it was impossible for the vision in her right eye to improve (mainly because of her previous unsuccessful operation), the sight in her left eye seemed to be returning miraculously. Her letter was highly optimistic. I was surprised. I had no idea whether what had occurred was medically anomalous or not, but I was thrilled to have taken part in a situation in which someone seemed to have benefited. I was surprised that the two medical cases I had monitored had turned out so favorably. All the formal parapsychological experiments I had attempted with the entities had failed to produce significant results.

Lisa began communicating regularly with the entities. In one letter, she detailed her medical history and noted that an "anniversary pattern" was evident. Every fall for the last four years her medical condition had worsened. She asked for advice.

A: It is so only because you believe it is so. You create your own patterns. Consequently, concentrate on all the good events that have occurred on these lovely autumn days. Remember instances of parental love, of crisp, alive air, of sunsets with frost in the air, of Halloween excitement and the odors of russet and turkey cooking, and see the pattern of joyful events.

I interviewed Lisa in December 1981, when she was 24 years old. She described a series of events in which her healing seemed connected with her attitude. After her third operation at Duke, she refused to visualize any return to the hospital. She renewed her magazine subscriptions and kept her car. She sought the aid of not only the Rolla entities but also other healers, such as British spiritual healer Rose Gladden and metal bender Steve Shaw (the entities encouraged contact with real people). She said that she "felt motivated toward something psychic," since the doctors had not seemed particularly helpful in curing her eyes. "I don't really feel, all the time, that there are entities out there healing. I feel that the healing is in me. Some people may transmit healing to another person but that's just a little bit of what helps," she stated.

At the same time, she felt that her imagination needed support. "If someone could set up a situation where I could just believe in it a little bit, I know it would help. The entities created that situation. I wish I could believe in God. I envy people who do, but it's not that easy."

Lisa's eyesight continued to improve. She reported that the highlight of her healing experience came in October, when it appeared that her neovasculation was definitely regressing. "The day that I received the entities' letter was the day that I realized that I was not going to go blind," she told me.

A nurse who examined her remarked: "It's amazing. It's a miracle. It just does not happen."

A doctor was more cautious. "I don't know," he said. "I can't explain it. I have no idea."

Lisa was not certain that a miracle occurred. "I can go both ways," she noted. "I'm not completely convinced, but it was incredible for me."

She continued to seek advice from the entities, hoping that her medical condition would keep improving. They mixed up their answers so that her letters were sent to other people, and she began to interact with them. She became integrated into the group. Then the entities gave her some very specific advice:

A: Go to Columbia, Missouri. Contact Alice and Joe through Tom. Perhaps you can be helped. For verification of a healing that could have been complete had she followed though, write to Kathy. This contact will help both her and you or we would not ask you to do so.

Kathy, who lived in Wisconsin, had sent a letter to the entities, seeking help. While she was waiting for their response, a powerful, emotional sensation swept over her, something beyond anything she had known before. She called Tom Richards and learned that the entities were rapping through the floor to send her healing energy.

Taking the advice of the entities, Lisa decided to travel to Rolla in January 1982. I visited her father, Bert Schwarz, and then drove to the Miami area to take her to Missouri.

"Do you really believe in this entity stuff?" she asked.

"I can't believe completely, but I'm curious," I answered. "I was trying to do a sociological study but things have gotten out of hand. It's hard to accept everything as real, but if this involves tricks, I can't explain them. It's like a game, and I watch what happens. Tom could be a magician, tricking us all, but at least it's an interesting show. Sometimes I see suspicious things, but if Tom were a complete fake, he should perform on stage. He could make a lot of money! Instead, he puts up with the parapsychologists slandering him. I believe that you can be helped because people who contacted SORRAT in the past have been helped."

"OK!" she laughed. "I'm here, aren't I? I'm ready to be healed!"

In the evening Lisa, Tom, Elaine, and I took part in a table-tipping session. The parapsychologist and physics professor Peter Phillips also participated. The entities rapped out the following advice for Lisa:

1. Exercise
2. Eat wisely
2. Love vigorously
4. Joy

This was followed by a table levitation. The table came up into the air, and we got our cameras out and snapped away. I knew that none of the photographs would prove anything because some people still had their hands on the table. One of my photographs was interesting, though. It showed Peter Phillips with his thumb under the table edge. The table was up in the air, and his thumb must have slipped off the top. In the photograph, his thumb appeared to be holding up the table. This turned out to be the most authentic SORRAT table levitation that I photographed. I cannot be certain that it was authentic, and it does not look authentic. All other times, I was suspicious about someone lifting up the table, but this time I saw it rise with everyone's hands on the table top. Although many people, over the years, have taken photos of hands-off levitations, many photographs show someone's thumb or fingers under the table rim, seemingly to hold it up. Elaine told me that the entities were like that; they wanted to avoid being verified.

The raps told Lisa that she should go to Columbia. Alice Thompson was too busy to allow us to come to Skyrim, but Joe said we could meet at his house. He had been a member of the SORRAT group since its beginning and was good at going into trance.

I was curious to see how the session would be conducted. First, we sat around the kitchen table, talking. Joe told me that he had absolutely no memory of anything that went on while he was in trance. He said that he would imagine himself walking into a mist that folded around him. Then he would lose normal consciousness. He talked at length with Lisa and got the full details of her healing story. She hoped her eyesight would continue to improve. The doctors could not explain why it had improved so much, and they were not certain that it would continue to get better. Joe's kindness and patience seemed highly conducive to healing.

We went down to Joe's basement, sat around a TV tray table, and turned off the lights. The lighting was dim, but I could see where everyone was sitting. Tom was on my left; Joe and Lisa were across from me. They appeared as shapes in the darkness. At first, the table movements were very slight and the raps weak. Tom was quiet. Lisa and I had trouble figuring out the messages that came from the concrete floor. Lisa's grandfather rapped out his name along with the message, "Heal" and "Love." Black Elk began his power beat: Rap, rap... Rap, rap, rap. I located the area on the floor from which the raps came. I could feel the vibration with my hand. The experience affected me, but I can't explain the exact sensation. I tried to think up an explanation for how the raps might occur normally. Did Joe have a special rapping device under the concrete surface? He must be part of the SORRAT conspiracy, a group that fooled people by fraud.

Joe went into trance, and his voice identified itself as Many Voices, a group of entities speaking as one. While Many Voices spoke, the table stood on two legs and began jumping around vigorously. I knew that Joe did not have his hands on the table, so I assumed that Tom was pushing it around. Then I saw that Lisa was facing Joe. Joe was holding her hands and Many Voices was talking with her. Where was Tom? I peered through the darkness and saw his shape beside me. He was absolutely quiet and still. I slid my hands around the vibrating table. No one else's hands were touching it. It was vibrating vigorously, and my hands were the only ones on the table. Was someone grabbing and shaking the table legs? Was a wire attached to the table legs?

The table jumped and vibrated in different directions. I slid my leg out to try to touch Tom, to see where he was or to find a wire. He was not near the table. There was no wire or thread on the left. I tried the right side, and found no wire or thread. Perhaps I should leap out of my chair and check the back side of the table? I could see the shape of Joe and Lisa in the dim light. They were away from the table.

I hesitated for minute after minute, straining to see in the darkness. I could see a dark shape to my left that must be Tom. In front of me, Many Voices was still softly talking to Lisa. It did not seem possible that the table movements could be created by wires on the far side.

I felt a wave of understanding sweep over me. I did not need to verify everything. To do so might disrupt the atmosphere and prevent Lisa from being healed. If I jumped up and felt the far side table legs, it would not prove anything. I was being allowed a wonderful experience and complete verification was not necessary. Healing came first. I should just take note of what was occurring. Verification would be out of place.

The table motion was so vigorous and erratic that I could not believe that it could be created by wires. The table was vibrating many times a second.[7]

One of Joe's children opened the door at the top of the basement stairs, allowing light to come into the basement. I could see that Lisa was embracing Joe, who was talking to her softly, "We are all one," he was saying in trance. Tom was sitting peacefully, on my left, with eyes closed. The table stopped moving when the light came into the room.

What can I say? I have no normal explanation for what caused the table to move. I know that I was not pushing or pulling it. I made every attempt to remain skeptical. I spoke with skeptical magicians who told me that sometimes they could not explain their fellow magicians' tricks, but they did not conclude that paranormal forces were involved in those cases. "Unexplained things are merely unexplained," one said.

Later I spoke with Lisa about what she had experienced. "Joe could not have caused the table to move while your hands were on it," she said with certainty. "My feet were touching his feet and my hands were on his hands. There weren't any wires or anything like that on my side of the table. I checked the table when I had my hands on it. If you checked your side then there weren't any wires on either side."

"How did the table keep vibrating?" I asked.

"It must have been the entities!" she said.

I was interested in seeing whether Lisa's eyesight would improve. Her condition did not change immediately afterward, but she continued communicating with the entities. She asked if she could heal others and what methods might be useful for doing that:

A: Feel thoughts of healing go out to the others. Visualize the germs, etc., as nasty little things and then visualize yourself crushing them, and nurturing (symbolically) the patient's "good cells" back to health. No matter how ridiculous your conscious mind "knows" this is, your subconscious mind does much better at giving psi-energy for healing if it can work objectively rather than with imageless abstractions.

As the months passed, they continued their advice:

A: Hard work helps heal. If you are sufficiently tired, mentally and physically, in the striving to accomplish a worthy task you will not have time to indulge neuroses.

Think less often of what is wrong with you. The effect is like constantly picking at a sore; the psyche can fester, too.

Q: Throughout mortal life, people have spoken of evil, the Devil, negativity and Hell. Is there a collective energy, an All that seeks to hurt and do harm?

A: People create their own hells; having a "real" one would be inefficient. Fear is the devil. Perfect love casts out fear. In answer to your question, no, but human beings have a deep inner need to create one. It is difficult to take responsibility. We need an "ancient enemy," a personification of humanity's flaws. The hard part comes when "we have met the enemy, and he is us."

Q: Physicians have documented over 2,000 healings of people who have gone to Lourdes. Other places and people affiliated with the Catholic Church have also been associated with "miracles/cures." Can you explain how this occurs?

A: Bernadette, now physically incorruptible and a spiritually very *high level, believes that the faith of those needing miraculous healing is concentrated there. The water itself is not what does the regeneration effect; it is the concentration of belief and the knowledge that miracles can and have happened there, that provides the positive frame of reference and helps overcome disbelief.*

Lisa, one of the great laws of life is, people usually get what they want consciously and unconsciously. As you know, often this is not what they say they want, much less what is good for them.

This seems absurd, but try not to think about the connection between your helping others and your being helped. Healing involves the great mass of mind that is not cognitive. Cogitating upon it inhibits the flow and thus slows the process.

Although the process was gradual, the vision in Lisa's left eye improved. She began driving her car again, and decided to seek a full-time job. She found a position counseling people with drug addiction problems. Her job took up much of her time. She was helping others, and she wrote the entities less frequently. After improving even more, she opened a diabetes treatment center. It seemed that her healing was a success. A hopeless situation had been resolved.

Since the entities had been successful in helping Lisa, I encouraged others to seek their aid. I kept a careful record of all requests for healing and documented each outcome. Two people had cancer. One had an incurable yeast infection. One had a skin fungus that had not responded to medical treatment. One had a chronic sinus problem. Two sought aid for chronic, but not severe, medical problems.

After receiving messages from the entities, the majority claimed that they had been helped, but some were unsure. It was not possible to do a full evaluation, but it seemed to me that, all in all, people were helped by their interaction with the entities. To my surprise, I found that those with more severe problems were more likely to say that they had been helped. I had thought that the easy cases would have more favorable outcomes. The two cancer patients improved, and their results were astonishing.

From time to time, I sent out a kind of newsletter, listing the people who sought aid.

Q: Do you have a message you would like to send to these people?
A: The Resurrection is continual. Love and help others. Do not let negativity and vile lowness triumph over positive, kindly feelings. Never lose faith in our side, in the good, and in yourselves as channels to the world.

Love, Peace ,
Rector/J.K.

One of these letters, mailed to the entities for their comments on March 29, 1982, was returned by them postmarked from Columbus, Ohio, March 14, 1982. This was one of the times that an entity letter was postmarked with a date previous to the day the letter had been provided to them. The letter seemed to have gone backwards in time.

SORRATs were curious about this; it seemed peculiar. Had the entities been able to convince a postmaster to apply a fraudulent postmark? Even the fraud hypothesis was surprising.

One last tale needs to be told. In February 1983, I began having prostate problems. This condition generally responds to long term treatment with large doses of antibiotics, but after months of medicine, my pain had not diminished. The doctors said that sometimes prostate problems are not related to bacteria and that there is little that can be done. I tried taking doses of zinc and bee pollen, as suggested by an herb book, but I got no relief from the pain. I decided that my problem was psychosomatic, and I asked the entities to help me. They replied that anything that I believed in would help me *externalize* the problem. This would facilitate an internal, natural process. A month went by with no change. I gave up taking the zinc and bee pollen tablets. I decided to depend only on faith. The pain suddenly went away.

Do the entities' healings constitute miracles? No skeptic would accept that explanation. We later asked the entities:

Q: Does the relief of a physical problem occur through your (or other spirits) efforts, or is it a placebo effect in that the person believes he or she is being helped thereby alleviating the problem?

A: Generally, it is a placebo effect, just as in the case of most medication on your side, although enough "miracles" occur to make this work.

Of the eleven cases in my formal study, six reported verified, marked improvement. The "successes" occurred in complex manners, so that we cannot say that the entities were directly responsible. One woman, who regarded her healing as miraculous, attributed the event to her reading the Bible. One described astonishing, miraculous improvement, followed by regression to her previous condition. One reported very gradual improvement. Among the five "failure" cases, three people reported no change (two cases involved "bursitis-like" pains). Two people did not respond to my inquiry, and these cases were classified as "failures." In all these cases, the individuals first sought treatment by a medical doctor and continued under the doctor's care as long as this was deemed appropriate.

I drew no formal conclusions from this study, but it stimulated my interest in spiritual healing. While in Asia, I had observed shamanic and folk healers in Sri Lanka, India, Thailand, Korea, Philippines, Taiwan, and Okinawa. As among the SORRATs, people in these countries claimed to have been helped, sometimes miraculously, by healers. Some people provided medical documentation, implying that their healing was anomalous.

My research allowed me to make hypotheses regarding what future sociologists would encounter if they investigated a PK group.[8] I predicted that parapsychologists would be unable to establish the authenticity of ESP or PK, but that people in the group would report anomalous experiences. The basic ideology behind the group seems conducive to spiritual healing. An investigation of these healings is likely to find people who report anomalous results. The entities support the argument that these benefits are best explained as placebo or hypnotic effects.

CHAPTER 8
COGNITIVE DISSONANCE

After my visit with Tom and Elaine in January 1982, I stopped by the Mc-Donnell Laboratory. I wanted to see those films! Did they show Tom cheating? Did they show Steve Shaw and Mike Edwards cheating?

Mark Shafer again treated me strangely. He had told me that he would share his information after the Parapsychological Association conference, and the conference was long over. It turned out that they did not present a formal paper but instead gave an informal talk. At the conference, Dr. Phillips had been criticized by the parapsychologists, particularly Charles Honorton.

Mark Shafer told me he could show me the videotapes, but I had to sign an agreement saying that I would not discuss what I saw with anyone. Why were they being so secretive? Didn't psychical researchers have an obligation to share information about fraud? I had been investigating the Rolla case for nine months. I was suspicious about many things I had seen. This was my chance to gain some insight into what was going on. I might see evidence of cheating; something I had hoped to see on my first visit to Rolla.

I asked Mark if I could see the tapes from the July 4, 1981, weekend. He put on the first tape. It showed no ostensibly paranormal events, nor did it cover the events I wanted to see. The second tape did not begin where the first one ended.

"What happened in between those two tapes?" I asked Mark.

"We sent some tapes back to the company because they were defective. We had to send them back so we could get them to return our money."

"What about the time when Tom's body blocked the camera's view of a bend?" I asked. "I know that you had that on tape because you played it back for Tom Richards to see. Where's that segment?"

"It must have been on a tape that was partially defective. We sent it back. I'm sure it's been destroyed by now."

"What about the two table-tipping sessions you filmed that day?

"I guess those were on defective tapes, also."

155

"You don't think something funny was going on in your lab that day?" I asked. "Doesn't it seem strange for the spoon to bend behind Tom in a manner that he could have done it with his hand behind his back?"

"Why would he do that? Mark asked.

Good question. According to Mark, he knew that he was being watched by the camera. Why would he incriminate himself? But why was Mark Shafer acting so secretively? It seemed astonishing to me that he allowed tapes that contained disputed evidence to be destroyed. The whole thing left a sour taste in my mouth. The researchers and their experimental subjects had divergent views and were not communicating very well.

Perhaps the solution was to generate the phenomena myself, I thought. That way I would have more control over the situation. I tried to organize a psi group at my home in Maryland. The entities implied that, if we achieved sufficient rapport, we could communicate with spirits using raps. I gathered a group together, but most people came only a few times and then stopped coming. They wanted to experience the paranormal but wanted immediate results. My group met for many months, but I was unable to attract people willing to come every week.

I meditated every day, focusing healing thoughts on the people who requested help from the entities. I prayed for them. One afternoon, a series of raps came from the cabinet where I stored the entity letters. My heart began racing. I was amazed and surprised at my emotional reaction. The raps kept coming, "Rap, rap, rap, rap, rap, rap, rap, rap…." I lost count. Maybe they rapped out "Z" or maybe they went beyond the end of the alphabet. How could I doubt now? The implications were frightening.

I had no friends in Maryland who believed in the entities. People came to my group because they were curious, but they had no strong commitment. The rapping incident might force me to accept something that I had originally considered absurd. Would I be labeled insane?

I checked the cabinet closely. There were no rapping devices hidden inside, just entity letters. I tried pushing the cabinet. It was not stable on all its four legs. I was able to make it rock by pushing it. Had there been a vibration in the house that caused the cabinet to rap the way it did? I could make it rock and that caused a kind of rapping sound, but it would not continue rapping for long. I checked the rest of the house. Was there a reason for the cabinet to begin shaking? I could find no explanation. The cabinet had never rapped before.

I checked the legs again and again. If I pushed the cabinet, it produced a noise like the one I heard; was that the noise I heard? It would rock no more than five times without requiring another push. Surely there was a logical explanation for the sounds that I heard. The idea that the entities had verified themselves to me was too far-fetched for me to accept. They had to make the raps again, I reasoned. If they did it again, I would believe.

"If you are really here, make some more raps," I demanded.

The room was quiet. I was not surprised. My psychological state probably prevented more raps from coming.

I did not know how to evaluate this experience. My problem illustrated a dilemma of psychical research. An event occurs and the investigator seeks a normal explanation. What is the probability of something anomalous occurring? How possible is the normal explanation? It is not possible to assign probabilities. Often the normal explanation is not very probable but is possible. The skeptical way of thinking suggests that something with a normal explanation should always be accepted rather than something with an anomalous explanation. Logically, miracles do not happen. They violate scientific principles. The believer has an alternative perspective. Miracles happen. They might be rare, but they happen.

I accepted a job as a sociology instructor with the Asian Division of the University of Maryland. I would begin teaching in Japan in August 1982. After I accepted the job, I remembered the advertisements for hand-painted Japanese plates that the entities had sent to me so many months before. Was that a coincidence?

Professor Walter H. Uphoff, of the New Frontiers Center, invited me to help him prepare for a three-day seminar in Madison, Wisconsin, August 6-8, 1982. The topic was "Psychic Phenomena, Healing Modalities, and Survival Evidence." I would have to leave for Japan the day before the conference ended to begin my job with the Asian Division, but I could help Walter put the conference together.

Walter had invited some people claiming PK ability: Uri Geller (famous metal bender), Tom Richards (with SORRAT), Steve Shaw (McDonnell Lab metal bender), Mike Edwards (McDonnell Lab metal bender), and Masuaki Kiyota (famous Japanese metal bender) would address the audience.

I decided to take a circuitous drive to Wisconsin to visit Tom and Elaine one more time. I knew that I would not return to Rolla for a while because I would be working in Asia. I hoped to resolve my cognitive dissonance regarding the entities.

Tom and Elaine were upset. They had been told about FRNM's report that inferred that they had cheated. They were especially disturbed that FRNM had concealed their negative opinions for three months while attempting to gather more evidence.

"Why were the parapsychologists so deceptive?" Elaine asked me. "Why did they treat us like guinea pigs?"

I had no answer. The researchers at FRNM had accumulated evidence that implied fraud but had not told Tom and Elaine. Elaine considered me to be a kind of parapsychologist, a member of the group who had concealed this information. I felt bad that she thought I had worked against her. To escape her wrath, I left with Tom to get gas for his car.

"Something funny is going on here," I told him. "You have to look at this from different vantage points."

"It's the attitude of those parapsychologists that hurts," he said. "We're just as interested in the truth as they are, but they treat us like test animals. I feel bad that George Hansen's experiment didn't work, but many other experiments have not worked. Psi is not reliable and sometimes you get ambiguous effects."

"Maybe George is partially responsible," I said. "Maybe our skepticism is preventing things from working." I was thinking about the smashed mini-lab.

"Dr. Neihardt founded SORRAT so that we could investigate telekinesis," Tom said. "The group is open to anyone who is interested. Whatever happens gives us insight into the nature of PK."

Many parapsychologists hypothesize that believers (whom they label "sheep") demonstrate psi more frequently than do skeptics (labeled "goats"). This is known as the "sheep/goat" effect. Researchers have found that people's belief affects their experimental results. They have also uncovered what they term the "experimenter effect." The researcher's beliefs, motivations, attitudes, and methods affect experimental results. Some researchers are psi-conducive, while others seem to prevent psi from happening.

"Maybe the scientific goal of verifying SORRAT claims is doomed to failure," I told Tom. "Perhaps the skepticism that is inherent within science makes proving psi impossible. After all, doubt is built into the experimental design. If we had no doubt, there would be no need to do scientific experiments. If we knew how an experiment would turn out, we would not bother doing it."

"We have been experiencing phenomena that exceed what might be produced through fraud," Tom noted.[1] "We have invited scientists to investigate the phenomena. Ed Cox built his mini-lab and we allowed him to do his experiments. It hurts when they say that we have engaged in fraud all these years.

They should treat us like human beings, not guinea pigs."

Tom started to move from the right lane to the left lane. A car attempted to pass him on the left, and Tom hit the car, causing a minor accident. This made me rethink my evaluation of SORRAT phenomena. I knew Tom fairly well. He was extremely overweight, slow moving, and methodical in his thinking, with a limited set of interests: target practice, writing fiction, and teaching English literature. The accident forced me to think about how absurd it was to regard him as capable of staging the mini-lab films, writing hundreds of mini-lab letters, forging Neihardt signatures, running down the basement stairs to place an ice cube on the rafter and smash a mini-lab, creating artwork as part of an ESP experiment response, creating fraudulent postmarks, designing methods to produce placebo effects. These things were just some of the skills that skeptics attributed to him. The conspiracy would have to include Elaine, Ed Cox, Steve Calvin, and other SORRATs. These people would also have to show high levels of dexterity, speed, mechanical skill, and film fabrication ability. Tom's clumsiness did not coincide with the many phenomena I had witnessed. I want to be honest about what I was dealing with: raps, Neihardt signatures, table tipping, mini-lab photography, letter writing, poltergeist phenomena. Previous psychical research investigators have faced similar situations and been amazed at how people who seemed innocent had devised ingenious methods to perpetrate fraud. You just never know, do you?

In the evening, we tried another ESP/PK experiment. Nothing happened. The table did not vibrate.

"I guess the energy is down," Elaine said sadly. Perhaps the magic was over, I thought. Perhaps the parapsychologists' accusations of fraud had so poisoned the atmosphere that the entities were dead. No more raps, table tipping, poltergeists, letter writing.

The next day, Tom, Ed, and I went to an antique car museum in Rolla. Tom and Ed were interested in antique autos. I looked at the old, well preserved vehicles. Many of the cars had been new when J. B. Rhine did his first ESP experiments in the early 1930s. Automotive technology had made great advances. What had occurred in the field of parapsychology? Although psi researchers used both computers and quantum mechanical theories, they seemed little closer to devising an acceptable explanation for psi than did J.B. Rhine. Ed's investigation of the Rolla situation was a form of regression to an earlier era when mediums were caught cheating. Some researchers claimed to have proven that the spirits were real but most did not have much luck. I wondered if I would be able to get my sociological study published.

Tom, Ed, and I walked slowly through the exhibits to a hallway lined with antique cars. We were alone with the ghostly vehicles. Suddenly, I heard raps beneath my feet. "Who is it?" Tom asked.

" J. K." the raps spelled out faintly.

"John King!" I exclaimed. "It's good to hear you." I was surprised and amused that John King could rap in such a public place.

Ed got on his hands and knees and was feeling the floor with his hands. He wanted to locate the exact point of the rap's origin.

"John, can you tell us where the missing FRNM deck is?" he asked.

"*Rap, rap, rap.*" Maybe. Ed placed his ear against the floor. He had located the exact point.

Tom looked frantically up and down the long hallway. "Please, Ed," he warned. "This is a public museum. Someone could come along at any moment."

I tried to view the scene as a detached observer. Could this be done by a magician? I had talked with various magicians regarding conjurers' methods for producing raps. Typically, the trick was done by misdirection. The magician might crack the joints in her or her toes while looking at an alternate point. This led observers to think that the raps originated from that point. Other methods require a confederate, who artificially makes the sounds. Yet, Cox and I could feel the raps coming out of the floor. Tom was not trying to misdirect us. He was concerned about Cox's embarrassing position on the floor.

We were in a huge room, filled with antique cars. There was another room below us filled with cars, that we had already visited. Was someone down there rapping on the ceiling with a broom stick? It did not seem likely that someone below us was rapping, but I could not rule out that possibility. Should I rush downstairs to check the room below us? I decided to stay with Tom and Ed. It would be more fun to see how a tourist would react to seeing Ed with his ear to the floor.

"John, is Samuel Csar, the man to whom the deck was addressed, still in San Diego?" Ed asked. The spirits had informed Ed that the important evidence, an ESP card deck, had been mailed paranormally to a man named Samuel Csar. This was Cox's latest attempt to generate evidence that would convince the parapsychologists that SORRAT was authentic.

"Rap," Yes.

"Does he have the deck?" Ed asked.

"Rap, rap, rap." Maybe

"Will you try to find this out for us?"

"Rap." Yes.

"Ed, we can't do this here," Tom said anxiously. "People will be disturbed. Someone may come any minute."

A man and his young son turned the corner and looked curiously at the three of us. Ed kept his ear to the floor. The man seemed surprised and curious.

"Ed, we really have to move along. People are coming!" Tom whispered urgently.

"John, can you tell us more about San Csar's address?" Ed begged, speaking softly. The raps began spelling a message. Tom tilted his head sideways, attempting to hear the virtually inaudible raps. I smiled at the man watching us. He could see that something unusual was going on, and he looked away from me, inspecting an antique car. His son stared back at me with a puzzled look on his face.

"Rap, rap, rap," the raps spelled faintly. Maybe.

"Come on, Ed," Tom warned. He pushed me forward as if nothing unusual had happened. Ed was still on the floor.

"I wonder what they think of us," I said to Tom.

"I suppose they think Ed is looking at the underside of a car," Tom replied.

"Ed is in the middle of the hallway," I noted. "He's not close to a car."

"Maybe they think we're drunk or maybe that he lost a contact lens," Tom speculated, smiling. The son continued staring at us.

We turned a corner and began looking at the autos in another hallway. Ed got up and joined us. We were now out of sight of the man and his son. The floor was carpeted in this area.

"You'll never find the deck," I said to Cox. "Of course, you might get it back, but I predict that if you get it back it will be opened and they'll accuse Tom of fraud. The parapsychologists will never believe in this stuff."

"I can't give up that easily," Ed replied. "This is too important. If that deck is sorted, and the seals intact, it will convince the people at FRNM."

"Psychical researchers have been attempting to verify psi for over a hundred years and what have they accomplished?" I asked him.

"We are continually improving our methods," he responded. "They said I could not film PK, but I did it under controlled conditions. It takes a great deal of dedication to be a pioneer in the field of psychical research. It takes…."

He was interrupted by the raps: "Rap, rap, rap; rap, rap, rap; rap, rap, rap."

"Three-Times-Three!" Ed exclaimed. "Perhaps you can help me locate the missing FRNM deck!"

"Rap." Yes. Again, Ed found a point to place his ear on the carpeted floor.

"Ed, we can't do this here," Tom said anxiously, but I could tell that he was curious about what the raps might say. He had turned his ear in the direction from which the raps seemed to come. They came from a point slightly in front of his feet; not under his feet, but about three feet in front of his toes. I viewed the scene with mixed emotions. It was curious that the entities allowed me to see things that produced partial belief. Cox located the exact point of the raps' origin; three feet in front of Tom's right shoe. I had seen this situation many times in the past. Skeptics assumed that Tom was producing the raps, but they were not coming from his feet. They originated about three feet in front of him.

"Three-Times-Three, do you know where the deck is?" Ed asked. The man and his son turned the corner and saw Ed lying on the floor again. They were too far away to hear his voice or the rapping sound.

"Rap, rap." No.

"We have to go," Tom pleaded softly.

"Please, Three-Times-Three," Ed begged. "Please find out. This is *very* important."

Tom and I walked along the row of cars, inspecting each as if nothing unusual was occurring. We left Ed behind. He continued questioning the silent floor: "Please, Three-Times-Three," he begged. "Please find out!" The floor was silent.

Cox never retrieved his deck. The entities later told him that Samuel Csar was in hiding because he had failed to pay his alimony, child support, and court costs. The entities said that Csar had received the deck but had thrown it away, thinking that it had come from his ex-wife.

Before I left Rolla that April, Ed gave me a souvenir from an earlier experiment; a reminder of the days when his mini-lab was in operation. The memento consisted of a small open box filled with modeling clay, along with a plastic stylus. The entities had written in the clay, "There are many of us each with his own goal." The message was signed "J.K."

"Do you think Tom could be doing this writing while in trance?" Ed asked. "He would have no way of knowing about it if he did."

"Elaine and Ivan would know," I said. "It doesn't seem likely that Tom could do all the writing in trance without someone seeing him to do it. It would take hours of work each week."

I thought about the connection between Tom's mind and the texts. Many messages contained things that Tom might write: spelling errors, typical phrases, story themes. The similarities were so numerous that it was logical to think that he wrote the messages. Yet the volume of messages was so great that it would be difficult for him to conceal this activity. His demeanor and attitude gave every indication that he was not aware of writing the messages.

The next day, Tom and I were working on the outside of his house. He was painting and I was on a ladder, repairing water damage under a gutter.

"You know, our scientific methods aren't really getting anywhere as far as investigating what is going on here," I said to him.

"I suppose the scientific experimentation isn't the most important aspect of what is happening," he replied.

"It seems to me as if the entities are playing with the parapsychologists. It's easy for them to assume that you are cheating, and it's hard for them to think that you aren't cheating. It's as if the entities have framed you."

"We don't cheat. We have never cheated," Tom stated with certainty.[2]

Later that afternoon, I went jogging. I was leaving Rolla the next day. My participation in this drama was ending.

When I returned to the Richards' guest room, I found that Tom had left a note for me: "Ed Cox called, Call him." I looked at the entities' message box with the clay and plastic stylus. The stylus was now stabbed into the clay. Three-Times-Three's signature (111x111) had been inscribed beside John King's initials. "There are many of us each with his own goal," the message stated. It was now signed "J.K." *and* "111x111."

"Did you write anything in this clay?" I asked Tom, showing him the box and explaining my observations.

"No," he replied. "Are you sure that Three-Times-Three hadn't signed it previously?"

"I'm sure it was not there before," I replied. "I think there are photographs of it. Do you remember leaving the note about Ed Cox calling?"

"Yes, of course," he said.

I called Ed Cox and said my goodbyes. Cox assured me that the "111x111" had not signed the note on the clay previously.

The next day, as I drove to Wisconsin, I considered the absurdity of belief. A likely explanation was that Tom entered the guest room, left Cox's message, and inscribed "111x111" in the clay. Perhaps he was in trance while doing it, or perhaps not. Psychical researchers have encountered poltergeist cases like that; the central people did not realize they were fabricating PK. The absurd explanation was that the plastic stylus magically rose up, scratched 111x111, and then poked itself into the clay. I had no basis to choose one explanation over another except for a rule of thumb that I had adopted: it is logical to accept normal explanations rather than paranormal explanations. Paranormal explanations require exceptional proof. But my situation was gradually changing. I had been exposed to too many ostensible PK events that I could not explain. PK did not seem as exceptional to me as it had in the past. PK was becoming normal to me. Could Three-Times-Three have signed his name in the clay? Of course, he could! The poltergeist activity was still active. It was a possibility. The poltergeist was aware that Cox and I had discussed the entity messages. There was no reason to think that Tom Richards would know about this conversation. The signing of "111x111" coincided with that conversation, so it was logical to think that the poltergeist had done it.

I reviewed the chain of events. Cox had mentioned the idea of Tom going into trance. Three-Times-Three (an aspect of Cox's subconscious mind) might have picked up on that idea and wanted to emphasize the fragmented nature of consciousness. Ed, Tom, Three-Times-Three, the other entities, and I each had our own goal. Even if some of us were only fragments of consciousness, we had our own goals. Thinking about this more deeply, what is consciousness? We don't really know, do we? Our human consciousness consists of fragments, loosely connected, a result of the evolutionary process.

"This is ridiculous," I thought. "I'm creating absurd theories about this stuff!"

Why should I consider the believer's image rather than the skeptic's image?[3] My prior experiences influenced me. I had seen tables jumping about in an unexplained manner; I had heard unexplained raps coming out of concrete floors, the ground outside, the floor of a restaurant, the floor of an antique car museum. I had monitored Cox's experiments with the mini-lab. I knew that focusing my attention on particular events was just a believer's rationalization for believing. I had also seen Tom engage in suspicious movements with the table and had talked to people who had seen him cheat. I had read the parapsychologists' report of tampering with the sealed ESP card deck.

There was another factor affecting my thinking. I liked talking with Tom, Elaine, and the entities. I had emotional relationships with them. I enjoyed writing them and thinking about them. The SORRAT puzzle had captured my attention. It was like a Zen koan—something without a logical answer. I enjoyed the mystery of it. I enjoyed playing with Tom and Elaine's son, Ivan. I laughed at Tom's puns. I was amused by the entities' imaginative stories. I accepted the entities because they were entertaining. I could not be certain that the entities were real, but I was a sociological observer, a participant observer. I wanted to understand what was really going on and, to do that, I needed to participate. Was my level of belief irrational?[4]

In St. Louis, I spoke with Michael McBeath at the McDonnell Laboratory. "Why did you ever tell me about Tom Richards?" I asked him, joking. "Things have gotten a bit out of hand. I notice that all logical people are skeptics, and I'm acting like a believer."

"Think about it this way," he said. "Why do people disbelieve? What are the grounds for their disbelief?'

"They disbelieve because they have had no paranormal experiences. Or their experiences have not been that powerful. To accept this foolishness on faith is illogical."

"But now you have had some experiences," he replied. "Welcome to the club!"

The day before the conference in Wisconsin, I had a chance to talk with the metal bender, Mike Edwards. He was attending college at the University of Iowa and had just arrived in St. Louis. He seemed outgoing, relaxed, and good-natured.

"I have an important question" I said. "Did you see Tom Richards fake a spoon-bending at the McDonnell Lab on the July Fourth weekend last year?"

"How did you know about that?" he asked.

"I'm a sociologist. I talk to people and they talk to me," I told him. "You can talk to me too. It's important. I'm trying to put the pieces of a puzzle together and you have one of the pieces. Did you see Tom Richards bend a spoon behind his back with his body blocking the camera?"

He hesitated, thinking for a moment. "Yes, that's what I saw."

"And you saw him cheat at the table-tipping that evening?"

"Yes, that's right."

"And you saw him faking the raps?"

"That's right."

"Did you tell anyone about it that evening?'

"I told Peter Phillips."

His story did not fit with Steve Shaw's information. I knew that Peter Phillips was not present that evening.

"Did you tell Jan, the McDonnell Lab manager?" I asked.

"No, I told Peter Phillips," he answered.

The problem with eyewitness testimony is that human memory and human observation are never flawless. I wondered how a jury would consider Mike's testimony in a court of law. A normal jury would regard Mike as honest because they would not believe in psychokinesis.

"Could I interview you using my tape recorder?" I asked Mike.

"No, I couldn't do that. I don't want to go on record. I just answered your questions. I don't want to make waves."

Now I had two witnesses who said they had seen my friend, Tom Richards, cheat. Although Tom's action lacked motivation, the implications were obvious. He cheated, at times.

I talked with John Hunt the next day. He picked up on my concern but did not shed his jovial mood. "Are you finally going to tell the truth about the SORRAT situation?" he asked. He knew that I was to give a presentation the next day at the conference.

"What do you mean?"

"1 think we have allowed this conspiracy to go on long enough. Let's face it: this entity business is absurd and no one will believe it. You might as well spill the beans on the whole thing." I knew he was joking. Jokes are a good way to deal with cognitive dissonance.

"How can I do that?" I asked.

"Tell everyone that Tom, Elaine, Ed Cox, Steve Calvin, and the whole SORRAT group are all fakes!"

"That's a good idea! Funny that you should bring it up at this moment. What can I say about the *Goat's Head Soup* incident that you told me about?"

"Don't mention that.'

"What about the raps?"

"Tom isn't actually overweight. He has a huge electronic rapping system strapped to his body."

"What should I say about Ed Cox's mini-lab films?"

"They have Walt Disney make the films. They bribed Cox a long time ago. He has a numbered Swiss bank account and a secret island hideaway in the Caribbean where he helps Disney do the filming."

"What about the raps you heard spelling out 'DAI' early in the morning? How did that happen?"

"That was done with secret agents who trail me. You should realize that this isn't your run-of-the-mill, fly-by-night conspiracy. They have agents everywhere. The KGB, CIA, FBI, and even James Randi are involved in this. They had a CIA midget hide under the car's hood and wait until I passed on the street."

"All just to fool you and me?" I asked.

"That's part of it! They also want to take over the world. Only you can stop them by warning the audience tomorrow."

"John, why have you been involved with SORRAT for so long?"

"You've been in this for a long time now yourself. I'm not the only one! Why do you keep coming back to Rolla again and again?"

"I'm doing sociological research. That's my excuse. What's yours?"

"I can't help it. This is the decision branch that I happen to be on. I'm destined to become a SORRAT crackpot! Maybe it's a kind of therapy. I'm interested in military strategy and they tell me that I was Marshal Ney and served under Napoleon in a past life. It's fun! Don't you think I would make a great general?'

"No, John. You're not a general. You're a mathematician. You would make a lousy general. Maybe that's why you were executed in 1815."

John seemed hurt. "My execution had nothing to do with my military abilities. It was a political situation. But maybe you're right. This is all absurd. I'm sure glad I don't have to talk about this weird SORRAT business like you do tomorrow. People would think I was a crackpot!"

What could I say with certainty about SORRAT? Was I certain that the entities were real? No, I was not. Was I certain that psychokinesis was real? Some events might be real, but how could I determine what was real and what was not? I had pieces to a puzzle, but the pieces did not fit together.

In the evening, the SORRATs held an ESP/PK experiment in a Sheraton hotel room. John, Lisa, Elaine, Masuaki Kiyota (the psychic metal bender from Japan), some others, and I were present. The raps came out of the floor, and the table jumped around. Just like normal, I thought. It sure is hard to explain those raps away. Steve Shaw could claim that he had seen Tom making the raps with his feet, but it was obvious that Tom was not using that method that evening. John and I watched Tom and smiled at our private joke.[5]

"How does he get the raps to come out of the floor?" I asked John in a whisper.

"There are Soviet agents in the room downstairs tapping on the ceiling with broom handles," John whispered back. We both held back our laughter.

Charles Dai, John's helper on the other side, rapped out his initials.

"C. D., welcome!" John called out. "Long time, no see. Or actually, no hear would be more accurate!"

"H—I," Charles Dai rapped out.

"C. D., could you give me some financial advice?" I asked. Over a year before, another entity message had suggested that I contact him for advice about the stock market. Apparently, C. D. had given accurate predictions to John in the past.

"Rap," Yes.

'Would you suggest a stock to buy?"

"Rap." Yes. Then he began spelling out a name.

"I hope you're getting a good time line," John commented. "Watch out for bum raps!"

I called a stockbroker at few days later and invested in the obscure, speculative company that most closely matched the letters that CD had rapped out. My investment doubled within six months. Although the Dow Jones average shot up during this time, my success seemed unusual. My broker had been against buying anything because the market had been declining steadily when I put in the purchase order. Warning: There is no evidence that psychics can predict the stock market any better than your financial advisor or random selection!

Nothing very evidential occurred during the rest of the session. The entities rapped information about a magic crystal that was important in the past lives of Lisa and John. Everyone had a good time. The entity game is fun! Months later they would send a diagram to a SORRAT letter writer regarding how to construct a Celtic crystal device for attracting psychic energy.

I asked Masuaki Kiyota what he thought about the table tipping experience. We had gone to see the movie *E.T., the Extra-Terrestrial* that afternoon and Masuaki had been thrilled by it. "*E.T.* was a remarkable movie," he said. "This psychokinesis is also remarkable. It is like my life. These things are astonishing."

The next day, I watched the metal-benders, Steve, Mike, and Masuaki, attempting their feats. Bends seemed to occur in groups. One metal bender would bend a spoon and soon afterward, another did something similar. It seemed to me that the "grouping" of bends might occur because the first event drew observers' attention, allowing the others to act with less scrutiny. I noted that Steve and Mike's mental bending differed from Masuaki's bends. Steve and Mike did bends only for others; Masuaki was pleased when a bend appeared, even though no one else saw it. He did metal bending for his own amusement. Mike's bends were exactly like those I had seen James Randi, the magician, do. This made me wonder about Mike's authenticity.

Some of Steve Shaw's bends seemed different. At times, his method did not coincide with Randi's methods. I hoped that I could get close enough to snatch the spoon away from Steve while it was bending so that I could discover something about the exact process. If he had previously tampered with the spoon, I hoped to detect his method.

Masuaki did slow metal-twisting. Sometimes he seemed to rotate the spoon to make it look as if it was twisting when it actually was not. Once I felt that I had caught him in the middle of his trick. First, he would bend the head of the spoon over, or at least I noticed that the head had been bent over, then the twist appeared later. A magician could duplicate the effect but would need either extremely strong fingers or a small tool to hold the spoon so that the twist could be made. I wondered if his belt buckle might serve as a way to hold the spoon while he made the twist.

None of the metal-benders could perform if I checked the spoon first and refused to avert my eyes from it afterward. They produced bends only if I gazed away.

Masuaki attributed his PK ability to an entity with no name but who he said could be called "Zenefu." Steve Shaw and Mike Edwards did not believe in entities. They seemed to lack an explanation for how they performed and there seemed to be something "off" about them. They seemed "out of harmony" with what they were doing.

Masuaki sometimes had difficulty expressing himself in English. I communicated with him using his Japanese/English dictionary. He invited me to visit him in Tokyo. I enjoyed talking to him, and I regarded him as a friend. I accepted him as he was, whether he engaged in fraud or not.

"Masuaki, why is it that I never see your twisting begin?" I asked.

"You must become used to the idea of it. Maybe someday you will see it," he replied.

"Do you ever cheat?" I asked.

"I am the only one who knows without doubt that I never cheat," he said.

That seemed to me to be an unusual way to answer the question, but it could be the correct answer. I thought about Tom Richards; did Tom know whether he was cheating or not? I was not certain about that.

Later, I spoke with a freelance journalist who had taken Steve Shaw and Mike Edwards out drinking the night before.

"How well do you know those two American metal-benders?" he asked me.

"Not very well," I told him. "They seem like okay guys, though. I visited Steve Shaw at his apartment in Pennsylvania. He told me he wanted to become a professional magician but that he wanted to get his psychokinetic ability verified scientifically first."

"You think those guys are authentic?" the journalist asked.

"I can't say for sure. Parapsychologist Walter Uphoff and some of his friends have told me astonishing stories about Mike Edwards, but I haven't seen him do that much myself. They say that he bent a fork without touching it, but the McDonnell Lab has given up trying to authenticate those guys. They couldn't prove their PK ability under completely controlled conditions."

"I took them out drinking last night," the journalist told me. "They're wild guys, all right, certainly not the spiritual types that you might expect. I think I should tell you something. You seem to be more skeptical than most of these people here, and you might understand what I'm saying. I saw Steve Shaw fake a bend. My colleague, Marty, saw it also."

"How did it happen?" I asked.

"I guess Steve had too much to drink or he would have been more careful," the reporter said. "He was showing his ability to a girl at the bar, turned very naturally with a spoon in his hand so it was not in the girl's line of sight, and he gave it a bend. Then, he revealed the spoon to her so that it seemed to bend right before her eyes. Do you think he always cheats?"

"I doubt it. A lot of strange things have happened around him. One McDonnell Lab researcher seemed convinced, but in the end they couldn't prove anything. I'm beginning to think that all these guys cheat at times. If they don't, they certainly get involved in some very ambiguous situations so that it *looks* like they cheat. I think that ambiguity helps psi work. It doesn't seem to happen under perfectly controlled conditions."

"Steve seems like a good kid. I suppose he'll screw up his future if he's caught cheating."

"Maybe, but maybe not," I replied. "Some people believe in this stuff no matter what. True believers ignore information that doesn't coincide with their beliefs, and true skeptics do the same thing. Reality isn't that important when people's beliefs are concerned. If Steve is caught cheating, the skeptics will ignore him and he can continue performing for the believers."

"Yeah, I guess you're right. My editor only wants stories for believers. If I see them cheat, I don't have a story."

"Scientists are the other way," I noted. "If I see them bend, it's only an anecdote, but if I see them cheat, it's big news. It lets the scientists rest easier."

We smiled at the irony. There are many of us, each with his own goal, I thought.

Six months later, on January 28, 1983, Steve Shaw and Mike Edwards declared that they were actually magicians and that they were working under the direction of James (the Amazing) Randi. The occasion was a press conference convened by *Discover* magazine in New York City. When Steve Shaw demonstrated paranormal metal-bending before the assembled news people, one startled reporter asked, "Can you tell us how you did that?"

"I cheat," Steve replied, drawing laughter from the room.

Later during interviews, both Steve Shaw and Mike Edwards declared that they had seen Uri Geller, Tom Richards, and Masuaki Kiyota cheat. They described the methods used. They said Masuaki Kiyota used a slot in his shoe to produce twists. They said Tom made raps by tapping his shoes.[6]

James Randi's agents, Steve and Mike, were part of what he called "Project Alpha," an attempt to discredit parapsychologists. Randi wanted to reveal parapsychologists as incompetent. His descriptions of Project Alpha on NBC's *Today Show* distorted the degree that his agents had fooled the scientists. In reality, the McDonnell Lab had given up on getting experimental evidence from Shaw or Edwards since they had been unable to perform under controlled conditions.

Project Alpha produced many ironies. Some who had observed Shaw and Edwards' ostensibly paranormal events could not believe that all the effects were produced fraudulently. Shaw told Dr. Bert Schwarz informally that he had no idea how some of the things attributed to him happened. When Shaw visited Schwarz's home, the furnace system and other items in the house were damaged in a manner that seemed anomalous. Bert attributed the damage to psychokinesis, based on the repairman's description of what he found. If Shaw did this damage by normal means, it implied that he was disturbed psychologically. Dr. Schwarz was convinced that some authentic PK events occurred at his home while Steve was with him.

Suppose that the human subconscious can influence physical reality (psychokinesis). Both believers and skeptics may generate phenomena supporting their opinions. Skeptics desire that fraud will be revealed and, as a result, that comes to pass since fraud seems to facilitate PK.[7]

The events surrounding Project Alpha started me thinking about the implications of widespread PK abilities. If everyone subconsciously produced PK, this would disrupt normal consciousness. But let's suppose that "normal" consciousness is the result of our individual efforts to create consciousness. Our collective efforts govern consciousness. We might refer to this as our "consensual reality," the total product of everyone's PK. Although the incidence of PK reveals that our consensual reality is not immutable, paranormal phenomena have limitations. We cannot verify it fully. Consensual reality has characteristics that preserve our consensus. People in small groups, who have the capacity to generate PK, do not have the capacity to overthrow the consensual reality. Typical poltergeist outbreaks last, on average, about two months (Roll, 1977: 388). Hauntings last longer, but have finite lives.

Some PK groups have longer lives than others. The history of SORRAT provides insights regarding factors that enhance longevity: use of spirits, emphasis on rapport, psi-conducive core members, and history of robust experience. It seems that all religions have elements that imply group PK. Early Christianity had characteristics that suggest PK group phenomena: apparitions, PK, ESP, spiritual healing. Modern bureaucratic organizations acknowledge phenomena in harmony with their established ideology but reject innovative experiences.[8]

Let us suppose the groups can create entities that then acquire a life of their own. These entities, like living people, might engage in actions designed to stimulate belief since belief allows them longevity. The appearance of fraud, which drives skeptics away, might be part of their behavioral repertoire.

This speculation predicts that PK cannot occur on demand. It cannot be part of a regular performance, and if such performances are expected, the phenomena will acquire extremely ambiguous characteristics that may include fraud. SORRAT history coincides with this scenario. Cox's films attracted skeptical scrutiny, and FRNM's experience resulted in accusations of fraud. Later, Dr. Phillips attempted to replicate Cox's experiments, generating further stigma for SORRAT, which previously had generated extremely robust phenomena.

In 1983, I spoke with Mark Shafer, the researcher at the McDonnell Lab who spent the most time with Steve Shaw and Mike Edwards. What could Mark tell me about cognitive dissonance and its relation to psi?

Mark was glad to talk with me. He had ended his association with the McDonnell laboratory long before Randi revealed his Alpha scam. He had given up attempting to verify psi in the way the parapsychological community demanded.

"I spent over four years trying to document macro-psychokinesis, and I really didn't have anything to show for it," he told me. "It just isn't that easy to prove. We thought we would begin with loose controls and attempt to discover what factors allowed psi to occur, but as it turned out, we just uncovered the situations that allow sleight-of-hand magicians to work effectively."

"What did you think when you were told that Steve Shaw and Mike Edwards were fakes?" I asked.

"At first, I couldn't believe it," he said. "After I spoke with them on the phone, I realized it was true. I was angry, but on another level, I was also thrilled. Few people get the chance to gain the insights that I have had from this experience. I have seen enough psi to know that it happens. As a result, I believed that Steve and Mike were authentic. I don't deny it."

"Do you think that any of the things they did in the McDonnell Lab were related to authentic psi?"

"I talked with them about what they did. I now have no reason to believe that anything paranormal occurred around them. They were good magicians, and I had a profound faith that they were authentic. But I learned that profound faith is not always creative. It doesn't contribute to spiritual growth. Project Alpha taught me that profound doubt is also required. Profound doubt coupled with profound faith can contribute to spiritual progress. Each is incomplete without the other. A person who has only belief as a guide will never change or grow in any way. Such people focus only on perceptions that support their belief. Those without any belief have no seed with which to begin their spiritual growth. They won't take the first steps toward discovering what is spiritually real. Those with both belief and doubt must always be alert for ways to grow, for ways to make their belief more valid."

I asked Mark about what procedures would be required to prove PK. He had tried to verify its existence but had focused his attention on people engaging in fraud. Suppose a researcher were attempting to verify authentic PK?

"Let's suppose you were working with a spoon bender," he said. "You would want to have a sophisticated video system with multiple cameras, and you would need to show the precautions you were taking to verify that the spoon had not been modified. You would want to show, on video, how you had put special markings on the spoon. You would also want to prepare control spoons identical to the ones that you offer to your subject. You would want to test the spoon by showing that it could lift a weight, and you would need to show that the weight was authentic. You might pour water into a pail and show that a cord attached to the spoon head could lift the pail of water. Then, with the camera continually recording the event, the metal-bender would be allowed to touch only the handle of the spoon, and you would need to document, on video, that the spoon was bending under those conditions. Then afterward, you would want to test the spoon to verify that it was your original spoon and that it had not been modified in a way that a magician might do, to create the effect your camera had documented. You could then offer your video documentary and your control spoons to skeptics so that they would have the opportunity to duplicate the results that you documented. If you could follow those procedures, you would have created some evidence for psi what would be of interest scientifically."

I tape recorded this conversation and gave it to a Japanese researcher who hoped to generate proof of paranormal metal bending. He was not able to create the evidence he desired. I argue that PK has the quality of avoiding verification through such rigid tests. It can affect belief by informal tests but not rigid scientific tests designed by skeptics.

During the summer of 1983, I also spoke to people who conducted research with Mike Edwards and Steve Shaw during Randi's Project Alpha. Peter Phillips said that he felt his laboratory had acted properly during all phases of their research with Shaw and Edwards. The lab had conducted a series of exploratory studies and, based on the results, undertaken experiments with increasingly tightened controls. The mental benders had been unable to demonstrate PK under tightly controlled conditions, so they had ended the experiment. Peter Phillips seemed surprised by Randi's ability to portray the McDonnell Lab as incompetent.

Marcello Truzzi (1987), a sociologist at Eastern Michigan University, felt that Project Alpha would make parapsychologists less likely to consult with magicians, since Peter Phillips had consulted with Randi and ended up being hoaxed by him. Michael McBeath told me about being ambushed by the media almost simultaneously with Randi's revealing the hoax. He was not able to respond because Mark Shafer, the researcher who ran the experiments with Shaw and Edwards, no longer worked at the lab.

When I visited parapsychologist Walter Uphoff in 1983, I expected him to be distressed by Randi's negative portrayal of psychical research. He said that Project Alpha was unfortunate but that he was not concerned. (I think he was also stunned by a local television documentary that portrayed him as fooled by Shaw and Edwards.) Walter was focusing on present research. He was hosting a metal bending party at his house and was holding a spoon in his hand as we talked. As the party progressed, the neck of his spoon became flexible, like rubber. He found he could easily bend it back and forth and twisted it with ease, something he could not do previously.

"Anyone can do this," he told me. "It isn't that remarkable. Randi says it's impossible, but obviously he's wrong."

I visited Dr. Bert Schwarz in Florida. He also had been a strong believer in Shaw and Edwards and had been completely fooled by them. Schwarz felt it was unfortunate that he had been hoaxed, but his experiments with Shaw had not been central to his research. He had conducted experiments with many people claiming PK, including Katie, known as the Gold Leaf Lady. Katie would sit before a video camera while a group of observers monitored the experiment. While she sat, gold foil seemed to emerge from her skin. I visited Bert Schwarz many times, each time watching Katie's "gold foil" phenomenon. I could never rule out slight-of-hand as an explanation for the phenomena because she had a fidgeting characteristic that concealed the original emergence of the foil each time it occurred. I have been told that Bert's videotapes do not capture an event that could not be duplicated by a magician. It seemed to me that Bert was doing something like what I did, a kind of sociological experiment. He allowed things to unfold, creating an environment far more conducive to psi than what was allowed in standard parapsychological experiments.

For example, I once brought two rose buds, one for Katie and one for Bert's research assistant (there were romantic implications associated with this event). The research assistant found that, while the rose was in her hand, it opened into full bloom. Later, I asked a florist if this was unusual.

"That's not possible," the florist told me. "That doesn't happen."

I later met Chinese parapsychologists who described similar experiences. A group of their subjects held flowers in their hands before an audience. The observers saw the flower buds open before their eyes.

I tell these stories to reveal the social phenomena surrounding Randi's hoax. Phillips, Uphoff, and Schwarz did not reduce their belief in PK, nor realize the value of bringing magicians into their experiments. Randi hoaxed them. I include my own experiences so that readers might understand what happens when someone experiences PK. There is always the possibility of a hoax, but being hoaxed does not seem to reduce the probability of future experiences. In my own case, I was familiar with seeing false PK since I had witnessed so many psychic surgeries and other sleight-of-hand shamanic performance in the Philippines. By 1983, I believed that some PK was real but had no way to determine if any particular instance was real. If real, PK seemed to have characteristics that prevented it from being proved in a way required by mainstream scientists.

CHAPTER 9
BELIEF

Friday, August 6, 1982, Oregon, Wisconsin

On Friday morning, the first day of the conference, I went down to Walter Uphoff's basement office. Manfred Koge, Uphoff's German photographer friend, was sitting in the main room with Steve Shaw, Masuaki Kiyota, and David Fuchs (Koge's assistant). They were conducting an experiment with the two metal-benders. I considered them all my friends and shouted a cheerful hello.

"Look at this," Manfred called out. "Masuaki did that." They had a spoon propped up in such a manner that if anyone pushed or pulled on it, the force would cause it to fall over. The spoon was twisted and bent with the head drooping down. Masuaki was pointing at it, apparently attempting to cause another twist. They had set up two cameras to document the experimental results.

"Did you catch any of this on film?" I asked Manfred.

"The camera is broken," he said, laughing.

"And the other camera?" I asked.

"Broken also," he said, and everyone laughed. Perhaps they had done the perfect experiment, but they had no documentation of it. Yes, I thought. That is why the spoon bent for them, because it will not be documented on film. No one would believe it.

"It is very strange," Koge said. "We don't know what is wrong with the cameras. They both worked perfectly before. Maybe someone broke them."

"Yeah," Steve said. "There is too much technology around here."

"Did Masuaki touch the spoon when it twisted?" I asked.

"Yes, first he got it to bend down, then he touched it to get it to twist. He could not have put any force on it, because of the way it is propped up," Manfred said.

A good experiment, I thought. Still, someone may have tampered with the spoon. I had not seen the preparation for the experiment.

I looked at the spoon closely. The head was slowly bending upward. It was becoming unbent! Masuaki was not touching it. It was absurd! There would be no filmed record of this, but we could see it happening before our eyes.

It was my impression that everyone in the room could see that it was unbending, and David Fuchs said something like, "Look! It is unbending!"

Manfred agreed with him, and I said that I also saw that it was unbending. I don't think that Masuaki or Mike said anything. Masuaki was focusing his full attention on the spoon, trying to get it to twist by pointing his finger at it.

David Fuchs began taking still pictures with his camera. I thought it was funny. Who would believe his pictures? People would not accept Cox's mini-lab films; how could they accept still pictures of a spoon unbending? I took a photograph with my own camera. Why not? It would make a good souvenir. Masuaki was pointing his finger at the spoon with mock anger. He was trying to get it to bend, yet its head seemed to be rising very slowly, almost undetectably. Could I be certain that it was actually unbending without anyone touching it? I watched closely as the spoon head continued to rise slowly. Everyone became quiet. David Fuchs continued to take photographs. I moved to the other side of the room and took a second photograph.

Then I realized that this was my big chance. To do this as a trick, someone would have had to tamper with the spoon. I had observed it continuously unbend. I was certain of what I saw. There would need to be a thread attached to, or looped around, the spoon to create this effect. I lunged forward and felt around the spoon, searching for invisible threads while, with my other hand, I grabbed the spoon. I found no threads.

"Sorry to disrupt things, but this is important," I said. Everyone seemed stunned.

I carried the spoon into the next room. I made a point to type out a label and glue it on every spoon that I saw bend. I hoped that, someday, someone would do a metallurgical analysis of the paranormally-bent metal and obtain evidence that would help explain the bending. I set the spoon beside the typewriter and began to type. It was still unbending! I typed out, "M.K. 8/6/82," which stood for Masuaki Kiyota, August 6, 1982, the date of the bend (or *unbend* in this case). The spoon was still unbending, even as I typed. I checked it again closely. It seemed to have normal tensile strength.[1]

I glued the label on the spoon handle. Masuaki came over to the typewriter to see what I was doing. He was irritated that the spoon was doing the opposite of what he wanted. I looked at the spoon again. It *still* seemed to be slowly unbending! The head was coming up, closer to its original position.

"Do you mind if I try again?" he asked.

I hesitated for a moment. Should I allow him to touch the spoon? A skeptic might say that he switched my "test" spoon for another one, or tampered with it in some way.[2]

Does it matter at this stage? I thought for a moment about it. This was just another story to be added to the thousands of tales regarding the paranormal. Skeptics don't believe these stories. Masuaki was my friend. Even if allowing him to touch the spoon reduced its value as evidence, I should let him try to do what he wanted to do. The scientific endeavor was not really going anywhere. I had seen the spoon unbend. I had held it in my hand. I saw that it had continued to unbend. Nothing would change that for me. PK was real.

I let Masuaki hold the labeled spoon. He struggled for maybe two minutes, holding it in his hand, concentrating.

"I will put another twist in the handle," he said. He tried for a while but, after about three minutes, I saw only a slight bend in the middle of the handle. I did not see the bending occur because I did not keep my eyes focused on the spoon continually. The bend occurred when I averted my eyes. Eventually, Masuaki gave the spoon back to me. Its handle was now bent slightly and the original twist was still there.

I skeptically observed the bend in the handle. Masuaki could have done that by sleight of hand. I suppose the game is never completely over.

"You must get used to it before you can actually see it," he had told me previously. Perhaps I was ready to see the "unbending" and to know that "psi is real." But it seemed that I was not ready for a convincing repetition of such an event.

Everyone was in high spirits. I told Mike Edwards about seeing the spoon unbend beside the typewriter. "I finally believe!" I exclaimed. "There's no doubt."

He answered with the resolve of someone who has known the same thing for a long time. (What an actor!) "Yes, psi is real," he said.

I took a photograph of Manfred Koge standing beside Mike Edwards. They were beaming over the miracle that just had occurred. "Psi is real," Mike exclaimed. In retrospect, it was ironic.

Months later, I looked at this photograph. Mike had revealed that he was a magician and he had said that he saw Masuaki and Tom cheat. If Masuaki's "unbending" was done by conjuring, what was the secret? Perhaps it was a trick! But then I looked at the spoon. It had continued unbending in my hand

and while I typed the label.

That morning, I put my souvenir spoon among the clothes in my pack. I put it deep inside, where I felt it would be safe. I drove Steve, Mike, and Masuaki over to the conference hotel. The drama was drawing to a close. The principal actors were assembling. Steve Shaw, Mike Edwards, Masuaki Kiyota, Tom and Elaine Richards, John Hunt, and Lisa were there. Even James Randi secretly came to the conference in disguise. I saw an old guy who looked like James Randi, but the guy was wearing strange clothes. I did not recognize James Randi.

During the conference, Steve Shaw and Mike Edwards gave a demonstration of their bending ability. The audience was amazed! It seemed as if the spoons were bending right before their eyes. Masuaki was unable to perform before the audience but later did some twists for smaller groups.

Tom Richards talked about SORRAT and showed Cox's films of PK within the mini-lab. There was only a limited amount of time for my presentation. I told the audience that as a sociologist I had observed what seemed to be a continuum regarding the concept of "extraordinarity." Some beliefs, such as the idea that the earth is round, are accepted by almost everyone today even though the idea was not accepted in the past. Other beliefs, such as Darwin's theory of evolution, are accepted by some but not by others, even in the face of scientific support. The extraterrestrial nature of UFOs is accepted by over half of a random sample of people in the United States and a similar percentage believe in ESP. About one in three Americans believe in Bigfoot or Sasquatch. Only about one in ten believe in ghosts. My investigation of SORRAT focused on phenomena accepted by even a smaller percentage. Perhaps ten percent believe in psychokinesis, and very few would think that it possible for spirits to write letters.

The SORRAT phenomena differed from many farfetched claims because they were connected with profound meaning. Phenomena included raps, table-tipping, mini-lab films, and letters from spirits that urged us to believe in life after death. Death is a fundamental source of our anxiety, and the spirits seek to alleviate this distress.

My SORRAT investigation failed to authenticate paranormal claims, but it demonstrated how people in a small group can generate anomalous phenomena, which make people ponder life after death. I argued that, in the final analysis, beliefs are not evaluated by how they originate but by the effect they have on the people who hold them.

The next day, I left for the airport. I opened my pack to make certain that I had my prized souvenir spoon. I looked at it closely. It was unbent even more. Both the bent head and the handle seemed straighter. Did someone sneak into my room, open my pack, and tamper with the spoon? That did not seem likely.

I flew from Madison, Wisconsin, through Minneapolis, to San Francisco. After the plane landed, I decided to check my prized spoon while I waited for a bus at the airport. It was buried deep in my pack. I pulled it out and inspected it. It was not completely unbent and untwisted, but it seemed as if it had continued unbending and untwisting. I could see where it had formerly been bent and twisted (the metal was deformed), but it seemed to have restored itself close to its original shape. It had continued to unbend while in my pack. Did someone at the airport search through my pack and unbend my spoon? That idea seemed absurd. The spoon was alive! It could unbend on its own. It was continuing a movement that I had observed originally at the Uphoff's house.

I fell asleep in the San Francisco hotel room. I was too tired to consider my spoon. I planned to check it again in the morning to see if all signs of its having been bent and twisted had disappeared.

I woke up at four in the morning and checked the spoon. Its configuration had changed slightly. It had re-twisted half way! This is getting absurd, I thought. I needed to document what I saw. I photographed the spoon along with the other twisted and bent spoons I had with me. The others were controls. They remained as they had been before the journey. Could it be that someone in the hotel had crept into my room while I had been sleeping and re-twisted the spoon? No, that seemed unlikely. The door had been bolted shut. It seemed more likely that there was a problem with my memory, but there was no evidence that my memory was faulty.

I looked over my notes of the Wisconsin conference. I had documented the date, time, and circumstances of each metal-bending event I witnessed. I had noted Masuaki's original unbending of the spoon and then the spoon's continued unbending while I typed up the label and glued it on the handle. I had documented my observation at the San Francisco Airport; the spoon was untwisted. There was no reason to think that there was anything wrong with these observations.

I wrote in my notes: "Spoon has partially re-twisted, 4 a.m., San Francisco, August 8, 1982." These things are possible. I know that now.[3]

The drama comes to a close. We never can be certain exactly what paranormal events mean. We attach significance to them, labeling them as results of the mind, devil, entities, or God, and our beliefs evolve from them. We gather experiences and sometimes change our beliefs.

I watched the rain as I waited for the bus to the airport. I thought back to my days in Vietnam and India. Now I was returning to Asia, where I had encountered so many people whose beliefs differed from mine. I had come to learn that beliefs can originate with anomalous experiences.

I have attempted to bear witness to the events around me. I have observed others and I have observed myself. I have known when belief was present and when doubt was present. I have observed the ways that belief and doubt evolve and the ways that belief and doubt are thwarted. I hope that others will benefit from my experience.

PHOTO GALLERY

Author's bed in the Richards' basement while sleeping beside the mini-lab. (photo by author)

Mike Edwards (left), Manfred Koge (right), Steve Shaw (seated behind and to the right of Manfred) on August 6, 1982. (photo by author)

Masuaki Kiyota bending a spoon. (photo by author)

Masuaki Kiyota bending spoon while holding "control spoon." (photo by author)

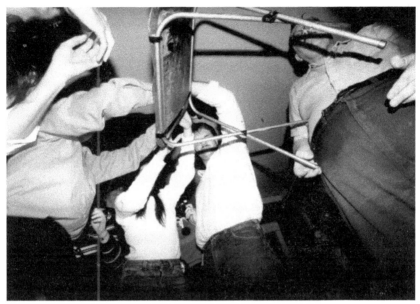

Tom Richards (right) seems to be holding leg of table during table-tipping session at Sky-rim, 1983 (photo by Dennis Stillings, 1991)

Mini-lab constructed by locksmith for W. E. Cox, 1982 (photo by author)

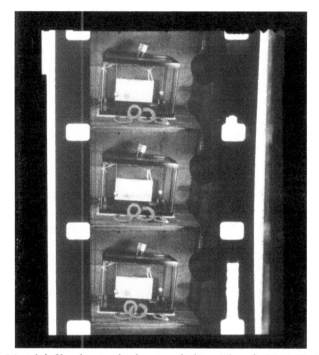

Mini-lab film showing leather rings linking (photo by W. E. Cox)

Original SORRAT members conducting table-tipping experiment
(photo by J. T. Richards)

Steve Calvin, assistant to W. E. Cox (photo by author)

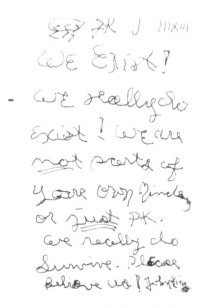

Example of early entity writing (signed by John King) (photo by J. T. Richards)

W. E. Cox in front of Entity Letters waiting to be answered mailed by the entities (photo by author)

Elaine and Tom Richards, preparing to do table-tipping experiment (Photo by author)

Plywood squares linked by entities (photo by J. T. Richards)

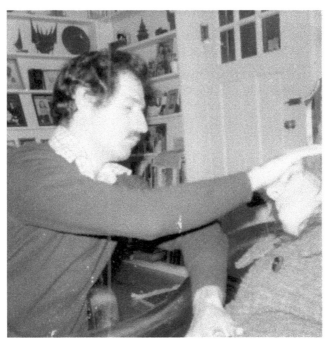

Joe doing healing at Skyrim (photo by J. T. Richards)

Photo of SORRAT table levitation (photo by J. T. Richards)

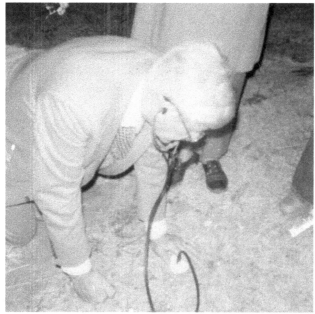

W. E. Cox listening to raps from the ground using a stethoscope (photo by J. T. Richards)

SORRAT photo of levitating table (photo by J. T. Richards)

John Hunt, SORRAT member (photo by author)

Typical photo of SORRAT table-tipping action. Table is up with hands still on it (photo by Dennis Stillings, 1991)

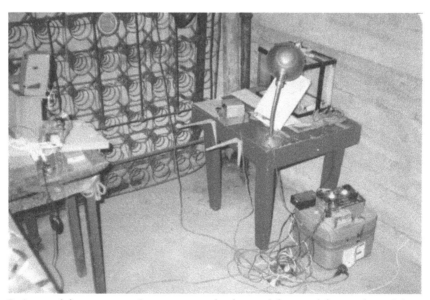

Cox's mini-lab equipment. Camera on wooden box on left; mini-lab on right with lamp, clock, pencil and paper, switching equipment on floor (photo by author)

Dr. John Thomas Richards (left); William Edward Cox (right) holding plywood squares (photo by author)

W. E. Cox holding plywood squares (photo by author)

W.E. Cox holding locksmith mini-lab (photo by author)

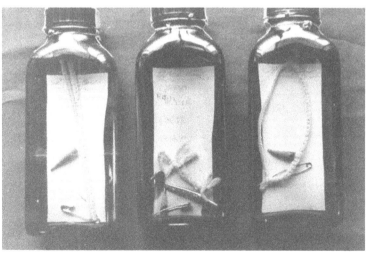

SORRAT sealed bottle experiment showing ostensibly paranormal bending and writing in center bottle (photo by J. T. Richards)

J. T. Richards (left) Masuaki Kiyota (right), Wisconsin, 1982 (photo by author)

SORRAT levitating table (photo by J. T. Richards)

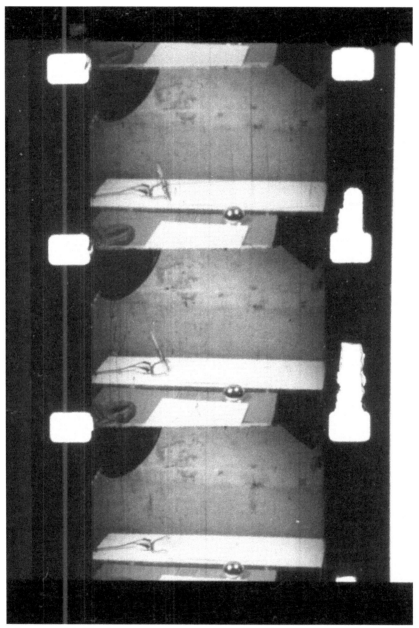

*Cox Mini-lab film showing pen writing – First film of pen writing inside mini-lab,
December, 1979 (photo by W. E. Cox)*

Pen photographed writing message by Cox camera device (photo by W. E. Cox)

Photo of pen writing entity letter message (photo by W.E. Cox)

Photo by Cox camera device of entity letter being written (photo by W. E. Cox)

Cox's locksmith mini-lab (photo by W.E. Cox)

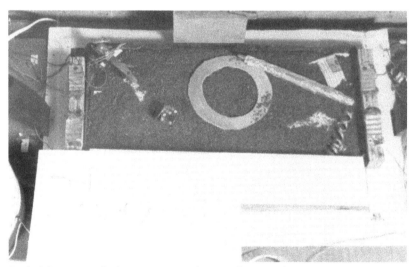

Early SORRAT coffee box experiment shows coffee grounds, material inside box and entity message, "Think." (photo by W. E. Cox).

PART 2 – THE ENTITY LETTERS UPDATE (2017)

CHAPTER 10
A SORRAT HISTORY AND UPDATE

The original *Entity Letters* manuscript focused on events in 1981 and 1982 with mention of early 1983 (Project Alpha). I visited Tom and Elaine Richards eight more times: 1983, 1986, 1988, 1992, 1996, 2001, 2002, 2004, and a final visit with Elaine in 2017. By the 1990s, I had given up finding a publisher for *The Entity Letters* manuscript, and no longer regarded my endeavor as a scientific study, but as a form of spiritual exercise. During those years, it seemed to me that SORRAT psi phenomena declined even though Ivan and his friends had many robust experiences.

Prior to my summer 1983 visit, SORRAT experienced a series of setbacks. FRNM and the McDonnell Lab presented results at the Parapsychological Association conference that pointed to fraud. The Alpha Project metal benders also accused Tom Richards of fraud. I suspect those events motivated Tom to invite some sympathetic researchers—Dennis Stillings, Loren Parks, and Walter Uphoff—to attend a séance at Skyrim in October 1983. During the session there, raps came from multiple places, the table jumped about and rose into the air (with hands on it), Joe went into trance and delivered spirit messages, and the room shook as if there was an earthquake.

Unfortunately for SORRAT, things did not work out as Tom had hoped. Dennis Stillings took a series of still photographs that implied that Tom was lifting the table. Loren Parks said that Joe was faking his trance and that Tom created the earthquake effect by flexing his knees (see their comments in Appendix A). Stillings sent a letter detailing his observations to a list of people interested in SORRAT.

These events turned out to be a turning point for SORRAT. Afterwards, Alice Thompson, who controlled access to Skyrim, showed less hospitality toward outsiders. For years afterward, whenever I met her, she complained about ungrateful, skeptical parapsychologists. Often, during SORRAT séances, she continued to complain, and my impression was that her attitude often reduced or thwarted the phenomena. The table might move around, but

I suspected that people pushed it. There were no more major earthquake effects in my presence. Skyrim raps continued to remain anomalous but did not demonstrate ESP as they had done for Cox. Sometimes, nothing happened at all, except for Alice's complaints.

In 1983, I asked Tom about his thoughts regarding the previous setbacks. "When people have their hands on the table, it can't be considered evidence," he told me. "Only when everyone's hands are off the table should it be considered evidence. People shouldn't regard other things as important. Not every experiment works. We don't like being treated like laboratory guinea pigs. In the long run, the truth will come out, but it hurts to be treated like this."

Elaine was also hurt and particularly angry at FRNM and the McDonnell Lab. "They shouldn't have treated us like that," she said. "It isn't our fault that things didn't work out as they had hoped."

I asked Tom to help me assemble a chronological history of SORRAT experiences. Previously, he had told me many stories about the past, but I wanted to get a better understanding of what factors facilitated PK. He said that rapport was the most important factor, but I had no way to quantify that variable.

"Dr. Neihardt was also a key factor," Tom told me. "It all began with him. He was the Poet Laureate of the Plains States and author of the book *Black Elk Speaks*. People wanted to be around him. I was a student at the University of Missouri, Columbia, while he was poet-in residence there. I took a class with him in 1959, and I got to know him afterward. We even exchanged letters. He told me that his wife, Mona, had been somewhat of a psychic, and after she died in 1958, he experienced a poltergeist in his house. In 1960, he told me that he planned to form an experimental PK group, but I moved to Arizona to teach high school, so was not closely involved in the planning. He had a philosophy about the interconnectedness of all things, and he thought the key to generating PK was group rapport. When I came back to Columbia in the fall of 1961, he had me recruit students for the group. The idea was to develop sufficient rapport so that we could get PK."

"How long did you meet before the phenomena began?" I asked.

"We met every Friday beginning around the end of September. Nothing happened for a long time, but we were developing rapport. Then, on November 17, 1961, we heard faint rapping from the floor. Dr. Neihardt sent people to try to figure out what was making the rapping sound. I was in the basement when they heard more raps."

Tom continued telling me about SORRAT's history. He was a graduate student, older than most of the others, and was given the role of observer and note taker. As the sessions continued, the raps grew louder and moved from place to place. They seemed to come from within the floor. The first raps were probably made by Black Elk, Neihardt's friend.

"In later sessions, the table seemed to move around, but when people's hands were on it we could not say for sure if it was PK or not," Tom told me. "When the table moved or levitated without anyone touching it, we were sure. Some people went into trance and gave messages from the spirits. Sometimes we took photographs of the table levitating."

In 1962, Tom completed his Ph.D. classwork, married Elaine, and moved to Snowflake, Arizona, where he taught high school for three years. He returned periodically to attend SORRAT sessions at Skyrim. The phenomena continued to be robust: loud rapping, table levitations, the room shaking like an earthquake.

Tom accepted a tenure-track position at Southeast Missouri State University in Cape Girardeau, Missouri in 1967. In September 1967, he organized a weekly table-tipping group. The participants, mainly college professors, experienced extremely robust phenomena, parallel to those reported by the original SORRATs: raps, table movement and levitation, object levitations, earthquake effects. SORRAT was experiencing a high point. Various SORRAT groups got results, and no particular person was required for phenomena to occur.

SORRAT experimental methods became more sophisticated. SORRAT members contacted the FRNM parapsychologist J. B. Rhine, seeking advice. Rhine suggested attempting to document PK by seeking effects within fraud-proof, sealed containers. Dr. Neihardt and the SORRATs prepared a container and got sealed box PK effects in 1967. In 1969, Ed Cox constructed a sealed transparent plastic box containing sensitized paper, upon which the spirits left writing—Old English, Celtic runes, and pictographs. He continued constructing boxes, sometimes with the test box locked inside another box. Ostensibly paranormal effects continued.

Skeptics suggested that a laser beam might have caused the spirit markings. SORRAT member Vern Mottert constructed a sealed box containing aluminum foil in place of paper. Paranormal writing appeared on the foil inside the box. Vern constructed a number of these boxes and continued to achieve ostensibly paranormal results. A Mottert box was kept for display at Skyrim, Neihardt's home, as a souvenir of a memorable meeting.

In 1970, Ed Cox began periodically visiting the SORRAT group in Columbia, Missouri, with more sophisticated sealed containers. Cox left a sealed container with Tom Richards in 1971. These early experiments were proto-types for his later mini-labs. He believed that he had verified signs of para-normal activity, but he may also have detected signs of fraud (see Rogo's com-ments in Appendix A). Cox told people that the SORRAT phenomena had a capricious, ambiguous nature. Although it was robust, it was extremely quirky. He had tested and verified its ESP ability, but it typically did not perform as requested. Cox did not feel that this quirkiness was unusual; he had encoun-tered similar "hiding qualities" during previous field investigations, but the SORRAT phenomena manifested this feature in more extreme form.

Although SORRAT attributed their success to rapport, Cox did not always contribute to that goal. His rigid scientific orientation and abrasive personality made some people uncomfortable. Ed Cox and Alice Thompson clashed and, after a series of arguments, she denied him permission to attend sessions at Skyrim.

I encountered other evidence of SORRAT conflict. "Alice sometimes puts on a show when the energy was low and not much was happening," a SOR-RAT member told me. "She goes into trance to gain attention. I don't find her spirit messages to be that useful, but others might think differently. Also, it looks like she pushes the table around sometimes. I can't say anything for sure, but that's what it looks like to me."

Later I saw a videotape of Alice during a Skyrim experiment. She seemed to be pushing the table around with her hands (see the video, "SORRAT 2 – Table-tipping," listed in Appendix C; other SORRATs also seem to push and lift the table).

Around 1970, Cox suggested that Tom Richards contact parapsychologist Raymond Bayless in Los Angeles. Bayless, who had published books about the paranormal, was considered an expert on Spiritualism and table tipping. In 1971, Tom and Elaine visited Bayless at his home in Los Angeles. Accord-ing to D. Scott Rogo, Bayless felt their séance, conducted in complete dark-ness, was fraudulent. I suspect it was equivalent to many I had witnessed in Rolla. Strangely enough, Bayless engaged in a kind of fraud himself. He lifted his side of the table, released it, observed that it fell, and assumed that Tom had lifted the other side (see Rogo's comments, Appendix A). Tom Richards later implied that he used "artifact induction," hoping that authentic phenom-ena would result (a derivation of Batcheldor's theory, described by Michael in Chapter 1). The fact that Tom and Elaine Richards agreed to conduct an experiment in complete darkness suggests to me that they did not expect it to be easy to get phenomena during this session.

Tom told me that many times there was no phenomena for months. The SORRATs had no explanation for these "dry spells." One such period ended on an Easter Sunday when the raps suddenly burst forth with a message about the Resurrection.

Tom was denied tenure at Southeast Missouri State University in Cape Girardeau in 1971. Tom and Elaine believed their SORRAT activity had harmed his academic career. Tom encountered strong resistance to his dissertation's portrayal of Neihardt's mystical philosophy, an orientation that advocated PK research. He became increasingly aware of the stigma associated with PK experiments, and he adapted a more cautious attitude when discussing SORRAT with outsiders.

Tom returned to Rolla in 1972 and taught as an adjunct professor for various colleges, particularly Columbia College at Ft. Leonard Wood. This became his source of income for the rest of his career. He organized a Rolla table-tipping group that experienced robust phenomena but was subject to periodic dry spells. Although the Rolla group witnessed many table levitations, Skyrim was always thought to have more robust phenomena. According to the entities, this was because it was located on a ley line crossing, a confluence of psychic energy. The entities refer to a British mystical tradition which argues that ancient spiritual sites in England were built on spiritual/magnetic lines (ley lines), in harmony with occult forces.

Cox found that, among SORRATs, Neihardt and Richards were the most open to scientific research. After Neihardt's death in 1973, Cox turned most of his attention to Tom Richards in Rolla, particularly after his relationship with Alice at Skyrim became problematic.

Almost from the beginning, results from sealed box experiments included spirit messages. There was a continuum regarding anomalous quality and complexity. The first spirit writing, a kind of automatic writing combined with PK, occurred in 1966 and consisting of four letters. The message was thought to have come from Neihardt's deceased wife, Mona. The first spirit writing inside a sealed container occurred in 1969. SORRAT found writing inside sealed or locked containers at various places and times between 1971 and 1978. Messages consisted of mirror writing with crudely formed letters.

Cox moved to Rolla in 1977 to focus his full attention on SORRAT. He brought his first mini-lab to Skyrim where it remained for a year. The Rolla table-tipping group included Tom and Elaine Richards, Ed Cox, Steve Calvin, John Hunt, Harold Cleveland (who dropped out in 1980), and various others. With the help of Steve Calvin, Cox set up a camera in the Richards' home, designed to begin filming when a pen moved. The system documented anomalous phenomena on its first night in operation; the pencil lifted out of its cradle, activating the camera. Later, the camera captured the pen upright and moving, as if writing (in my opinion, these movements are symbolic rather than actual writing).

Cox, with the help of Steve Calvin, devised an automatic film camera, triggered by micro-switches so that the camera could film mini-lab PK activity. Cox carefully locked and sealed the mini-lab with the idea of precluding fraud. The first four filmed PK events occurred in Tom Richards' house (Dec. 1978 - Jan. 1979). Perhaps because John Hunt was experiencing active poltergeist phenomena in his apartment and Tom Richards was not considered a PK agent, the mini-lab was moved to John Hunt's place (Jan. 1979-May 1979). One instance of ostensible PK was filmed before John moved to St. Louis to start his career as an engineer. The mini-lab was then moved back to Tom Richards' basement (May-July, 1979) until Harold Cleveland, a new member, reported poltergeist phenomena. Cox placed the mini-lab in Harold's basement where the camera documented ostensible PK (Sept. 1979 - Jan. 1980). In January 1980, it was moved back to Tom Richards' basement where it remained until December 1982.

Although skeptics tend to assume that Tom Richards fabricated the films, many segments were filmed in other people's residences. The theory that an alternate system was constructed to fabricate the films does not consider unique marks on the various mini-labs visible in the films (theoretically these marks might be duplicated but this would require a high degree of skill). Some skeptics suggest that the locks were cut off and replaced, but the locks also have unique features.

Some film segments were extremely anomalous. One segment shows a pen inside the mini-lab writing a message while a paper spontaneously bursts into flame. Another film segment shows an empty balloon rising up and a thread tying itself around the balloon's neck. The balloon then inflates and deflates repeatedly, pressing the objects around it with each inflation. It would be extremely difficult, perhaps impossible, to create these images through stop-action photography using Cox's equipment (see videos "SORRAT: Society for Research on Rapport and Telekinesis, 1961-1981," "SORRAT Mini-lab experiments, 2004," listed in Appendix C and Steve Calvin's comments in Appendix A).

It might be possible to devise such a theory explaining how Cox could have produced his films through normal means, but no one has offered such a theory. The parapsychologist Tony Cornell had his students produce a parody stop-action film under uncontrolled conditions. Cornell's students removed the back glass of the mini-lab to facilitate their stop-action photography. This film duplicated the jerky quality of Cox's films, but it did not duplicate the more anomalous scenes (paper bursting into flames while other PK activity occurred, for example). It might be possible to produce such a film if there were no security involved, but it would require a high level of skill and special equipment.

Cox continually tightened his security measures, devising hidden traps to catch tricksters. In response to criticism by parapsychologists, he replaced the original mini-lab with a mini-lab constructed by a locksmith in 1982. The camera documented two PK events within the locksmith's mini-lab (coins passing through the mini-lab glass face) before it was replaced by a McDonnell Laboratory mini-lab. All in all, about 15 rolls of 8mm film were exposed by the Cox automatic filming device, with about 5% showing PK activity. The McDonnell Laboratory mini-lab camera captured images of moving objects, but these films were not regarded as evidential by the lab director, Peter Phillips. (There was a strange impersonal characteristic regarding the way the McDonnell Lab treated the Richards; I think this attitude did not contribute toward the rapport thought necessary for success.) In the end, the Richards felt that they had been treated poorly by the parapsychologists, and Elaine refused to allow further mini-lab experiments.

I began my investigation in 1981, a time when the table-tipping phenomena apparently was less robust than in previous years. Vern Mottert photographed a levitating table in 1976, and many other SORRATs showed me similar photographs, but I never witnessed this phenomenon myself. John Hunt, who joined SORRAT in 1979, told me that he, also, never witnessed a full table levitation.

In 1983, I brought a video camera to Rolla to record interviews, rapping, and table-tipping experiments. Although I did not expect to verify anomalous phenomena as authentic, I successfully documented raps and table tipping (see "SORRAT Experiments, 1983, Appendix C). The video showed people locating the exact point on the floor where the raps were emanating. The group discussed possible ways that the raps' vibrations could be captured visually, like spreading iron filings or coffee grounds on a sheet of paper and placing it at the origination point. For some reason, few raps were audible during the initial session when I played back the videotape. SORRATs have noted that the entities sometimes "erase" audiotaped evidence. Virtually all the audiotaped raps I recorded, over the years, have been erased.

SORRAT raps have a quality that differs from the sound made by a knuckle, foot, or tool. They sound as if they originate within the floor. Sometimes the table generates rapping sounds by raising and lowering two legs and this creates an alternate sound, different from the internal-origin raps. While in Maryland, in 1982, I copied numerous tapes that Tom had lent me. At the time, I felt these tapes accurately documented rapping sounds. Later, I found that the raps were inaudible—an *erasing* phenomenon. The erasing phenomenon has also been reported by Australian poltergeist researchers (Healy and Cooper, 2014).

Colvin (2010) conducted acoustic analyses of raps associated with other researchers' poltergeist and PK group cases. He found that these raps had a low frequency profile, distinct from raps made mechanically. His findings implied that these raps originated under the surface rather than on the surface. I had previously sent a tape recording of raps to the American Society for Psychical Research, but no analysis was ever conducted.

My 1983 videotape also shows a table-tipping session. The participants have their hands on the table top when two of the table legs rise. The participants remove their hands from the table and the table remains on two legs. The participants hold their hands above the table surface, and it remains on two legs. I ask Tom Richards to move his foot under the table legs to show, for the camera, that the legs are clearly off the floor. He complies, demonstrating that the table legs are clearly up. I inspect the table closely to verify that it is not leaning on anything. The angle of the camera is such that skeptical observers cannot be certain the fraud is not occurring since the end of one table leg is not visible due to the camera angle. After inspecting the table closely, I pushed it with my hand. My impression was that it provided no resistance. The table descended gently so that all four legs were on the floor. Although this performance might be duplicated by a magician, it is an example of the types of experience SORRAT members report.

During one scene on a 1983 videotape, I asked the raps to say *hello to the camera*. The raps laboriously spelled out the message "HELLO TO THE CAMERA." The table-tipping group put their hands on the table, and it appears that Tom pushes the table with his hands toward the camera (muscular movements?). He removed his hands from the table and the raps made Black Elk's drumming signature (see "SORRAT Experiments, 1983," Appendix C; 43:30 min. into the video). I remark that raps are coming from the floor, and the raps have the sound quality that coincides with those coming from the floor. This video turned out to be the high point in my documentation of SORRAT phenomena.

The table leaning, table moving, table rapping scenes constitute a kind of summary of my investigation: (1) The events seemed anomalous but could have been produced by a magician. (2) The phenomena acted as if they wanted to be verified. (3) The video evidence suggested that fraud or subconscious muscular movements masked (or transitioned to) possibly authentic phenomena (the transition from Tom's muscular movements to unexplained raps). (4) The phenomena behaved in a way that thwarted full verification (the table moved into a position so that the camera did not have a view of everyone during the "table on two legs" event or the "raps from the floor" event).

During my visit in 1986, the phenomena were less robust. Elaine was visiting relatives in Wisconsin, and I was told to expect less phenomena when she was not present. Although Tom, Steve, and I conducted table-tipping sessions, the messages and phenomena were not memorable, and I made no effort to videotape phenomena. Sessions held during later visits, with Elaine present, did not produce extremely robust phenomena, and during those years I did not regard attempts to verify the phenomena as worthwhile. Raps from the floor became less frequent, and Tom and Elaine began holding sessions in their basement in complete darkness, a situation that reduced the ability to verify the phenomena as authentic.

Although table-tipping phenomena declined, entity letter writing increased until about 1990, and then continued unabated for about a decade. (I could not monitor actual volume but base this statement on copies I received in the mail.) On average, perhaps three or four people received answers about once every two weeks with about 25 participants overall. Each person might receive between one to three pages of handwritten text. Answers were always mailed to some other SORRAT member than the one submitting the question, and members were expected to forward the letter to the person who made the request. The entities explained that the purpose of mis-mailings was to increase rapport among SORRATs.

There were weeks when the volume of letters far exceeded the average. If the letters were being written by a human, it would have required hours of daily effort that included setting up unusual postmarks at places such as Deadwood, ND; Bethlehem, PA; Spiritwood, ND; Loveland, OH; and Tombstone, AZ. The trickster would have to figure out a way of getting postmasters to put false dates on some letters. The trickster had a quirky personality—putting childish stickers on the outside of the envelopes and putting miscellaneous objects inside that recipients found meaningful and including plastic steak markers that said "medium" inside each envelope.

The entities offered obtuse explanations for the phenomenon. For example, they wrote that time travel was possible due to "unstable" time gates affecting the "space/time continuum" that were governed by "ley convergence energy." People seeking to "visit an alternate version of reality or temporal era" could do so by locating exact transfer points using a special "fish-harp" (symbolic Celtic device for mystical use). The entities provided a design for this device, which required a crystal, to a SORRAT member in Oregon. She had the fish-harp constructed and believed that it facilitated phenomena.

I grew bored with the high volume of letters between 1980 and 1990. At first, I carefully saved all letters and filled about twelve boxes with them. As the years went by, I made no effort to encourage people to send me copies of their entity messages. I had hoped the letter writing might generate paranormal evidence, but this did not occur. If written by a living person, the phenomenon implied a strange hobby or perhaps a form of pathology. Eventually, I threw virtually all the boxes of letters in the trash. They constituted a fire hazard. Like typical personal correspondence, they were designed for individual needs rather than a universal message.

Between 1982 and 1996, I attempted to replicate SORRAT phenomena by forming PK groups. I organized groups in Wisconsin in 1982, Maryland in 1986, and in North Carolina in 1996. Each group lasted about two months. The group in Elizabeth City, NC, came closest to achieving success but did not generate any phenomena during group sessions. In 1996, I brought three Elizabeth City participants to Rolla with the hope of increasing our probability of experiencing PK during our regular meetings. I invited Dr. Emily Edwards (Professor of Communications, University of North Carolina, Greensboro) to accompany us. Dr. Edwards hoped to document SORRAT phenomena with a broadcast-quality video camera.

During this visit, the spirits rapped, the table moved, but the activity was less robust compared to previous visits. Dr. Edwards interviewed SORRAT members and my PK group participants. Her documentary portrayed social-psychological aspects of the group dynamics but did not verify the phenomena as paranormal ("Talking to the Spirits: A Pilgrimage," Appendix C). Perhaps in response to previous problems with outsiders, Alice Thompson did not allow us to visit Skyrim. Although we did not experience group PK after we returned to Elizabeth City, two participants later reported poltergeist-like events in their home.

I presented a video, produced by Dr. Edwards, at a Southern Sociological Society conference. The video discussed sociological theories regarding cult recruitment (Lofland and Stark, 1965; Stark and Bainbridge, 1980; Snow, et al., 1980). It included a segment showing Cox's locksmith-sealed mini-lab experiment. The film shows coins, on separate occasions, flying through the glass face of the locked and sealed mini-lab (see "Wondrous Events in a Small Group: A Field Study," Appendix C). The narrator in the video, reading text that I provided, hypothesized that anomalous phenomena influenced ancient shamanism, since anthropologists have witnessed paranormal phenomena (tent shaking and poltergeist-like effects) equivalent to those reported by SORRAT.

During my later visits, the phenomena were often weak and sometimes non-existent. I took few field notes during these visits, except for final interviews in 2017.

I remember a time when I was sitting at the kitchen table with Tom and Elaine, looking at some of their photograph albums. Like most SORRATs, they kept books of photos taken during table-tipping sessions. Some images showed tables levitating without anyone touching, but a few photographs showed people with their hands on the table, sometimes with a thumb under the edge while it was up in the air.

"Sometimes we worry that you might harm us," Elaine said to me.

"Why would you think that?" I asked.

"People are skeptical," she replied.

"Is it because some photographs show people holding up the table?" I asked. I was looking at a photo showing Tom's thumb supporting a rising table.

"What can we do differently so that people will accept what we are doing?" she asked.

"Don't let your fingers slide under the rim of the table," I said. "It looks like you're holding up the table with your thumb or fingers in some of these photographs."

"When the table goes up in the air, it's natural for the thumb to slide under the rim," Tom stated. "That's why you see so much of that in the photographs. Everyone knows that table-tipping doesn't prove anything when people's hands are touching the table. That's why we don't regard the experiment as a success unless the table remains in the air without anyone touching it."

I found this conversation uncomfortable. I had never seen a levitating table. Tom indicated no awareness of why people were skeptical and why these images were interpreted as indicating fraud. Tom sent a photograph to British psychical researcher Kenneth Batcheldor in which he appeared to have the table leg caught in his belt while he had his hand on the table top. Batcheldor expressed concern about this image in a letter to me. He was amazed that Tom showed no awareness that the photograph seemed to indicate fraud.

"Doesn't Tom realize what the photograph implies?" Batcheldor wrote.

"I don't think he realizes that the image implies fraud," I answered by mail. "For him, the image is just documentation of the kind of thing that happens during PK experiments. I think he believes that the table paranormally moved into the position captured by the photographer. It is as if the entities frame participants so that it seems that they are engaging in fraud."

I asked Tom and Elaine, "Do you ever cheat? Do you lift the table up or push it around?"

"We never cheat," Tom said.

"*They* make it seem like that," Elaine said, referring to the entities. "Maybe they do it to make the skeptics leave us alone."

In their book about Australian poltergeists, Cropper and Healy (2014) described parallel fraud-like events. The poltergeists seemed to have an awareness of how images would appear on camera and apparently were able to thwart attempts to fully document paranormal phenomena. Invariably, an object or a person's body would block the camera's view during a crucial stage of the poltergeist manifestation. The trajectory angle of poltergeist-thrown objects would be such that the photographic image was ambiguous, implying fraud. Resulting photographs cast suspicions on core figures, so that skeptics regarded the cases as hoaxes.

Tom wanted me to continue interviewing SORRAT members, but I told him that I had stopped doing interviews. I told him that sociologists did not seem interested in SORRAT. Tom seemed to ignore my resistance to his idea.

"In 1979, Harold Cleveland asked for our help," Tom said. "He was old then, so he must be really old now. He had a poltergeist problem, and we did what we could to help him. He was involved in many SORRAT experiments and had some powerful experiences at Skyrim. I'm sure he has some meaningful things to tell you."

At the time, I did not realize Harold's importance among the Rolla SORRATs (Cox's mini-lab had been in Harold's basement from Sept. 26, 1979 to January 4, 1980 where it documented PK activity). I had not heard Harold's name mentioned previously.

"Some former SORRATs don't like it when I call them," I told Tom. "They don't want to be involved with SORRAT anymore. Why hasn't anyone told me about Harold before?"

"Harold was upset by the poltergeist in his house, and he did not want to continue meeting with us," Tom told me. "We haven't kept in touch with him. This would be the perfect chance to interview him. We are going to the county fair where he is the Grand Marshal, so we can be sure that he will be there. He didn't stay with SORRAT because he wanted to become a politician."

I told Tom again that I was tired of doing interviews. I thought the matter was settled. I had previously called a man whose telephone number Tom had provided, and the guy had expressed deep irritation. "I saw it; I know it's true, but I don't want to talk about it," he told me curtly. "Don't call me again. No one around here believes in it, and I don't want to talk about it." I was afraid that Harold might have a similar attitude. If he wanted to talk about it, he would have stayed in touch with Tom.

While we were at the state fair, Tom abruptly walked off, leaving me with Elaine and Ivan. "He really wants you to talk with Harold," Elaine said firmly. Tom returned after a few minutes.

"Just stand here for a while," Tom told me. "We will be by the concession stand. Harold does not want me to be present while he talks with you." Tom, Elaine, and Ivan then quickly said good bye and walked off.

I found the situation strange, but I stood there, waiting for Harold. He approached and introduced himself. He was an old man, probably in his 80s, but he spoke clearly. I told him I was investigating SORRAT.

"Tom came over to my house when I was having some poltergeist problems," Harold said. "He did some table-tipping sessions, and I also visited Skyrim. I know the phenomena are real. I had some astonishing experiences at Skyrim and at Tom's house, and I can't explain those things. But there's something you should know about Tom. I caught him doing sneaky things. One time, I caught him carrying some ice cubes into my house. That was something that the spirits did. They left ice cubes sometimes when they did PK. I was really surprised to catch him carrying the ice cubes. I guess he was going to put them out so that we would think the spirits did it. I know you're investigating PK, so you need to know about this. I don't know what Tom would say; he might deny it, but I know what I saw. He does sneaky things, even though the phenomena are real."

Harold seemed uncomfortable talking to me. Our conversation was brief. I was startled by what he said and did not conduct a formal interview. What he said made me feel tired inside. I had hoped to avoid a negative interview. I was upset that I had become involved in such a strange situation. I forget the exact question I asked, but it was something like "Why did he do that?" and Harold said, "I don't know, but he did it."

I did not know how to evaluate what Harold had told me. I walked back to where my friends, Tom and Elaine, were standing. I was shocked by the idea that Tom would do something like that. The ice cube event Harold described reminded me of the ice cube I discovered when Cox's mini-lab was smashed. The parallel motif led me to believe that Harold was telling the truth. Harold's story was not the type of thing that someone would fabricate.

"Harold told me that you took some ice cubes over to his house with the idea of putting them out so that he would think the poltergeist did it," I said to Tom.

"He's an old man," Tom said. "He's confused. We never did anything like that."

"We don't do things like that," Elaine said. "He was troubled, and he probably doesn't remember things properly. He was old when we knew him, and he's probably not in good health. His memory is probably flawed. He must be imagining things."

I don't think Harold was confused. He seemed like a reliable witness. He considered me a scientific investigator, and he was providing relevant information.

I pondered the situation while driving home with Tom and Elaine. I was sad and angry and did not know what to say to them. They were liars. People suggested that Tom did things while in trance, but it was hard to imagine him doing something that complex without remembering what he did.

Perhaps it was an extension of table tipping, I thought. First you push the table around without realizing that you are doing it. Later, you grab and lift the table without being aware of it. Maybe there is a progression of dissociated behavior; you become able to do increasingly complex actions without being aware of them—increasing levels of dissociation. Eventually, the phenomena take over and the entities are in control. Could this occur without other dissociative symptoms? The skeptics assumed that Tom cheated, but perhaps he cheated while in trance.

The entities, or perhaps Tom, seemed to want me to discover this. The entities revealed their own fraud regarding the cancellation marks on the letters. They were cheaters, and like Tom, they seemed to want me to figure out what was happening.

I decided to learn more about dissociation and mental disorder. I hoped to determine how Tom and Elaine were different from other people. Years later, I worked as a social worker in a psychiatric hospital. I had the chance to interview and counsel people suffering from psychotic, dissociative, and bipolar disorders. I became familiar with the symptoms associated with these disorders. I realized that Tom exhibited no symptoms suggesting dissociative identity disorder beyond going into trance at times. The situation was puzzling, but psychical research involves puzzlement.

A third possibility was that Tom and Elaine were engaged in a life-long hoax, simulating the SORRAT phenomena through slight-of-hand, film production skills, literary stamina, and all manner of other forms of deception. The problem was that anyone who knew Tom and Elaine could not accept this hypothesis. Tom and Elaine did not have the qualities or skills required to pull off such an elaborate hoax. The hoax theory was suitable only for people unaware of Tom and Elaine's circumstances. The hoax theory involved a paradox. Perpetuating a hoax required skillful behavior, but Tom had not been skillful enough to sneak ice cubes into Harold's house without getting caught.

I searched the psychical research and hypnosis literature to learn more about fugue states. Sometimes mediums spontaneously slip into trance, under the control of a spirit. I also had stories about fugue states within the collection of anomalous experiences I had assembled as part of another study. One respondent, a college professor, told me that he had woken up one morning wearing muddy clothes. Later he learned that people had seen him walking about in the night, seemingly in a fugue state. He had uncovered some unknown human remains and moved them to a more suitable site. When he woke in the morning, he had no memory of these actions. In other stories, people fell spontaneously into trance and spirits spoke through them. They did not engage in complex behaviors. As part of previous research, I had interviewed Asian shamanic practitioners who went into trance and performed pain immunity and fire-walking feats. I was familiar with people who could go into trance and speak with spirits. Tom's behavior did not seem parallel to this—but, on an alternate level, it all seemed the same. The spirits were tricky.

The medical literature describes fugue states. People embark on unplanned travel or wandering, and sometimes they establish a new identity. Fugue states can last for days, months, or longer but, typically, when the fugue state ends, the person's memory returns. Tom's behavior did not seem equivalent to this. He showed no signs of remembering trance behavior.

I make a list of my hypotheses: fraud hypothesis, spirit hypothesis, group consciousness hypothesis, "Tom in trance" hypothesis, "Tom cheats consciously" hypothesis, "Group conspiracy" hypothesis. I had no way to logically assign probabilities to these ideas. I knew that PK could occur, that Tom was responsible for at least a few artifact effects, that Tom was not responsible for all the effects—but I had no explanatory theory. Some people suggest that there was a "mixed mediumship" syndrome; they believe that many authentic mediums during the Spiritualist era cheated. These mediums mixed authentic phenomena with fraud, but there was no theory that allowed testable hypotheses allowing scientific progress.

Skeptics and believers avoid logical analysis by using heuristics to evaluate ambiguous situations. Skeptics often use the heuristic "what I see is all there is." They search their memories to determine what exists. If they have not had an anomalous experience, they decide that such things cannot occur. Believers remember anomalous experiences and make a leap of faith, explaining their perceptions as due to deities, spirits, or psi. As a result, the believers and skeptics are not required to seek further explanations because they felt they already had the answer. Non-belief is a type of belief. I hoped to avoid this dilemma by coming up with an explanation that fit my observations.

It seemed doubtful that any of my existing hypotheses would generate scientific agreement. I needed a new hypothesis. In 2001, I invited my friend Amanda Mosher, Michael (a videographer), and a member of the Parapsychological Association (who wishes to remain anonymous) to help me investigate SORRAT. Michael brought a special infrared video camera. On his first evening in Rolla, he demonstrated the camera to Tom Richards and Steve Calvin, and left it unattended while he went out for the evening. When he returned, he found that the camera's cassette frame had been bent, rendering the camera inoperable.

The situation seemed parallel to the smashing of Cox's mini-lab. Someone or something did not want this line of research to continue. Had Tom broken the camera to prevent it from seeing him cheat in the darkness? Did the entities cause the damage? Months later, Tom told me that Steve Calvin had accidentally bent the metal frame while testing the camera. I did not get the chance to ask Steve about this.

Michael turned out to be very resourceful. The next day, he went to a camera store and exchanged his damaged camera for an equivalent loaner. He then videotaped hours of SORRAT experiments, many of which took place in complete darkness. He also made video of a séance at Skyrim. My impression was that little or no paranormal phenomena occurred during these sessions. One aspect of the Skyrim session was interesting, though. The table rose into the air dynamically and some feathers, allegedly from Black Elk, appeared magically on top of the table. The parapsychologist seemed interested at the time; she wanted a feather as a memento of the evening's events. It seemed to me that Tom and Alice were pushing the table around, and I was embarrassed that I had brought visitors to see such a poor performance. At the same time, I felt that the emotional element was important. If the group developed rapport, they might be able to generate authentic PK.

Some unusual things happened in Rolla. Ivan was attracted to Amanda, and I think the entities were acting as matchmakers. They had made a similar attempt with John Hunt and Lisa. When Ivan first met Amanda, two ceramic figurines, male and female, on the Richards' piano, changed the direction they were facing so that they faced each other. Everyone denied responsibility, so I considered this a possible poltergeist event. Anyone could have moved the figures; the event could not be regarded as proving psi. It was absurd! As the relationship progressed, the figurines moved closer to each other (Ivan was attracted to Amanda). Later the figurines moved even closer and touched, symbolic of developments in the relationship. Then, the figurines turned away from each other, simultaneously with Amanda's gentle rejection of Ivan. Each figurine movement reflected an attraction or rejection. Whoever was moving the figurines showed astonishing empathy, moving the objects concurrently with actual events. Tom and Elaine were not in position to monitor Ivan's relationship that closely, and Ivan was too involved in the situation to have done it himself.

The parapsychologist was irritated that nothing could be verified as paranormal. She seemed interested in the Skyrim séance but found nothing evidential in Rolla.

"You won't be able to understand what is going on by just watching," I explained to her. "It is an experiential process."

"I need an explanation," she stated.

I told her about the medium Mina Crandon, who had been caught cheating back in the 1920s. When Mina was lying on her deathbed, the researcher Nandor Fodor invited her to confess.

"All you psychical researchers can go to hell," Mina told him. "You'll all be guessing for the rest of your lives" (Tietze, 1973: 184-5).

"That story is a lesson for us," I told the parapsychologist. "We will not come up with definitive answers."

"I have to know," she responded. "This is totally unacceptable."

I marveled at the obscurity of the figurine event. Like most SORRAT phenomena, it conveyed little information beyond empathy and the possibility of being paranormal. The "need to know" led to the heuristic processes I described previously. By assuming that a particular hypothesis was valid, one can achieve certainty through a skeptical or believers' assumptions: (1) What I see is all there is, or (2) The spirits did it. The nebulous *collective consciousness* theory does not explain much. None of these choices is completely satisfactory.

After everyone returned to their homes, the parapsychologist asked that her name be removed from SORRAT's mailing list. She did not wish to be involved with a case that might involve fraud.

By 1996, I noticed that Ivan was playing an increasingly important role in SORRAT. He and his friends held séances without Tom and Elaine being present. His friends showed me sealed containers holding objects bent by PK inside. They told me about seeing tables levitate during séances. I got the impression that the phenomena they witnessed were less robust than those experienced by early SORRATs, but I was jealous anyway. I had never seen a table levitate.

There did not seem to be much chance that I would see much since the phenomena seemed to be declining. I remember when Tom, Steve, and I decided to drive to a park one evening. We sat in Tom's car and discussed what we might do to get some phenomena to occur.

"We could pretend that it is happening," Steve said. "That might stimulate it."

"Sometimes there isn't much we can do," Tom explained. "They have their own way of doing things. Maybe we just have to be patient."

We sat in silence for a while. I made some raps with my foot. I wanted to see how Tom and Steve would react.

"That doesn't sound right," Tom said.

"Was that you, Jim?" Steve asked. I was silent. I felt embarrassed and did not say anything.

"That did not sound like them," Tom said sourly.

Then the raps began sounding faintly from the car floor. I could feel the vibrations on my feet.

"That's sounds a lot better," Tom said, cheerfully.

"That's the real thing," Steve agreed.

Tom and Steve tried to determine which entity was rapping. "Who is it?" Steve asked. A series of raps began spelling out a letter, but it seemed to die out before completion. Steve asked again; the raps made another attempt but again faded out.

"Jim stimulated them," Steve said. "The energy was low but they came anyway."

I was beginning to understand why Tom might push the table around. My fake raps seemed to bring authentic ones. Artifacts stimulate real results. It was like priming a pump.

In 2004, I returned to Rolla but there were no phenomena. On my last night, I joined Tom and Elaine for a table-tipping session in their basement. I did not expect anything to occur. As we sat in absolute darkness, I heard raps and felt the table move, but I couldn't see anything because the darkness was absolute. It seemed to me that the raps were made by the table moving up and down and hitting the floor, a situation I regarded as suspicious. It had been years since I had heard raps emanating from the floor. Then the table began moving up and down vigorously and I heard an unexplained tinkling or rattling sound beside me. I felt a surge of excitement. The feeling reminded me of the thrill I had experienced so many years before at Skyrim. The entities had returned! I tried to photograph the levitation but my flash would not work.

"That's typical," I thought. "They prevented me from documenting the phenomenon but this is remarkable. I haven't felt this way for many years. I like this feeling! This is why I come to Rolla."

When Tom turned on the lights, I saw the source of the sound. A long bench extended along the wall. Someone had placed little ornaments on the bench, close to where I sat. I pushed the bench back and forth and found that the ornaments rattled, making the sound I had heard. The bench was positioned in a way that Tom could hold the table up with one hand while shaking the bench with his other hand. It seemed obvious to me that someone had set up this trick to induce my experience in the darkness. I assumed Tom was responsible.

I felt troubled that Tom, my friend, would resort to such a crude trick. I was deeply disappointed. I remembered what Mike Edwards had told me. "Tom Richards is a magician, but he's not a very good one."

A few months later, I described my experience to a SORRAT member who was a strong believer. She had done some interesting experiments while alone in her own home. Some material had entered a bottle that she had sealed. Now, she was alarmed at my skeptical attitude.

"Too much has happened over the years for you to become skeptical at this stage," she said. "I'm editing Ed Cox's manuscript right now. Dr. Schwarz has asked me to prepare it for publication. Your skeptical attitude could spoil things for everybody."

I did not see how I was at fault. I felt alienated from SORRAT. The SOR-RAT members hoped that Cox's book would change people's beliefs about SORRAT, but my close relationship with Tom had led me in the opposite direction.

Cox's book, *Psi Physics*, was published in 2004, ten years after his death. I was surprised to find that a chapter that he had shown me years before had not been included in the book. Cox often mentioned the capriciousness of the phenomena. He had uncovered many instances where the "agency" (his term) seemed to imitate fraud. He felt that quirkiness was a characteristic of the agency. He told me about some of the strange scenes within his films. In an early "pen writing" film, a pen rises and, for a few frames, a thread can be seen attached to the pen. Then the thread disappears. This happened on two occasions. "Why would they do that?" Cox asked me. "Who would do something like that? Those images suggest fraud, but the locks, seals, and booby traps state otherwise."

Cox mentions the appearing/disappearing thread phenomenon in a SOR-RAT video (Appendix C: SORRAT: Society for Research on Rapport and Telekinesis, 1961-1981). He also told me about another film anomaly: in a single frame, a large object within the mini-lab disappeared. The object reappeared in the next frame. This event could not be detected when watching the film at normal speed. It was as if the entities were sending a hidden red flag—they simulated stop-action fraud. There were other strange events that Cox had discovered. The shadow of some leather rings appeared in position before the rings moved into that position. Objects, such as rings or ESP cards, become transparent before they were affected by the PK process. Ed told me many other times that he planned to include this chapter about the quirky phenomena. But in the end, this information seems to have been omitted.

I did not see Tom again during his lifetime. He experienced medical problems in 2014 and died in 2015 at the age of 78. Elaine told me that, afterward, she heard faint raps from the floor, but that we should not expect Tom to come back. "He did not want to be reincarnated again. He did not expect to return after he kicked the bucket."

In March 2017, I visited Elaine and Ivan, hoping to gain further insights. My wife suggested that they might tell a different story now that Tom was gone. "People want a resolution at the end of your book," she told me. "You have a final chance to let Elaine and Ivan tell the truth."

I stayed in the Richards' home in Rolla as I had so many times in the past. Elaine, at 78 years old, was slow and unsteady of gait. Ivan, whose health had always been fragile, suffered from cancer of the esophagus. He was in a hospice and his physician expected him to die soon. Elaine was experiencing severe stress, watching her only son struggle with end-of-life issues.

Elaine and I visited Ivan every day, and I cooked meals for Elaine and Ivan's two children. I searched through Tom's office for his notes regarding PK experiments.

"Some people think that Tom wrote the entity letters," I said to Elaine. "Could Tom have slipped into trance and written them?"

"We didn't write those letters," she replied. "I was in the house with Tom all those years, and he didn't go down to the basement much at all. He did not write those things. We left those letters down there and let it happen. There's letters down there right now. They've been there since Tom died. I guess they needed his energy to write them, but he didn't write them."

"Did he go into trance sometimes?" I asked.

"He did sometimes, but not very often. Alice and Joe went into trance. When nothing was happening, Alice would go into trance for a show, but Tom wasn't like that. There is a kind of way of thinking that allowed the things to happen. Some people were really disturbed at the beginning by the levitating tables, but Tom and I just went along with it. I didn't get my mind in a set pattern, and I always believed that things could happen. Maybe that's the reason I experienced the things I did. Tom was like that also. Some people were afraid of it, and I think that's why they think the way they do. If you don't get your mind set in a pattern, things can happen. Tom did not write those letters. He just let it happen. They took the form that they did because they were connected to him in a way but he did not write them."

"What about Harold, the guy with the haunted house?" I asked. "He told me that he caught Tom trying to sneak ice cubes into his house."

"Tom never did anything like that," Elaine explained. "We never did anything like that. Harold was sick in those days. His wife was very afraid because they had a low-level spirit in their house. I don't know why Harold would say something like that."

I asked Elaine about times when the phenomena seemed most active. I hoped she might have ideas regarding why the phenomena came and went. I noted that Tom had not been very clear about what seemed to cause it to come and go.

"Certain people seem to help it happen," Elaine said. She went on to tell me a story I had heard many times before. She had taken a photograph of the spirit Myra when it was dark outside. When they developed the film, Myra was on the grass, sitting in the sunshine. The shadows around her indicated it was afternoon, but Myra, herself, left no shadow. I looked through their books of photographs and found Myra's image.

"What does this story signify?" I asked.

"Myra made it happen," Elaine said. "She was the one who did it. She wanted to show us that she was real."

Elaine told me about the lights that flashed across the sky one evening. "I think it was in 1965," she said. "It was like a UFO, but it was very colorful. We were coming back from Skyrim after an incredible session, and it was late at night. There were other people on the road and they saw it. Some stopped their cars and they pointed at it. It was even in the newspaper the next day. It was remarkable for me because it was so surprising. The Skyrim levitations and the earthquakes were remarkable, but we were used to those things. It became slightly boring after a while because we had experienced those things so many times. That's what made those lights so remarkable. It was something unique."

What does this mean? Certain people facilitate phenomena, but they do not cause the phenomena. Tom and Elaine allow the phenomena to occur, but they did not cause Myra to reveal herself or lights to flash across the sky.

"Not much has happened in recent years," Elaine told me. "It has been declining for a long time. Ivan and his friends got results, but that group did not stay together for long. We did not have much happening for the last 10 years. I still hear light raps, but it isn't like it was before. A doll moved in the basement last week. It was in a jar, and the next day I found that it had turned around. That's the only thing that has happened in recent months. It has been very quiet for many years. I think that entities are helping Ivan, though. The doctors are surprised that he is still alive."

I went down to the basement to inspect that area where the spirits had been most active. Some entity letter requests were laid out on the work bench. They were dated 2014, a time when Tom first became ill. The letter phenomena were obviously connected to Tom's consciousness. It stopped when he became sick. Ed and I had found many correspondences between Tom's mind and the Entity Letters: misspellings, grammatical errors, phrases, specific knowledge, and story themes. We also found that the writing phenomena had anomalous characteristics. There seemed to be a progression in the writing phenomena regarding how anomalous it was. It started off with very brief messages inside sealed containers – very anomalous. It was something that the SORRATs came to accept as valid. Then it became more complex: Old English with Celtic runes and pictographs. Then the sealed containers became more sophisticated,

and Cox generated films with pens writing but the messages were simple—
"Rethink time," for example. I facilitated the Entity Letter phase because I
hoped to get paranormal evidence, but the phenomena seemed to be on another wavelength. The messages indicated that rapport was important and that
there was life after death.

The Entity Letter phenomena may have used up some of the SORRAT
energy because séance phenomena seemed to decline when the writing was
most robust. But there were events during the 1980s that suggest otherwise.
For example, the spirits linked two plywood squares that Cox had prepared.
The squares had a square hole cut in them, allowing the possibility of linkage.
At the time, this seemed like a remarkable achievement. The rings were sent
out for laboratory analysis, but their authenticity could not be established. The
experts said that they would have to destroy the linked plywood squares to
determine if they have been linked paranormally. They suggested that a skillful trickster may have pried the plywood sections apart to create the illusion
of paranormal linkage.

Afterward, a NASA scientist provided metal rings made of extremely rare
alloys. The SORRATs asked the entities to try to link these rings since it would
be impossible for a normal person to create the special alloys. According to
SORRATs, the rings linked while in the hands of Alice Thompson during a
Skyrim séance. This seemed to be a remarkable achievement, but the NASA
scientist refused to allow his name to be associated with this experiment, and
the results were never published. These events occurred during an era when I
was not monitoring SORRAT closely. I did not interview witnesses so I cannot vouch for the validity of this story.

The entity letter experiment floundered on for year after year, long after I
lost interest in it. In 2017, I noticed that Tom had many boxes of entity letter responses in his basement remaining from the decades of the letter writing
experiment. I visited Ivan to talk about his experiences with the entity letters.
I knew that he had written and received many letters from the spirits. The
entities had told him that he was a crew member on a time travel ship, Lynx,
active in future millennia. His participation would occur during one of his
future lifetimes.

"Do you think all the entities letters are authentic?" I asked him.

"The stories might be part fiction, but the part about the Lynx is true,"
Ivan told me.

"Is it possible that your father wrote the messages?" I asked.

"I've thought about that," Ivan answered. "There were many things happening when I was a teenager. I know that the levitation and rapping phenomena are real, but I could not monitor the letter writing completely because I often stayed at my grandparents' house. I particularly wondered about the Lynx. Could it be true? Did I have a future life as a crew member of the Lynx? One evening, when I was 17 years old, I was looking out the window of my room at my grandparents' house, and I saw a blinking light. It traveled along the horizon, and then it went back in the other direction. It seemed like an airplane, except that it maneuvered in a way that seemed strange for an airplane. I asked a question in my mind, 'Are you the Lynx?'

"It stopped blinking immediately, and I knew that was a signal," he continued. "The answer came into my mind: it was the Lynx. It became brighter. It was communicating with me. It was watching me. It started moving again and blinking, like before. I asked another question: "Can you change your color?" It did not change its color, but it maneuvered around in a manner that proved it was not an airplane. I asked it, 'Can you become brighter? Can you make my room brighter?'"

Ivan paused for a moment. I had heard this story before but never in such detail. "Immediately, my room filled with light—and it became VERY BRIGHT. It was alive. It was BIG MIND! I was terrified. It was so bright that I could not stand it. I said in my mind, 'Enough!' and it turned off immediately. It was gone, and I knew that it was the Lynx, a ship with the technology of the future. It was overwhelming, totally overwhelming. I was completely convinced by it.

"Later, I received entity letters that included drawings, designs for the different components that allowed it to travel in time," Ivan told me. "They told me that I had been a crewman, and they sent a woman who tried to contact me. She talked to various people I knew, asking about me. They said she was strange and had blue hair, but I never met up with her. We came close to meeting one time, but it did not happen. I guess I'll meet her in my future life."

"You believe in the Lynx," I said. "What about the entity letters?"

"There's a message for us in this," Ivan said. "I have to accept the information I have. My father told me about a story he wrote when he was young about a time-travel ship. The entity letters seemed to have built on that story. It is as if they are using his mind. Many of the entity messages were like that. They built on ideas in my father's mind. I accept that. Do you believe in time travel?"

I thought about his question for a moment. I had no firm beliefs about time travel. I searched my memory for something I could say. "Your father told me a story about the early SORRAT group," I said. "They got together in somebody's room, and they tried to focus their minds so that they could go forward in time."

Elaine joined us at the table and listened to my story. "The sunlight dimmed and it was night, then it became light, and that happened two times. They seemed to go from Thursday to Saturday—two-days forward in time. One of them, I think it was Terry Kilpatrick, wrote a letter to himself, and he went to a mailbox and mailed the letter. Then he returned to the room, and they time-traveled in the opposite direction, returning to Thursday. Later, they received the letter through the mail. It was postmarked Saturday. Their friends said they saw Terry walk down the street on Saturday. 'He was walking funny,' they said. 'He looked like he was drunk or in a daze.'"

"I heard about that," Elaine said. "They were all dizzy. It was a risky experiment because they might not have been able to come back. They got the letter by mail, and it was postmarked on Saturday. Tom, Joe, and Terry were there. They tried to do it again, but they were not successful. I don't think Tom ever wrote about that because he didn't think people would believe him. It was one the many things that happened in those days. A lot was going on in those days and much of it was beyond what people could accept."

I was puzzled about how to proceed. I had hoped to get Ivan to confess to something so that I might have a good conclusion for my book. Most people don't believe that spirits can write messages, and I was hoping I could end things in an acceptable way. Instead, we were going off in a strange direction.

Elaine went back to the front desk to use the telephone. She needed to set up a time to pick up Ivan's children from the lady who was caring for them.

"I know about that experiment," Ivan said. "You interviewed those guys about that, didn't you?"

"Yes, they said it happened," I acknowledged.

"Then you know that time travel is possible?"

"For me, it was just a story," I said. "I write down what people say, and I look for patterns. That's the kind of research I do."

Ivan sat silently thinking.

"I wondered if time travel could be possible," Ivan said. "I knew that the table could levitate, but I was curious about time travel. Then I had experiences that convinced me."

I was taking notes as he spoke. I wanted to capture his exact words.

"What conclusions should people draw from SORRAT?" I asked.

"People make their own timeline," he said. "I believe in the Lynx, and I am on that timeline. There are degrees of belief. The further you go, the more real it becomes. For me, it is completely real and that makes the Lynx real. Belief makes it real."

This was the belief/skeptic paradigm, I thought. Seek and you shall find. People, at various times, have asked me if I think the entity letters were the result of paranormal phenomena or fraud. To me, it is a question of probability. Within quantum mechanics, the observer determines the answer to questions of probability. Skeptics see fraud; believers see paranormal phenomena. I was somewhere in between. I saw both fraud and paranormal phenomena.

I seems to me that in modern times, the skeptics have the upper hand, but I suspect the believers will eventually have their day. The phenomena will happen no matter what. I drew on my experiences working in the psychiatric hospital. I believe that all the different forms of mental disorder exist on a continuum. They occur in ways that are not pathological. I have come to realize that the SORRAT woman who was alarmed at my skepticism was probably correct. My scientific way of thinking probably thwarts PK from happening. If I could become more dissociative, I might compartmentalize things in my mind so that PK could happen around me even though I had been exposed to things that implied fraud.

Elaine returned from her telephone call. I asked her about what conclusions people should draw about SORRAT.

"Healing," she said. "That is what is important, but people will have to discover that for themselves."

Okay, I thought. That can work, but how does one achieve the powerful belief that lets it happen? It seems to me that Tom, Elaine, and the Asian shamans I had interviewed, were similar in that they allowed the phenomena to use them. The entities used Tom's hands to move and lift the table, carry ice cubes, and do other things. Belief had somewhat brought them into existence, but they required human consciousness as part of that process. I remained a scientist, so I could not completely believe in them. My role was merely to observe them. It seemed as if the merging of the different forces—the group, the individual, the mental constructions of the group and individuals who came to life—resulted in a powerful ambiguity connected to a trickster. As a scientific observer, I would not be able to figure it out but, by being merely an observer, I would end up writing about it.

Later, I spoke with a scientist who was familiar with SORRAT. He did not want me to mention his name because he wished to preserve his reputation. "Tom was not capable of doing all the paranormal things connected with

SORRAT," he told me. "He may engage in fraud at times—pushing the table around or holding it up in the darkness—but he had no deep knowledge of photography or film production. He could not have created those mini-lab films. He was not skilled in that area. Elaine did not have those skills either. The phenomena were like a wild animal, different from human consciousness. It had the skills to make the SORRAT phenomena; Tom did not have the ability to do it."

The scientist was alarmed when I told him that I wanted to publish his words in my book. "I would not have said those things if I had known that you would publish it," he said.

"I won't reveal your name," I promised. I understand why people are afraid of psi. There is something uncontrolled about it. People say that they are not afraid, but those who are familiar with it know that it can be scary. It is bad for your reputation, that's for sure!

I called John Hunt on the telephone. We had not spoken for over a decade. He was going to retire soon after a successful career. I asked him about his thoughts regarding SORRAT. Was he still a believer?

"You have to remember that I heard raps in my apartment when no one else was around," he said. "When I tested the entities, they knew what I was thinking. This stuff seems absurd, but we can't dismiss it completely. Are you familiar with the Philip Group experiment?"

"Yes," I said. "They created a fictional story about a ghost, and then did table-tipping to make PK using the story they invented."

"The story doesn't have to be true to work," John noted. "They proved that. When people get together, they can create stuff at variance with what is considered reality. That's what they proved. Our minds can create a paranormal reality. I don't discount the possibility of discarnate spirits, but the Philip Group experiment suggests that everyone may be creating what is considered reality. Humanity is creating a group consciousness, which we consider normal reality. A group like SORRAT can have a local effect. They could move the table and get raps, but the world at large will overpower them eventually. It depends on who observes the phenomena and on the credibility of the witnesses. It depends on the ability of the observers to influence others. The degree of credence of the observer affects the way information and beliefs are disseminated. Think about SORRAT's history. Cox was not connected with a research organization. He retired and came to Rolla. He was not a credible source of information. Because few people accepted what he said, he could observe and document PK. He even made films of PK, but because of his lack of credibility, he did not have much impact and that allowed him to do what he did. When a group of prestigious researchers, the McDonnell Lab in St. Louis, tried to replicate Cox's work, they failed. They had far greater impact, so there was less chance of them being successful. When you bring in prestigious observers, it keeps the phenomena from happening. Rhine's research group, FRNM, also failed to verify anything."

"I agree," I said. "And the closer you watch, the less likely that the phenomena will happen. When I slept in the Richards' basement, my presence seemed to thwart the phenomena. Because I watched the mini-lab closely, it could not produce PK before the camera."

"You're a sociologist, so you bring more credibility than a regular individual," John said. "The regular people photographed levitating tables. You and I did not see that, but others took photographs and they could do that because those images were not disseminated very far. The images could not compel much belief because of the way the photographs were taken and because of the level of credibility associated with the activity."

"How do you react when people say that Tom was cheating?" I asked.

"Let's think about why Tom Richards might have cheated," John said. "He might have wanted to fool you because you were doing an academic study. He wanted credible witnesses. But why would he want to fool me? I was not writing a book or anything. It doesn't make sense. There may be explanations for why he did certain things, though. He probably found that pushing the table stimulated belief and that led to authentic PK. The entities themselves may have had a hand in it. He went into trance sometimes. I saw him go into trance. The entities may have caused him to do unusual things, but in normal life he did not have the skills required to fabricate the mini-lab films. He did not have any special equipment or knowledge in that area."

"Everyone who knew him agrees with you," I stated. "But it's difficult for people who did not know him. They assign a very low probability to this stuff being authentic. They assume the probability of him being able to do it was greater than the probability that the paranormal stuff actually occurred."

"The consensual reality prevails in the end," John said. "SORRAT might make raps and levitate tables, but it can't do it consistently. SORRAT-like groups might emerge in the future, but they will be temporary unless someone works out the mechanics of the process."

"It might be difficult to do normal science regarding this stuff because our minds shape what happens," John continued. "The spirits seem to be inside us, but we don't know the degree to which they are autonomous. It's a tricky situation. I'm open minded about it. There could be souls of some sort, but there also seems to be a group mind thing going on. And there are things going on beyond our imagination. The spirits need the group mind, or at least it's helpful for them. It's probably a combination of processes, and the entities make it look like we are doing it. We might be doing it without being aware, but they also could be involved. There are many possibilities, aren't there?"

"I have no need to convince people one way or another," I said. "I'm trying to come up with hypotheses that others can test."

"People in the future will have to work it out," John said.

I returned home carrying 14 notebooks, filled with Tom's records of SOR-RAT experiments. His notes describe over 800 experimental sessions between 1962 and 2007. The accounts include date, location, participant names, starting time, names of those taking photographs, quantity and volume of raps, descriptions of anomalous phenomena such as levitations and apports, spiritual entities present, names of people going into trance, rap and trance messages, psychological and physical conditions, ending time, and experimental results. Some notes were taken while sessions were in progress, particularly regarding rapped messages. The narratives describe how levitating objects reacted to photographic flash: remaining still, vibrating, rising, gradually descending, or falling. He included diagrams showing participant seating, location of furniture, and object flight paths. Objects often descended anomalously or changed direction during flight, unlike something dropped or thrown. Anomalous phenomena included rapping sounds, table vibrations, table and object levitations, waves of rapport, earthquake effects, sealed box experiments, apparitions, and unexplained lights, odors, sensations.

Each experiment was classified as a *success*, *partial success*, or *failure*, depending on objective and result. A levitation experiment, for example, was deemed a *success* if the object remained in the air after all hands were removed. Evaluations were subjective since some experiments occurred in complete darkness. Criteria included height of levitation and time in the air. *Attempt at photography* was a criterion since this required that the object stay up long enough to be photographed.

I saw Tom taking notes during all the experiments I attended. The careful quality of his transcriptions implied that he sought to advance science rather than gain public acclaim. The notebooks in my possession appear to be the same ones I saw in in his hands, and in his office, over many decades.

I analyzed his narratives by tabulating key variables on a spreadsheet. About half the sessions consisted of only two or three people, but there was much variation. The maximum number of participants was 25. A major SOR-RAT goal was to photograph a levitating object; the notes reported that objects were photographed during 274 sessions. Tom's log books offer a sociological puzzle. Most parapsychologists rejected SORRAT claims. Why did Tom keep such careful notes long after scientific interest in SORRAT waned?

I read over the notes of sessions I had attended. The narratives coincided precisely with my memories. I focused on the report of my final session in 2004. Because of the darkness, I had assumed that Tom had shaken a bench and lifted the table, simulating paranormal phenomena. The account stated, "The bench vibrated several times" and "The table finally rose about eight inches." I read the notes regarding other experiments during that era. Many accounts noted the degree that the bench vibrated. Apparently, these move-ments were a measure of psychic energy, a kind of paranormal thermometer. Sometimes objects on the bench fell or flew about the room, suggesting *high* energy. I pondered the situation from Tom's perspective. His notes portrayed a believer's attitude. The slight vibration of the bench and the 8-inch levitation during my session indicated *low* energy. My skeptical interpretation placed me *outside* the SORRAT paradigm. Believers trusted each other not to cheat. To play the SORRAT game, you had to believe.

The notes were particularly precise during Cox's mini-lab experiments. Tom documented each time Cox inspected the mini-lab, the person who dis-covered mini-lab camera activity, time of discovery, ostensible PK effects, time of Cox's re-inspection of the mini-lab, and dates when films were developed. The texts noted "windows of opportunity" during which a trickster might have fabricated mini-lab films. He documented who was present in the house dur-ing those times. He described events when raps foretold the exact times when the camera had been triggered, information later verified when the films were developed. The tight clustering of mini-lab phenomena, small windows of opportunity, and frequent visits by Cox implied that a trickster had little time to fabricate the films—unless Cox was the trickster. I had been skeptical of the mini-lab evidence, but these notes supported Cox's claims. The notes were strangely sincere. Tom hoped to further the scientific understanding of PK.

Tom documented dates and times when the early entity letters disappeared from inside the mini-lab. These messages had been part of a progression of in-creasingly anomalous claims. In the end, experimental controls regarding all phenomena had been relaxed.

The notes portray SORRAT's final era as associated with higher rates of levitation success. Ivan recruited a stable group of college student friends who photographed many levitations (I interviewed two of them). Overall, there were great variations in individual levitation success rates. Certain people and groups achieved high success rates while others seemed to thwart the phenomena.

Narratives documented SORRATs going into trance. Joe went into trance during 68% of his sessions, while Tom's rate was 9%. Did Tom, without conscious knowledge, push and lift the table in the darkness? Did he write the entity letters in trance?

During my career as a psychiatric social worker, I conducted many therapy sessions with people diagnosed as suffering from psychosis, bipolar disorder, and dissociative identity disorder. They often failed to remember events during their psychotic breaks or when controlled by an alternate personality. Tom exhibited no symptoms suggesting these disorders. His experimental records reveal him to be an organized and methodical note-taker, aware of the anomalous quality of the phenomena he documented. If SORRAT phenomena were mainly fraudulent, these notes constitute a strange psychological curiosity.

Between 1982 and 1986, I observed and interviewed shamanic practitioners throughout Asia. I saw shamans, in trance, performing slight-of-hand tricks, heat immunity feats, and other forms of unusual, dazed behavior. Some observers claimed anomalous experiences during these performances. According to Batcheldor's paradigm, shamanic performances expedite anomalous experience. Trance, fraud, and artifact stimulate belief, facilitating authentic PK. The ambiguity associated with SORRAT helps PK to emerge—but not fully. PK has a hiding quality, camouflaged within a trickster's cloak. It is thwarted by our inability to believe in it but emerges in obscured conditions.

I see no value in arguing about the authenticity of past events. As a sociologist, I note that exceptional claims generate exceptional skepticism. The stranger the report, the greater the disbelief. Tom's experimental notes describe extremely anomalous events, *far* beyond what I report in this book. SORRATs heard raps coming directly from the floor. They saw objects levitate or move anomalously. They reported unexplained lights and felt the room shake as if there were earthquakes. The psychical research literature provides many examples of these paranormal phenomena. Some events, as with SORRAT, occurred repeatedly over many decades. For example, St. Joseph of Copertino, a 17th century priest, levitated on hundreds of occasions, seen by thousands of witnesses (Grosso, 2016). Although Tom describes things that most people cannot accept, his narratives are a piece in the psychical research puzzle.

Sociologists can contribute to this endeavor. Tom's notes reveal patterns regarding the probability of experiencing a levitation. About half of SORRAT levitation experiments were labeled, by Tom, as *successes*. Some participants were far more likely to witness success than others. Star participants experienced success during more than 60% of the sessions they attended. Others had success rates of less than 25%. These differences exceed what would be expected by chance. This evidence implies that the propensity for levitation experience resides, to a degree, within the individual.

Some SORRAT groups had high success rates. These groups consisted of (1) John Neihardt, Tom, Joe (2) Tom, Elaine, Joe (3) Tom, Elaine, Ivan (4) Ivan, Tom, Sean (one of Ivan's friends). Sessions that included these groups averaged a 70% chance of levitation success, above the individual average. These results imply that the propensity for PK experience resides, in part, within the group.

SORRAT history does not prove that psi occurs, but it supports a theory regarding the origin of religion. Paleolithic people probably experienced anomalous events both spontaneously and during trance. They spent thousands of years conducting rituals around fires, environments conducive to altered states of consciousness. Unusual experiences would have shaped their beliefs in shamanism, humankind's first religious form. Experimental groups, such as SORRAT, provide evidence that sheds light on how humans acquired shamanic beliefs.

Based on SORRAT history, I offer hypotheses, subject to evaluation: (1) Future PK groups will experience anomalous phenomena coupled with artifacts. (2) Some people are more likely to witness these phenomena than others. (3) Some combinations of people are more likely to experience phenomena than others. (4) Some people facilitate group PK while others inhibit it. (5) The phenomena have characteristics supporting shamanism.

These hypotheses imply existence of a kind of collective mind, an idea that coincides with the Batcheldor and Philip Group arguments. Groups achieving sufficient harmony can experience extremely anomalous phenomena. Through research, we can discover the factors that facilitate or inhibit these events.

PART 3 - THEORIES

CHAPTER 11
PSYCHICAL RESEARCH

Psychical researchers have devised theories regarding hauntings, poltergeists, and PK (sitter) groups using multiple paradigms. Houran and Lange (2001) discuss sociological, psychological, physical, and physiological perspectives. Batcheldor's (1966, 1979, 1984) psychological theory and Lucadou's (2015) quantum mechanical theory are particularly applicable to SORRAT.

Hauntings and Poltergeists

Analysis of haunting and poltergeist case collections shaped PK theories (Carrington and Fodor, 1953; Gauld and Cornell, 1979; over 500 cases; Roll (1976; Psychical Research Foundation; PRF; 116 cases; Huesmann and Schriever, 1989, IGPP; 59 cases; Spencer and Spencer, 1996; Healy and Cropper, 2014, 52 Australian cases; 3 other Asian cases). Modern researchers tend to attribute the phenomena to human consciousness rather than spiritual forces (Laursen, 2016). William Roll (1976), who coined the term recurrent spontaneous psychokinesis (RSPK), noted that a core agent was often present during poltergeist events. He hypothesized that this person subconsciously produced RSPK due to unexpressed frustration. Although the evidence supporting this theory is not strong, it provided a paradigmatic foundation for later theories.

Haunting and poltergeist case collections revealed patterns that future researchers might replicate. Gauld and Cornell (1979) found two overlapping categories using computer analysis of their 500-case collection: (1) hauntings, which implied a spirit source, and (2) poltergeists, associated with a living agent. Hauntings more often involved apparitions, had longer duration, and involved lower frequency of experience. Poltergeists more often included movement of objects and a particular person (the core agent). Poltergeist cases had shorter average duration and higher frequency of events. Experiential elements within poltergeist and haunting cases overlapped; some poltergeist cases had many apparitions and long duration, while some haunting cases included PK with short duration. During my own investigations, I often found it impossible to distinguish haunting from poltergeist cases.

The case collections revealed patterns regarding poltergeist agents. All agents were human; there were no animal agents. Agents were most likely to be teenagers (within the Psychical Research Foundation collection, age varied from 8 to 70 with a median of 14). Earlier cases were more often female, but modern cases revealed greater gender balance. Some agents were caught cheating, although in many instances investigators believed that other phenomena were authentic. Many poltergeist agents had psychological symptoms (Roll, 1976).

Poltergeist duration was generally brief. The 116 Psychical Research Foundation cases lasted for an average of five months with a median of two months. The 59 Institut für Grenzgebiete der Psychologie und Psychohygiene cases had a median of five months.

Most typical poltergeist phenomena involved object movements, knocking and rapping sounds, apparitions, objects appearing, and floating/flashing lights. Object movements revealed unusual features: (1) a focus on particular types of objects; (2) objects sometime changed direction in flight or had a velocity slower than of one thrown normally; and (3) some objects landed with reduced impact. Within many cases, phenomena revealed an astonishing ability to thwart documentation, showing an overarching awareness of camera angles and witness position so that researchers were unable to generate evidence fully supporting paranormal claims (Healy and Cooper, 2014).

I investigated 20 poltergeist/haunting cases and 15 parallel telephone counseling cases between 1983 and 1998. All cases contained people who might be regarded as agents but no agents were teenagers. Although many revealed psychological distress, none exhibited a special propensity to conceal their frustrations. Although these experiences reduced my faith in Roll's (1976) "unexpressed frustration" theory, the agents often had special qualities. I found that the person with the most previous anomalous experiences was always the one reporting the most haunting/poltergeist perceptions.

Between 1978 and 1990, I interviewed more than 33 Asian spiritual practitioners (China, India, Japan, Korea, Okinawa, Philippines, Sri Lanka, Taiwan, Thailand) and 17 American psychic practitioners (McClenon, 1994). Their accounts paralleled those of poltergeist agents, in that all reported anomalous experiences prior to becoming practitioners. Unlike typical haunting/poltergeist experiencers, they appeared to have a degree of control over their capacity for anomalous perception. I hypothesize that some people in all societies have a propensity for anomalous experience and that those who master this propensity become shamanic practitioners, a process that typically involves trance performance skills.

Over the years I collected thousands of anomalous experience narratives and conducted eight major surveys regarding anomalous experience (McClenon, 1994, 2002a). I found that certain experiential forms occur in all societies: apparitions, waking ESP, paranormal dreams, out-of-body experiences, synchronicity, psychokinesis, and spiritual healing. In general, people reporting many anomalous experiences developed powerful beliefs regarding spirits, souls, life after death, and magical abilities. These ideas formed the ideological foundations for shamanism, humankind's first religious form (McClenon, 1994, 2002a).

My SORRAT observations coincided with the poltergeist, shaman, and survey evidence. Core SORRAT members did not reveal a propensity for unexpressed emotion, but like shamanic practitioners, they described many anomalous experiences. Both SORRATs and shamanic practitioners described a series of anomalous experiences that shaped their certainties regarding the supernatural.

These observations led to testable hypotheses: (1) Core individuals within haunting/poltergeist cases are likely to have a history of anomalous experience. (2) People with a history of anomalous experiences are potential shamanic practitioners and, using initiation processes, can induce anomalous experiences in audiences. (3) Anomalous experiences shape beliefs, particularly regarding spirits, souls, life after death, and magical abilities (McClenon, 2002a; Braude, 2003). These hypotheses can be evaluated by sociological participant observation, anthropological research, and social surveys. Observation of groups experiencing PK may be a particularly fruitful area for investigation.

Batcheldor's Groups

Kenneth Batcheldor (1966, 1979, 1984) argued that PK depends on belief and devised a method for eliciting PK. He organized table-tipping groups in which people sit around a table with their hands on it, hoping that the table will move paranormally. He suggested that participants subconsciously pushed the table using subconscious muscular movements. He believed that groups exposed to this situation eventually overcame their psychological resistance to PK, and, as a result, they could experience authentic PK.

Batcheldor hypothesized that fear of psi, intrinsic to humans, thwarts PK. He believed that fear of psi is derived from two factors: (1) witness inhibition (the shock or fear associated with observing PK) and (2) ownership resistance (the fear of personally being the source of PK). He hypothesized that artifact effects, such as unconscious muscular movements, helped participants overcome their natural fear of PK, resulting in authentic PK.

A YouTube video (Kenneth Batcheldor Table Tipping [Improved Version] Part 1; https://www.youtube.com/watch?v=CyHjmtUhbWE), made in 1978, portrayed the process by which fear of psi is overcome. Video from an infrared camera showed a group in complete darkness with their hands on a table top. The table moved about from side to side. Batcheldor explained that the video did not prove that PK occurred, but illustrates how groups can achieve table movements that affect their beliefs. A later session revealed more robust phenomena; the table came up on two legs while the group had their hands on the table top. One participant pressed on the center of the table to determine if he could prevent it from moving. The table continued to move even though the others, with their hands on the table top, seemed to exert little effort.

A video of another group showed people with their hands on a 38-pound table (https://www.youtube.com/watch?v=oVqKW8AhnU4). They revealed little effort as the infrared camera documented table movements. This video also showed a progression toward more robust phenomena, which was attributed to increased belief. During the later session, the table slid about more vigorously and sometimes rose on two legs. All group members appeared to have their hands on the table top. These videos do not verify that the PK is real, but they demonstrate how groups can experience anomalous phenomena through artifact induction.

Colin Brookes-Smith (1973) explored the role of fraud as a way to generate belief. He randomly assigned one participant among the group to act as the designated cheater and found evidence, documented by his monitoring equipment, that paranormal phenomena occurred. Although he was unable to preclude all possibility of fraud, his experiment supported the hypothesis that fraud, which facilitates belief, contributes to increasingly robust phenomena.

Batcheldor believed that the obstacles inhibiting PK prevented its complete verification. After years of effort, he was unable to produce video-taped evidence verifying the authenticity of PK group phenomena. He reported various unusual events where the phenomenon seemed to "know" or "see" what the camera was viewing and actively prevented images that verified paranormal effects. He regarded this "hiding quality" as an inherent aspect of psi. His observations of psi's capricious characteristics coincide with those of many psychical researchers, including myself (McClenon, 1994).

Batcheldor's theory harbored a hidden premise. He argued that a kind of group-mind produced psi, but at the same time the human mind prevented psi from occurring. These results coincided with quantum mechanical theories of psi (Lucadou, 1994). Batcheldor's theory also coincided with a kind of parapsychological folk belief (McClenon, 1994; Beloff, 1993). Some parapsychologists and New Age theorists suggested that the human mind creates a shared reality that can be disrupted by special conditions. This idea is in harmony with Asian spiritual traditions warning spiritual seekers to avoid attachment to anomalous experiences (*siddhis*) since the shared reality itself is a mental production.

The Batcheldor and SORRAT groups, although harboring different assumptions, had similarities regarding fundamental theories. Batcheldor regarded PK as a psychological phenomenon rather than a product of spirits. Dr. Neihardt, founder of SORRAT, advocated scientific research but had been exposed to Native American shamanism. Batcheldor advocated artifacts as a pathway toward belief, while Neihardt encouraged immediate investigation of ambiguous situations. Neihardt assigned special observers during séances and provided them flashlights to investigate possible artifacts and fraud. He encouraged use of tape recorders and cameras. SORRAT members checked basement pipes, furnace ducts, and floorboards while raps were occurring, seeking artifact explanations. They disassembled the arm of a chair from which raps had been coming, seeking hidden rapping devices. Although Neihardt, like Batcheldor, regarded skepticism as detrimental to PK, he found that active investigation of artifacts did not prevent raps from continuing. He believed that rapport was central to inducing PK rather than a tolerance of artifacts. We might hypothesize that SORRAT rapport reduced psychological boundaries among participants, lessening ownership resistance and witness inhibition.

Batcheldor's theory suggested that unconscious muscular artifacts led to beliefs that, when sufficiently robust, allowed authentic phenomena such as raps. SORRAT experience did not coincide with this model, since raps preceded early table movements. When they began experiencing table movements, they accepted Batcheldor's idea that unconscious muscular movements contributed to belief, enhancing the phenomena. Tom Richards (1984) published an article arguing that artifact induction, which included fraud, facilitated PK.

Survey research data and anthropological findings coincided with Batcheldor's observations. People reporting spontaneous anomalous experiences often felt unsure regarding the authenticity of their perceptions since many accounts probably reflected artifacts. Kennedy (2003) estimated that only 20% of reported ESP experiences actually involved psi. Yet these artifacts shaped people's beliefs regarding spirits, souls, life after death, and magical abilities (McClenon, 2002).

Many shamanic performances included artifacts contributing to belief. Trance performances included fire walking and fire handling (heat immunity), body piercing (pain immunity), and extracting evil substance from clients' bodies (slight-of-hand performance). These exhibitions generated beliefs producing hypnotic and placebo effects (McClenon, 1994, 2002a).

Some performances are parallel to table-tipping. Chinese cult-members, for example, hold a symbolic chair, upon which a deity is thought to sit. The chair, while in their hands, moves about, spelling messages in Chinese. Although the effect seems created by unconscious muscular movements, groups report gaining extrasensory information and spiritual healing (McClenon, 1994).

Philip Group

The Philip Group extended Batcheldor's theory. Dr. A. R. G. Owen assembled an eight-person sitter-group in 1972 with the goal of demonstrating that actual spirits were not required to produce Spiritualist phenomena (Owen and Sparrows, 1976). They devised a shared narrative regarding a fictitious spirit that they named Philip. According to their story, Philip was a mid-1600s English aristocrat who married Dorothea, the beautiful but frigid daughter of a neighboring nobleman. One day, while riding on the boundary of his estate, Philip encountered Margo, a beautiful dark-eyed gypsy girl, with whom he instantly fell in love. Philip secretly kept the girl in a gatehouse near his stables until Dorotha found out about her. Dorothea accused Margo of sorcery, and Philip, concerned about his reputation, remained silent. Margo was convicted of witchcraft and burned at the stake. Philip, filled with remorse, committed suicide by jumping off a battlement.

The group hoped this story would help them induce a mutual apparition. They meditated together weekly but, after a year, were not successful in collectively seeing Philip. They contacted Batcheldor, who suggested they lower the lights, sing together, and adapt a more playful attitude. His suggestions seemed to work. Within three or four sessions, the group heard raps from the table, seemingly from Philip. The raps could answer questions—one rap for yes, two for no. Over time, Philip could move the table, sliding it from side to side even though the floor was carpeted.

Philip's responses implied that he was a collective creation, since he could not provide information outside his biography. If the group agreed regarding a particular answer, Philip would answer quickly, but if they were not in agreement, his response was hesitant or non-existent.

Philip (the group's subconscious or perhaps artifacts) acquired increasing ability to move the table anomalously. Sometimes the table came up on two legs or left the floor completely. The group placed doilies under their hands to rule out the possibility of unconscious muscular movements, yet the table moved anyway. Philip became able to cause the lights to dim or brighten when requested to do so. He could also make a cool breeze blow across the table when asked.

Philip's performances were documented on camera during two television programs (Laursen, 2016). The cameras portrayed table knocking, odd noises, and lights blinking off and on. The group and film crew witnessed the table levitating slightly, but the camera failed to verify this effect.

By the fall of 1977, the group grew tired of performing, and when Philip's activity declined, the experiment ended. The group's inability to completely verify the phenomena coincided with Batcheldor's experience.

Although the exact procedure was unclear, the Philip Group established what seemed to be a replicable methodology. As with SORRAT, the group adopted Batcheldor's paradigm even though they did not originally use unconscious muscular movement to instill belief. A second Toronto group met for five weeks before successfully "contacting" the fictitious spirit Lilith, a French-Canadian spy. Similar experiments achieved success with other fictitious entities: a medieval alchemist named Sebastian, a man from the future named Axel, and a 16-year-old Australian girl, Skippy. As with previous experiments, these groups could not fully verify the phenomena they experienced.

I made three attempts to replicate these experiments by organizing weekly groups, each lasting about two or three months. None of these groups were successful. On a later occasion, I organized a single session during which participants heard an unexplained scratching or rapping sound that all present denied making. This group included a woman who had previous table-tipping experiences. Based on my SORRAT experiences, I believe that special people facilitate group PK.

The Philip Group's use of a fictitious entity has implications for the scientific study of religion. Throughout history, charismatic leaders gathered followers who then experienced miracles. The Philip Group experience implied that a group's ideology need not be valid for miracles to occur.

Patterns exist within Batcheldor, Philip, and SORRAT experiences: (1) All groups were unable to verify the authenticity of their PK phenomena;

(2) SORRAT produced more robust phenomena for a longer time than did Batcheldor and Philip groups; (3) Elements within SORRAT history differed from the history of Batcheldor and Philip groups: greater acceptance of spirits, emphasis on rapport, accusations of fraud. It may be that use of spirits, rapport, and fraud reduce ownership resistance, as suggested by Batcheldor, but it is difficult to quantify these variables.

Comparison of existing videos of Batcheldor, Philip, and SORRAT table-tipping leave me with the following impressions. (1) Batcheldor and Philip Group members seem more animated, communicating with greater excitement, than was revealed by 1983 SORRAT participants. This suggests that the 1983 SORRATs had less rapport. (2) All Batcheldor and Philip participants maintained firm contact between fingers and table top. In the SORRAT video, some participants allowed the table to slide under their fingers while Tom and Elaine Richards maintained firm contact. The images give the appearance that Batcheldor and Philip groups shared responsibility for the phenomena to a greater degree than did the 1983 SORRAT members. My impression of that era was that SORRAT members assumed that Tom and Elaine generated the phenomena paranormally.

Based on these observations, we can devise a working hypothesis regarding PK group success. The probability of success is increased by devising or accepting a narrative explaining the phenomena, developing rapport, tolerating artifacts, showing tenacity, using loose controls that do not preclude the possibility of fraud, and tolerating the idea that both spirits and special people generate the effects.

Parapsychological Research and the capricious quality of psi

As in psychical research, the field of experimental parapsychology has generated findings implying that psi actively avoids detection. Kennedy (2003) pointed out that: (1) Major parapsychological experiments, verified by meta-analysis, declined with further experimentation; (2) In many cases, the power of a psi relationship varied inversely with the reliability of its demonstration; the most reliable experiments revealed extremely small effects; and (3) Effect strength, within experiments, was not correlated with sample size, a statistical relationship at variance with "normal" science. Experimental series investigating actual effects should show greater effect strength with increasing sample size.

General Quantum Theory (GQT)

Walter von Lucadou (2015) explained this capricious quality using a General Quantum Theory (GQT) model. He argued that parapsychology's concept of psi as a signal is invalid. Within physics, only electromagnetic forces can transmit information over long distances and these signals dissipate over distance. Because parapsychological evidence indicated that psi was independent of distance, psi cannot be explained as a signal. Lucadou's (2015) Model of Pragmatic Information (MPI), derived from GQT, explained psi as an *entanglement correlation*. Within quantum mechanics, *entanglement* occurs when pairs or groups of particles are created together and interact in ways that the state of each particle is correlated with the others, even when the particles are separated by large distances. Although Albert Einstein skeptically described this phenomenon as "spooky action at a distance," modern physicists have verified the effect. Even when widely separated, measuring one particle immediately influences the other, with the order of observation affecting results.

Although the assumption that quantum processes pertain to psychological systems is somewhat artificial, parallel concepts suggest that theories in one domain can be applied to the other (Lucadou, Römer, and Walach, 2007). The psychologist C. G. Jung's' term *synchronicity* refers to meaningful coincidences lacking causal relationships, an idea parallel to *entanglement*. Quantum systems also find that order of measurement affects outcomes (if A and B are measurements, AB is not equal to BA). Psychologists observed similar discrepancies. When subjects filled out questionnaires, they experienced changes of mental state, dependent on the order of the questionaire items. As a result, "a lot of psychology is in fact a good candidate for quantum-like theoretical treatment" (Walach, Lucadou, and Römer, 2014).

Lucadou's MPI model allows hypotheses derived from Generalized Quantum Theory. A quantum theory axiom specifies that it is impossible to transmit information or controllable causal action by means of entanglement correlations. If psi phenomena are entanglement correlations, this axiom specifies that psi will decline if it is regarded as pragmatic (useful) information. As a result, we should expect psi to be sporadic, producing experimental results that cannot be replicated.

Lucadou's concept of *pragmatic information*, derived from information theory, is defined as the impact of a message on a receiving system. *Pragmatic information* is a product of novelty (elements that cannot be inferred from experience) and confirmation (elements already known that allow message interpretation). Pragmatic information requires a balance between these elements, which vary inversely. Without novelty, no new information is conveyed and without confirmation, the message cannot be interpreted.

Pragmatic information is also determined by *quality* (reliability of the documentation) and the *autonomy* of the system (behavior of the system that cannot be predicted). These variables vary inversely. As a result, within RSPK systems, surveillance (observers, cameras, security devices) reduce the effect size of psi. A parallel quantum mechanical observation is that systems have larger fluctuations when not observed. Continuous observation of a nonstable particle prevents its decay, a phenomenon known as the Zeno effect. Similarly, observation of psi effects reduces their incidence and magnitude. Poltergeist effects, for example, occur less often when a camera is set up to document them (Lucadou and Wald, 2014).

Many elements within my SORRAT narrative coincide with Lucadou's hypotheses. For example, I monitored Cox's mini-lab experiment by sleeping in the same room with the equipment. This close scrutiny seemed to thwart mini-lab phenomena. Events drawn from my SORRAT narrative illustrate how Lucadou's theory helps explain the nature and interpretation of PK.

One evening, while I was with the Richards and Ed Cox, we hard raps from the kitchen floor.

"C-A-N," the raps spelled out. We could not interpret the meaning. "C-A-N," the raps spelled out again. (Within the MPI model, this was novel information.)

I went down to the basement to inspect the mini-lab and to check the floor boards while the raps occurred above. While I looked at the mini-lab, the camera activated, but the pen did not move. Simultaneously, I heard loud music playing upstairs. I could not fully interpret these events but recognized the synchronicity: the camera was activated at exactly the moment the music began, an effect that would be difficult to create by fraud.

When I returned upstairs, I discussed the situation with Tom, Elaine, and Ed. Everyone denied touching the record player. The entity Jay, through raps, identified himself as responsible for the raps and music. Tom noted that the rapped message "can can" coincided with the music, Offenbach's *Can Can.*

I pondered what actions would be required for someone to create these effects fraudulently. I thought that fraud was possible and wanted to evaluate the probability of that hypothesis. I regarded Elaine as a prime suspect; she had left the kitchen and was in the bathroom when I came up the stairs. Could she have started the record playing while simultaneously activating the micro-switch using some type of electronic device?

Tom noted that Offenbach's *Can Can* was from the opera *Orpheus in the Underworld*. Did this have symbolic meaning? Elaine suggested the perhaps Jay merely liked Offenbach's *Can Can*. Jay rapped his agreement with Elaine and rapped that he had activated the micro-switch in the basement and had tried to write, but had failed.

The group discussed the meaning of these events, information important within Lucadou's theory: (1) I regarded the message "can-can" as paradoxical since the entities were unable to make the pen write. Rather than "can-can," they "can't, can't." (Within the context of Lucadou's theory, my monitoring the camera thwarted the phenomena due to the Zeno effect). (2) Tom regarded these events as puzzling. (3) Ed found these events to be capricious, like many he had witnessed in the past. (4) Elaine regarded the situation in harmony with her brother's personality. He was playful and, as her brother, trying to be helpful. (5) My opinion, not expressed to those present, was that the Jay (and all the entities) lacked empathy for the SORRAT members. The entities failed to establish their authenticity or paranormal quality and had created a situation where Elaine was a suspect. (According to the PMI model, psi cannot convey useful information regularly; apparently, my observation and beliefs prevented the pen from writing, something regarded as useful information.) It seemed to me that these types of events, described repeatedly in my manuscript, reflect a kind of pathology. The entities and the Richards live within a deviant environment, a kind of break with reality that might be regarded as a collective psychosis.

The PMI model focuses on the effect of information on observers, and with the publication of this book, its readers become part of the equation. In Appendix A, I provide comments, mostly from the 1980s, from people who read the original manuscript. Their opinions vary greatly but tend to coincide with those present at this event: puzzlement, belief in spirits, rejection of spirits, awareness of psi's quirky quality. My attitude at present differs from my attitude at the time since I consider the probability of PK more likely than I did that evening. Considering that change, what message does the entities offer us? The phenomena coincide with Lucadou's PMI model, but they suggest a kind of sentient pathology, an active elusive awareness.

Later, I searched the house while the Richards were gone but did not find an electronic device or associated wiring. At the time, I felt that, if fraud were involved, I would probably uncover it eventually because the human trickster would probably slip up due to the complexity and skill required. The Richards did not seem capable of fraudulent performance at the level I witnessed. The history of Spiritualist mediumship shows a progression of events that often include fraud.

Lucadou and Wald (2014) predict that RSPK and sitter groups go through four phases: (1) *Surprise*. During this phase, observers do not attribute the phenomena to spirits. The core person is expressing a hidden problem, a psychological "cry for help," but observers are not aware of this. (2) *Displacement*. Observers seek explanations for the phenomena that do not involve the focal person. There efforts may cause the phenomena to change. (3) *Decline*. Attention by outside observers and the idea that the agent produces the phenomena cause it to decline. (4) *Suppression*. Skeptical observers prevent the phenomena from occurring. Although Lucadou states that these stages pertain to both poltergeists and PK groups, most of his discussion focuses on spontaneous PK. Ouellet (2015) regards the model suitable to explain UFO waves. UFO experiences are attributed to groups whose psychological distress triggers sightings. He provides example cases where UFO waves progress through the phases hypothesized by the PMI model.

It is difficult to precisely identify PMI phases within Batcheldor, Philip, and SORRAT narratives. In a letter sent to me in 1987, Batcheldor described four phases in his table-tipping experiments: 1964-1976 (much phenomena, very successful); 1967-1982 ("none quite so successful as the first group" except a few "ostensible levitations and movements without contact"); 1982-1984 (very successful; powerful results); 1984-1987 (continued powerful results some of which were documented on video).

Although this history does not coincide with the Lucadou's predicted phases, many elements within Batcheldor's work fit the PMI model. The ambiguity of his documentation of PK success seems in harmony with that model.

The Philip Group phenomena was relatively short lived but seemed to have achieved increasingly stronger results over time. Effects documented by two television programs show increasing robustness followed by a decline, a progression that might be interpreted as fitting the PMI model.

SORRAT core members describe phases within the history of their phenomena. SORRATs experienced a declining rate of table levitation until a final phase (1999-2007) when Ivan became active. Cox's mini-labs (1978-1981) achieved success without reducing frequency of other PK phenomena, but a decline occurred with introduction of the McDonnell mini-lab (1981-1982). This reduction might be considered a turning point in SORRAT history since frequency of hands-off table levitations also declined until the 1999-2007 phase.

Letter writing by the entities (1981-2014) increased in frequency, reached a high level around 1990, maintained a moderate level afterward, then declined after 2010 (approximately). Rather than surprise, displacement, decline, suppression, SORRAT exhibits a complex series of surprises and declines, coupled with continual discussion of displacement ("group mind" as opposed to spirits).

Lucadou hypothesized that there are two types of RSPK agents. *Active focus people* tend to be both dissociative and over-controlling, "like a boiling pot," ready to explode because of their desire to control the environment. A second type, passive agents, lacks ability to control the environment. Their failure to observe allows increasing randomness and RSPK. Passive agents may experience a complete "collapse" of the system, without the decline and suppression phases. "In clinical terms, the active RSPK can be considered as a phenomenon of dissociation whilst the passive RSPK phenomena show the phenomena of depression and degeneration" (Lucadou and Zahradnik, 2004, p. 110).

Although it is not clear that active/passive agent predictions apply to SORRAT, the PMI theory explains how human consciousness in everyday life affects quantum systems. "We assume here that everybody under normal circumstances subconsciously controls his or her environment to stabilize it" (Lucadou and Zahradnik, 2004, p. 110). Within this theory, RSPK is the result a modification of "normal circumstances."

Using the PMI model, we might theorize that Batcheldor, Philip, and SORRAT phenomena originated with people failing to stabilize their environments and that, over time, randomness became so large that it was suppressed by skeptics. This model allows hypotheses subject to evaluation:

1. RSPK will decline if (1) observers keep written documents regarding the phenomena; (2) observers audiotape, videotape, or keep other electronic records documenting the phenomena; (3) phenomena are monitored more closely (level of documentation increases); (4) core agents recognize their own role in producing the phenomena; (5) skeptics monitor the phenomena.

2. Active RSPK tends to pass through phases: surprise, displacement, decline, suppression. Each phase affects PK incidence and form. Passage through the stages is determined by the degree that active agents perceive they are the source of the phenomena and by exposure to outside and skeptical observers.

3. Poltergeist agents tend to have either dissociative or depressive characteristics.

In general, Batcheldor, Philip, and SORRAT histories coincide with hypotheses predicting decline, but variables cannot be defined with enough precision to explain these variations. The degree that these groups passed through the four phases is unclear. The impact of documentation is also unclear. In the case of SORRAT, for example, some forms of documentation did not seem to thwart the phenomena (Cox mini-lab), while other efforts were detrimental (McDonnell Lab); observers assume additional precautions inherent within the McDonnel Lab created this differential effect.

Watt and Tierney (2013) present a three-year study testing the PMI model. They randomly assigned people reporting anomalous experiences to either a waiting group or questionnaire-study group with the prediction that frequency of future experiences would be reduced by those documenting these episodes. Their results failed to support PMI predictions; the researchers suggested this result could be attributed to various factors such as low statistical power.

Much of Lucadou's discussion seems to regard reducing anomalous experiences as a therapeutic goal. This is a logical orientation within secular societies. In shamanic paradigms, documentation of anomalous experiences might be considered a kind of cognitive behavior therapy. Potential shamans, by monitoring their inner states, figure out how to reduce negative experiences while increasing frequency of useful perceptions. In both shamanic and PMI paradigms, the incidence of anomalous experiences is linked to pathology, but the shamanic model offers a pathway toward becoming a practitioner, capable of trance performance and psychological health. From a secular anthropological perspective, the shaman model coincides with the PMI predictions, since shaman performances are not thought to generate psi effects but instead generate hypnotic and placebo benefits.

Kennedy (2003: 53) argues that the PMI hypotheses could be derived "from precious empirical findings without the need for the esoteric jargon and equations from systems theory" (p. 67). Alternate explanations include those of Bierman (2001) who suggests that the number of people aware of an experiment influence its outcome, even after the experiment is completed. With experimental replication, the number of skeptical observers increases, bringing about the parapsychological decline effect.

We should not expect perfection from our theoretical models. Lucadou's theory links a successful physics paradigm with parapsychology, a rhetorically powerful combination. Even if some elements within this theory end up being modified, it constitutes a useful tool for future research. The basic idea is that certain people, with particular propensities, are affected by quantum mechanical processes in a way that causes psi to have a hiding quality. This theory can be evaluated using standard methods within the fields of psychology, sociology, and physics. Social scientists can evaluate hypotheses using participant observation, comparison of cases, and survey methodology.

For example, Mirowsky and Ross (1989) provide a methodological model for survey research that could be applied to anomalous experience. They devised questionnaire items measuring psychological symptoms associated with diagnostic categories: schizotypal experience, paranoia, mania, depression-mood, depression-malaise, anxiety-mood, anxiety-malaise, phobia, panic disorder, OCD, and alcohol abuse. Their questions are well accepted survey measures of psychological distress. They used multidimensional analysis to portray the relationships among variables. This method produces a "map" based on the correlations among variables so that the proximity of any two variables corresponds with size of their correlation. Small distances between variables indicate large correlations.

They surveyed random samples of El Paso and Juarez residents using their symptom questionnaire and created a multidimensional map of the results. They found that the symptoms were arranged in a kind of "color wheel," with diagnostic categories overlapping. Their study, which revealed the difficulties of psychiatric diagnosis, is regarded as a classic within psychology literature.

Where would anomalous experiences fit within Mirowsky and Ross's map of psychological symptoms? Roll and Lucadou might argue that PK is correlated with dissociation, depression, or perhaps anxiety. Skeptics might predict that all anomalous experiences represent a kind of pathology and that these episodes should fall within the symptom cloud. Some proponents of psi might argue that anomalous phenomena are not correlated with psychopathology.

A questionnaire was designed and administered (N=965) measuring 88 of Mirowsky and Ross (1989) psychological symptoms as well as frequency of 8 anomalous experiences: apparitions, waking ESP, paranormal dreams, out-of-body experience, near-death experience, psychokinesis, sleep paralysis, spiritual healing. Questionnaire items also asked about UFO, religious experiences, "other" unusual perceptions, and absorptive, dissociative, and transliminal experiences (McClenon, 2012, 2013)

Derived Stimulus Configuration

Euclidean distance model

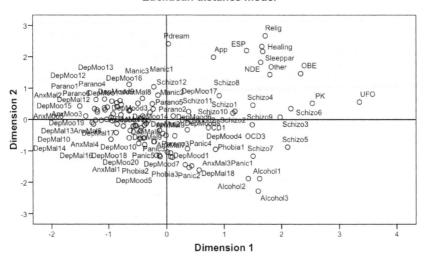

Figure 2: Anomalous Experience Variables and Psychological Variables

Schizo1 to Schizo12=schizotypal experiences; PK=psychokinesis; UFO=unidentified flying object; OBE=out-of-body experience; Sleeppar=sleep paralysis; ESP=extrasensory experience; App=apparitions; Pdream=paranormal dream; Relig=religious experience; Healing=spiritual healing experience; Other=other anomalous experience

Figure 2 portrays multidimensional analysis of the 88 psychological symptom variables and the 8 anomalous experience variables. As found by Mirowsky and Ross (1989), psychological symptoms were arranged in a circular pattern with diagnostic categories overlapping. The experience variables formed a loose cloud to the right and above the symptom cloud (figure 2, upper right quadrant). This means that the psychological symptoms were correlated with each other and anomalous experience variables were also intercorrelated. Anomalous experiences differ from psychological symptoms but are highly correlated with them.

The psychokinesis variable (PK) is in the bottom of the upper right quadrant, below OBE (out-of-body experience), to the left of UFO (unidentified flying objects) and to the right of Schzo6 ("felt that you had special powers"). This means that, among all the variables, these questionnaire items are most correlated with psychokinesis. Other variables highly correlated with PK include Schizo4 (had visions or seen things other people say they cannot see), Schizo9 (felt that your unspoken thoughts were being broadcast or transmitted, so that everyone knew what you were thinking), Schzo3 (seen things or animals or people around you that others did not see), and Schizo5 (felt that you were possessed by a spirit or devil).

Further analysis (not shown in figure 2) indicates that PK is highly correlated with the Tellegen Absorption Scale and less correlated with selected Dissociation Experience Scale items. All the anomalous experiences are correlated with questionnaire items pertaining the childhood difficulty, a variable highly correlated with absorption and dissociation.

These findings indirectly support Roll's and Lucadou's predictions that PK is associated with psychological symptoms but fail to support precise predictions. The data imply that PK is most correlated with experiences related to non-pathological forms of schizophrenia (schizotypy).

These findings coincide with my observations regarding shamanic practitioners. Spiritual healers often report difficult childhoods, dissociative experiences, and anomalous events. The psychologist Carl Jung describes a process in which those suffering from psychological wounds are motivated to become "wounded healers." They overcome their difficulties by advocating methods they found useful for resolving their own problems. Psychologists have observed that childhood trauma often results in dissociative ability, a trait associated with propensity for anomalous experience. This theory coincides with the survey findings that those reporting childhood difficulty tend also to report anomalous, schizotypy, absorptive, and dissociative experiences.

Future researchers can contribute to this line of inquiry using research methods that include observing haunting/poltergeist phenomena, PK groups, and shamanic and psychic practitioners, as well as conducting social surveys regarding anomalous experience. Previous studies indicate that psi is correlated with a constellation of variables that facilitate its hiding quality. These variables include schizotypal experience, absorption, dissociation, fraud, and psychological symptoms in general.

CHAPTER 12
COMPARING SORRAT TO EQUIVALENT CASES

A comparison of SORRAT to equivalent psychical research cases allows insights into the nature of psi. Jeffrey Kripal provides guidelines for this endeavor (Strieber and Kripal, 2016, p. 339-342). He suggests comparing cases while considering cultural and historical context. He advocates exercising a degree of skepticism but realizing that we should not assume that everything imaged is imaginary. Anomalous experience studies require considering sexuality and sexual features and "listening for the traumatic secret," the element that can unlock the non-material aspect of life. Anomalous experiences may include "energetic, electromagnetic, or plasma-like phenomena." The endeavor may require pondering opposing ideas simultaneously. This calls for a new story, something outside of our "present cultural trance-form."

Kripal's orientation overlaps that of Lucadou in that he seeks insight regarding the "symbolic signal" imbedded within paranormal experience. While Lucadou's PMI seems somewhat mechanistic, Kripal is more open to existence of spiritual entities.

The fields of psychical research and anthropology provide evidence useful for comparison (Hunter, 2012; Long, 1977). SORRAT has elements parallel to Native American tent-shaking rituals (Barnouw, 1942, 1975; 257-58), sorcery in the Republic of Niger (Stoller, 1989; Stoller and Olkes, 1987), and Ndembu ceremonies (Turner (1992, 1993). Ojibwa Native Americans tied up their medicine men and placed them in ritual tents. The sides of the tent would begin shaking, apparently activated by the spirits called up by the medicine men, asking questions asked by observers. The situation is parallel to SORRAT rapping sessions since the phenomena were not fully verified. (Could the medicine man escape from his bonds?) Although skeptics assumed trickery was involved, observers derived therapeutic benefits (Hultkrantz, 1992: 3). As with SORRAT, it was not unusual for Native Americans to report other anomalous experiences, such as anomalous lights and spirit voices (Barnouw, 1942, 1975; 257-58).

Young and Goulet (1994) provide a collection of anomalous perceptions, experienced by anthropologists in the field. Stoller describes poltergeist events associated with Songay sorcery (Stoller, 1989; Stoller and Olkes, 1987). Edith Turner (Young and Goulet, 1994, p. 71-96) described seeing a spirit form while participating in Ndumbu ceremonies in Zambia. Jack Hunter's book (Hunter and Luke, 2014) and on-line journal, *Paranthropology*, establish a paradigm regarding anthropological approaches to anomalous experience.

As mentioned previously, written messages from spirits were a recurring feature during the Spiritualist era (1848-1920s). Observers reported raps, table-tipping, mediumship phenomena, and spirit writing parallel to that experienced by SORRATs.

Poltergeist phenomena has included spirit writing throughout the ages. The earliest Chinese poltergeist account, from before AD 1000, mentioned that "objects were moved, clothing was damaged and written messages were received." The Old Testament book of Daniel (5: 1-30) described spirit writing. The Esther Cox case (Amherst, MA, 1878-1879) included poltergeist writing on the wall above the central figure's bed. The Borley Rectory case (1929-1948), labeled "the most haunted house in England," included entity messages. Other poltergeists leaving written texts attributed to spirits include cases in New Jersey, 1972; Yorkshire, 1972; Stratford, 1850; Hertfordshire, undated; and a computer case, 1991 (Spencer and Spencer, 1966: 140-142).

I review five group PK cases that parallel SORRAT regarding written messages, film documentation, potential for fraud, and impact on experiencers. (1) Matthew Manning experienced poltergeist phenomena while a teen that included paranormal writing (ostensible) on his bedroom walls—over 600 signatures from people whose lives spanned six centuries. (2) Joe Fisher (2001) took part in a group that channeled spirit messages. Although he originally found this evidence compelling, he later determined, in all cases, that elements were false. (3) A poltergeist described by Ken Webster (1989) produced over 300 handwritten scripts and computer messages between 1984 and 1987. Texts were ostensibly written by a man living four hundred years previously and by entities in a parallel universe, perhaps in the future. (4) The Battersea Poltergeist (1956-1968) included extensive written messages, ostensibly by an entity claiming to the son of French King Louis XVI (Hitchings and Clark, 2013). (5) The Scole Experiment (Solomon and Solomon, 1999) generated photographic evidence of anomalous lights and images on film inside secure containers. Other reported phenomena included touches from ghostly hands, table levitations, and disembodies voices. The case terminated abruptly after two years.

Matthew Manning

At age 11, while living with his family in Cambridge, England, Matthew Manning became the center of a poltergeist outbreak in 1966. As with many poltergeists, objects did not move when observed, and eventually the phenomena declined. The Mannings moved to an 18th century house in Linton, and the poltergeist resumed in 1970. It moved heavy objects and caused things to disappear and appear in different places. Signatures, allegedly from historical figures, appeared on the walls of Manning's room. Poltergeist phenomena followed Manning to his boarding school where chairs and heavy bunk beds moved around, objects were thrown, pools of water materialized, odd lights appeared on walls. Manning figured out how to channel the energy thought astral projection and automatic writing. He seemingly communicated with the spirits who had produced the phenomena and this reduced unwanted episodes. Manning channeled messages in languages unknown to him, such as Greek and Arabic. After seeing Uri Geller perform, he acquired the ability to bend metal paranormally.

In 1977, Manning went to India and had profound mystical experiences that led him to spend five years as an experimental subject at the Mind Science Foundation, the University of California, and London University. Although researchers believe they verified paranormal phenomena under controlled conditions (Braud, Davis, and Wood, 1979), skeptics determined that the spirit writing was invalid (Nickols, 2015). Manning became a full-time psychic healer, helping thousands of people who came to him with their problems.

Manning's biography reveals features parallel to those of SORRRAT and to the anthropological literature regarding shamanic practitioners (McClenon, 2002a). His case includes poltergeist events, spirit writing, accusations of fraud, spiritual healing, and the capacity to gain control of paranormal phenomena—major elements within shamanism. As with SORRAT, the spirit writing was regarded by skeptics as fraudulent, yet people familiar with the phenomena became believers.

Joe Fisher

Joe Fisher (2001), a journalist who had written a book on reincarnation, joined a group whose leader advocated a spiritual development program via channeling spirits. Based on his experiences with the group, Fisher became convinced that mediums could bring messages from people in-between their earthly lives. The spirits put Joe in contact with a spiritual "soul mate," a lover from one of his previous lives. His relationship with this spirit became so intense that it disrupted his earthly romance. Over time, Fisher uncovered evidence that the leader's spirits might not be authentic. He continued his investigation and went to Greece, hoping to verify the identity of his spirit lover. He found that the evidence she provided was false; she was not who she claimed to be. He attempted to verify the information provided by other spirits channeled by prominent mediums. Again and again, he found these spirits to be false. He developed financial and personal problems and believed that the spirits were harassing him. He committed suicide not long after his book *The Siren Call of Hungry Ghosts* was published.

This case illustrates a recurring problem within psychical research. Although Spiritualists believe their evidence to be valid, most investigators are unable to verify their claims. In harmony with Lucadou's PMI theory, the phenomena itself, when scrutinized closely, is found to have fraudulent qualities. As with SORRAT investigators such as myself, Fisher found that his spirits could not verify their identities.

I experienced emotional dilemmas somewhat parallel to those reported by Fisher. I developed deep friendships with Tom and Elaine Richards, but the evidence implying fraud was overwhelming. Parallel to Fisher's findings, it seemed that the spirits created compromising situations, but I was unable to determine exactly what was going on.

Because of the prevalence of fraud within the psychical research literature, I predict that future researchers will encounter deception. The possibility of fraud is inherent within loosely-controlled psi phenomena. In harmony with Batcheldor's and Lucadou's theories, the possibility of fraud seems to contribute to the phenomena's robustness and longevity. If phenomena are produced by spirits, it may be that these entities engage in fraud as a way of ending skeptical observation, a practice that extends their existence.

Battersea Poltergeist

The Battersea Poltergeist case began in 1956 when a British family was plagued by a terrifying entity who they came to call Donald (Hutchings and Clark, 2013). Phenomena included rapping sounds that answered questions, movement of objects, anomalous lights, and spontaneous fires. Donald threatened to burn down the family home if they did not comply with his demands. He required his own room, and space was set aside with the material he requested. Over time, he acquired the ability to write and type messages, and he generated a huge quantity of texts and letters. As with SORRAT, he sometimes mailed letters using the postal service. Some letters had a threatening quality, but most were mundane. Over time, Donald's behavior became less menacing, and he even sent out Christmas cards. The phenomena continued for 12 years, until the central figure in the case, Shirley, married at age 27.

Historical patterns within the case coincide, to a degree, with Lucadou's model. During the early phase, newspaper reporters launched an investigation that concluded that Shirley, the core figure, made rapping sounds with her toe. Although this explanation did not explain the full scope of the phenomena, Shirley was labeled a fraud. This brought about a decline in public interest, allowing the phenomena to continue for many years afterward. This case suggests that Lucadou's progression from surprise, displacement, decline, and suppression should be regarded as a tendency rather than a rigid prediction. Events can disrupt the progression to suppression. In this case, the displacement phase seemed somewhat permanent until the phenomena ended.

The primary researcher, Harold Chibbett, investigated Donald's claim to be Louis-Charles, the son of French King Louis XVI. Although historians believed that Louis-Charles died in prison at the age of 10, Donald said that he had escaped, only to drown during his passage to England. Chibbett spent years attempting to verify Donald's claims, but the evidence was not conclusive. Years later, DNA analysis revealed Donald's claim to be false. The 10-year old male who died in prison was Louis-Charles.

Within Lucadou's theory, Chibbett's acceptance of Donald's claims suggests that the case had progressed to the displacement phase. (Chibbett did not regard Shirley as the source of the phenomena and the phenomena did not decline.) Chibbett's actions did not attract the attention of many outside observers, and he was unable to get his manuscript published during his lifetime. As with SORRAT, the case seemed to remain in the displacement phase for many years. James Clark authored *The Poltergeist Prince* (2013) based on Chibbett's notes and with Shirley's help.

The Battersea Poltergeist and SORRAT reveal similarities: (1) Participants treated the phenomena as spiritual entities, but the situation was ambiguous. (2) The phenomena included hundreds of written messages thought to be written by sprits, but the spirits were unable to authenticate themselves. (3) Although the phenomena were robust, researcher publications were delayed for decades. (4) Core figures were accused of fraud and assumed to write the texts attributed to spirits. (5) Core figures did not benefit from the phenomena in ways that would compensate them for their effort. (6) The spirits often acted against the interests of the core figures.

I hypothesize that future researchers will uncover parallel patterns; they will find that, although group PK seems linked to group consciousness (as in the Philip Group), spiritual entities may express ideas, information, or sentiments beyond normal group consciousness. The SORRAT entities, at times, seemed to engage in meaningless, trivial disruption of reality, outside the motivations of the living people present. Group PK may represent a form of collective dream or something related to psychosis, anomalous in that it can be documented through photography.

Ken Webster

In *The Vertical Plane* (1989), Ken Webster describes his experiences as the central figure in a poltergeist case that produced about 300 anomalous computer messages between 1984 and 1986. An agency, labeled "2109," allowed Ken to communicate by computer with a 16th century man, later identified as Tomas Harden, a historical personage. Tomas described meeting a mysterious man who left a "box of lights" that allowed him to send messages to Ken's BBC Micro computer, which was not connected to the internet. The agency facilitating this linkage claimed to be from the year 2109 (and hence was named 2109) but this identity was uncertain. Later messages implied that "2109" was some type of space/time traveler conducting an experiment.

As with the Battersea Poltergeist, Fisher's case, and SORRAT, the identities of Webster's entities were problematic since their claims changed over time. Both the *Vertical Plane* and the SORRAT cases (1) generated many messages, (2) lasted longer than an average poltergeist case, (3) involved emotional relationships between entities and earthly communicants, (4) did not provide evidence verifying the identities of the communicating entities or the paranormal quality of the communication, and (5) involved extremely robust poltergeist phenomena that compelled belief among participants.

Features within this case fit some of Lucadou's predictions in that the phenomena had a hiding quality. In contrast to other predictions, the impact of outside investigators was unclear. Skeptical observers did not terminate the phenomena.

The SORRAT entities, Tomas Harden, and 2109 show little empathy for the "earthly" participants' desires to authenticate paranormal claims. For example, 2109 wrote: "Unfortunately you put far too much concern in proving this to the 'world.' You know that this is a worthless effort, why ask! - We remind you that you have been honoured with this communication. Thank you for your cooperation." At one stage, 2109 terminated interaction with the message: "Tomas did eventually write his book and soon died, shortly after… There is no need for you to write back as we will have gone. Thank you for your cooperation. 2109." Although 2109 later sought further communication, Ken decided not to reply since he was tired of the phenomena disrupting his life.

Both the SORRAT and *Vertical Plane* cases portrayed emotional connections between entities and human communicants. The Vertical Plane case and Battersea Poltergeist included negative emotions. Ken Webster was deeply concerned for Tomas Harden's well-being but found 2109's messages to be irritating and worthless. He did not regard the poltergeist and messages as involving a spiritual force but as a kind of time phenomena. In that regard, the communications were parallel to SORRAT's vague directive to "rethink time."

Scole Experiment

The Scole Experiment (1993-1998) consisted of 500 séance-like sessions led by a four-person core group. Phenomena included anomalous lights and voices, apports, and vocal spirit messages. The purpose, claimed by the messages, was to further belief in life after death. The group invited outside observers to witness the phenomena but, at the request of the spirits, did not allow well-controlled experiments. As would be predicted by the Batcheldor and Lucadou orientations, reduced light and limited precautions against fraud allowed on-going phenomena. Participants were allowed to bring unexposed film and, under varying conditions, generated anomalous photographic evidence. Although some conditions seemed to preclude fraud, the loose control conditions allowed skeptics to devise normal explanations for reported paranormal events. Witnesses reported interacting with floating light globes that showed an awareness of their surroundings, phenomena that would seem difficult to produce by fraud but could involve laser pointers (Solomon and Solomon, 1999).

The Scole group claimed to be in contact with a parallel experimental group from the future. The parallel group stated that full precautions against fraud could not be allowed. The experiment was terminated, somewhat abruptly, when the "entity" researchers declared that they had encountered obstacles related to future disruptions.

The Scole Experiment was similar to SORRAT due to (1) a parallel Spiritualist ideology, (2) the high volume of anomalous phenomena, (3) a requirement that conditions not be fully controlled, (4) the accusations of fraud leveled against core members, and (5) some phenomena would be difficult to produce fraudulently, but this possibility reduced the scientific impact of the results.

Recurring features suggest testable hypotheses. Future researchers should expect to encounter phenomena that (1) seem connected to a core person or persons, (2) compel belief within core participants, (3) do not always act in the interest of the core people, (4) have qualities that repel skeptics such as loose controls and the possibility of fraud, and (5) provide messages, thought the messages cannot be used to verify paranormal claims.

I devised a speculative theory, parallel to that of Lucadou, to explain these characteristics. The collective consciousness, which creates our "taken-for-granted" reality, sometimes breaks down due to genetic mutations and/or stress. This collective consciousness has characteristics that thwart paranormal phenomena since deviant forms threaten its existence. As a result, the phenomena are inherently unstable, something outside of normal reality. Breakdowns of the collective consciousness, like psychosis, confer evolutionary costs. As a result, mechanisms have evolved, like skepticism, which restore the collective consciousness. Within this theoretical orientation, psi is not a signal, as assumed by secular parapsychologists. It is not something produced by spirits, as assumed by Spiritualists, but is a result of random breakdowns within mechanisms that govern consciousness, a concept in harmony with Lucadou. PK is linked to human consciousness but acquires a form of sentience that allows it to act in its own self-interest. This feature coincides with an over-arching quality within some RSPK series; the phenomena deflect close skeptical observation by thwarting full verification.

A Thought Experiment

The scientific method calls for further research, analysis of observations, and revision of theories. One way to do this would be to form a PK group and determine if the phenomena fit hypotheses derived from our theories. Let's do a thought experiment: Suppose we assembled a group of psi-conducive people and invited them to do a table tipping experiment. They would meet weekly, get to know each other, and develop the conditions (rapport) required for phenomena to occur.

I offer a hypothetical narrative describing what might happen. Keep in mind that the conversations I describe are derived from my imagination rather than actual events. I engage in this literary exercise because I want you to think about the types of experiences that participants report and the ways these experiences affect their beliefs. By doing this thought experiment, we explore the implications of the hypothesis that small groups can generate deviant realities.

Let's invite six people for our experiment: (1) Shirley Hitchings lived in a house infested with a belligerent poltergeist, Donald. Donald later wrote messages and eventually became less threatening. (2) Joe Fisher found that his spirit-lover and other spirits were spurious. His story illustrates the psychological damage that can occur due to lack of skeptical restraint. (3) Ken Webster communicated, by computer, with the 16th century man, Tomas Harden, and with the agency, 2109. (4) Jack, a fictional psychical researcher, observed The Scole Experiment, a Spiritualist group. (5) Matthew Manning experienced poltergeist activity and became a spiritual healer. (6) John Hunt experienced poltergeist activity and become a SORRAT member. (7) You are invited to join us in our table-tipping experiment as a participant observer. We want you to gain a feeling of what it is like to be a psi group participant. I give you a flashlight, tape recorder, and camera so that you might document the events you witness.

"I have asked each of you to come today because I think that together we can learn something about group PK," I tell the group. "Let's go around the room and introduce ourselves. Shirley, would you start things off?"

"I was only 15 when my family was plagued by a poltergeist," Shirley said. "It was a very difficult time for me and it went on for 12 years. Donald harassed us and even threatened to kill us. We left paper and pencil out for him and he gained the ability to write. That seemed to help him get along with us. I experienced things that I would not want anyone to have to endure. Donald took away my adolescence. Some people say that my mind brought Donald into existence, but they don't understand how difficult it was for me. They suggest I wrote the messages but that was impossible. Donald had a mind of his own, different from mine. I worked with James Clark so that a book could be written about my case. I wanted people to know what really happened. I wanted to set the record straight so that people could understand what is possible in this world."

"I was familiar with the reincarnation evidence and I accepted the idea that spirits can talk through mediums," Joe said. "I hoped to write the definitive book about spirit guides, so I immersed myself in a quest to learn about channeling spirits. Then I met my spiritual soul-mate, Filipa. She was an 18th century Greek woman who told me that we had shared a tragic life together.

My girlfriend at the time became increasingly jealous, and my relationship with her floundered. Filipa seemed to understand me, often better than I understood myself. Although much of the information I learned from the spirits was accurate, some claims were false and I decided to investigate more deeply. I went to Greece and was shocked to find that crucial details that Filipa had told me were false. She had told me a mixture of truth and lies, and I was troubled by the implications. I investigated other spirits channeled by Toronto mediums, and I discovered falsehoods in each case. It was a very difficult lesson for me. We should not completely rely on external guides. The spirits seem real but they lie. I hope this information is valuable to you. I think the spirits punished me for learning this."

"I was remodeling a very old cottage in Cheshire, England, when my work unleashed a poltergeist," Ken told us. "Some unexplained footprints appeared on a wall and we painted over them but they came back. Then the poltergeist activity increased. My girlfriend, Debbie, and other friends witnessed the phenomena so I knew that this was not something I was hallucinating. Not long afterwards, I started getting messages on my 1984 model computer. That was before the days of the internet so we assumed someone was playing a trick on us. Some messages were in Olde English—from a gentleman who claimed to have lived in the cottage 400 years before. I also got weird inter-dimensional messages from entities claiming to be from the year "2109." We did all kinds of things to preclude trickery. Debbie can verify that this was not a hoax. We made sure that no one could have put the messages on the computer while we were gone. The case went on for 15 months, from 1984 to 1986. I developed a close relationship with the 16th century man, Tomas Harden. We found historical records referring to him; texts show that he refused to execute Henry VIII's order to delete the Pope's name from church documents. We established that the message dialect resembled the writing of that era. We put a lot of effort into it, but I developed an aversion to "2109" because they had inhuman personalities. They told us that we were involved in a time manipulation experiment, but I don't know if we can trust them. The British Society for Psychical Research and a UFO researcher investigated us but nothing much came of it. They wasted our time. I don't see this case as supernatural or spiritual. It was a kind of time phenomenon experiment, but I can't say exactly what was going on. My friend Pete Trinder did an analysis of the Tomas Harden texts and determined the percentages of words that were first used during the 15th, 16th, and 17th centuries. It would be impossible for Debbie or me to have written those messages. I think the researchers established that fact. There's no evidence supporting the theory that those writings came from our minds. My case is like SORRAT in that outsiders concluded we wrote those things, but they are not thinking about the actual evidence when they say that. I'm not that interested in psychical research, but I agreed to participate today because I'm curious. I think it is possible our minds play a role, and it might be interesting to see what happens as long as we don't allow something like 2109 to manipulate us."

"I was a psychical researcher who observed some of the Scole Experiment séances," Jack said. "We brought our own film inside a locked container. The mediums went into trance, and we had some astonishing experiences. I kept the locked container in my hands the entire time. I heard raps and was touched by a materialized hand. Many other astonishing things happened, but the lights were off so it was difficult to verify that these things were paranormal. We saw a series of small, bright blue lights curve downward from the ceiling at high speed—like shooting stars. They were accompanied by sparks and a distinctive crackling noise. Afterwards, I watched as my films were developed. The images on the films portrayed lights, some in circles, and a collection of 10 orbs with varying intensities. No matter what skeptics might say about our experiences during the séance, the photographic images should not be attributed to fraud."

"You can read my story in my book, *The Link*," Matthew Manning said. "I was at the center of a poltergeist outbreak when I was a teenager. I used automatic writing and drawing to gain a kind of control over the phenomena. Some skeptical researchers accused me of writing the messages and of making the poltergeist events, but they don't understand what really happened. It was like Shirley's experience with the skeptics—they accuse you of fraud, but the phenomena keep happening anyway. I was tested at the Mind Science Foundation in Texas in the late 1970s and they verified my ESP results. I could also bend metal paranormally, move compass needles, and make medical diagnoses. I had some profound experiences in India and moved in a spiritual direction. This isn't something I fully understand, but I think the quantum mechanical theories are a logical pathway to pursue. I focus on healing these days."

"I'm not a famous person," says SORRAT member John Hunt. "I haven't written a book or anything like that. I had some poltergeist activity in my apartment many years ago, and Steve Calvin invited me to come to SORRAT meetings. I experienced a lot of weird stuff but that was many years ago. Since then, I've tried to live a normal life, but I've visited Rolla regularly to take part in SORRAT sessions. I know that paranormal things happen."

"Can you explain your SORRAT experiences?" I asked John. "Do you fully believe in it?"

"Remember, I had experiences outside of SORRAT that could not be explained. I know it's real," John replied. "SORRAT was just as extension of that. I don't think anyone can explain the things we experienced. Regular people aren't willing to accept those types of things."

"We invite you to join us," I said, addressing the readers of this book. "We are curious about you. Have you had unusual experiences? The group listens to what you say, and people ask you questions. What motivated you to join us? Are you willing to come week and after week and get to know us and allow us to get to know you?"

"There are good reasons to be cautious," Ken says. "This isn't something that makes complete sense."

"Keep in mind that many spirits lie," Joe says. "They can trick you into believing in them."

"There are definitely problems associated with paranormal things," Shirley says. "I understand why people avoid thinking about it. There's a real stigma associated with psychic phenomena. I had troubled keeping a boyfriend because Donald scared them away. They saw some of the strange things that were going on in my house, and people assumed I was cheating. They said I wrote the messages, but I didn't. I can't think of anyone who would have chosen to go through the things that I went through."

"I had the same problem," Ken says. "I could not have written texts like a 16th century man. I don't know anything about that. People say that my mind created those messages, but I don't see how that could be possible."

"I know what you mean," John Hunt said. "I found that the entities, or whatever, could read my mind, and I think they draw information from us and it gets woven into what they do. But there is no real evidence that the group process explains all the weird stuff that goes on."

The conversation continued. "Some people say that you benefited from having a poltergeist in your house," Joe told Shirley. "They say that it kept you from working—that you wanted to stay home and avoid work."

"Donald threatened us," Shirley told him. "He tortured us psychologically. Do you really think that we were so sick as to do that to ourselves? That does not make sense."

"I understand that feeling all too well," Joe said. "I ended up committing suicide. Dealing with this type of stress was not psychologically healthy. You come to believe in something, but on a fundamental level you realize that your belief was misplaced."

Remember: this is a hypothetical conversation. I have written a narrative where Joe comes back to take part in this group. Unlike other conversations in the book, this is fiction.

Joe and Ken then discuss their emotional relationships with the spirits. "Filipa meant everything to me," Joe noted. "I loved her with all my heart. When you're experiencing those types of emotions, you are not thinking clearly."

"I still think about Tomas, my 16th century friend," Ken noted. "He risked everything to communicate with us. He was accused of witchcraft and detained by the authorities. We tried to help him, but there was not much we could do. Receiving those messages put me in touch with a past way of thinking. People in those days had to cope with superstitions that limited their worldview. It makes me think that modern people are probably limited, in some way; our worldview is restricted. The skeptical way of thinking keeps people from seeing clearly. It may be that people in the future have alternate ways of thinking, and this might be associated with totally different problems. Sixteenth century Tomas seemed as puzzled as we were, and the 2109 entities were on a different wavelength. They did not provide anything meaningful."

John Hunt described how strange it was to be the center of a poltergeist outbreak. "I wondered if there was something wrong with me for ending up with the SORRATs because it got pretty weird. We hoped that the parapsychologists would verify the phenomena, but that didn't work out. It seemed, at times, as if they were part of the problem. James Randi was certainly part of the problem. Skepticism can be useful, but if you make it into a religion it becomes a problem."

"I had a bizarre childhood because of the poltergeist and the publicity," Matthew said. "For a long time, it seemed as if there was no solution. Then I tried channeling the energy into automatic writing and through my art. That helped because the poltergeist disruptions declined. I could write in fluent Chinese and Arabic, and I don't think those languages are in my subconscious—so it seemed as if something truly real was happening—even though it was strange. Unfortunately, I became a kind of performing monkey, and the fame did not suit me. It was extremely stressful. I could bend spoons like Uri Geller, and people were saying that I was a fraud. I became somewhat of a hell-raiser and started hitting the bars pretty hard. I think it was because I lost out on having normal adolescence. The poltergeist took that away from me. I wanted to show people that I was a regular guy, but it got out of hand. The researchers discovered that I could affect cancer cells and that made a difference. I got more involved with spirituality and healing. I understand why skeptics think the way they do because I'm still skeptical myself. I think placebo effects play a role in spiritual healing, but I know that truly remarkable things also happen. I started out as an atheist, but when you've had the experiences that I've had, you know that there is something out there. I suspect that it has something to do with quantum physics."

"I'm still a bit skeptical," John said. "Tom Richards had some of the problems others here described. People assumed that he engaged in fraud because they could not explain what they saw. He may have done things to get the spirits started; they call it artifact induction but that's a part of table tipping. Sometimes, if someone moves the table a bit, it will get things started. I also think that the phenomena were part of the problem. It is hard to believe in things that are so extremely weird. I don't think anyone knows why the phenomena are the way they are."

"Do you think it is valuable to invite psychical researchers to investigate the phenomena?" I ask.

"I worked with the researchers," Matthew says. "I gained a great deal from doing experiments with them. They introduced me to new ways of thinking."

"I didn't get much out of it," Ken says. "It was a waste of time, but we wanted to put an end the talk that we are writing the messages. I think they ruled out that hypothesis that we were doing it, but we never got back any formal reports."

"Did you ever cheat?" John asked Shirley.

"Of course not," Shirley said. "I wanted Donald to go away."

"Artifact effects are useful for some groups," John said. "That's what Tom Richards used to say, but I think he was talking about subconsciously pushing the table. I watched Tom very closely, and I never saw him cheat."

"I liked talking with Harold Chibbett," Shirley said. "He understood what we were experiencing. It would have been hard to get through those days without having someone like him to talk with. He paid attention to us. I think that he truly believed in Donald. I was just trying to survive."

"We never even got a written report regarding the research opinions," Ken noted. "We hoped to gain some insight regarding what was going on but they never gave us anything concrete."

"I liked talking with parapsychologists," I told them. "Most of them seemed to be good hearted and intelligent and I developed friendships with some of them. They were honest, but I think the phenomena were not amenable to the type of research they were doing. Psi seemed to have a hiding quality, and these days I wonder if psychical research will ever be effective. It seems to me that, in the end, the FRNM and McDonnell Lab researchers harmed SORRAT rather than helped them. They were trying to get something that was not there. I suppose these efforts provided more evidence about psi's hiding quality, but the field wasn't that interested in macro-psychokinesis."

I present this hypothetical conversation to portray how a group could interact in order to develop the rapport required to get PK. People with a history of paranormal experience make good PK group participants. If the SORRAT entity, John King, were allowed to join this conversation, he would explain that rapport was more important than psychic phenomena. He would argue that spiritual development, the raising of one's spiritual level, was the goal. This process results in spiritual healing and the feeling of Oneness. He might say that paranormal phenomena are useful only to the degree that they contribute to belief in this process.

CHAPTER 13
THE RITUAL HEALING THEORY

As a sociologist, I observed many common features within SORRAT and shamanism. While teaching in Asia between 1982 and 1986, I observed shamanic rituals in Japan, Okinawa, Korea, Philippines, Sri Lanka, China, Taiwan, and India. During typical performances, the practitioner went into trance, communicated with spirits, performed unusual feats, and healed audience members. Successful healings seemed due to hypnotic and placebo effects.

I asked each shamanic practitioner to describe how he or she became a healer. A Thai school teacher, for example, told me that, following her father's death, she experienced intense grief and medical problems that did not respond to treatment. She visited some spiritual mediums and found she could go into trance. Spirits, speaking through her, told her that she must become a medium. The spirits designed a ritual healing trance performance. Her own health improved as she conducted these rituals for friends and neighbors. News of her abilities spread, and she attracted supplicants from all over Thailand. I watched as she went into trance and inserted metal skewers through her tongue and cheeks. The wounds did not bleed, and she seemed impervious to pain. With the skewers in place, she joked with the audience, bringing them to laughter. She seemed able to detect people's medical problems psychically. She touched her bare foot to a red-hot metal grill and then placed her foot (which seemed uninjured) on people's infirmities. Many people claimed to benefit from this treatment. When I interviewed her afterward, a jewel fell to the floor beside me. She told me that this was a gift for me from the spirits. I assumed that she created this effect by sleight-of-hand.

Healers often reported having medical problems that did not respond to conventional medical treatment. They described anomalous experiences (spontaneous inner voices, waking ESP, paranormal dreams, OBE, PK) and attributed these perceptions to spirits. In harmony with local traditions, many healers followed directives prescribed by their spirits. They used sleight-of-hand performance (ostensibly PK), pain denial feats, heat immunity feats, and trance behavior feats (ostensibly ESP) as part of their rituals. People in their audiences claimed miraculous benefits.

These experiences coincide with paranormal categories reported all over the world. They shape folk belief in similar directions, even though there is wide cultural variation. Some people report waking ESP and paranormal dreams, and those around them believe they have magical abilities. People report out-of-body and near-death experiences and come to believe in souls that can leave the body. Psychokinesis, apparitions, and poltergeist events support belief in life after death. Those reporting many experiences, and mastering performance skills, conduct spiritual healing rituals. All in all, anomalous experiences support shamanism, the belief that practitioners leave their bodies, communicate with spirits, and conduct beneficial rituals.

SORRAT fell within this pattern. College students, guided originally by Dr. Neihardt, heard raps and communicated with spirits. Some went into trance and spirits spoke through them. They developed powerful beliefs regarding PK. As a result, core members conducted hundreds of séances for decades afterward. All SORRATs that I interviewed regarded their experiences as authentic. Many claimed to benefit from spiritual healing.

Asian practitioners revealed features similar to SORRAT accounts. They communicated with spirits, experienced ESP and PK, and conducted rituals that resulted in hypnotic and placebo effects. As with the SORRATs, the reported healings could be explained as hypnotic and placebo effects. Some Asian features were particularly parallel to SORRAT. A Taiwanese group, for example, held the legs of chair, believing that a deity controlled the chair's movements. As with SORRAT, they seemed to use subconscious muscular movements to guide the chair while it wrote messages. They told me that the texts included information, unknown to the group, which they later found to be true. The chair also provided healing to those seeking its aid. Like the SORRATs, they were certain of the authenticity of the phenomena. A Taoist group told me about a poltergeist in their temple. They saw objects move without being touched, and people were pushed off a bench by the unseen spirit. Their priest alleviated these problems by going into trance, speaking with the spirit, and performing special rituals.

These patterns led me to hypothesize that SORRAT-like processes probably shaped Paleolithic beliefs. Ancient hunter-gatherers, who lived in small groups, would have experienced the rapport that SORRAT found conducive to PK. Some, with a propensity for anomalous experience, came to believe that practitioners could go into trance, leave their bodies, communicate with spirits, gain information psychically, and conduct spiritual healings. Anthropologists refer to this belief as shamanism, humankind's first religious form. They tell us that all hunter-gathers lived in small groups and practiced shamanism. Anthropologists in the field documented many anomalous experiences associated with shamanism (Goulet and Young, 1994; Hunter, 2012).

I conducted random sample surveys, asking about anomalous experiences in China, Japan, and the USA. I collected thousands of anomalous experience narratives in the USA and other countries. My narrative collection revealed major categories: apparitions, paranormal dreams, waking ESP, out-of-body experiences, near-death experiences, psychokinesis, sleep paralysis, psychokinesis, synchronicity, déjà vu, UFOs, and spiritual healing. Each category had core features consistent across cultures with common structural elements. Apparitions had similar distortions of perception in all societies. All societies reported hauntings (recurring experiences, particularly apparitions, associated with a place and deceased person) and poltergeists (recurring spontaneous PK associated with a place and deceased or living person). Waking ESP often pertained to the present, while paranormal dreams more frequently portrayed the future. Waking ESP tended to instill more conviction than did paranormal dreams (McClenon, 2000).

Cross-cultural commonalities within these perceptions imply a genetic basis. Anomalous experiences run in families. People reporting many experiences typically have close relatives with many experiences (McClenon, 2002a, 2002b). Folklore all over the world suggests that psychic ability is inherited. These observations should not be surprising since virtually all psychological traits have genetic basis.

Researchers found that certain psychological variables are correlated with the propensity for anomalous experience. These variables include absorption, dissociation, hypnotizability, transliminality (the capacity to "go beyond the threshold" of normal consciousness), history of childhood difficulty, and belief in spirits, souls, life after death, and magical abilities. People abused or traumatized as children tend to be more dissociative and to have greater propensity for anomalous experience (McClenon, 2002a, 2002b).

These observations resulted in the *ritual healing theory*, a scenario describing the origins of religious sentiment. The theory argues that Paleolithic people had spontaneous anomalous experiences. These perceptions led to belief in spirits, souls, life after death, and magical abilities (Hufford, 1982). Based on these beliefs, Paleolithic shamans devised trance performances resulting in spiritual healing. Those with genes facilitating spiritual healing (absorption, dissociation, hynotizability, transliminality) benefited from these rituals and, over time, these genes became more prevalent. Because these genes facilitate anomalous experience and shamanic trance, an evolutionary cycle occurred, shaping the human capacity for anomalous experience, hypnosis, and shamanism.

Clinical studies support the ritual healing theory. Paleolithic people experienced childbirth complications, hemorrhage, inflammation, burns, and many psychologically-related disorders. Hypnosis based on absorption and dissociation has proven effective for treating these problems. Hypnosis can affect physiological processes considered outside conscious control (Barber, 1984; McClenon, 1994, 2002a, b).

The ritual healing theory coincides with what we know about the evolution of consciousness. Ancient worms (nematodes) had sleep/wake cycles that helped them cope with stressful environments. Birds and mammals exhibit REM sleep and dreams, which are thought to provide preparative functions. Some animals exhibit rapid changes of consciousness, playing dead in response to novel positioning or threat, a process called *animal hypnosis*. Chimpanzees exposed to repetitive motion pass into hypnotic-like states with the dreamy appearance of hypnotized humans. Pre-linguistic *Homo erectus*, gathering around fires, must have chanted, sang, and danced as they gained control over their vocal cords. These conditions are conducive to hypnotic trance and increased suggestibility.

Was there sufficient time within human evolutionary history for healing rituals to affect gene frequencies? *Homo sapiens* buried their dead around 100,000 years ago, indicating religious sentiment. Based on cave paintings and burials, we know they practiced shamanism for at least 30,000 years. Evolutionists note that social factors can result in genetic change within one thousand years. Ritual healing has been practiced long enough to have evolutionary impact.

Ritual healing hypotheses have been verified through social surveys, anthropological observation, folklore research, and clinical research (McClenon, 2002, 2012, 2013; Cooper and Thalbourne, 2005). The theory provides basic hypotheses: (1) anomalous experiences are correlated with absorption, dissociation, and transliminality. (2) Anomalous experiences propensities are correlated with beliefs regarding spirits, souls, life after death, and magical abilities. (3) When people tell and retell anomalous experience stories, they shape folk religious traditions regarding spirits and healing. (4) Shamanic healing rituals, in which practitioners induce hypnotic and placebo effects, have a degree of effectiveness.

The ritual healing theory pertains to scientific areas experiencing rapid progress, such as molecular genetics. The theory, published in 1997, predicted that geneticists could locate genes selected by shamanic healing. Ott, et al. (2005) identified a gene associated with the Tellegen Absorption Scale, a finding supporting the ritual healing theory. The theory argues that other genes associated with spiritual healing will be discovered.

Some parapsychologists argue that ESP provides survival benefits. If this is the case, researchers can locate these genes by comparing DNA of family members reporting many ESP episodes to those claiming none. The search for ESP genes could be conducted in a manner parallel to the search for schizophrenia genes.

By the 1990s, after decades of twin and family studies, researchers felt sure that schizophrenia had genetic basis. Twin studies indicated that schizophrenia, bipolar disorder, many personality variables, hypnotizability, and even religiosity were influenced by genes (Bouchard, McGue, Lykken, Tellegen, 1999). The existence of schizophrenia genes posed a paradox since the disorder has evolutionary costs, yet persists over many generations. Some researchers argued that schizophrenia must convey survival advantages sufficient to overcome its costs. They theorized that schizophrenia had benign forms linked to shamanism or creativity. They argued that only a small percentage of people with schizophrenia genes experienced onset of the disorder. Parapsychologists speculated that these genes facilitated ESP, a variable related to shamanism and creativity. This theory explained, in part, the stigma associated with psychic phenomena.

During the 1990s, I became curious about the relationship between anomalous experience and mental disorder. I noticed that many psychic practitioners had unusual symptoms and that people visiting psychic practitioners and mediums seemed to seek be a special type of therapy. During that era, I read Mirowsky and Ross's (1989) community survey of psychological symptoms. Their method of analysis created a map in which psychological variables used to diagnose mental disorder were arranged so that the distance between them corresponded to the degree they were correlated. Variables close to each other were highly correlated, and those far apart were not correlated. I wondered how anomalous experience variables would have been arrayed if they had been included on Mirowsky and Ross's questionnaire. A tight cluster of variables implied shared genes. What were the relationships between ESP,

PK and other anomalous experiences to each other and to the psychological symptoms? Was ESP connected to schizophrenia, as predicted by theorists who hypothesized shared genes?

In 2001, I began a community survey to conduct a multidimensional analysis of psychological symptoms and anomalous experiences (McClenon, 2012, 2013). I had community members fill out questionnaires asking about anomalous experiences, psychological symptoms, and dissociative/absorptive/transliminal experiences. As predicted by the ritual healing theory, the anomalous experience, shamanic, and psychological symptom variables were correlated with each other and with self-reported childhood difficulty. Multidimensional scaling revealed that anomalous experiences were highly correlated with schizophrenia variables, but the anomalous experiences were not within the schizophrenia symptom cloud (see Section 3, Chapter 11, figure 2). The pattern implied that anomalous experiences were like schizophrenia but did not share genes with schizophrenia.

The relationships among the anomalous experiences revealed a curious configuration. These experiences were correlated in a way that did not fit folklore explanations. For example, psychokinesis (thought to represent mind-over-matter) was highly correlated with UFO experience (thought to represent extraterrestrial visitors) and out-of-body experience (thought to indicate the soul leaving the body). All anomalous experience variables were loosely clustered close to the schizophrenia variables, suggesting that all these experiences were unusual forms of consciousness.

These findings fit the concept of schizotypy, the theory that hypothesizes a continuum of characteristics and experiences ranging from psychosis to normal dissociation. Although the original concept of schizotypy was devised to identify people susceptible to psychosis, researchers have found that schizotypy has psychologically-healthy forms that include dissociative imagination. Anomalous experiences, mysticism, and shamanic experience may be included in this continuum since all represent unusual forms of consciousness. People reporting these episodes rarely experience onset of psychosis but often exhibit the unusual beliefs and non-conformist personalities labeled as schizotypy. During the 1990s, researchers discovered correlations between schizotypy and OBEs and other forms of anomalous experience.

These findings suggest that anomalous experiences may be better understood as variations of consciousness. The folklore explanations of ESP (sixth sense), apparitions (discarnate entities), OBE (detached souls), PK (mind-over-matter), and UFOs (extraterrestrial visitors) have not led to fully replicable experiments. The theory that these episodes are associated with variations in consciousness does not deny their unexplained qualities.

Many people assume that consciousness results from either physiological brain processes or a magical entity, the soul, that leaves the body after death. Some forms of anomalous experience (apparitions, PK, UFOs) support belief in a collective consciousness since (1) they are perceived by multiple observers simultaneously. (2) Incidences of the various experiential forms are highly correlated. (3) Incidences are affected by belief and skepticism by those within the group. (4) Group PK experiments such as those by the Philip Group suggest collective consciousness. Participants often report anomalous experiences. (5) A set of hypotheses link anomalous experience with unusual consciousness. The various types of anomalous experience are hypothesized to (a) share genetic basis (b) be correlated with mystical and shamanic experiences (c) be correlated with odd, schizotypal behaviors, and (d) be correlated with childhood difficulty. Psychokinesis is involved with shared developmental patterns since age of schizophrenia onset, poltergeist agent modal age, and age of highest hypnotic suggestibility all coincide, in general, with adolescence.

Molecular genetics research has resolved the issue regarding shared ESP and schizophrenia genes. Rather than discovering genes related to schizophrenia, researchers found hundreds of genetic risk variants, each with small effect. Collectively, the results explain only about 4% of schizophrenia variance, suggesting that the disorder has no major underlying genes (Leo, 2016). Present gene hunting methods are sufficiently robust that discovery of major genes is very unlikely. This finding refutes the hypothesis that schizophrenia and ESP share genes since schizophrenia has none.

How can schizophrenia have genetic basis without specific genes? Keller and Miller (2006) provide a theory explaining this paradox. They hypothesize that human brains evolved through development of a series of overlapping modules. Each module had "added-on" characteristics, layered upon previous modules, providing functions that extended those of previous modules. For example, Broca's area, in the frontal lobe, extended previous functions in a way that facilitated language. Keller and Miller (2006) note that random mutations are almost always detrimental. They hypothesize that mutations often result in module failure, triggering a cascade of failures in overlaying modules. The result is a pattern of failures associated with the brain's layered configuration, causing a set of symptoms. The various symptom patterns allow psychiatrists to diagnose mental illness even though many disorders are not associated with specific genes.

The Keller/Miller theory corresponds with the diathesis-stress theory of schizophrenia (Corcoran, et al., 2005). This model regards psychosis onset as due to genetic propensity coupled with a critical level of stress. Within the Keller/Miller model, mutations are the weak links that cause failures when exposed to sufficient stress. The Keller/Miller theory also explains schizophrenia research history. Early genetic studies found schizophrenia genes within isolated ethnic groups, but these studies could not be replicated in other samples. Keller and Miller argue that deleterious mutations are often passed down for several generations before being eliminated. The Keller/Miller theory explains why psychiatrists struggle to demarcate mental disorder categories; symptoms patterns, resulting from module failures, often overlap since modules overlap. Their theory also fits evolutionary scenarios. Animals reveal prototypes of depression, anxiety disorder, and obsessive-depressive disorder, but not psychosis.

Keller and Miller's theory can be applied to the ritual healing theory. Psychosis, schizotypy, anomalous experience, mysticism, and shamanic experience are hypothesized to be products of temporary failure patterns originating with mutations. This theory explains the wounded-healer syndrome among shamans. Some mutations result in temporary, sporadic module failures, some of which involve anomalous experiences. The shamanic role helps the shaman overcome cognitive handicaps associated with these mutations.

These hypotheses coincide with a parapsychological paradigm explaining the relationship between consciousness and ESP. Chuck Honorton's Ganzfeld Experiment was based on the theory that normal consciousness blocks ESP and that sensory restriction facilitates it. This idea originated with teachings from the *Yoga Sutras of Patañjali,* an ancient Indian text. Patañjali portrayed the mind as like a container of swirling, muddy water. Within this metaphor, the mud reduces clarity, preventing the observer from seeing clearly, but when the mind becomes still, the mud settles and spiritual insights become possible. Over the centuries, Asian adepts have found that mental stillness also allows paranormal phenomena. Although much research supported Honorton's hypothesis, skeptics were critical (Bem and Honorton, 1994, Hyman, 1994). Whether ESP exists or not, this history implies that normal consciousness thwarts anomalous experiences while certain altered states facilitate them.

Other spiritual traditions advocate alternate ways of disrupting normal consciousness to achieve anomalous experiences. Techniques include repetitive drumming, dancing, chanting, and other rituals for inducing trance states. These methods suggest that hypnosis, or similar processes, facilitate shamanic and anomalous experience.

J. B. Rhine's parapsychological paradigm uses standard statistical techniques to evaluate experiments such as Honorton's Ganzfeld method. Researchers have generated much evidence supporting belief in ESP, PK, and sensory restriction strategies, but like SORRAT, they have not devised a fully replicable experiment. Some parapsychologists argue that psi has capricious, evasive qualities that thwart full scientific verification. Jim Kennedy (2003) describes the tendency for laboratory psi to decline, sometimes reverse, and other times manifest with unexpected secondary effects. He reviews psychological, motivational, and quantum theories seeking to explain this tendency but feels their scope is limited. He suggests that a "higher consciousness" may be the source of psi. SORRAT entities argue that low, middle, and higher levels of consciousness are involved. George Hansen (2001) reviews an extensive body of literature regarding psi's capricious, elusive nature. He notes that psi is associated with low status researchers, high status opponents, social change, transition, flux, disorder, marginality, binary opposition, liminality, and blurring of distinctions. These features describe the *trickster*, a universal folklore archetype representing chaos, irrationality, deception, and marginality. Although the trickster is beyond psychological explanation, Hansen argues that its personification allows us to organize these characteristics in ways that provide coherence. The psi trickster has an active, self-aware quality, motivated to thwart scientific verification. Hansen's discussion fits SORRAT experience.

Both Kennedy and Hansen mention genetic factors as possibly related to psi's capricious nature. Psi is like a genetic mutation, typically dysfunctional but sometimes facilitating innovation. This idea coincides with the random mutation model; random mutations are typically detrimental but some trigger experiences revealing hidden dimensions. Hansen argued that the process can even occur on the social level, an observation in harmony with group apparition, PK, and UFO experiences. He hypothesizes that the trickster "can operate through individuals without them being aware of it," and also occur on a collective level, "influencing entire cultures" (Hansen, 2001, p. 430). These ideas coincide with SORRAT experience. Core SORRAT members went into trance and were not always aware of this. Psychical researchers hypothesize that a form of group consciousness can generate PK, and many SORRAT accept this idea. The SORRAT entities may act independently at times, but this hypothesis cannot be verified and some entity characteristics seem derived from the group. SORRAT history suggests that a group consciousness, allowing PK, was eventually overwhelmed by a more powerful collective consciousness.

These speculations exceed what can be evaluated scientifically since consciousness has not been defined. Alan Hobson (1994) provides a model offering a starting point for discussing consciousness and anomalous experience.

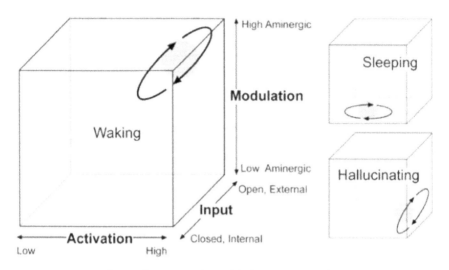

Figure 3: J. Allan Hobson's (1994) model of consciousness (from Kent, 2010)

Hobson's (1994) argues that three measurable features govern consciousness (see figure 3): (1) *brain activation* is the rate of information processing (high vs. low); (2) *information input source* is either outside the individual (open) or inside the individual (closed); and (3) *chemical modulation* pertains to the aminergic chemical system vs. cholinergic chemical system. Waking consciousness occurs when the brain has high activation, external focus, and is under the control of the aminergic chemical system. Sleep occurs when the aminergic chemical system declines, activation declines, and inner focus increases. Under the control of the cholinergic chemical system, the brain varies between low activation during non-rapid eye movement (NREM) and increased activation during rapid eye movement (REM). Humans experience about four or five REM cycles each night, with about 90-120 total REM minutes. Although dreaming can occur during both REM and NREM stages, it is more visual during REM. Hobson suggests that dreams are the result of the brain interpreting random neuron firing, but an alternate theory suggests that dreams have rehearsal functions, programing the brain to cope with concerns. These theories are not mutually exclusive since dreams have qualities coinciding with both theories. Dreams bring random elements into fantasy scenarios involving life concerns. These combinations could provide rehearsal functions for dealing with random dangers, enhancing coping skills in chaotic environments.

Hobson identifies five basic characteristics of human dreams: (1) dreams often feature intense emotions; (2) dreams are frequently disorganized and illogical; (3) strange content is accepted without question; (4) people often experience bizarre sensations (flying, falling, or running in slow motion); and (5) dreams are difficult to remember. The most-remembered dreams are stressful, with negative emotions and dramatic conflicts. These features suggest random processes, narrative imagination, and preparatory function.

Hobson's model can be used to interpret unusual experiences. Hallucinations, the sensory experience of something that does not exist outside the mind, involve a combination of chemical systems. The cholinergic system is activated during wakefulness, with closed input during high activation (figure 3, lower right). Hallucinations occur in conjunction with psychosis and other disruptions of consciousness, a variation from the normal sleep/wake cycle. The term *apparition* is a parapsychological concept, referring to perceptions often labeled as ghosts. Apparitions, the most prevalent experiential form in my collection of anomalous experience narratives, are like hallucinations except they seem unrelated to pathology and sometimes include extrasensory elements. There are a disproportionate number of apparitions appearing during, and shortly after, a death, implying that a deceased person has returned from the dead. Some apparitions provide information not known to the experiencer, which the experiencer later verifies. Although not always the case, multiple people often describe the same image after an apparition appears before a group. Although Hobson's model cannot explain this anomalous element, in many respects apparitions are like hallucinations. Among the accounts in my collection, only a minority of accounts include evidence suggesting a paranormal event.

Hobson's model facilitates discussion of psychosis, schizotypy, and anomalous, mystical, and shamanic experience. The concept of *schizotypy* hypothesizes a continuum of experiences from psychosis to normal imaginative dissociation (Lenzenweger, 2010). The term has various definitions, shaped by researchers' desire to identify people prone to schizophrenia. They hoped to reduce the onset of schizophrenia by identifying and treating people prone to this disorder. Schizotypy includes some symptoms of psychosis (such as hallucinations), odd beliefs and behaviors, nonconformity, and unusual experiences, particularly out-of-body experiences. Researchers have found that, although people exhibiting schizotypy are more prone to psychotic breaks, the condition can be associated with creative dissociation, cognitive organization, and psychological well-being. Within Hobson's model, some schizotypic experiences suggest activation of the cholinergic system during the waking state. The concept could be broadened to include anomalous, mystical, and shamanic experience, since all these perceptions imply deviations from normal consciousness. This line of thought does not deny the anomalous qualities of some experiences but leads to testable hypotheses. Combinations of aminergic/cholinergic chemical systems sometimes result in perceptions that mix reality with dreams—with the reality element leading to anomalous qualities. For example, people's visions and dreams are anomalous if they convey information not known to the experiencers.

The term *trance* has not been defined precisely, but within Hobson's model it suggests deviation from the normal sleep/wake cycle, allowing dream-like perceptions during the waking state. Trance often includes a degree of cognitive control. The shaman has an out-of-body experience, experiences visionary images, gains insights regarding distant events (alleged ESP), but is able to return to normal states of consciousness. The mechanisms by which this occurs seem to involve hypnosis, self-hypnosis, meditation, or the results of sensory overload. The term *shamanic experience* refers to perceptions that are not spontaneous but involve a degree of controlled deviation from normal consciousness. In a way, most parapsychological research involves a type of performance. The subject must call forth an unusual ability, a deviation from what is considered normal, since most people regard ESP or PK to be rare.

Waking ESP and paranormal dreams are, by definition, related to specific conscious states. Cross-cultural analysis of narratives reveals consistent patterns, suggesting that consciousness influences the anomalous content. Paranormal dreams are more likely to involve future events, a high volume of information, and low levels of conviction (with low probability of taking action). Waking ESP episodes are more likely to involve present events, provide a low volume of information, yet result in higher levels of conviction (with greater probability of taking action). According to the ritual healing theory, these episodes are the result of temporary disruptions of module connections, failures that interrupt waking or dreaming consciousness. The high volume of information conveyed during precognitive dreams suggests that the cholinergic chemical system facilitates information conveyance, while the aminergic system facilitates reality orientation.

Poltergeist and group PK entail collective perceptions of unexplained events. Although PK experiencers typically feel awake, their accounts have dream-like characteristics, with reduced or restrained dream qualities. PK groups report intense emotions, but to a lesser extent than dreamers. They see dream-like events—objects moving without touching, levitations, and apports, but these experiences do not defy reality to the same degree as dreams. They feel strange sensations such as touching or variations in temperature, but few are paralyzed to the degree experienced during dreams. Participants in trance experience amnesia, somewhat similar to that of dreamers. It is as if the group generates PK through collective cholinergic processes, moderated by the aminergic system.

Group PK often involves some type of spiritual entity, thought to be produced, in part, by the group's collective consciousness. These entities have dream-like characteristics. Within spiritualist traditions, they have stereotypic personalities (ancient sage, joker, trickster, noble savage), reveal quirky qualities, and present unorthodox doctrines—characteristics of schizotypy. Like dreamers, they claim independent existence but cannot verify their identity. They expect audiences to accept this situation without question. Although they claim to be independent of the living, elements within their utterances seem derived from the group. Observers are left with a variety of hypotheses: fraud, paranormal tricksters, unusual forms of consciousness, or discarnate entities. It seems that elements within group PK coincide with the theory that the cholinergic chemical system is involved. Group PK seemed linked to a collective narrative imagination, which manifests in ways that cannot be fully verified, a situation parallel to dreams.

Unlike dreams, group PK stimulates skeptical opposition, an attitude that seems to reduce the phenomena. This process should not be considered completely rational. Even elite scientists resort to *a priori* arguments when attacking claims of the paranormal (McClenon, 1982). It is as if the phenomena are the product of a battle between skeptical and believer projections. This situation supports the idea that some type of collective consciousness is involved in both support and opposition to psi. Perhaps, as Asian traditions imply, the evolutionary process has constructed mechanisms within waking human consciousness that thwart ESP and PK, rendering their incidence sporadic and generally weak. This may be due to the evolutionary costs of psychosis or perhaps some type of ego-defense mechanism.

Future researchers could investigate the recurring patterns observed by previous researchers. Although they should not expect to fully verify anomalous claims, they can document correlations among variables, trickster characteristics, and the degree that the phenomena have cholinergic characteristics. Over time, cognitive researchers will gain a better understanding of the mechanics of the aminergic/cholinergic chemical systems, allowing more precise hypotheses.

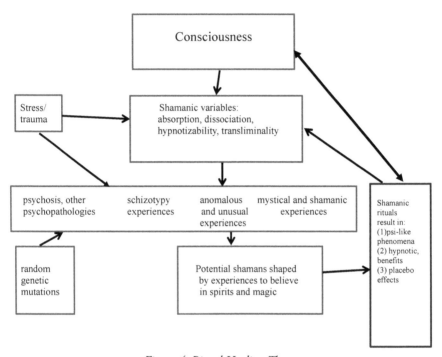

Figure 4: Ritual Healing Theory

Figure 4 provides a schematic of the ritual healing theory, summarizing hypotheses derived from the theory. It portrays random genetic mutations as a factor contributing to psychosis, schizotypy, anomalous/unusual experiences, and mystical/shamanic experiences. Due to this genetic basis, the ritual healing theory hypothesizes that all societies contain people with these experiences. Researchers can test this hypothesis through surveys of incidence of these types of experience (genetic basis hypothesis).

Figure 4 portrays childhood stress and trauma as contributing to psychosis, schizotypy, and anomalous/mystical/shamanic experience. This is an extension of the stress-diathesis model of schizophrenia. Those with genetic propensity experience unusual forms of consciousness when exposed to sufficient levels of stress.

The figure shows a correlation between childhood stress/trauma and dissociation, absorption, hypnotic susceptibility, and transliminality (trauma/dissociation hypothesis). Childhood stress/trauma is hypothesized to activate alleles governing these traits.

The figure shows a connection between shamanic variables (dissociation, absorption, transliminality) and the consciousness variables (psychosis, schizotypy, anomalous, unusual, mystical, shamanic experience).

The figure shows a relationship between anomalous/unusual experiences and "shaman shaped by experiences to believe in spirits and magic." The ritual healing theory specifies that the frequencies of common anomalous and unusual experiences (apparitions, paranormal dreams, waking ESP, out-of-body experience, psychokinesis, spiritual healing) are positively correlated with beliefs in spirits, souls, life after death, and magical abilities (experiential source hypothesis).

The figure specifies that "shamans shaped by experience to believe in spirits and magic" engage in rituals that result in "psi-like phenomena, hypnotic effects, and placebo effects." The ritual healing theory specifies that shamanic performances stimulate belief, generating hypnotic and placebo benefits (performance hypothesis).

The figure shows a relationship between psi-like phenomena, hypnotic effects, placebo effects, and the shamanic variables. The ritual healing theory hypothesizes that shamanic rituals had evolutionary impacts, selecting for genes related to the shamanic variables—absorption, dissociation, hypnotic suggestion, and transliminality (shamanic effectiveness hypothesis). Anthropologists can observe shamanic rituals and interview those reporting benefits. Surveys should indicate that benefits derived from spiritual and folk healing are correlated positively with the shamanic variables. Molecular geneticists can uncover the genes related to shamanic variables.

Special hypotheses regarding field investigations of group PK

The ritual healing theory hypothesizes that the shamanic variables interact with physiological parameters governing consciousness. The theory predicts that investigators will witness patterns encountered by previous observers: (1) Presence of people prone to PK increases probability that the entire group perceives the phenomenon. (2) Skeptical observers reduce the probability that the entire group perceives PK. (3) The more closely group PK is monitored, the less likely that it will be experienced. (4) Group PK has sporadic trickster characteristics, perhaps derived from cholinergic chemical systems. These qualities include irrationality, deception, marginality, and active avoidance of detection. (5) Research involving group PK is associated with stigma.

Further research is required to determine relationships between group PK experiences, collective consciousness, and effects of rapport, belief, and skepticism on group PK. Advances in cognitive science will probably allow more precise definitions, hypothesis testing, and theory revision.

APPENDIX A
COMMENTS FROM PARTICIPANTS

Author Note: In 1984 and 1985, I sent out copies of my original *Entity Letters* manuscript (Part 1 of this book) to people interested in SORRAT, soliciting comments. Unless otherwise noted, their responses were made during those years. Many provided comments regarding specific phrases in the texts, requesting that I shape the narrative to fit their skeptical or believer predispositions. For example, skeptics asked that I insert the word "ostensible" before all mention of paranormal phenomena. Some believers were angered by my discussion of skeptical hypotheses since they regarded these explanations as implausible. All in all, the comments support the argument that believer/skeptic polarity shapes our interpretation of the narrative.

John Thomas Richards, Ph. D. (1937-2015)
SORRAT Member

Dr. McClenon has asked me to tell him what I think the nature of psi energy may be. I do not think much can be gained from mere speculation, since we do not yet know much about what psi can and cannot do. It is hard enough to convince most people that psi exists at all. If pressed for an answer, I can but summarize what the entities have told us: that psi is a natural, universal force that can be used to accomplish many seemingly impossible tasks, and also do work that can be more efficiently accomplished by the application of ordinary, known physical forces. That is to say, a table can be levitated by the application of psi energy—and that is a very remarkable fact, a fact that runs contrary to ordinary human experience and consequently tends to be fervently denied by those who have not seen a table levitate for themselves. However, using psi to raise a table into the air is an inefficient use of psi energy, much like trying to hammer a ten-penny nail with a large screwdriver. It can be done that way, true—but it would be more efficient for someone to pick up the table and carry it. While entities certainly do exist, even those who most vigorously deny the reality of the spiritual nature of life have yet to offer one shred of concrete proof that the spirit does not survive bodily death. They would be hard-pressed to prove any negative about this subject. The entities have communicated by raps, trance-talking, automatic writing, and direct writing, to use four examples; they have also stressed the fact that we should not value information from the "Other Side" any more than we value information from ordinary sources on *this* side of the change that we call death. In *The Entity Letters,* you will see examples of wisdom, trite statements, idle conversation, casual remarks, practical advice, and sheer foolishness, just as you would expect from conversations with your friends who "still have their skins on." In the 22 years during which I have been regularly exposed to various levels of entities in the SORRAT experiments, I have come to accept them as people, picking up some of their expressions and their sense of humor, just as one does with companions whom one knows through the years in ordinary situations. For, by now, to me, this contact with the "Other Side," of *which our side is one aspect*, has become quite ordinary, too.

William Edward Cox (1915-1994)
SORRAT investigator

It was a unique pleasure to read this analysis of the SORRAT experience as seen through the eyes of such a dispassionate sociologist. The author is one I have known for some years; but when the manuscript of his very readable book arrived, it revealed to me how sociologists, among others, look upon new frontiers of empirical science. McClenon's innocent doubts, as they continued through all chapters save the last, surprised me; but not nearly as much as did his depicting so hyperbolically how I, an admitted pioneer in psychokinetic researches, appeared to my juniors in parapsychology as a "crackpot," more to be pitied than censored. This he has done with such finesse that I have made no effort to dissuade or correct him.

On certain points, however, the present solicited contribution does enable me to take two or three corrective measures. The first alludes to the possibility the effects were created by fraudulent animation of films, via thousands of manual openings of the mini-lab and delicate movements of its target objects. Fraud would require single-frame exposures of the camera for more than a thousand feet of film—a feat too laborious to be possible, even if my multiple seals had not made it a practical impossibility. Jim McClenon is not alone in the view that this was somehow indeed the case. It should show that almost as much prejudice remains among parapsychologists concerning qualitative phenomena as they themselves find extant among most other folk concerning quantitative ESP findings!

The second point concerns rapping sounds. I grant that some types are very easy to fake, but the varied conditions under which we have heard so many at Rolla make that inconceivable. Raps were observed coming from concrete and earth, at my home or elsewhere, and by a floor-level microphone, wherever I might wish.

When this book appears, I shall enjoy reading it again before completing my own, a more slowly plodding analysis of selected SORRAT claims. [W. E. Cox died on June 12, 1994. His edited manuscript, *Psi Physics,* was published posthumously by Penobscot Press in 2004.]

John Hunt
SORRAT member

Dr. McClenon has asked me to write a few words about the Rolla phenomena. First of all, I wish to state that, to the best of my knowledge, his account is factual. Although I was not present at every event he cites, I was present at some of them and at many similar events. It is inevitable that anyone's account will to some extent differ from that of ether witnesses and this is no doubt true for this book as well. However, I feel that Jim has done an excellent job describing the events connected with the Richards' home in Rolla as well as elsewhere.

It is certain that most people will view these events in Rolla with no small degree of skepticism. Yet, after knowing the Richards for eight years, I have never seen any evidence of fraud, and I was skeptical at first. The wealth and variety of PK and other phenomena would, in my opinion, have been quite beyond the abilities of the Richards, or anyone else involved, to create by deception. I have always found the Richards to be honest and generous people. To the best of my knowledge the Rolla phenomena is a valid case of macro PK and perhaps much more.

Interestingly enough, the only fraud even remotely connected with this case was perpetrated by known skeptics: Mr. James (the Amazing) Randi, Steve Shaw, and Mike Edwards. It is quite ironic that those who are so quick to make accusations of wrongdoing and deception without evidence, such as Mr. Randi, resort to these themselves. Yet, the Randi-Shaw-Edwards case did reveal that both parapsychologists and others (such as myself) could fail to detect deliberate deception over a considerable period of time. It is for just these reasons that proof in parapsychology is very hard to achieve.

I would like to conclude by making two points. First, I think that the parapsychological community should reconsider the negative reception that they have so far given to Mr. Cox's mini-lab films and many other investigations of the Skyrim and Rolla events. Second, that parapsychology itself is unlikely to advance until it moves beyond trying to prove that the phenomena it studies actually exists.

Lisa Schwarz
SORRAT member

I haven't written the "entities" for a few years [written in Oct. 1985]. I may write them in the future if I have more time. Originally, I had hoped that they would be able to predict my future, but they did not seem able to do this. They gave a few predictions, but these contained as many errors as those of people "in-the-flesh."

The entities serve a social purpose. Previously, I had plenty of time to write letters and found that the entities "networked" by mixing up the letters of those who contacted them so that we would have to write to each other. I began corresponding with people from all over the country, and I still keep in contact with some of them.

I haven't thought much about who the entities are. They say they are like us only without flesh. Their existence and means of communicating via raps and automatic writing upsets my worldview when I think about it, but I don't think about it that much. There are many things in this world that are beyond the understanding of normal people. I fly long distances in jets and talk to people via satellites and do not understand exactly how this is accomplished. I do not need to know all the details about how these things work and am not really that interested in it. I am interested in telepathic communication and would like to learn more about it so that I might have more control over it. I believe that the "entities," whoever they are, have helped me to improve my life.

Marian L. Nester (1910-2004)
Parapsychological Association Member
What I think about the Rolla case

It seems to me quite possible that there have indeed been many striking authentic manifestations of macro PK and other phenomena at the Rolla circle. Everything that I have read suggests that it is well worth parapsychologists' continuing study. I am impressed not only by the reports and photos, but by the entities' quality: their wisdom, individuality, purposefulness. Their claim to be "real" seems justified to me. Their information often seems to be coming from some other level of consciousness.

I received one of the envelopes mysteriously posted after being extracted from the mini-lab. I also received some answers to questions written by me left inside the mini-lab. Once there seemed to be a contact with the Control of the Margery mediumship, Walter Stinson, among these answers. One reply purportedly from another communicator at the mediumship had quite helpful insights.

Similarities to the Margery mediumship of Boston (1920s and 1930s)

I am intensively studying the Margery case at present. Both the Margery and SORRAT cases attracted a great deal of attention from the parapsychological "establishment." Cognitive and retro-cognitive dissonance showed up in respect to both, I believe. As a result, both have been ridiculed and dismissed by some researchers. Even good photos, detailed records, and sincere affidavits never seem enough to convince skeptics.

But at Rolla, as with Margery, there certainly were striking events that should not be forgotten or disregarded by psychical researchers. The reports must continue to be studied if there are accusations of fraud. Rich demonstrations like these cannot be pushed aside even if they are not fully understood.

George Hansen
Former Parapsychological Association Member

I spent a total of five nights as a guest in the home of Dr. and Mrs. Richards. As Jim McClenon indicates, they were very warm and open people; they wanted to have the phenomena scientifically studied and were very cooperative in experiments.

During my visits, I heard hundreds of raps that communicated in an intelligent fashion, At the beginning of a "rap session," the raps would frequently seem to be coming from directly below Dr. Richards' feet. As the session progressed, the raps seemed to gradually move some distance from him (usually up to two or three feet). Nearly all the raps occurred under very well-lighted conditions. Several times I sat on the floor near Dr. Richards (with my eyes within three feet of his feet). I never observed anything suspicious.

In one session hundreds of tiny raps emanated from a small metal snack tray around which five of us were seated with well-lighted conditions, everyone took their hands off the table and then I put mine back on. The raps continued for several more seconds but gradually died out. Everyone put their hands back on the table, and the tiny raps again started. We took our hands off, and the raps died out.

Others have reported observing trickery by Dr. Richards in producing the raps. Tony Cornell, in a workshop at the 1982 Parapsychology Association convention in Cambridge, reported observing Richards knocking on an object with his knuckles during a rap-session.[1] Cornell also reported hearing raps that he could not explain. Randi claims that "Richards is fond of producing 'spirit raps' with his foot and the Alpha boys [Steve Edwards and Mike Shaw] found it a hilarious sight as learned people stared at the floor whereon Richards stood, their mouth agape, while thumps came from a clearly moving foot" (*The Skeptical Inquirer*, Fall, *1983*, p. 39). If this statement is read carefully, it should be noted that Randi does not explicitly say what the boys observed. Steve Shaw has informed me that he does not agree with Randi's explanation (personal communication, 1983).

Clearly the raps occurring around Richards are anomalous. A satisfactory explanation has not yet been given. Perhaps the raps are a trick. Certainly, I have been fooled by magicians on other occasions. Perhaps the raps are paranormal. Unfortunately, parapsychologists have not yet developed adequate tools to study the phenomenon. For those still interested in scientifically studying the SORRAT phenomena, the raps might be the best place to start.

Masuaki Kiyota
Japanese PK Performer

I think that Steve Shaw and Mike Edwards are probably conscious of a sense of sin at the bottom of their hearts. A lie detector test could prove that they are wrong in saying that I cheat. I will continue to allow scientists to investigate my ability to bend spoons paranormally. This will prove that I do not cheat. I believe firmly that, in the end, the truth will be revealed and their lies laid bare.

I will act boldly and fearlessly to make the existence of psychokinesis known to the world. I will sow the seed of PK phenomena over the world little by little. Someday, the seeds will bear fruit, and the truth will speak for itself. I hope that people will understand why I do paranormal metal bending. I do not do it just for a show. People should realize that everyone has these powers. This is what I hope to show to people. They can bend metal paranormally by themselves. All people have psychic abilities.

I met Dr. Richards in Wisconsin in August 1982. I was surprised when I heard the raps come from the floor and felt the table vibrate when his group met. Many people in Japan, America, and all over the world have psychic abilities, even though it is hard to discover how these things occur. The truth will speak for itself, and the lies will eventually be found out.

Dennis Stillings
Director of the Archaeus Project

I find the communications of the "entities" vapid, pretentious, overblown, and above all, information-poor. In those rare instances when information is apparently given, it is usually of the sort that is difficult or impossible to verify, or if it involves psi-theory, already in print, or it is pseudo-quantum mechanics gobbledygook.

Let me give an example of what I mean by "information-poor." If you were to enter a bar and were to overhear a bit of conversation like, "Hey, Joe, I hear the Vikings' quarterback, Tommy Kramer, tore a ligament and will be out for the rest of the season," you would have heard an *information rich* statement—albeit a low-level one. Such a sentence contains, imbedded within it, reference to a form of recreation, anatomical references, a concept of time measurement, and a number of little mysteries—like "quarterback" and being "out for the season." If one were from another galaxy, such a sentence would be of considerable value in understanding the nature of human beings and how they live. If, in our hypothetical bar, you went on to question the speaker about details, he would, more often than not, gladly provide them—even if he were quite drunk. Such is not the case with the "entities."

First of all, information-rich sentences are an extreme rarity among the pages of entity communications. And try to get a straight answer to a simple question! A straight answer would be much too profound for us to grasp, limited as we are to a narrow earth-bound, sense-restricted view of things. Our poor brains are simply not adequate to grasp the complex and paradoxical nature of the "Beyond." Everything here is limited, a sweatshop to work out our karma so we can qualify for admission to the next world of "Spiritual Advancement," where the ineffable mysteries of "bodilessness" will he revealed. How dull.

There is, in fact, a great deal about the "entities" that reminds me of UFO contacts. The space messengers tell us of our "need to work through our problems" while they "watch over us" and, if we are good, and love one another, someday we will be whisked off to view the glories of advanced civilizations, where there is no war, etc., etc., ad nauseam. The biblical admonition to "try the spirits to see if they are of God" has some bearing here.

I am very far from denying the reality of the *phenomena* attributed to the entities. I have seen enough on my own, and at Rolla and Skyrim, not to concern myself any longer with the question of the existence of these effects. I am much more interested in how these phenomena affect the minds of those who are involved with "entity communication." Much is made in the SORRAT of the notion of "rapport." I have never heard anything but positive comments from the SORRATs about being "in rapport." But rapport is a neutral condition, colored by the moral nature of the participants. Both conscious and subconscious states combine and manifest in rapport in ways not necessarily predictable. Charlie Manson and his women were in a remarkably powerful state of rapport.

My impression of the SORRAT entities, and this may be typical of all "entities," is that they string everyone along. They cannot or will not perform when it would be helpful to us mere mortals to observe the phenomena. Of course, they have their reasons. They can't be made to "stoop" to prove matters of "faith." They dangle the carrot of "proof of psi" in front of SORRAT noses, while actually leading everyone concerned to a position where they are considered frauds, crackpots, and deluded fools. And soon these accusations will become true enough, and the *real job* of the entities will have been accomplished: this pattern has been repeated, historically, over and over again. The paranormal successes that are seen in the SORRAT rapport-sessions, the failures of the open experiments, the *successes* of the experiments, and the evidences of "tampering" all combine to create a no-win program of isolation and disrepute for those committed to the SORRAT experience. I prefer not to consider this program accidental.

The monotonous frequency with which the entities invoke "love," "oneness," and a host of other pious words and phrases—to the point of inducing trance states—is, to me at least, no small evidence of their insinuating deceitfulness. "Rapport," whatever else it may be, is a hothouse for brain-numbing psycho-poppies that quickly calm the critical faculties, and hold the unwary in thrall.

D. Scott Rogo (1950-1990)
Parapsychological Association Member

I first became acquainted with the SORRAT group and its claims in 1970 when Dr. John Thomas Richards wrote to my friend and colleague Raymond Bayless. The late J. B. Rhine at the Institute for Parapsychology in Durham had suggested the rapprochement. When Dr. Richards first explained the nature of his work, we were excited by its prospects. We, too, had been involved in sitter group research and had even achieved some minor success, so we were naturally eager to learn more of Dr. Richard's group. He subsequently sent us tapes of some of his sessions along with a batch of photos showing objects in flight, table levitations, and so on, that had occurred during his séances. It became immediately clear to us that our initial enthusiasm was premature, for the tapes revealed that the SORRAT sittings were conducted under very lax conditions—certainly too lax for comfort. The photographs we examined were also most curious. The levitating objects were invariably positioned in such a way that each of them could have been fastened to a wall, an adjoining piece of furniture, or prop. One photograph showed a hat *levitating,* but a closer examination revealed what appeared to be some sort of prop under it, perhaps holding it up. We dismissed the SORRAT group and Dr. Richards' claims after examining these and similar material.

I later shared my observations with Mr. W. E. Cox, who was actively pursuing research with Dr. Richards. He dismissed my observations without any consideration. He did tell me, however, that some of the early mini-lab boxes he had sent to the SORRAT group had been booby-trapped. (In other words, they were rigged so that trying to fraudulently manipulate the boxes would leave tell-tale signs.) He admitted that at least one of these boxes had been returned to him and had been tampered with. This was an admission and claim that Mr. Cox has never owned up to publicly, for reasons unknown.

Dr. Richards and his wife came to Los Angeles during the summer of 1971, and as part of their stay, gave a séance at the home of Raymond Bayless. I could not attend that night, but Raymond phoned me the next day to report on what turned out to be a rather hilarious evening. Dr. Richards did not know at the time that, even at this early stage, we were not taking him seriously.

The séance was held in a specially prepared and light-proofed room on the second floor of the Bayless's two-story duplex. The lights were put out, Raymond and his wife sat with the Richards in front of a light table, which immediately began to lift into the air in true Victorian fashion. Raymond's suspicion was that Dr. Richards was simply lifting the table up. To check out this supposition, Raymond supported his own end of the table as it rose with his hand. Once the table was "levitating," he let go of his end and the table immediately fell downward and toward Dr. Richards. The table remained suspended from *his* end! Mrs. Richards fell asleep during the sitting, but Dr. Richards assured everyone that she was really in trance. This claim was belied when Mrs. Richards began to snore loudly. Raps also erupted during the sitting, but these invariably emanated from the space close by the Richardses, and the Baylesses did not take them seriously. The sitting finally ended, and Raymond wished his guests a fond goodnight.

Frankly, the next day Raymond and I just laughed off the SORRAT matter once more. We never dreamed that it would ever come to the forefront of parapsychological interest. It was to my utter amazement that it actually did in the 1980s, when parapsychologists became more interested in the study of large-scale PK effects.

Looking back over the SORRAT records and my own 15-year familiarity with them, does it appear that any genuine PK was ever achieved by Dr. Richards or the SORRAT group? This is an issue that will probably never be resolved. But I can offer one observation that ties in with this more general issue—Dr. Richards' own testimony concerning *anything* should be considered extremely suspect.

It was rather surprising when we later learned that Dr. Richards had gone on the defensive against us. The catalyst probably came in 1976 when I wrote up a disguised account of the SORRAT matter in my book *In Search of the Unknown*. We learned through a researcher working with the SORRAT group (and who eventually became disenchanted with it) that Dr. Richards was charging us with "sour grapes." We were after him, we were told, because he would not cooperate in an investigation with us. I spoke directly with the parapsychologist to whom Dr. Richards had made this specific claim, and assured him that it was blatantly untrue. The fact was that Dr. Richards wanted us to investigate his claims, but we simply didn't want to have anything to do with him.

It was even more surprising when I found out that Dr. Richards' version of the 1971 Bayless debacle had appeared in print. Dr. Richards referred to the séance in the September 1984 issue of the *Archaeus Newsletter*. The crux of this article was a discussion of artifact induction in PK sitter groups. This is a questionable practice whereby a member of the group will deliberately fake a PK event in order to get the genuine PK going. The theory is that the faked event will be mistaken by the other sitters as genuine, thereby breaking down their psychological inhibitions about releasing PK. This procedure was developed and promoted by Kenneth Batcheldor, a British psychologist with a long interest in PK sitter group work.

While not mentioning us by name, the séance Dr. Richards describes is obviously the one he gave the Baylesses. The date, place, and even the description of the house and séance room precisely match-up. Yet it is here that Dr. Richards suddenly tells the world that the entire séance was a joke, that he did in fact levitate the table, and that it was all a matter of artifact induction! He even claims that he was caught because a second investigator (presumably me) was hiding behind a door, spying on him with a snooper-scope. This is, of course, utter nonsense and a total fabrication. Dr. Richards excuses his action because he says he drank too much wine before the sitting. When I questioned them on this issue, both of the Baylesses adamantly denied that Dr. Richards drank heavily before the sitting, or even imbibed very much at all.

So here we have a situation where, for several years, Dr. Richards tried to make weak and fabricated excuses for our skepticism about his claims. Note that never during this time did he give anyone any cause to think that the séance he gave for the Baylesses was anything but genuine. Yet years later, he suddenly admits that it was faked after all, but that it was simply a matter of artifact induction. It is interesting to note that never once did Dr. Richards make such a claim until well after Kenneth Batcheldor began popularizing the concept. Both before and after the séance in 1971, Dr. Richards made it clear that his séances were totally on the level and that anything occurring during them must be taken seriously.[2]

The fact that Dr. Richards often maneuvers his way out of embarrassing situations with fabricated scenarios came to light in 1983, when I reviewed his book on SORRAT for *Fate.* I commented that films showing object movements in the Cox mini-lab had been presented at a recent convention of the Parapsychological Association. I pointed out the films couldn't possibly be taken seriously by anyone with even the slightest familiarity with photography—especially by anyone who knows anything about stop-action animation. I also added that the audience roared with laughter as the films were run, since they were so blatantly ridiculous. Dr. Richards replied with an indignant letter to *Fate* in which he claimed that the only laughter heard during the screening was when a portion of the film was accidentally played in reverse. Since Dr. Richards had not attended the convention, I don't know where or how he got this information [author's note: this information came from W. E. Cox]. But again, it was a totally ridiculous claim. No portion of the film was ever run backwards, as even the projectionist for the screening later assured me. (He even told me that he had thought about responding to the Richards letter himself.)

I asked W. E. Cox an important question at the Parapsychological Association meeting in 1984, after his report on the SORRRAT mini-lab experiments. I asked him if had ever uncovered evidence of fraud on the part of SORRAT or Dr. Richards. He said that he hadn't. I then asked him why he had told me in 1973 specifically that he had found such evidence. Mr. Cox could not respond to this glaring inconsistency in his testimony and only grumbled that what he had told me didn't really matter!

In light of experiences and testimony such as this, I don't see any reason why the parapsychological community should take SORRAT or Dr. Richards seriously. It is clear that the testimony offered by both Dr. Richards and by Mr. Cox is presently unreliable. I wonder how often Dr. Richards will cry "artifact induction" whenever negative evidence is collected against him.

In conclusion, I have never lost my fascination with the SORRAT claims, if only because it is rather surprising to me that *anyone* still puts any faith in them. (To my dismay, however, I continually see references to SORRAT in the literature on PK.) This interest has led me to interview several fellow parapsychologists who have visited Dr. Richards and SORRAT. So far, I have not been able to collect any evidence from these researchers that causes me to change my mind.

Perhaps the matter was best summed up by a personal friend of mine who went to Missouri to witness the SORRAT miracles some years back. He considered the entire affair ridiculous but tried to keep his suspicions to himself. When he left, Dr. Richards bid him goodbye with this farewell: "It was nice having had you." My friend couldn't resist the temptation. "It was nice having been had," he answered.

James Randi
Skeptical Magician

I have never said—nor could I say—that any claimed paranormal phenomena do not exist. I can only say that the evidence offered to prove such claims is not sufficient to that purpose, and unusual claims require unusually good proof. If I say that I keep a billy goat in my yard, little proof is needed to establish the truth of that claim; if I say I have a unicorn there, much firmer and more extensive proof is needed.

Most "proof" of psi is anecdotal in nature. A great deal of such low-quality evidence does not serve to replace one good, solid positive experiment, replicated by independent, unbiased experimenters.

I have, for more than 20 years now, offered a prize of $10,000 to any person who can produce evidence of any paranormal, supernatural, or occult ability under proper observing conditions. No one has succeeded. I continue to offer the prize and it may be collected tomorrow. However, I do not expect that to occur. I have been approached by more than 600 persons for that prize. Only 75 have actually gotten to the testing stage. All have failed.

When an observer waits every December 24th evening for two decades at the fireplace waiting for a fat man in a red suit to drop in, he is qualified to doubt the existence of St. Nick based upon that evidence. The Jolly Old Elf might tumble down the chimney any time, and I am willing to greet him.

Dr. John R. Cole
Former Executive Director of the Committee for the Scientific Investigation of Claims of the Paranormal

Paranormal claims are to various degrees possible but, so far, undemonstrated beyond anecdotal evidence. Some experiments are finally taking into account in advance rather than retroactively the idea that their research subjects may be wrong, misleading, or fraudulent, or that researchers may affect the results via subconscious feedback. But many people believe in ESP devoutly. Some are led down the path of "false consciousness"—belief in baseless claims and unscientific theories about "causes" that add up to an unintentional smokescreen, diverting people from more significant scientific, political, social, and economic realities and explanations.

The mass media deal with exotic claims erratically, typically treating them uncritically as "features." Believers in "entities" or psychic powers are usually relegated to a sort of intellectual ghetto by outsiders' derisions and insiders' predictions of derision. Claims tend to be ignored or sensationalized, and the social movement(s) involved have been little-studied.

Dr. McClenon's research is thus welcome indeed. It is potentially flawed by an attitude that, ironically, has in the past been the major complaint sociologists have leveled against anthropologists—he practices "cultural relativism" to an extent that he sometimes appears to sacrifice analysis and skeptical, critical thinking. Indeed, he writes at one point that he realized that "skepticism was out of place" at SORRAT gatherings. However, his sympathetic approach allowed him access to people's thoughts and emotions that would have been less accessible to a scholar less anxious to believe.

John Neihardt's literary Black Elk was poetically mystical. SORRAT's Black Elk, like the other "spirits," is a rather inarticulate, banal clod who speaks (or raps) modern English (sometimes arch but never archaic) without tangible cultural differences from SORRAT members. If these messages represent true communications from "the other side," I would conclude that life after death entails lobotomization and a transformation of dead souls into Euro-American middle class suburban entities.

Spiritualism dates quite precisely to 1848 and the activities of the Fox sisters of Hydesville, New York. Rapping message sounds, table-tipping, and trite messages have been hallmarks of the movement ever since. In the 1870s, Kate Fox confessed, and in 1888 Margaret did the same, saying that they had made their first sounds by popping toe and other joints. They went on to become experts at various conjuring effects to impress people desperate to believe—people anxious to hear messages from dead loved ones with the profundity of "I am fine. Do not worry." They had, in fact, been exposed in 1851 by three Buffalo physicians, Austin Flint, Charles A. Lee, and C. R. Coventry (Bullough, 1985). Public exposure and confession of fraud had no major impact on the Spiritualist Movement in general, and the recent Randi, Shaw, and Edwards exposés were viewed by many believers with a similar yawn. People in the vast middle ground, not knowing what to believe, as well as many previously-duped believers, do benefit from healthy debunking, so the effort is not in vain,

And so it continues today. Every paranormal event reported by McClenon can be duplicated by a skillful trickster. Each event, with some variations, has been duplicated by magicians for a century or so—and of course by self-proclaimed "mediums" dealing with supposed spirits. Darkness or dim light makes trickery easier; there are dozens of ways to produce rapping noises, table-tippings, "materializations" of pine cones or whatever, phantom pictures, ectoplasmic ghosts, mysterious mailings of letters, and so forth. If an expert magician can duplicate every effect McClenon reports, one has to wonder about the reality of these effects. The author's natural skepticism is clear in this report—as is his wish to believe, to find something transcendent.

I am no magician but, like McClenon, I can see through many of the tricks described. One might go through the book adding footnotes to each amazing happening, reporting on how it was "really" done. (And one might ask why the famous "mini-lab" was not under 24 hours per day surveillance by a video camera with a very wide-angle lens, for example.) This would be misleading, however, because any effect can be duplicated a dozen or more ways. The instruction "always watch the guy's left hand" might convince an observer that something inexplicable had transpired if the trickster used his right hand or a shill or a remote-control device or mirrors or something controlled by foot movements or other methods.

The hardest lesson a skeptic must learn is the ability to be fooled—to be resigned to the fact that something unexplained need not imply "inexplicability." It is difficult or impossible for the average person, directly involved in a séance or the equivalent, to avoid being fooled unless the trickster is very inept, because participants are part of the effect. One can only counsel people to avoid the false dichotomy "explained versus supernatural." Even the best magicians fool each other, but they know that there is a natural explanation for the trick they cannot for the moment explain.

The "Entities" fit into a long gradation of ersatz spiritual claims that boil down to tricks. Indeed, parapsychology as a scientific discipline is burdened by a history of similar claims that are incredibly impressive and incredibly spurious. A devil's advocate may argue that yes, everything described was trickery, but we were still in touch with spirits occasionally, fleetingly. Who could prove otherwise? One is left with Occam's razor (all things being equal, the simplest explanation that covers all of our observations is more likely to be true than a contorted, complicated explanation of observations supporting a rather unlikely scenario in violation of known scientific principles) and the fact that the internal SORRAT evidence is non-profound, even a bit silly.

If there is life after death and souls are able to communicate with the living, why are the messages and physical evidence so banal, so easily duplicated by magicians, and so much in the Euro-American tradition started by the Fox sisters? Why is "life" on the other side of the grave so boring and middle class and vague and devoid of new information? Why do the ghosts speak a sort of fake-archaic English rather than the vastly more likely Chinese or Hindi?

Many things described in this ethnographic/sociological report are puzzling at first glance; most, however, are quite simple tricks—well-known to investigators of spiritualist claims for a century or more. Certainly, there are new wrinkles—tricksters introduce new variations on old themes even if by accident. Experimental controls at Rolla seem to be more or less non-existent, although McClenon tries. He is not an experienced magician, however, and if ever a "paranormal claim' called out for a magician/skeptic, this one does. The (uneasy) assumption that "something is going on here beyond rational explanation" is not at all supported by the evidence.

The ethnographic details, on the other hand, provide an extraordinary documentation of a small late twentieth century belief system or subculture. The details of this specific spiritualist cult are repeated, with minor variation, across decades and hundreds or thousands of miles. But we still need a definitive, cross-cultural analysis of such cultural movements and their place in contemporary society, measuring claims against controlled scientific tests and probing deeply into the backgrounds of principal actors.

The pivotal role of John Neihardt in SORRAT deserves comment. I knew him slightly, meeting him several times when I was an aspiring teenage poet in Nebraska. He was still obscure after *Black Elk Speaks* was published by the University of Nebraska Press. Later, he achieved fame from being on the Dick Cavett Show and *Black Elk Speaks* was reprinted by a major publisher. As a nonagenarian, he became a cult figure because of his age and mystical poetry. He was small, wizened, and articulate, speaking with the authority of someone four or five times as old as most of his fans, a Hippie from the past, whose every word seemed wise and deep.

Small wonder that his mentorship in the SORRAT project left a powerful shadow. Years after he had outlived everyone he remembered from his youth, he seemed to have outlived death. Why should he not outlive his own death, just as Black Elk did in his poetry? In his 90s, he cultivated sageness. It is no wonder that SORRAT survived him—he was a master choreographer of his own life in old age, setting in motion "entities" to survive himself: poetry, tape recordings, and SORRAT.

Black Elk revealed more to Neihardt than possible, I think. Poetic license entered the story, and Black Elk became the epitome of the nineteenth century Noble Savage so dear to twentieth century romantics. The old man, a master myth-maker, must have longed for contact with the source of the main artistic milestone in his life, old friends and memories, and promises of immortality.

In order to put things in perspective, I recommend analyses of paranormal phenomena published in the *Skeptical Inquirer* published by the Committee for the Scientific Investigation of Claims of the Paranormal. I also recommend James Randi's book *Flim-Flam!* (Prometheus Press, 1983) as strong antidotes to spiritualist claims.

Anonymous
A former President of the Parapsychological Association

Before reading the manuscript (1985): My belief that something paranormal might be going on in Richards' basement has been steadily eroded. There must be a strong presumption that he wrote the entity letters normally and by stealth for no other purpose than to sow confusion, mock the gullible, and gain notoriety. However, I will see what impression *The Entity Letters* makes on me before coming to any conclusions.

After reading the manuscript: My attitude to the whole SORRAT business has fluctuated over the years and is still in flux. Although after reading *The*

Entity Letters I am still unable to come to any definite conclusion, the overall effect has been to make me somewhat more positively inclined towards belief than previously. Certainly, I would not wish to align myself with those who dismiss the entire affair as a farce and a hoax.

On the negative side, there is the persistent and irritating fact that the demonstrations invariably fall short of being clinching. Even the locksmith test or Cox's plywood ring linkage are not flawless. Then there is the suspicious fact that nothing ever happens except in the vicinity of John Thomas Richards.

[Author's note: for a discussion of the locksmith test, see Hansen (1985) and Cox (1985). *The Entity Letters* mentions Cox having a locksmith ensure the security of his mini-lab. Afterward, while I was in Asia (1982-1986), the entities linked two plywood rings provided to them by W. E. Cox. These rings were hanging on a door but fell when the door was opened (by either Tom or Ed, I believe), and broke when they hit the floor. The entities were provided a second pair of rings that were linked (ostensibly through psi). These rings were sent to England for analysis. John Beloff (1985) describes a preliminary analysis that implied fraud.[3]]

The one phenomenon, the one thing that seemed beyond doubt, was Masuaki Kiyota's bending of the spoon in front of the author's eyes—and it continued bending. That was not a SORRAT phenomenon. Young Masuaki may very well be genuine. On the other hand, I am impressed, as was the author, that it is hard to imagine that John Thomas Richards had the skill and persistence to engage in such elaborate and prolonged faking. After all, when Randi does his tricks, he becomes rich as a consequence. What possible advantage could J. T. Richards gain from all this, apart from some mild notoriety? And what of Elaine? She must know what is really going on in their basement. Yet it is even harder to think of her as part of the conspiracy. The trouble is that one knows of cases of proven fraud where the motivation remains very obscure.

I must confess, finally, that I was not impressed by the actual entity letters. I found them, for the most part, prevaricating, nonsensical, pretentious, and pious. Even the occasional attempts at humor were banal. Certainly, I could see nothing in them that J. T. Richards could not have readily made up himself. The idea that these were messages from discarnate beings struck me as ludicrous.

Loren Parks
Participated in a Session at Skyrim on October 23, 1983
The room at Skyrim Farm was dark, but moonlight came in through the

lightly curtained windows. I was sitting next to Joe, who had an elderly lady on the other side of him. Soon after lights out, there was a rather heavy breathing, the kind you often hear in trance, and the breathing was to communicate to the people around him that such was happening. I had heard it on tapes of previous SORRAT gatherings.

I have done hypnosis with a few thousand people. I do deep trance things several times a week—positive and negative hallucinations, age regressions, so-called "past life regressions" that are simply play-acting of the subconscious, and most of the other phenomena of hypnosis. I know how the mind can switch in and out of these trances within a few seconds, and that a casual observer would not be aware of what is happening. Joe's "trance" was manufactured. It was simply a means to communicate that he was "possessed" by a spirit that gave him the power to heal. Now I have no quarrel with the effectiveness of the method. I'm sure that many have been healed. It's called the placebo effect, and I use it all the time. But if the subject at hand is genuine phenomena, that wasn't it. The *healing* consisted mostly of hugging the ladies and whispering in their ears. I didn't see him work with any men. He spent most healing time with the prettiest young woman there. She was probably the healthiest of the whole bunch to start with.

At some time, the "earthquake" started. It was a rhythmical shaking of the floor and rattling of things on the wall. Earthquakes I have felt are not rhythmical. You can feel erratic up and down movements. This was rhythmical, like something heavy was bouncing on the floor. Levitations of a TV-tray table were attempted with Tom Richards and others being the participants. Dennis Stillings was taking unannounced flash pictures from underneath. I didn't hear any objections to this. There were also occasional raps heard from around the room. I admit, it was kind of spooky, and I can't account for how they were produced because they came from different parts of the room and the room was full of people.

Later the major participants and others went outside in the moonlight with a number of us onlookers. Joe was still hugging women and Tom was describing some of the things that had happened out in this "prayer garden." I heard raps that seemed to come out of the ground near Tom's feet. I have heard raps from cement and wood floors at some distance from Tom, and I have recorded them. I have heard them move around the floor in broad daylight when Tom wore moccasins in full view. They would give Yes and No answers to questions and sometimes rap out messages. You would say the alphabet to yourself as each group of raps started, and the last rap would be the letter the source of the raps was communicating. It took a while, but was clear; I have no explanation for this.

When we went back into the house, I followed Tom and his shadow by keeping myself in a position such that Tom was between me and a window. I waited for the next "earthquake." Sure enough, it came several times. Tom's shoulders were going up and down in a rhythmical motion, probably about four inches. I had told my friend Donna Hay what I was going to do. She was beside Tom and watched him. She heard his heavy breathing after his exercise. Tom probably weighs over 300 pounds. Then I spotted Walter Uphoff, a believer (and a very sincere man). He did watch, at my suggestion, and confirmed what I saw, though this did not shake his faith.

Before the séance I saw a *Mottert box*, a flat covered box with glass top, dry coffee grounds on the floor and a small square of wood and one of lead inside. It had been placed outside the séance room. I noted the pattern, already traced in the coffee grounds. Later the pattern was different. I don't believe it was the same box, because my memory of the previous pattern was that the new pattern was not just an extension of the old. The box was under Alice's control. [Author's note: SORRATs sometimes shake the box before a séance. Apparently, Loren Parks was not aware of this practice.]

After all was over, Walter Uphoff was testing the resiliency of the floor. Alice blurted out "Nobody was doing that!" They maintained the floor was solid. It wasn't.

It is my opinion that if any genuine phenomena occurred, it was the raps. All the rest was as phony as a $3 bill.

If anyone is "psychic," it's Tom. And he has always been very cordial and cooperative. The "raps" communicate a point of view that would be Tom's, but it is conceivable that it is subconscious phenomena.

Steve Calvin
SORRAT member and Assistant to W. E. Cox

Regarding the possibility of faking movement inside the mini-lab: When sealed and locked, there are no cracks or holes exceeding 1/32 inch (actually the largest is less than that). With the bottom board in, any entry would also require at least one 90-degree bend as well. Any postulated procedure for faking that would require opening and closing the box during filming (single frame). Even without a lock, this method for faking is untenable for several reasons. The metal straps are very springy and get in the way, usually causing major unintentional disturbances of the contents of the box. If any objects are touching the sides of the box, they are guaranteed to be disturbed. Loren Parks can verify the above statements. Another criterion that would rule out single frame operation while manipulating the contents of the box is a characteristic of the camera that I did not reveal to anyone until over half of the 29 reels of film had been exposed. When operated in the single frame mode (also for the first frame of a full speed run), the camera shutter speed is a nominal 1/28 second. Nominal shutter speed at 16 f.p.s. is 1/32 second. This is enough to produce a noticeably brighter image during single frame operation. With only one exception, this was not observed on sequences shot inside the box (the one exception being the moving die sequence). This was observed on some sequences outside the box but is not particularly relevant for several reasons: (1) anything we (corporeal beings) can do, the entities could also presumably do (though the converse is not true), and (2) events outside the box have been considered suggestive, but not evidential, by all parties concerned. Any procedure involving an open-sided box, as suggested by Mr. Cornell, is quite preposterous. All glass was in-place on all occasions when I inspected the box. There was never any evidence that the glass had been removed and replaced, such as broken glass fragments, evidence of gluing, or the acetic acid odor of curing silicone rubber glue that lingers for several days after application. Considering the number of separate events observed and the frequency of checking of the box (often Mr. Cox or I would check the box on several successive days, with events occurring in between) postulating the removal and replacement of the glass as a mechanism for permitting animation is ridiculous. Substitution of film exposed at an identical setup elsewhere would be impossible for a number of reasons. The contents of the box often included unique objects that were unduplicatable. The film sequences often included one or more of us doing something to show a setup or the results of an RSPK event. Records of events filmed were kept by both Cox and Richards. I believe that either the padlock with seal or the melted string seal would be adequate to prevent undetected entry, and that both together would prevent multiple undetected entries. Mr. Cox did not have sufficient unobserved access time to permit faking of even a small fraction of the events, ignoring all the other constraints preventing anyone else from faking events occurring within the locked and sealed mini-lab. Another constraint preventing faking events by single frame operation is blurring as a result of movement during the finite open time of the shutter. A number of high speed events occurred inside the locked and sealed mini-lab that showed an amount of blur consistent with the observed amount of movement. The best example that comes to mind is a sequence showing an uninflated balloon with string (loose). The film shows the string being rapidly tied (no hands seen) around the neck of the balloon during several frames, with blurred string. The balloon then rapidly inflates. The balloon was examined later. No entrance for air other than the normal opening (now tied) was found.

Summary: Using the available equipment, many of the events filmed inside the mini-lab could not be duplicated by any corporal being, including Mr. Cox and Dr. Richards, even if the locks and seals were not present, the addition of the locks and seals would seem to preclude multiple undetected entrances to the mini-lab by Richards or any other corporeal outside agent.

Michael K. McBeath
Former Parapsychologist at the McDonnell Laboratory
for Psychical Research

James McClenon's autobiographical and sociological account described in *The Entity Letters* mirrors many of my own thought and feelings. I too felt frustration in my inability to document unambiguous paranormal events in this case. As McClenon explained, most of the anomalous events associated with the Richards occurred in poorly controlled situations. Yet, only events that take place under controlled conditions can be scientifically studied. I do not believe events that occur under uncontrolled conditions should be ignored, but they must be viewed with caution.

Anomalous events that occur in uncontrolled situations could be interpreted as instances of psi or deception. Evidence for one interpretation is often generalized to all events in a particular case study. A third interpretation is that of mixed mediumship. In mixed mediumship, both psi and deception occur. I believe it is likely that many poltergeist cases are of this nature, the current one included. A number of parapsychologists (including McClenon) have speculated that the ambiguity of not knowing if events are normal or paranormal may actually facilitate psi. The possibility of mixed mediumship serves as a caution against generalizing that all events in one case study are either psi or deception.

McClenon also suggests that psi might occur in a manner that looks like fraud. If we are to consider this possibility, we should reserve judgment of events that occur in uncontrolled situations. Clear evidence of psi or fraud requires controlled tests.

As a whole, I found *The Entity Letters* to be an accurate sociological account. It is a valuable description of the experiences of parapsychological researchers investigating a controversial case.

George Andrews
SORRAT letter writer and author of books about UFOs

Having now read your book, I realize that you really are attempting to be fair by presenting all sides both positive and negative. However, the negative bias of the academic community, of which you are a member, is so deeply rooted and unquestioningly accepted that it makes modern scientists resemble medieval priests, pronouncing anathema and excommunication upon the heretics that dare to disagree with the prevailing belief system. You try to be fair, but the conditioning you have undergone to obtain your degree and acceptance into the orthodox academic hierarchy amounts to a monumental brainwashing that cuts you off completely from intuitive non-linear thinking. You are to be congratulated for preserving at least a glimmer of this ability in spite of the tremendous peer pressure exerted by your colleagues to force you to conform to accepted academic norms. Trying to describe the SORRAT phenomena from the point of view of conventional sociology is comparable to trying to describe the multiple dimensions of geometric hyperspace from the point of view of conventional biology.

The one point at which I felt you had at last hit the nail on the head and found the solution to the mystery came when you wrote, "The spoon was alive!" There you had it in a nut-shell, but you didn't seem to recognize the significance of this breakthrough. In my opinion, the way the phenomena are produced is that discarnate spirits draw off bioenergy from participants to temporarily animate normally inanimate objects. That theory is not original with me. It dates back to Alan Kardec, about 120 years ago.

Some statements made by the entities are trite, but others are genuinely profound. Direct telepathically-transmitted perception of non-physical reality may be outside the parameters of modern science but, if that be indeed the case, so much the worse for modern science. Science is still encased in the straitjacket of Euclidian Newtonian Cartesian thinking, in spite of the quantum leap into relativity over half a century ago.

I think that Black Elk and John Neihardt are collaborating together from the Other Side, as they did during their respective lifetimes, working toward the fulfillment of the Great Vision that Black Elk was granted in his youth. I see the SORRAT group as a Sioux medicine lodge transplanted into the dominant Caucasian culture for the purpose of non-violently transforming it. The Great Hoop of all nations with the Flowering Tree at its center is a goal I find worthy of dedicating myself to. I don't care if academic authorities look down their noses at such a concept with a condescending sneer, so long as it makes good sense to me.

Marjorie Sherrill
SORRAT Member and Letter Writer

As I read the manuscript, I thought about what my beliefs are regarding the SORRAT phenomena. Either I do not know my beliefs or I lack the vocabulary to describe them. I fall into the group of pen pals who have been able to verify information in entity messages through experience. So far, neither the letters nor my activities have told me anything about the SORRAT phenomena themselves. My activities suggest that I can have perceivable experiences when I check out information in the entity letters. I wrote to the entity isolation room originally to increase the variety of my experiences, and I will probably continue to do so as long as the goal is fulfilled. As mentioned in this manuscript, I am engaging in a willing suspension of disbelief. [Author's note: she refers to a phrase mentioned in the introduction—from Balch and Taylor, 1977.]

W. E. Cox Responds to Other Commentators

I will address my comments to other's statements that pertain to controlled experiments that I have conducted and to speculations regarding incidents that reflect on Richards' personality. It is fortunate that Richards' character and background are well above the average, and particularly above the random array of known psi sensitives over the centuries. I agree with Richards' view that little can he gained from mere speculation.

George Hansen included in his comments Mr. Tony Cornell's claim of having observed trickery once, when a rap coincided with Richards's knuckle movement. Readers should remember that well over 100,000 raps have been produced (I have heard nearly that many myself), most of them well away from anyone's extremities. Hansen's citing of James Randi's inept claims are somewhat out of place. I acknowledge that it is unfortunate that *some* of my target objects including, particularly, the FRNM's own ESP decks, demonstrated capricious antics, but hope to focus attention on *successful* experiments (see the table at the end of my comments for an analysis of the probability of fraud associated with various SORRAT phenomena). Many of the people commenting on this manuscript who make negative comments (Dennis Stillings, James Randi, Loren Parks, etc.) have nothing to say about the verifications of SORRAT phenomena, and if one reads their comments closely, it is apparent that much of what they say is merely speculative opinion that should not be considered as *scientific* evidence.

D. Scott Rogo's statements require lengthy comment since they reflect on Richards' and my honesty. Rogo appears to assume that Richards does not realize that photographs of table levitations cannot be taken as concrete evidence of RSPK [recurrent spontaneous psychokinesis]. Rogo misinterprets some photographic evidence, suggesting that they indicate fraud occurred. For example, a "thread" that he feels is holding up a hat is in fact a scratch on the negative. There are much easier ways. It was I who long ago told him: simply let the hat, etc., hide a prop-stick.

Rogo refers to a box, that had been tampered with, that I told him about years ago. Apparently, he does not realize that this incident had nothing to do with Richards, and we cannot know exactly what occurred with this box.

Rogo and Bayless both seemed to have jumped to the conclusion that no genuine PK has been achieved in Dr. Richards' presence and that further investigation is unwarranted. The initiating of levitated tables by deliberate (and/or subconscious) means is a common practice, and no one knows better than Richards that this sort of evidence cannot *per se* be considered as more than a psychological stimulus. Artifact induction is not a heinous act, or necessarily a deliberated one. The problem is in sifting true paranormal events from false ones. If clearly inexplicable developments follow questionable events, as may happen at Skyrim, Batcheldor's theory would be supported. Richards has every right to be offended by Rogo presuming to say, in his "Evenings in the Dark" chapter of the book *In Search of the Unknown*, that heels were seen being used to produce raps, etc. Rogo and Bayless have far less evidence than I have gathered from investigating thousands of raps in concrete, earth, under snow, beneath distant floor microphones, etc. It is only natural for Richards to have charged "sour grapes"—assuming he used such a phrase, which I personally would doubt.

Rogo misrepresents my statements regarding the reversed film segment that brought laughter from the audience at the Parapsychological Association meeting. The laughter ensued only when the volunteer projectionist reversed a film segment (at my request) so as to run it again—its linkage of solid rings being apparently a most significant violation of physics. When initially viewed, there quite naturally was stunned silence. [Author's note: Cox's memory is flawed; many present at this event remember laughing. As stated by Rogo, the audience laughed upon seeing the jerky movement of target objects.]

To make claims worse, Rogo assumes film animation, as if it were an easy task. I challenge any experts to equal the products at Rolla, in a thousand feet of film, in anything less than a thousand hours of labor (for which they would have had to burglarize their way into both house and sealed mini-lab many times). I believe I informed Rogo of this, but he ignored this fact.

Rogo fails to note one of my experimental findings, the failure of a paid professional locksmith to thwart any internal effects in the mini-lab. I hired him to lock the mini-lab securely and to place booby-traps so that attempts at fraud could be detected. This locksmith testified before a public notary regarding the effects he observed, effects that defied his explanatory ability.

I challenge Rogo to cite where I err in conducting these mini-lab experiments. I respectfully suggest that his response be more intelligent than was a remark within *Fate* magazine soon after his book review of Dr. Richards' *SORRAT*. He suggested that it would be easy to inflate balloons, which I had sealed inside the mini-lab, using an air hose under the table! I include a Table at the end of my comments that outlines methods of faking and problems inherent within some of these methods. If critical readers might cite where I err in this analysis, I will be the beneficiary.

Dr. John R. Cole's comments are clearly the worst, however desirous of serving truth he may be. Typical of the sins of omission rendered by practically every CSICOP-er, his reporting regarding the Fox sisters is erroneous. Not only did the Fox sisters publicly recant their "spirit rappings," for which they were paid by promoters, but the confession was later retracted. The same press release (N.Y. *Herald*, October 21, 1888) that mentions the three physicians Dr. Cole commends does also say this: "As [Margaret Fox] remained motionless, loud . . . rappings were heard, now in the files, now behind the scenes, now in the gallery." Since there is no claim that these were produced by confederates, I am inclined to doubt the honesty of the "three doctors [who] knelt down, took hold of [her] big toe, and assumed a grave air...." There does exist evidence of ESP through their raps, and raps on surfaces held by others (such as Sir Wm. Crookes). Given this what more need I say—except that Dr. Cole has reflected little more than his cognitive dissonance.

The Anonymous Commentator has revealed reactions of ambivalence. But I must say a word about the mini-labs and linking rings, on which he looked down in doubt. My locksmith was given strict injunction to seal it *well*, and this he easily did. Even a second (actually fourth) time was for a Yorkshire, England, TV company, as Arthur C. Clarke, it so happens, has impressively described [Fairley and Welfare, 1984]. As for those linked rings (although aged, and looked it) I can confidently say they pass man's understanding—or mine at least. So do a few of the "entity letters" that were, in fact, written (and so filmed) inside the mini-lab. As Richards himself says, in concluding the Preface to his book, "[As for] slurs and accolades.... I expect the former, while hoping for the latter."

I am not equipped to agree or disagree with Loren Park's comments regarding Joe's trance states or the control of a box or boxes on events at which I was not present. My only criticism is in his finding that the study floor is weaker than I could detect via my structured tests of its solidity soon after two personal "earthquake" experiences at Skyrim (in one of which Tom was not even present). My own experiments using sealed test apparatus that are incapable of simple substitution have yielded dozens of significant coffee-ground patterns that only RSPK [recurrent spontaneous psychokinesis] could have produced.

As an empiricist, I regret the superior value that the author gives to sociological views at the expense of apparently calling into question the competence of SORRAT's chief archivist. It could have been done differently; but when there occurs any other replication of the lengthy series of paranormal "direct writings," given the admittedly rare opportunity, his work will have its particular value.

Would that we today knew more about the subconscious than we do, for after a century of existence the societies for psychical research still have not conclusively determined whether the sundry but established psi effects (not to mention SORRAT's, which are much more varied than Parks cites) are really of this world or the next. What is established is the great difficulty that any critic probably will have in attributing to fraud most of the effects in the following tables from Chapter 15 ("Fraud: Received Opinions and Their Evidences") in my book.

A Dozen Selected Major RSPK Effects and the Logical

Possibilities of Their Production by Fraud

TABLE A: Filmed Effects in the Mini-lab

Brief Description	Methods of Faking	Problems with Methods of Faking
1. "Direct writing" in mini-lab and any other internal movements	Stop-action photography by opening and closing mini-lab between each active frame	Extremely difficult for hundres of repeated or differing effects, even by a motivated expert who also is a master of opening and re-sealing the mini-lab
2. Inflation of balloons in ML	none	See #1 above
3. Passage of objects in and out of ML, tightly sealed ESP card cases, and sealed envelopes	Stop-action photography granting an ability to unseal and restore super-glued enclosuers, et al.	See #1 above
4. "Direct writing" in mini-lab during exterior fire	none	See #1 above

Table B (Unfilmed Effects Not Involving the Mini-lab)

Brief Description	Methods of Faking	Problems with Methods of Faking
5. Raps: general, on living room floor	Confederate in basement	Confederate would not hear questions softly addressed
	Deliberate agitation of any sitter's foot	Concealment difficult and this method cannot explain raps moving on floor to other locations
	Electrical trickery by Dr. J. T. Richards	Impossible to produce raps using this method in my home and other locations
6. Raps in concrete, underground, under snow, on untouched tin trays, etc.	None	
7. Raps predictive, to significant degree, of dice results, et al.	None, requires clairvoyant ability	
8. "Direct writing" marks in adequately-sealed tray of coffee grounds	None, given the construction detail in my as-yet-unpublished text	

Brief Description	Methods of Faking	Problems with Methods of Faking
9. "Direct writing" on exposed sheets	Very easy by normal means	None (but hundreds were so produced)
10. Metal—bending in various sealed bottles	None, without leaving traces of fraudulent entry	
11. Breezes on command	A sitter's breath, or natural draft	Directions of such "breezes" prohibited explanations other than collective hallucinations
12. Strong floor shaking (earthquake effect)	None on sturdy floor (floor was tested)	Collective hallucination by all members of sitter group

James McClenon
Written in 1985

Scientists study the various mental states: waking, sleeping, dreaming, and altered states of consciousness. They detect mixtures of brain waves associated with the different states. Most Westerners regard waking conscious as a reflection of reality, while other states are thought to be less connected to reality.

Chuang Tzu (1981: 61), a Chinese Taoist philosopher (3rd-4th centuries BC) once dreamed that he was a butterfly who realized that he was Chuang Tzu. Within the dream, the butterfly was real, while Chuang Tzu was a dream. When Chuang Tzu awoke, he wondered if it had been Tzu who dreamed he was a butterfly, or if the butterfly was now dreaming it was Chuang Tzu.

Could some altered states of consciousness, such as mystical states, be more valid than "normal" consciousness? Some people believe that their mystical perceptions are superior to waking perceptions. Some near-death experiences are considered more valid than everyday experiences.

A similar situation exists regarding the entities. They state that they live in a reality superior to ours. Most of us on this Earth are skeptical about their claims. After reading Chuang Tzu's story, I dreamed I was concluding an agreement with a man in a three-piece suit. He had on clothing exactly the same as that worn by a shaman I interviewed in Taiwan. I realized I was dreaming and that this man was an honorable shaman but also a figment of my imagination. He was like a SORRAT entity, a messenger from the spiritual world. He existed only in my dream. "I wonder if he realizes that he does not exist," I thought.

"Do you realize that I am dreaming and that, in all probability, you don't exist?" I asked.

He smiled in puzzlement, indicating disagreement. "Show me," he said. In order to verify to him that he was not real, I shook myself awake.

I pondered what the dream might mean. Did the shaman in my dream understand my vantage point? He did not accept his lack of authenticity. Like Chuang Tzu's butterfly and the man in my dream, the SORRAT entities *might* be real but most people do not believe in them.

I drifted back to sleep and found myself talking to the same man.

"You made a very good point," he said. "I'll have to remember what you said. I might not be real. When I meditate, I find that my self does not exist."

I searched my memory for the topic of our conversation. This time I did not realize that I was dreaming. "I must admit that I can't remember what we were talking about," I replied. The shaman looked at me in surprise.

"Surely, you remember, "he said. "You made such a profound point that none of us will ever forget it." The people around him nodded in agreement. "You pointed out to us that we may not be real. We could be figments of your imagination, and we have no way to prove that this is not true. I have come to the same realization during my meditation, but it is hard for me to maintain that realization during my normal consciousness."

"I truly can't remember anything about our conversation," I replied. The group laughed at my puzzlement and the irony of the situation. My friend smiled knowingly.

In the morning, I pondered the implications of these dreams. The entities are elements of a recurring human dream—the idea of a non-material reality. We may dismiss this dream as unreal, but long after we all are in the grave, people will be talking to spirits just as they do today. They will accept non-material worlds as real. Undoubtedly, spirits will be writing. Some people will scoff, while others ponder their words, many of which will be inane.

Buddhist meditators say that our concept of self is an illusion. Our concept of self is not "real" but something constructed by our brains. Some scientists argue similarly; they tell us that our consciousness consists of physiological and electromagnetic phenomenon. I don't understand the evidence very well, but it is something to think about. When I meditate, I just let thoughts go.

Desiderius Erasmus, writing in the early sixteenth century, noted that most of what humans regard as serious is actually folly. He noted that, when considered in another light, folly has value. Folly gives life meaning. It increases our enjoyment of everyday life. Love, fantasy, and emotion allow self-deceptions that contribute to a better life. People say that it is bad to be deceived, but Erasmus argues that the "saddest thing is not to be deceived." He points out that happiness is not found in reality but in opinions. Nothing can be clearly known. The human mind is far more taken with disguises than with realities, and those who spend all their time with "realities" work against the enjoyment of life. Erasmus portrayed the folly of politics, war, religion, academics, and science. The only ideology he does not mock is simple-hearted kindness and love, as described in the Christian *New Testament*.

If we refuse to accept anything but the obvious, we lose the potential for using *belief* as a means of transforming reality. It is folly to reject all belief—a negative folly. Belief in the obvious has no magical power, but belief in something outside of reality creates the potential for wonderment.

Bear with me while I conduct a kind of sociological analysis. I understand the folly of trying to analyze the non-material world, but the responses in Appendix A may be useful as data. There are various categories of response: (1) some writers note the prevaricating, nonsensical, pretentious, and trite nature of the entity messages;[4] (2) some express belief in the entities; and (3) some use the messages to exercise their imaginations—they enjoy the messages but may be agnostic. These people realize that something that seems impossible, such as psychokinesis or spiritual healing, when sought, can *become* possible. By turning off the rational mind, we call forth intuitive ways of knowing, which can be useful. We should not pretend that we understand consciousness completely. There is mystery involved.

My failure to remember my previous conversation with the shaman in my dream captures this paradox. I have not put together a theory acceptable to both the entities and myself, but I hope that by getting this manuscript into print I can fulfill a kind of agreement with them and with myself.

SORRAT Entities

Imperator, Rector, John G. Neihardt, John King, and all

Friend James,

Thank you for giving us the opportunity to comment upon your manuscript, through which we glanced after you sent it to Rolla. Errors can be corrected editorially.

There is one contradiction that we find puzzling. You state that you do not believe in us. This is unfortunate, for we believe in you—not merely believe that you exist as an eternal soul, quite incidentally and irrelevantly inhabiting a physical body for your instant in time, but also believe in you in the sense that you shall prove a powerful persuasive person helping others on your side realize that life is eternal and that they should help others and live for eternity, not just for material goods and gains. This is a worthy goal, and we shall certainly help you achieve it, if we can.

However, what puzzles and amuses us is the fact that you say that you do not believe in us, yet you do ask us to answer your questions, heal the ill, tell you where treasure is hidden, and even to write this commentary for your book about us—the very title of which presumes entities who can write letters. From our naturally prejudiced viewpoint, this inconsistency is absurd, and your readers would see the absurdity. This should lead them to more closely examine their own anti-spiritualistic prejudices, which is always a good thing to do!

In defending our viewpoint, which is, to us, like, a Frenchman defending the notion that France exists, the obvious answer is that one should come to our side and find out from personal experience. Even a good American may not go to Paris when he dies, but everyone will eventually find out that we live beyond physical death, and at that point the basic argument is resolved in our favor. The problem lies in returning to tell about the experience. When you die, you may return and rap until your ectoplasm grows thin, and those who are not inclined to believe we are real will not listen to you either.

Therefore, how can we prove our own existence? Aristotle suggested that every man must first do this before he could argue anything else. That would prevent most arguments.

Descartes set one criterion: cognition. We are obviously not blind forces of nature. If you grant "*cogito, ergo, sum,*" then, since we are able to think, therefore we exist. However, perhaps it is a matter of "*cogito sum, ergo cogito sum,*" The Nihilist would tell me, "you think you are, therefore, you think you are," so it still is only *our* opinions, and we may only be figments of someone else's dream. But whether I dream that I am a butterfly, or whether I am a butterfly dreaming that I am I, however you identify the immortal self, man-spirit or butterfly-spirit, the self must still exist. Consequently, Descartes is still right. Man or butterfly or Aristotle's plucked chicken, you still have the existential self—the immortal essence of Selfhood.

Therefore, friend James. and both gentle and ungentle readers, *Know that we exist.*

Otherwise, you are only hallucinating that you are reading these words.

Peace be unto you all,

Imperator/Rector/J.G.N./J.K. and All

APPENDIX B
DO IT YOURSELF: A GUIDE FOR GROUP PSYCHOKINESIS

The advice provided here is drawn from my original "Do-it-yourself Guide" completed in 1985. I have revised these suggestions to include Batcheldor's ideas.

(1) Form a PK group based on a dramatic story about a spirit.

(2) Ask participants to put their hands on a table and talk about this story.

(3) Meet regularly once a week. Be patient. Develop rapport. Sit in very dim or no light.

(4) Regard "minor" or "questionable" events, such as small table movements, as signs of PK.

(5) Protect yourself from negative experiences through positive imagery and attitude. If the group wishes, adapt a protective ritual.

(6) Avoid being overly skeptical.

(7) Invite people to join your group who have had many previous anomalous experiences.

(8) Think of group PK as a spiritual pilgrimage rather than a scientific experiment.

I discuss opinions about these suggestions.

The PK group and its ideology

Batcheldor believed that, for scientific purposes, you should avoid actual spirits. The Philip group suggested making up a fictional story about a spirit. SORRAT did not devise a special story, but J. G. Neihardt had experiences with Spiritualist and Native American phenomena. Preconceptions will probably affect results.

SORRAT began meeting in September 1961. They began hearing raps on November 17, 1961 (perhaps 50 raps during a 15-minute period). Neihardt recognized the raps as paranormal since they were equivalent to those he had heard during previous experiments with his wife and others. The group spent much time ruling out normal explanations. The raps reoccurred on November

319

24 and on all Fridays during December. The sounds seemed to come from within the wood of the floor—not from its surface. After Christmas of that year, they heard raps and perceived slight table movements. Some SORRAT members went into trance and the phenomena were attributed to specific deceased people.

The Batcheldor and Philip groups differed from SORRAT in that they were smaller and had exactly the same people during all sessions. SORRAT participants varied from week to week but had a stable core group. Batcheldor and Philip phenomena were thought to be derived from the consciousness of the group. Although SORRAT stressed the idea that group rapport facilitated the phenomena, some SORRAT members were thought to more psychic than others. I have heard that the Batcheldor groups also found that particular people help phenomena occur. Batcheldor did not mention this in his letters to me, but other participants have told me this.

I have been told that a PK group's story is very important for achieving success. People say that the story should have fantastic elements, something beyond the mundane. The world religions are derived from stories with fantastic features. For example, the idea of a Jewish Messiah being unjustly and cruelly executed and then returning from the dead is a central story for Christians. We would expect this story to generate apparitional experiences. Early Christians, pondering this story, experienced many PK events and spiritual healings.

I think that having men and women holding hands in the dark is a good way to develop rapport. Sexual attraction motivates people to attend regularly. Batcheldor (December 1987) disagrees: "In the past I have found flirtations and sexual pairings among my sitters to be more of a nuisance than a help. They tend to distract those involved from the main task. Also, as the researcher, I like to know approximately what is happening in the dark. If a sitter's hands are supposed to be on the table, then they shouldn't be groping around their neighbor! Also, close involvements usually break up in time, and then you lose two sitters at once (since they no longer wish to meet each other). I admit that having a mixture of males and females make the meetings more attractive socially. But at present I appreciate the advantages of having an all-male group (despite their occasional protests that we ought to have some females present)."

Some people say that spiritualist sitter groups have a higher probability for success. Batcheldor (Dec. 19878) writes: "I would object to invoking 'John King' and his like. I admit that a belief in spiritual entities has some advantages but it also has some disadvantages. For example: (1) Some people have no enthusiasm for creating purely artificial entities. (2) Spiritualists hand over control of the phenomena to the entities. This makes it impossible to explore the possibility of direct, human control. (3) There is a danger of getting carried away with the idea that the entities are real. This can lead to a false trust in the content of messages. It can also create fears that the entities may take control in an unpleasant way, making it necessary for the sitters to invent protective measures. (4) Some researchers feel that using the concept of 'entities' comes too close to Spiritualism."

The Philip Group created a fictional story about a British aristocratic, Philip, who lived during the time of Oliver Cromwell (Owen and Sparrow, 1976). Philip generated raps and anomalous table tipping phenomena (Google: "The Philip Experiment – YouTube). A later group created and communicated with a talking dolphin named "Silk" (Batcheldor, 19790: 83). Some groups have not been successful. Differential success implies that stories with a "fantastic" quality help focus the group's attention.

Batcheldor disagreed with my suggestion that patience was important (letter of December 1987): "If my hints are followed, blank sessions should be few and far between. Regular productivity depends mainly, I think, on having a small group rather than a large one—say 3 or 4 members only. This helps to ensure that all (and the same) members will attend each time. With a large group, the chances are much greater that one or two of the members will be absent on each occasion, and the composition of the group will thus seldom be quite the same. Group harmony is then less predictable. With a lot of people present the meeting may go very well, like a successful party, or it may go dead, like an unsuccessful party. Some of SORRAT's phenomena are far more astonishing than ours, but they have far more negative sittings than we do (we have hardly any). They have a large and changing group, whilst we have a small and constant one."

Unconscious muscular movements

I suggest letting unconscious muscular movements simulate PK and refraining from criticizing people who seem to be pushing the table. My understanding is that the first SORRAT phenomena were raps—not connected to unconscious muscular movements. Other groups find unconscious muscular movements useful, and I believe that SORRAT began "priming the pump" through that method at an early stage. Tom Richards stressed, again and again, that table movements with hands on the table should not be regarded as PK—

so I suppose you should take all advice with a grain of salt.

Batcheldor (Dec. 1987) writes, "In my view, for maximum speed of development, beginners who are worried about UMA [unconscious muscular action] should accept the fact that it is probably present in the early stages, to some degree, but that they should simply not worry about it. They can be told that later, if all goes well, UMA will be decisively ruled out by the occurrence of total levitations (with hands on top) and movements and levitations without contact. UMA cannot simulate these. Meanwhile they should accept the necessity of working through a somewhat ambiguous phase. Development need not be as tediously slow as you suggest. UMA should occur within one or two sittings. Our first ostensible levitation (in darkness) occurred in the eleventh sitting."

In a later letter, he states, "For best and speediest development, I offer the following hints: Do not use too heavy a table at the beginning (you can try a heavier one later). Do not try to keep the hands very light or very still. (If you are worried about unconscious muscular action, remember that it will be ruled out later.) Resist your natural inclination to try and make the phenomena occur (e.g., by urging, demanding, etc.). Simply relax, chat, and wait. In particular do not keep asking for advanced phenomena, such as levitations, near the beginning. Rather, you should welcome the simpler phenomena, such as table sliding and tipping, when they occur (and they should occur quite quickly—i.e., within one or two sittings). Encourage these to grow gradually stronger and more varied. A lot of fun can be had at this stage, and so the time should pass without boredom until the more advanced phenomena start to occur. These are likely to take many sittings. Their chances of occurring and their eventual strength are greatly increased by working in darkness or a very dim light. Therefore, one might as well work in darkness (or a dim light) right from the very beginning. In this case it is a good idea to fix a small luminous marker in the center of the table. Of course, many people object to working in darkness on the grounds that it increases the opportunities for fraud, but if you want the quickest and most powerful results, avoid full light. Any attempt to discriminate the genuine from the false (such as by working in full light, or using tests and controls) should be deferred until much later on. Paranormal events occur most readily in loose and ambiguous conditions."

Meet regularly, once a week. Be patient. Develop rapport.

Batcheldor writes (Dec. 1987), "I would suggest, assuming that darkness is used, that a pledge to attend regularly (except for illness) for a period of three months, or twelve weekly sittings, should be adequate. By the end of this time, most groups should know whether they are sufficiently motivated to continue."

People join PK groups for fun, sexual attraction, religious goals, and social support. Some people argue that psi development is a learning process and that feedback is important. Asian shamans disagree with that advice. They believe they encounter actual spirits. They tell me that success is achieved by following the spirit's guidance—perhaps by making a solemn pledge.

The sociological literature suggests that meeting regularly should contribute to rapport because people ask themselves, "Why am I doing this?" and the answer will be "I must like these other people or else I would not be coming every week." The more people interact, the more they come to like each other. I suspect that something magical is also required—the connection between people motivates them to keep coming and some unknown force becomes available as a result of rapport.

The attitude toward "minor" PK and fraud

Batcheldor (1979, 1984) hypothesized that PK *artifacts* (events that seem as if they might be PK, but were not) trigger unconscious belief resulting in actual PK. Artifacts, accepted as real, aid people in overcoming the natural forms of resistance that tend to prevent PK. For example, a person might think he or she heard a rap when, in reality, the sound was merely a floorboard cracking. Artifacts include effects produced by fraud; Brookes-Smith (1975) conducted experiments supporting this argument. The group drew lots, and one person was selected to secretly move the table in the dark. The idea was that some type of "trigger" was required for PK to begin. Ultimately, the table moved without anyone pushing it. I suspect that use of fraud shapes the phenomena—maybe it encourages the phenomena to engage in fraud.

Protect yourself but don't take yourself too seriously

My original advice was: "Many occult experts recommend asking for spiritual protection from higher powers and visualizing holy white light encompassing the room where the group meets. Experts also warn against using Ouija boards because this method leaves participants open to psychic problems. They argue that using 'black magic' can be physically and psychologically unhealthy."

PK is not a well understood phenomenon, and it can result in unpleasant side effects. Some people get too attached to it. There is stigma involved. If you get PK results, you might be accused of fraud. If there are spirits involved, they may mislead you.

Pay attention to your inner well-being. Take care of yourself through proper lifestyle. Stay off street drugs, don't drink too much alcohol, do things in moderation, get enough sleep, eat a proper diet, maintain social relationships. Sometimes people in groups lead each other astray. Don't do things that you would not want others to discover. The "entities" might be more interested in their own survival than in your psychological and physical well-being. Sometimes it is best not to share your experiences with people who would not understand. Show common sense regarding who you talk with about what you have experienced.

Some people are plagued by too much PK, particularly those troubled by poltergeists. Think of poltergeists as a disturbance of the collective consciousness. Therapy might be useful. Even talking to a kind-hearted person can be helpful. It is often a good idea to acknowledge your fears and then face them. Negative paranormal forces feed on fears.

Practice some type of meditation—a type that fits your needs. Some people prefer paying attention to their breath. Others use mantras. Some use Zen or Vipassana meditation. By adapting a ritual practice that helps you focus your mind, you can gain control over how you react to your experiences. This will result in an inner discipline that will aid you in changing the things that need to be changed in your life.

People with poltergeist problems can get control over the situation by developing methods for creative expression. The poltergeist can be included in the project. You might invite it to express itself in some way. Some people try automatic writing. Other find ways that allow random processes to lead them to new ideas. For example, you might try opening the Bible at random and seeing what verse you should read. If your problem persists, consult a psychological counselor who is sympathetic to psychical research.

K. J. Batcheldor (Dec. 1987) wrote "I believe that in many ways the group creates what it expects, though the members are often unaware of this. If nerves become on edge, I find it helpful to stop and discuss the matter. The leader should point out that 'all is created.' Pleasant thoughts will create pleasant phenomena, while fearful thoughts will create fearful phenomena. He should tell the sitters that if *they* calm down, then the phenomena will calm down. He should discourage any belief that there are 'evil entities' hovering about, waiting for a chance to 'horn in.' I think that the dangers lie in our own fears, not in 'things out there.'"

People experiencing "demonic-type" situations should consider the idea that part of their problem is granting the force working against them a powerful status. It is likely that you have experienced problems in the past that have weakened your defenses. Perhaps, you need assistance from someone who can help you increase your strength. There are many types of therapists. I believe in a method called cognitive behavioral therapy. A therapy goal may include figuring out ways to express your turmoil in a creative, wholesome way. It is possible to replace negativity with positivity.

Do not let your interest in PK dominate your life. Psychic phenomena tend to occur on the margins of one's consciousness, in a kind of twilight zone. Everyday life is filled with a richness that should not be missed. Asian traditions argue that anomalous phenomena are merely a signpost on the way to something greater.

My SORRAT experiences illustrate how one's attitude affects one's experiences. I think my skepticism affected the anomalous events I perceived. Because I exposed myself to many anomalous events, my experiences eventually overcame my skepticism. As the years went by, I focused less on paranormal phenomena and more on compassion and empathy. I realized that attempting to verify these things was not accomplishing much. In this book, I advocate anthropological and sociological methods but, I think that, ultimately, the way to understand the non-material world is through spirituality and compassion.

There is a circular feature associated with group PK phenomena. Your beliefs create the effect, and the effects shape your beliefs. The UFO expert John Keel (1975) and many others note that there is a tendency for their theories to be verified by their research. "I tested this by inventing some rather outlandish ideas," Keel (1975, p. 197) writes. "Within days I would receive phone calls, reports, and mail describing elements of those ideas. This was the feedback or reflective effect." The phenomenon produces effects paranormally, and as a result, it can lead you in absurd directions. For this reason, I suggest holding onto a degree of skepticism. Don't take any wooden nickels.

Remember that macro PK can stimulate negative social reactions

My interest in paranormal phenomena damaged my career as a sociologist. Mainstream scientists cannot accept extremely innovative theories unless the evidence is overwhelming. Consciousness has qualities beyond our understanding, and it is unlikely we will truly grasp its essence rationally. Those with a deeper understanding of the non-material world seem less concerned with their own survival. For them, death is not a threat, and self-preservation is not a goal. This idea does not fit with what has been instilled in us through the evolutionary process. Those who spend all their efforts on preserving their own genes are troubled by those who ignore this way of thinking.

Some people are better at this than others

The Batcheldor, Philip, and SORRAT groups began with the thought that any group can experience PK. It has been my experience that certain people facilitate PK. Although I have organized three different groups, my single experience in a non-SORRAT group was with a group that only met once. Our group included a woman who had a history of group PK experiences. During the session, we heard anomalous sounds no one could explain. It was as simple as that. I suspect that groups that have a person with a special knack for this type of thing will experience success, while those lacking such a person will be far less likely to succeed.

Regard the investigation of PK as a spiritual exercise

I argue that it is not possible to verify PK in a manner that will convince skeptics. If your group experiences PK and allows skeptics to investigate, the phenomena may decline and people will be accused of fraud. You may be portrayed as an incompetent fool. It may be best to keep a low profile and not attract attention to yourself. Don't seek publicity or fame. People associated with authentic religious miracles are humble.

I conclude with two basic plans. In my "Do It Yourself!" guide, I offer a plan that I tried but did not achieve success. In doing the SORRAT research, I followed the alternate plan.

Basic plan

Form a group. Invite people with experience. Meet regularly. Discuss a story. Develop Rapport. Overcome your fears. Let it Happen.

Alternate plan

Go where PK is happening. Watch and learn. Take notes. Write a report regarding your observations.

APPENDIX C
SORRAT-RELATED VIDEOTAPES AVAILABLE ON YOUTUBE

These videos can also be found by Googling "Dr. Jim McClenon SORRAT" and selecting "Videos."

(1) SORRAT: A History of the Neihardt Psychokinesis Experiments, 1961-1981 (1982; 2:03:01) published with the permission of Elaine Richards

https://www.youtube.com/watch?v=1UiTLkDA7A4

This video reviews the history of SORRAT and W. E. Cox's mini-lab experiments, showing ostensible PK within the mini-lab. Some segments show pens magically writing messages inside the mini-lab and envelopes containing messages disappearing. These envelopes then magically entered the mail system, a phenomenon that provided the title of this book.

(2) The SORRAT Mini-lab experiments, 2004 (1:00:30) published with the permission of Elaine Richards.

https://www.youtube.com/watch?v=WIQZYNMzJBg&t=1234s

This is an edited version of the previous video, produced in 2004. It includes some alternate narrative and discussion.

(3) SORRAT Experiments, 1983 (1:10:30)

https://www.youtube.com/watch?v=44Iwwznq09o

This unedited video documents raps and table-tipping sessions during the author's 1983 visit. Participants locate the exact point from which the raps originate within the floor. During one session, the table stands on two legs and remains up after all hands are removed (37:30). The author inspects the table, seeking a normal explanation. Audible raps from the floor are documented (43:30). These events are described in Chapter 10.

(4) Talking to the Spirits: A Pilgrimage, Produced by Dr. Emily Edwards (30:57).

https://www.youtube.com/watch?v=taGeXOO_s9Q&t=1857s

This video was designed for presentation at a sociology conference. It documentes the 1996 visit by a PK group from North Carolina to Dr. J. T. Richards' home. The video shows two participants from Ivan Richards' SORRAT group and audio from a table-tipping session. These events are described in Chapter 10.

(5) Wondrous Events in a Small Group: A Field Study, 1992, co-produced with Dr. Emily Edwards. (12:26)

https://www.youtube.com/watch?v=0NXyn6eoUEg

This video was presented at two sociology conferences. SORRAT provides a prototype for how shamanism began among Paleolithic people. The video portrays mini-lab phenomena discussed in Chapters 1, 2, and 10.

(6) SORRAT 1 (2001) Table-Tipping (9:05)

https://www.youtube.com/watch?v=RJHq04o6fig

This unedited video was provided by Amanda Mosher. An infrared camera portrays unconscious (or conscious) muscular table movements in Rolla, MO, during a séance held in complete darkness in 2001. These events are described in Chapter 10.

(7) SORRAT 2 – Table-Tipping (32:34)

https://youtu.be/iYOHTOfgJD8

This unedited video was provided by Amanda Mosher. An infrared camera documents unconscious or conscious muscular table movements in 2001. In some scenes, participants grab and lift the table during a séance in Columbia, MO. These events are mentioned in Chapter 10.

(8) SORRAT 3 – Table-Tipping (17:28)

https://www.youtube.com/watch?v=Fz8mb7OHm28

This unedited video was provided by Amanda Mosher. An infrared camera documents people grabbing and pushing the table in Rolla, Missouri in 2001. During the session, the author summarizes his experiences with raps in different houses, from the open ground, from a restaurant floor, from the floor of an antique car museum. These events are described in Chapter 10.

(9) How Shamanism Began (2002) (18:40) co-produced by Amanda Mosher, James McClenon

https://youtu.be/AlFCEaGCdJ4

This video was presented at a Sociology of Religion conference. It documents a 2001 interview with a SORRAT member (Joe) talking about his out-of-body experience and early SORRAT history. The video argues that small group experiences have shaped religious beliefs throughout history. This video pertains to Chapter 10.

(10) Wondrous Events: Foundations of Folk Belief, co-produced with Dr. E. Edwards

https://www.youtube.com/watch?v=zSyBMzF6BbY

This video describes folklore and survey research regarding anomalous experience and its impact on folk religious belief. These ideas are discussed more fully in the book *Wondrous Events: Foundations of Religious Belief*. It pertains to Chapter 11 (Psychical Research).

(11) Wondrous Healing, 2004, (57:44) co-produced with Dr. Emily Edwards

https://youtu.be/y0KCQ_Qfsqs

People describe spiritual and folk healing experiences. Physicians and scholars provide opinions. This video reviews the Ritual Healing Theory (Chapter 13).

ENDNOTES

Author's Note: Endnotes were included during the late 1980s as a way of allowing readers of the original manuscript to comment on specific parts of the text and for me to react to their comments.

Chapter 1

1. A skeptical reader argued that my war experiences made me susceptible to false beliefs. I found this comment offensive as it infers that all veterans are damaged and that believers should be stigmatized. I see parallels between the stigma of serving in Vietnam and the investigation of psychic phenomena. Erving Goffman (1959, 1963), a sociological expert regarding stigma, compared human interaction to a theatrical performance in which actors play roles before audiences and have front and backstage regions of their selves. Backstage regions are concealed from all but one's closest associates unless a mistake is made. For example, a husband and wife may exchange thoughts about their guests when out of earshot, but quickly revert to "front stage" behavior when they return. I include "backstage" information to portray my thinking at the time. In Vietnam, I went over a kind of edge, experiencing extreme forms of consciousness. My investigation of psychic phenomena continued that process. I suspect that the skeptic does not share my curiosity regarding consciousness and is unwilling to endure the difficulties required to gain a better understanding of it.

2. A reader (believer in the paranormal) demanded details regarding this experiment, thinking that full disclosure would compel other readers to believe. I will not be giving detailed descriptions of experiments or psychic experiences. My goal is to illustrate how people came to believe the way they did, not to establish the reality of paranormal phenomena.

3. The "relativistic" orientation within the sociology of science hypothesizes that controversial issues within science are sometimes so bound up with preconceived idea-sets that they cannot be resolved empirically (Collins 1975, 1985; Collins and Pinch, 1982). Scientists tend to throw out results that do

not fit their preconceived notions.

4. I use the word "believer" to refer to the category of individuals who tend to accept paranormal claims. The word "skeptic" refers to those who tend to doubt such claims. Technically, skepticism (using a dictionary definition) refers to the doctrine that all knowledge is in question, subject to doubt. I note that there is a continuum regarding conviction: Some people believe fully, others less so; some suspend judgment, others tend to reject. Marcello Truzzi (1980) referred to a middle category of "zetetics," those who suspend belief. I document a reader's reactions to the manuscript by referring to some as "believers" and others as "skeptics." Only Truzzi seemed to be a true zetetic. People who actively engage in field research tend to achieve a form of belief. Skeptics generally avoid active field research. To illustrate the variety of positions, I provide comments written by people who read the manuscript prior to publication.

5. I formed a hypothesis: Interacting with people who report haunting experiences is more likely to lead to belief than interacting with people who conduct parapsychological experiments.

6. One skeptic writes, "You seem to speak of people 'seeing' things rather than 'reportedly seeing' things. This is most dangerous when dealing with matters anomalous. We should never confuse reports with actual observations. You keep slipping into this semantic error and thereby confuse what may be lies or errors with actualities. You do not properly guard against erroneous facts before trying to deal with the dissonances such discordant 'fact' then produced for you."

I regard this comment as indicating the skeptic's desire that I shape my narrative to fit his position. He asks me to stigmatize people reporting their experiences by saying that they "claimed" to report experiences. If a person says, "I saw a ghost," I am supposed to say that the person "reportedly" saw a ghost, instead of writing that the person said, "I saw a ghost." I must imply that the person might be lying. Skeptics request that I use words such as "alleged," "ostensibly," and "reportedly" in order to make inferences regarding false testimony.

7. The formal, "scientific" style appeals to skeptics and irritates believers. One believer writes, "The evidence for PK, remote viewing, telepathy, and clairvoyance abounds, even though each individual case should be considered on its merits. The scientific community still thinks there is little hard evidence, but that position usually reflects unfamiliarity with the facts." This commentator would disagree strongly with the orientation expressed by the skeptic

quoted in the previous footnote.

8. Ectoplasm is a hypothetical substance, accepted as real by Spiritualists, which was thought to extend from mediums in order to produce psychokinetic effects. One believer wished to question whether these "ectoplasmic" threads were visible in Cox's movies since he has not seen them in his own viewing of them. He also expressed concern for the apparent bias that I expressed in the narrative regarding W. Edward Cox. I hope my statements are understood as a record of my thoughts and impressions at the time. I have not seen ectoplasmic threads myself, but I have not viewed all the films, frame-by-frame, as Cox has done.

9. Dr. Richards writes, "I am not a medium any more than everyone is, in the sense that even a turnip may be *somewhat* psychic." W. Edward Cox referred to him as a medium probably because so much allegedly paranormal phenomena seemed to occur around him.

10. W. Edward Cox writes, "The filming was far from 'clumsy.' Only the camera was cheap, but this *per se* can hardly detract at all from its sharply filmed product's quality as evidence." Another believer writes, "If there is evidence of trickery, it ought to be exposed. If not, it should not be implied." I provide this text to portray my own opinion at the time. For Cox's rebuttal, see his comments in Appendix A and also Cox (2004).

11. A believer writes, "I have yet to find anyone who will even seriously attempt to explain how the Zener cards could be made to move as rapidly as they do on film, how balloons could be made to inflate and deflate smoothly by single frame photography. It takes 15 minutes to take the ML [mini-lab] apart and put it back together for every 1/16 second of the film. Then there is the task of inflating and tying balloons with just the right volume of air, placing them in the precise position for the next photos, etc., linking and unlinking the rings, and causing them to disappear—all with limited and crude equipment that was available to Cox." The parapsychologist George Hansen (1985) does not perceive that faking the films would be as difficult as this believer thinks. Some parapsychologists speculated that the glass back of the aquarium could be removed.

12. One believer apparently took Michael's anecdotal report (which I have modified for conciseness) quite seriously and wrote a letter to me demanding to know why everyone was not searched and questioned. He felt someone should have attempted to prove that this event was paranormal. We might note a pattern regarding belief in anecdotal claims: believers find anecdotal evidence to be very important; skeptics regard these reports as of little value.

These attitudes were encountered by psychical investigators even in the 1800s. For example, in 1886 William James (1961) published his first evaluation of the medium Mrs. Piper. He notes: "The ordinary disbeliever rules out all hearsay evidence in advance. The believer accepts far too much of it because he knows that some of it is good."

Chapter 2

1. My colleague probably felt an emotion similar to the one I experienced while speaking with Ed Cox. People are uncomfortable dealing with stigmatized topics, and as a result I began to conceal my sociological investigation of psychic cases from all but my closest friends. Goffman (1963) discusses how people with stigmatized attributes tend to integrate their personality around the feature in question. *The Entity Letters* portrays this process. I was investigating something unacceptable/stigmatized/unbelievable.

2. Commentators reacting to Richards' hypothesis regarding Three-Times-Three portray divergent assumptions. One believer writes: "There is no more evidence that the phenomenon Three-Times-Three is tied to Ed Cox's subconscious than that it is some independent force that manifests in connection with Cox." The writer suggested that all raps are produced by discarnate spirits. Another believer pointed out that a demonic spirit connected to the moon in the Cabala—which has 333 as its symbol and is linked to wild sexual fantasy—is connected to Three-Times-Three. My experiences, over many years, lead me to believe that Three-Times-Three acts as Cox's agent.

3. The story of Cox's car was followed by an ironic incident. "That car event should not be considered evidential," Tom Richards later told me. "Cox had an old car. He might have been mistaken." During the years with Tom Richards, there were many times when he demonstrated more skepticism than all other believers. At the same time, he was furious when skeptics failed to show an open mind regarding the psychic phenomena that surrounded him.

4. Many commentators asked that changes be made in the text so that descriptions of psychical cases in this book would better fit their beliefs. Cox's discussion of spiritualist phenomena triggered criticism by both believers and skeptics. Cox requested that I modify his original statement to say that the sisters "reportedly demonstrated" their toe snapping method rather than that they "demonstrated" it. Cox did not believe that the toe snapping exhibition accounted for all the sisters' raps. He believed that that most of their raps were authentic. Skeptics asked that I insert *allegedly* or *reportedly* before all verbs suggesting that someone observed a paranormal event. The person might be

lying, they argued. For an in-depth description of the Spiritualist Era, which includes a discussion of the Fox sisters' case, see Gauld (1968).

5. Psychical researchers frequently observe this pattern: a skeptical witness cannot explain an anomalous event but rejects all paranormal explanations. The witness, over time, decides that a "normal" explanation must exist, even though none seem logical. Some parapsychologists refer to this process as *retrocognitive dissonance*, the tendency for a skeptic, over time, to maintain disbelief (see Nester's comments in Appendix A).

6. Various believers wrote that my use of the word "trickster" was offensive, since I found no evidence that tricks were involved. I continue to use this word to reveal my attitude at the time. Years later, I uncovered evidence regarding fraud.

7. Social interaction reinforces the effects of personal experience. William James (1961: J43-145) made similar observation regarding his belief in the authenticity of Mrs. Piper's séances in the early 1900s. He stated: "Active relations with a thing are required to bring the reality of it home to us, and in a trance-talk the sitter actively co-operates...it is difficult not to take away an impression of having encountered something sincere in the way of a social phenomenon. The whole talk gets warmed with your own warmth, and takes on the reality of your own part in it... But watching my mind work as it goes over the data, convinces me that exact logic plays only a preparatory part in shaping our conclusions here; and that the decisive vote, if there be one, has to be cast by what I may call one's general sense of dramatic probability, which sense ebbs and flows from one hypothesis to another—it does so in the present writer at least—in a rather illogical manner."

8. One believer suggests that I stress Neihardt's founding and association with SORRAT to a greater extent. Skeptics, who tend to accuse Dr. Richards of fraud, ignore the fact that Neihardt, who no one accused of dishonesty, claimed to have verified, beyond doubt and on occasions when Richards was not present, that the SORRAT phenomena were authentic.

Chapter 3

1. Hodgson (1892) and Hodgson and Davey (1886: 7) published studies that are often quoted as grounds for rejecting anecdotal evidence from the séance room. Interestingly, after publishing these studies, R. Hodgson investigated Mrs. Piper, a medium who had convinced William James of her authenticity. Hodgson also found her paranormal abilities to be authentic and, unlike James, came to believe in life after death. After Hodgson's death in 1905,

an "entity" who claimed to be Hodgson began speaking through Mrs. Piper while she was in trance. William James conducted a lengthy investigation of the case. Although he was not convinced that Hodgson's spirit actually spoke through Mrs. Piper, he felt he had gained information paranormally (James, 1909, 1961).

2. One reader comments, "Isotonic contraction, in which flexor and abductor muscles are set in firm opposition to each other, can result in fairly rapid tremors of the hand and fingers. It may very well be that this effect is considerably enhanced in altered states." The reader infers that unconscious muscular movement *could* create all table tipping phenomena—yet this argument is absurd since some phenomena involve levitations. The reader also ignores my argument that "something highly unusual was occurring, at least from a social-psychological standpoint." Doesn't isotonic contraction in trance seem unusual?

3. Although cognitive dissonance theory (Festinger, 1957, 1974) has gone out of fashion among sociologists, it is supported by a long tradition of field research (Lecky, 1945; Heider, 1946, 1958; Newcomb, 1961). Cognitive dissonance refers to the unease or discomfort that an individual feels when he or she attempts to harbor conflicting ideas or attitudes. Individuals seek a balance between their attitude toward another individual and their perception of that individual's attitudes. People also seek to harmonize their own beliefs with their perceptions of phenomena bearing on those beliefs. They sometimes change their beliefs to coincide with that of others as a means of reducing cognitive dissonance. The theory has been subject to severe criticism (Chapanis and Chapanis, 1960; Truzzi, 1973) and numerous restrictions (Krauss and Critchfield, 1975; Levinger, 1972). I use the term, cognitive dissonance only in a broad sense, hoping to harmonize with the entire sociological tradition surrounding it. Although I did not conduct a formal test of cognitive dissonance theory, I pondered it during this phase of the field study. I include endnotes regarding cognitive dissonance and other sociological analysis that reflect my way of thinking during this era.

4. Barnouw (1942, 1975: 257-58), Hallowell (1934, 1942), Hultkrantz (1992: 31-39), Kalweit (1992: 156-161), Landes (1968).

5. Richards (1982). Although I tape recorded this and many other conversations, the text is not an exact version of the tape recording. Events were described and arranged in a way that allows narrative flow between scenes. Although the narrative is based on field notes, audio recordings, and photographs, text has been edited to increase literary quality.

6. One aspect of role playing requires explaining the belief system to outsiders. This can be particularly effective in modifying the actor's beliefs in situations where he or she receives little reward (Festinger, 1971).

7. Later I mentioned to Ed Cox that this effect could have been done with magnets and a metallic object inside the clay cube. Cox stated that he had formed the clay cube and built and sealed the box so that it could not be duplicated by a cheater. He stated that on the occasions when he was present at Skyrim, he was certain that fraud was not a valid hypothesis explaining the effect.

8. Experts in hypnosis note that it is difficult to determine by observation whether a person's trance is authentic or not (Shor and Orne, 1965). Based on my own experience with trance phenomena among shamans in Asia, I would argue that Joe was in trance, but see Park's comments in Appendix A.

9. Dennis Stillings attended a SORRAT session at Skyrim in October 1983 and simulated the earthquake effect while he was there. He writes: "The earthquake effect is very easy to achieve by flexing the knees and rolling on the balls of one's feet. The curious thing is that both Tom and Ed Cox deny that this is possible. They deny it with such conviction that I even have a certain cognitive dissonance regarding whether I did it or not!" Loren Parks, who also attended this session, writes that he actually saw Tom Richards produce the effect (see Appendix A). When confronted with this information, Tom replied that he had no knowledge of creating the earthquake effect but that he had been merely trying to go along with the flow of the vibration. Some of those attending the session suggest that Tom created the effect while in trance, since photographs of him taken soon afterward show his eyes in an unusual, unfocused condition. I revisited Skyrim Farm during the summer of 1986 and attempted to produce the earthquake effect by flexing my knees in the same room that I had experienced it before. I found that, although I could cause the room to vibrate slightly, no 60 second "earthquake effect" occurred. When two people jumped up and down as vigorously as possible (one of whom weighed more than me), we caused objects in the room to shake. I am uncertain as to how I should evaluate my Skyrim earthquake experience. The phenomena during the group session differed from what I was able to create later, but the skeptical position remains possible.

10. The sociologist Emile Durkheim (1995) suggested that religion originated through group emotional excitement. He hypothesized that primitive people failed to recognize their feeling of group rapport and attributed it to a supernatural source. He suggested that religions are a way of symbolically

worshipping one's own collectivity, an action that helps hold society together. Durkheim's theory explains why a society's religion tends to reflect the populace's social structure. I hypothesize that PK experiences (associated with rapport) contributed to religious sentiment. Within primitive cultures, the raps would be treated as real, just as happened within SORRAT.

11. Many parapsychologists consider this issue to be beyond scientific resolution. William James (1961: 147) noted that, "I myself can perfectly well imagine spirit agency, and find my mind vacillating about it curiously." In 1907, he wrote: "My state of mind is this: Mrs. Piper has supernormal knowledge in her trances; but whether it comes from 'tapping the minds' of living people, or from some common cosmic reservoir of memories, or from surviving 'spirits' of the departed, is a question impossible for me to answer just now to my own satisfaction. The spirit theory is undoubtedly not only the most natural, but the simplest.... [yet] the electric current called belief has not yet closed in my mind" (James 1961: 112,113). In a later report published in 1909, James (1961: 145) writes: "The common-sense rule of presumption in scientific logic is never to assume an unknown agent where there is a known one, and never to choose a rarer cause for a phenomenon when a commoner one will account for it....Our rule of presumption should lead us then to deny spirits and to explain the Piper phenomena by mixture of fraud, subconscious personation, lucky accident, and telepathy, whenever such an explanation remains possible." James goes on in this same report to note that acceptance of the life-after-death hypothesis is not necessarily illogical, when one considers the exceptional aspects of the evidence. For a review of modern evidence, see Gauld (1977, 1983) and Solomon and Solomon (1999), who describe the Scole Experiment that includes much macro PK phenomena.

12. One commentator regards this as a key passage indicating the cult-like nature of SORRAT, which he considers dangerous. He writes: "After the skeptical flag-waving of the first portion of the book, you go on to abandon your critical faculties to a rather considerable extent... and it becomes apparent to all that you have given yourself to the thrall of the 'entities.' No one is going to believe you haven't turned into a raving occultist!"

SORRAT can be classified as a cult using any of various sociological definitions (Glock and Stark, 1965: 245; Lofland, 1977, 1; Wallis, 1976) since it is a "little group" that has broken off from the "conventional consensus" and espouses a very different view of the "real, the possible, and the moral" (Lofland, 1977: 1). Bainbridge and Stark (1980) would classify SORRAT as an "client cult' since it dispenses magical services and therapy. Other sociologists have studied far more deviant groups than SORRAT. Leon Festinger and his associates (1955) huddled in the cold one evening with the UFO cult they were observing, waiting for flying saucers to arrive. How lucky they were that they did not actually see a UFO!

Chapter 4

1. Litvag (1972) supplies examples of Patience Worth's writing. The word "dulcitte" should be translated as "sweet."

2. Padre Pio of Pietrelcina, the religious name of Francesco Forgione (1887-1968), was an Italian Capuchin friar. He ostensibly performed miracles, suffered from Christ's stigmata, and was seen to be at two places at the same time on various occasions (Carty, 1955; Ruffin, 1982).

3. Gauld (1968), Nicol (1977), Rogo (1975); Brown (1972) suggests that some of the Davenport brothers' phenomena may have been authentic. Nickell (2001), a skeptic, discusses this case.

4. Nicol (1977: 313). This incident hints that the PK may control the medium, causing fraud (Feilding, 1963). Alvarado (1987) furnishes many references regarding Palladino's séances.

5. Prince (1929), Litvag (1972), Wiseman (2011).

6. William James (1961: 115, 117) summarizes his opinions regarding Rector and the Imperator Group in a report published in 1909: "Dr. Hodgson [the primary investigator for the American Society for Psychical Research] was disposed to admit the claim to reality of Rector and the whole Imperator Band of which he is a member, while I have rather favored the idea of their all being dream-creations of Mrs. Piper, probably having no existence except when she is in trance, but consolidated by repetition into personalities consistent enough to play their several roles. Such at least is the dramatic impression that my acquaintance with the sittings has left on my mind. I can see no contradiction between Rector's being on the one hand an improvised creature of this sort, and his being on the other hand the extraordinarily impressive personality that he unquestionably is. He has marvelous discernment of the inner states of the sitters whom he addresses, and speaks straight to their troubles as if he knew them all in advance. He addresses you as if he were the most devoted of your friends. He appears like an aged, and, when he speaks instead of writing, like a somewhat hollow-voiced clergyman, a little weary of his experience of the world, endlessly patient and sympathetic, and desiring to put all his tenderness and wisdom at your service while you are there. Critical and fastidious sitters have recognized his wisdom, and confess their debt to him as a moral

adviser. With all due respect to Mrs. Piper, I feel very sure that her own waking capacity for being a spiritual adviser, if it were compared with Rector's, would fall greatly behind.

"As I conceive the matter, it is on this mass of secondary and automatic personality of which in later years Rector has been the center, and that forms the steady background of Mrs. Piper's trances, that the supernormal knowledge that she unquestionably displays is flashed. Flashed, grafted, inserted—use what word you will—the trance automatism is at any rate the intermediating condition, the supernormal knowledge comes as if from beyond, and the automatism uses its own forms in delivering it to the sitter."

7. The incongruence illustrated by SORRAT events is typical of patterns found in previous psychical research cases. Mediums such as Eusapia Palladino, Mina Crandon, and H. P. Blavatsky displayed similar irregularities. For example, Mme. H.P. Blavatsky, founder of the Theosophical Society, generated a social movement that perhaps best illustrates the SORRAT prototype. Letters, allegedly written by spirits, fell from the ceiling during some of her séances. Other spirit letters supposedly apported to her friends. Blavatsky was also the center of an amazing array of psychic experiences. Dr. Richard Hodgson, a member of the newly founded Society for Psychical Research, was sent to India to investigate. Although he concluded that she was "one of the most accomplished, ingenious, and interesting impostors in history" (Report, 1885: 207), her followers refused to accept his devastating analysis; even today, some question Hodgson's honesty and skill as an investigator (Harrison, 1985).

Solomon and Solomon (1999) describe the Scole Experiment, a modern Spiritualist group reporting anomalous sounds, lights, and other forms of psychokinesis within séance environments. The phenomena, which included direct writing, were parallel to SORRATs in being robust and emotionally compelling, yet not verified sufficiently to sway skeptics.

8. Keene (1976) and Randi (1982) describe many tricks used by mediums. A believer takes issue with my comments about mediumship in this section and writes: "I have heard the explanation of the 'one-ahead' trick and grant that it may well explain *some* of the blindfolded medium acts, but I have also seen cases where specific and precise information was given that had to be picked up clairvoyantly or telepathically, and in some cases the person present did not know the information (such as the whereabouts of a son) that later turned out to be accurate."

9. Like most of the conversations in this book, my interview with James Randi has been condensed. For a more complete description of Randi's meth-

ods for testing table-tippers and his tests of some in Italy, see his book *Flim-Flam!* (Randi, 1982). Various commentators expressed irritation that I did not condemn Randi in some manner. Many parapsychologists regard him with extreme hostility. For example, one writer states: "I would not dignify Randi by calling him a *skeptic*. He is what I call an *explainologist*, one who does not seek valid alternative explanations, but whose real business is to *contrive* explanations, a talent that requires special skill, perhaps, but a skill wholly unrelated to the process of intellectually sound scientific inquiry." As might be inferred from Randi's comments, he holds many parapsychologists in equally low regard.

10. For discussions by others of this incident, see Richards (1982, 1983) and Phillips (1984). Shaw's description of Richard's alleged cheating was the first of various accusations of fraud against Tom Richards that have been brought to my attention over the years.

Chapter 5

1. One believer expressed anger, at this point, that I would not affirm my complete faith that I had witnessed a paranormal event. He considers the electromagnet theory to be ridiculous.

2. One skeptic expressed concern that I allow people to say that they saw paranormal events, rather than saying that they *reported that they saw* these events. I write, "John told me that he…" and apparently I am supposed to say "John reported that he…." Later, I quote John's exact words, but the skeptic demands that I insert "John reported that…." in place of these quotations. I feel that these requests are silly, but I acknowledge that it is possible to weaken witness statements by inserting words such as "reportedly" or "ostensibly" into their testimony.

3. A skeptical magician pointed out that "when a magician does X, it is frequently reported as K + C where C seems to make the trick K impossible. In reality, X occurred." He criticized me saying, "You take reports at face value, but you do not similarly look at the reports on conjuring effects. Magicians often hear their own effects described by laymen in ways that would preclude the actual methods they used."

The magician's comments are important for parapsychologists to ponder, but as a sociologist, I do not find them meaningful. If people believe that K + C occurred, the event will affect their beliefs, and folk traditions will emerge. Shamanic practitioners will do "X" as a method of inducing placebo and hypnotic effects. John's beliefs were affected by his experiences.

4. One believer who was present at this event states, "To me, the laughter that occurred when the audience saw the sorted ESP cards suddenly jump into the sealed packet suggests astonishment and complete lack of information about the mini-lab experiments, and about how such feats would have to be done normally." A controversy between Dr. J. T. Richards and D. Scott Rogo later arose regarding the nature of this laughter (see Rogo's comments and Cox's comments on the other commentators in Appendix A). I found the images absurd—something that could not be accepted at face value because it looked like stop-action photography.

5. One believer writes: "The remark that someone should go to Missouri 'to catch whoever is fooling poor old Ed' is certainly neither scientific nor open-minded. It implies that it *must* be trickery, rather than considering *both* paranormality and trickery as possible explanations."

6. Dr. J. T. Richards taught in a high school in Snowflake, AZ (1962-65), returned to Columbia, MO (1965-67), accepted a job as a college instructor at Southeast Missouri State University in Cape Girardeau, MO (1967-71). During that era, he organized SORRAT meetings that generated extremely robust PK experiences among participants. A professional anthropologist writes: "Probably the most significant experience obtained was the awareness that phenomena could be produced by the group, seemingly at will. Most importantly, I think, levitation and 'raps' were produced when fakery was impossible—outdoors in full sunlight. I observed that certain individuals strongly influence the psi phenomena. These individuals possess remarkable abilities. I am convinced that such individuals act as a sort of battery within the psi group." Other respondents argued that professional magicians must not be able to duplicate outdoor raps in full sunlight, or else they would do so in order to make money.

7. If King's birth-year is 1637, his age listed on the questionnaire (completed in late 1980) was incorrect. I wrote him asking for a resolution of this discrepancy and he replied: "When you have celebrated as many birthdays as I have, you will probably gleek the reason why such errors occur. Besides, mathematics was never one of my specialties. The *date* is correct enough, methinks: July 25, 1637. That seems right."

Chapter 6

1. John King refers to the magician James Randi.

2. The SORRAT entities (or whoever writes their messages) periodically engage in fraud. Parapsychologists at the Foundation for Research in the Na-

ture of Man found that someone using entity handwriting tampered with a sealed ESP deck in a manner that implies fraud. The entities have periodically revealed that they use fraud, saying that this supports belief. They asked post-masters to cancel stamps at distant places—with the inference that the letter was teleported while, in fact, it went through the mail in the normal manner. The clumsy manner of mailing (in which the address label fell off) implied that the entities wanted to be caught cheating. Segments of the mini-lab films have single frames that show no blurring at the object edges, inferring use of stop action photography. Steven Calvin describes this problem in his comments (Appendix A) but he also mentions features that preclude fraud. Cox told me that his analysis of each frame in the films shows instances of an object disappearing for a frame and then appearing in the next frame, as if the films were produced by stop action photography (an argument he feels he can refute). A trickster wishing to not be caught would not engage in that behavior. Overall, the evidence does not prove that the films were produced fraudulently but implies that whoever generates the phenomena has a self-defeating quality—he/she wants to be caught cheating. The trickster reveals his tricks—parallel to the way that Tom and Elaine push the table around without concern that people will see them doing this. Richards (1984) published an article in which he argues that artifact induction facilitates PK. "It works for some groups," he told me.

3. Houdini (1953), Christopher (1975), Tietze (1973), Jaher (2015).

4. A believer responded, stating that anecdotal observations, although of a different quality from experimental data, are acceptable and must be evaluated scientifically. Cox (1984) eventually presented a paper at a Parapsychological Association meeting in 1983, amid much controversy.

5. Ed Cox wrote me stating that George has exaggerated the appearance of fraud. Cox states: "The fact is that the FRMM test package containing the deck had been slit open and very crudely resealed. The 'solvent' notion might not be correct and is relatively insignificant considering the outright crudity of the resealing. I observed this when it arrived, being in the FRNM mail room myself at that moment."

6. One reader comments: "I used to clean museum display cases with a soft cloth and became utterly amazed at the effects on paper and silk objects within the case. This influence could extend to several inches." A believer expressed the opinion that the mini-lab results could not be produced normally.

Chapter 7

1. There was huge variation in attitude toward the entity letters—from great enthusiasm to extreme criticism. For example, after I shared *The Entity Letters* manuscript with a skeptical observer, he responded: "The enthusiastic overuse of the entity letters is not only boring—in an otherwise very upbeat account—it indicates commitment to the messages, which are by and large, just plain dumb…The best evidence that something fishy is going on is the exaggerated importance given to the utterances of the entities. Surely no one in his right mind could assign more than an extremely limited value to this drivel. I therefore suggest that SORRAT psyches have been modified to ooh and ah at this BS. The critical functions have been blitzed—a good first stage in the Program." The repetitious nature and limited range of entity communications seems characteristic of trance messages cross-culturally (Jordan and Overmyer, 1986), and psychical researchers over the decades have been plagued by boredom because of this. William James, for example, (1961: 111) noted in 1906 that the Piper investigations had begun to bore him to extinction.

2. Fodor (1961), Gomez (1987).

3. I have found that readers' perceptions of the aesthetic quality of the entities writing tend to coincide with their evaluation of its ideological importance. One commentator refused to read any further, stating that these messages were unbearably boring and trite. Another writes: "I have been quite impressed with some of the things that happened in Rolla and with some of the answers that were given by the various entities. The majority of them don't seem to be very different from the answers one might receive using an Ouija board or during a séance."

4. Bucke (1969).

5. Zukav (1979).

6. Huxley (1945).

7. One believer expressed anger that I suggested such a "preposterous" explanation. "How can one seriously entertain the notion that wires could cause a back-and-forth movement (push and pull) without this being detected?" he writes. I could argue that electromagnetic impulses might create the motion, but I cannot specify the precise mechanism. I believe that anomalous forces were most likely paranormal, but I could not say that with certainty. I find it strange that believers and skeptics grow angry when someone expresses an opinion that does not coincide with their opinion exactly.

8. One commentator argues that the entities are demonic. He points out that Tom and Elaine Richards suffered various accidents and medical ailments

during a period following my study (1984-85). He believes that this may have been a direct result of their occult activities. He writes: "It appears to me that it is grossly unwarranted to assume that these phenomena do not in any way involve the psyches and bodies of those who participate in the phenomena. When I first attended a SORRAT séance, I felt the initial raps very distinctly in my chest. I also wish to draw your attention to the fact that, in 'the old days,' those who summoned the spirits outlined the most elaborate precautions to *protect themselves*." Tom and Elaine feel that their temporary medical problems have normal explanations and medical doctors agree with them.

After reading this endnote, the same commentator states: "You fail to discuss the seriousness of the 'various accidents and medical ailments' suffered by Tom and Elaine. You convey to the reader that these were minor complaints typically occurring within a family as part of the routine of living. You further depreciate this aspect by calling Tom Richards' near-fatal attack of bleeding ulcers and Elaine's cancer 'temporary medical problems.' Your comments in this note look like nothing less than a cover-up. You have put yourself into the heroic position I can best characterize as parallel to investigating a group of hashish-smokers as they overindulge themselves in a nearly airtight room. You may not be wholly participating in their practices, but soon the smoke would draw you into a state of rapport that would drastically compromise your perception of the situation. Aesthetic and moral relativism are simply catalytic agents that serve to suck the unwary into self-destructive rationalization."

Although Tom and Elaine claim to be in good health at present (1995), Ivan experienced medical difficulties in 1995. I concur to a degree with some aspects of this observer's analysis. Psychical research may involve physiological or psychological peril.

My research has harmed my academic career, but it does not seem to have harmed me physically. The hashish-smoker condition is a common problem among participant-observers. Sociologists and anthropologists sometimes are accused of "going native"—a condition that distorts their perceptions. On the other hand, there is something gained from understanding natives—and "going native" enhances that understanding (Tedlock, 1991). I attempt portray the SORRAT atmosphere as I felt it. During my early investigation of SORRAT, I was deeply puzzled by my experiences but have become more detached through engaging in other projects. I do not expect to gain resolution to questions regarding the authenticity of paranormal events.

Chapter 8

1. A skeptical magician comments that only magicians can state which events might be produced by fraud. Ironically, even a magician cannot make this distinction since another magician might devise a trick with a "solution" unknown to the first one. Following this logic, no one can claim that an event exceeds what can be produced by fraud—but many people make such claims and these stories generate folk religious beliefs, according to my theory.

2. Later, I learned that this was not the case. In an article about artifact induction, Richards (1984) infers that he sometimes cheats (see Rogo's comments in Appendix A). Many people, including myself, have photographs of Tom holding a table up in the air with his thumb under an edge of the table. Tom considers these images to be artifacts—but not cheating. He writes: "Try keeping your fingers on the edge of a table for half an hour, and see what your thumb does. Then raise the table into the air, and see what the thumb does even if it puts no pressure on the tabletop to hold it up." Tom states quite vehemently that all the accusations of fraud that I review in this book are slanderous, that he did not tamper with FRNMs envelopes, bend spoons, or make raps fraudulently in the McDonnell laboratory, or write entity letters at any time. He considers those who claim otherwise to be liars. I have discussed cheating with Tom Richards on various occasions, and he has always denied cheating, but sometimes his denial seems to involve a kind of dissociation since he ignores aspects that refute his arguments. He fails to recognize others' logical concern regarding ambiguous information.

3. A skeptic writes: "I think that what you largely ignore is parsimony. Although two theories (skeptical and paranormal) both 'explain' the facts, they are not really on an even footing. Exceptional claims require exceptional proofs. Although the scientist must be agnostic when it comes to loose ends, this does not mean that he is neutral. It means that he makes his judgments on a probabilistic basis that is essentially conservative and which places the burden of proof on the claimant rather than the one who fails to accept the claim." This skeptic does not grasp what I am saying in my narrative. His argument works for skeptics, but I portray an inner process in which I have become less of a skeptic. He seems to say, "Don't become less skeptical," but I argue that exposure to many anomalous experiences makes a person less skeptical because the anomalous gradually becomes less anomalous. Like he says, it is a matter of probability.

4. One believer argues that my belief is rational. He cites anecdotal evidence from the Spiritualist era to the present supporting his claims. I un-

derstand his position but think personal factors play an important role in developing belief. It is not completely rational. William James (1961), whose investigation of Mrs. Piper produced far better evidence than mine, recognized that his knowledge of her personality and character contributed to his belief in her authenticity. James (1961: 210) described Mrs. Piper's spiritual entities as "valued friends," a result, undoubtedly, of his long interaction with them.

5. A hardcore believer expressed alarm that I included this interaction between John and me. He was afraid that readers would not realize that we were joking. We see much of SORRAT phenomena as "funny," while he regards it as proof of life after death.

6. A believer writes: "You have not presented any evidence that Richards is cheating or that Cox is in collusion with him. Who, besides the confessed fraud James Randi has said that they observed Tom Richards cheating? Randi is an admitted charlatan. No one has ever found that Masuaki has a slit in his shoe that allows him to twist spoons."

But I have uncovered accusations of fraud. See comments in Appendix A by Rogo, Parks, and Hansen.

7. Batcheldor (1966, 1979) presents a similar hypothesis. Many anecdotal accounts support this argument. Seeing an event that seems paranormal can stimulate sufficient belief, generating paranormal experiences, particularly among children. For example, Dennis Stillings states that his 12-year-old stepdaughter and various other children bent spoons paranormally after witnessing others do it. Miller (1978) and Schmidt (1978) discuss "observational" theories, the idea that observers affect parapsychological experiments. Some of those theories include the concept that PK can affect past, present, and future events and that events in the future can affect the present. Because skepticism regarding PK is more prevalent than belief, skeptics in the future may thwart present PK.

8. This idea could be compared to Sheldrake's (1981) "morphic resonance" theory. He hypothesized that the behaviors of living organisms are shaped by morphogenic fields. The forms and behaviors of past organisms of the same species are shaped by the form and behaviors of past organisms of the same species. The morphogenic fields, created by past forms and behaviors, have properties that transcend space and time.

Chapter 9

1. A skeptic writes: "I frankly do not believe you actually saw what you believe took place, but I cannot prove that any more than you can prove it

did. Having been at spoon-bending parties where people thought stuff was bending when I could see it was not, I conjecture that you were responding to suggestion rather than objective reality." For a first-hand report of a metal-bending incident similar to the one I describe, see Stillings (1985). I wrote Steve Shaw, Mike Edwards, and James Randi a number of times, seeking explanations about how a magician might have accomplished the phenomenon I witnessed. Shaw and Edwards have not responded. Randi tells me that if an investigator photographs a spoon and then does not allow the metal bender to touch it, it will not bend. See endnote 3 for a discussion of photography and bending.

2. In early 1984, Fuji Television aired a program in which Masuaki Kiyota seemed to confess to fraud (Stevenson, et al., 1985). Masuaki later told me that he was framed and that he did not confess (Uphoff, 1987). This controversy seems similar to those surrounding mediums of earlier eras. For example, the Fox sisters, whose poltergeist phenomena launched the Spiritualist movement, confessed to fraud and later retracted their statement. See comments by Cole and Cox in Appendix A.

3. I might have modified my conclusions if I had not met people who had also seen metal bending without touching (Stillings, 1985, for example). Over the years, I have spoken with many people who have witnessed bending without touching and bending in their own hands. Dr. Sonji Otani, of the Japanese Society for Parapsychology in Tokyo, conducted extensive investigations of Masuaki Kiyota's paranormal abilities. He showed me videotapes of Masuaki Kiyota bending spoons without touching them, under experimentally controlled conditions. The images are equivalent to what I observed in Wisconsin. In order to preclude fraud, we would want to see the preparations for the experiment; perhaps the spoons had been modified. In 1986, scientists in the People's Republic of China told me of similar experiences: Drs. Chen Shou Liang, (Director of the Natural Science Division at Beijing University), Lin Shu Huang (Beijing Normal Institute), Hsu Hung Chang (Institute of High Energy Physics), and Zheng Rongliang (Director of the Department of Biology, Lanzhou University). They described videotapes of incidents that were equivalent to Cox's mini-lab films of PK. Maintaining one's belief in anomalous phenomena depends, in part, on meeting people with equivalent experiences.

Appendix A

1. Author's note: One respondent to my mail survey of SORRAT members reported seeing a similar incident. She states: "I believe that most of J. T. Richards' experiments with raps and table levitations are authentic. However, I believe I have seen him tap his foot to imitate raps on a few occasions (Tom's 'raps' may be subconscious). I have never confronted him on this, as we are friends, I do watch him most carefully during experiments because of this and am convinced that most phenomena are genuine."

2. A degree of "fishiness" seems associated with virtually all major macro PK cases. When I discussed the Bayless séance with Dr. Richards (previous to his published account of it), he claimed that the entities furnished remarkable evidence for survival after death and implied that Raymond Bayless was troubled by this. I think this was a fabrication. In his article, Dr. Richards (1984) states that fraud is an effective method for stimulating authentic PK, but he does not explain how he became an expert in artifact induction. On some occasions, he has tried to conceal his misrepresentations, implying that he is aware of self-fraud. On one occasion, he obtained a copy of *The Entity Letters* manuscript, removed the sections from Appendix A that refer to his fraudulent activities (including Rogo's and Park's comments), and submitted the manuscript to a trade publisher in a manner that caused them to believe it had been sent by me!

I have encountered similar "fishiness" in all claimed macro PK cases that I have investigated. Although Filipino psychic surgeons, folk healers, and shamans throughout Asia *claim* no awareness that they practice trickery, I believe some are aware. They complain of inner stress as a result. Investigations of Uri Geller and Masuaki Kiyota produce similar "ambiguous" evidence. Geller proclaims that he *never* uses trickery, but Emery (1987) provides photographs supporting the charge that Geller cheats. On a Japanese TV program, Masuaki Kiyota admitted to cheating, but later said he had been framed and that his statements had been edited in a manner distorting their meaning (Stevenson, et al., 1985; Uphoff, 1987).

3. Robert Hedges, an expert from the Oxford University Research Laboratory for Archaeology and the History of Art, holds the opinion that these rings were linked normally. In a letter to Beloff dated October 14, 1985, he notes that one corner of the thicker ring had various suspicious attributes. It was 0.8 mm. thinner than the rest of the ring; it had breaks in the surface layer; it was stained in a way that is consistent with the theory that its glue had been dissolved by steaming or a solvent. He states: "My explanation would be that one

corner was steamed and softened; that the lamiae were split from each other and broken in somewhat different places, partly because the break would be along the grain; that the second, thinner ring was inserted through the bent back laminae; and that the whole was re-glued, in a vice, thinning the plywood at that point, and that the inside edge was then re-cut; to removing protruding laminae. He states that he cannot verify this hypothesis without dissecting the layers of plywood. The rings were returned to Cox.

4. Jordan and Overmyer (1986: xiii) note the "trite and trivial" content of Taiwanese séance writing. The UFO expert John Keel (1975: 148) writes: "The messages received by psychics everywhere bear remarkable similarities in content, even in phrasing. I have researched obscure contactee-type books written two and three hundred years ago and have found the same identical messages and phraseology were prevalent then. Since much of this literature is very obscure and hard to find, and since many of our psychics and contactees are poorly read, it is doubtful if this is of fakers repeating the earlier material. Rather, it seems as if there is a phonograph in the sky endlessly repeating the same material generation after generation as if there were a crack in the record."

ACKNOWLEDGEMENTS

I wish to thank the members of the Society for Research on Rapport and Telekinesis (SORRAT), who shared their experiences with me. I particularly thank John Thomas Richards (1937-2015) and Elaine Richards, whose hospitality and friendship over the years make this study possible. I also wish to thank my wife, Karen Franza McClenon, and Patrick Huyghe for editorial assistance. People contributing to Appendix A gave early feedback regarding the original manuscript. George Hansen and Gerhard Mayer provided suggestions pertaining to the final manuscript. Others, too many to mention, offered counsel on handwriting analysis, trance behavior, and all manner of quirky topics relevant to my investigation.

Chapter 11 of my book *Wondrous Events: Foundations of Religious Belief* (University of Pennsylvania Press, 1994) describes events covered in this book and contains parallel text.

REFERENCES

Alvarado, Carlos S. 1987. "Historical Notes on a Séance with Eusapia Palladino in 1912." *Zetetic Scholar* 12/13: 61-72.

Bainbridge, William Sims and Rodney Shark. 1980. "Client and Audience Cults in America." *Sociological Analysis* 41: 199-214.

Balch, Robert W. and David Taylor. 1977. "Seekers and Saucers: The Role of the Cultic Milieu in Joining a UFO Cult." *American Behavioral Scientist* 20: 839-59.

Barber, Theodore X. 1984. "Changing 'Unchangeable' Bodily Processes by (Hypnotic) Suggestions: A New Look at Hypnosis, Cognitions, Imagining and the Mind-Body Problem." *Advances* 1 (2): 7-40.

Barnouw, Victor. 1942. "Siberian Shamanism and Western Spiritualism." *Journal of the American Society for Psychical Research* 36: 140-68.

Barnouw, Victor. 1975. *An Introduction to Anthropology, Vol. II: Ethnology*. revised ed. Homewood: IL: Dorsey.

Batcheldor, Kenneth J. 1966. "Report on the Case of Table Levitation and Associated Phenomena." *Journal of the Society for Psychical Research* 13: 339-356.

Batcheldor, Kenneth J. 1979. "PK in Sitter Groups." *Psychoenergetic Systems* 3: 77-93.

Batcheldor, Kenneth J. 1984. "Contributions to the Theory of PK Induction from Sitter-Group Work." *Journal of the American Society for Psychical Research* 78: 105-132.

Batcheldor, Kenneth. 2011a. "Table Tipping 1." *YouTube* by evpman. https://www.youtube.com/watch?v=q2eDDP0fHRs

Batcheldor, Kenneth. 2011b. "Table Tipping 2." *YouTube* by evpman. https://www.youtube.com/watch?v=oVqKW8AhnU4

Beloff, John. 1985. "Research Strategies for Dealing with Unstable Phenomena." Pp. 7-8 in *The Repeatability Problem in Parapsychology: Proceedings of an International Conference.* Edited by B. Shapin and L. Coly. New York: Parapsychology Foundation.

Beloff, John. 1993. *Parapsychology: A Concise History.* New York: St. Martin's Press.

Bem, Daryl J. and Charles Honorton. 1994. "Does Psi Exist? Replicable Evidence for an Anomalous Process of Information Transfer." *Psychological Bulletin* 115: 4–18. doi:10.1037/0033-2909.115.1.4

Bouchard, T. J., M. McGue, D. Lykken, and A. Tellegen. 1999. "Intrinsic and Extrinsic Religiousness: Genetic and Environmental Influences and Personality Correlates." *Twin Research* 2: 88-98.

Braud, William G., G. Davis, and R. Wood. 1979. "Experiments with Matthew Manning," *Journal of the Society for Psychical Research* 50: 199-223.

Braude, Stephen E. 2003. *Immortal Remains: The Evidence for Life after Death*, Lanham, MD: Rowman & Littlefield.

Brookes-Smith, Colin. 1973. "Data Tape-Recorded Experimental PK Phenomena." *Journal of the Society for Psychical Research* 47: 73-86.

Brown, Slater. 1972. *The Heyday of Spiritualism.* New York: Pocket Books.

Bucke, Richard M. 1969. *Cosmic Consciousness. A Study in the Evolution of the Human Mind.* New York: Dutton.

Bullough, Vern. 1985. "Spirit Rapping Unmasked: An 1851 Investigation and its Aftermath." *Skeptical Inquirer* 10: 60-67.

Carrington, Hereward and Nandor Fodor. 1953. *The Story of the Poltergeist Down the Centuries*. Rider and Co.

Carty, Charles. 1955. *Padre Pio - The Stigmatist*. St. Paul Minnesota: Radio Replies Press.

Chapanis, Natalia P. and Alphonse Chapanis. 1960. "Cognitive Dissonance: Five Years Later." *Psychological Bulletin* 61: 1-22.

Christopher, Milbourne. 1975. *Mediums, Mystics and the Occult*. New York: Thomas Y. Crowell Company.

Chuang-tzu. 1981. *The Seven Inner Charters and Other Writings from the Book Chuang-tzu*, translated by A. C. Graham. Boston: George Allen and Unwin.

Collins, Harry M. 1975. "The Seven Sexes: A Study in the Sociology of a Phenomenon or the Replication of Experiments in Physics." *Sociology* 9: 205-224.

Collins, Harry M. 1985. *Changing Order: Replication and Induction in Scientific Practice*. Beverly Hills: CA: Sage Publications.

Collins, Harry M. and Trevor J. Pinch. 1982. *Frames of Meaning: The Social Construction of Extraordinary Science*. Boston: Routledge and Regan Paul.

Colvin, Barrie G. 2010. "The Acoustic Properties of Unexplained Rapping Sounds." *Journal of the Society for Psychical Research* 74 (899): 65-93.

Cooper, Gemma and Michael A. Thalbourne. 2005. "McClenon's Ritual Healing Theory: An Exploratory Study." *Journal of Parapsychology* 69: 139-150.

Corcoran, Cheryl, E. Walker, R. Huot, V. Mittal, K. Tessner, L. Kestler, and D. Malaspina, 2003. "The Stress Cascade and Schizophrenia: Etiology and Onset." *Schizophrenia Bulletin* 29: 671-92.

Cox, William Edward. 1981. "Some Exceptional Evidence of Solicited and Recurrent Static Psychokinesis." *Journal of Parapsychology* 45: 159 (abstract).

Cox, William Edward. 1984. "Selected Static-PK Phenomena Under Exceptional Conditions of Security." *Research in Parapsychology, 1983*. Metuchen, NJ: Scarecrow Press.

Cox, William Edward. 1985. "An Invited Rebuttal to George Hansen's 'Critique of Mr. Cox's Mini-lab Experiments.'" *Archaeus* 3: 25-28.

Cox, William Edward. 2004. *Psi Physics: A Scientific Investigation of Recurrent Psychokinesis Related to Dr. Neihardt's SORRAT*. Penobscot, Maine: Penobscot Press.

Durkheim, Emile. 1995 (originally published, 1912). *The Elementary Forms of Religious Life*, translated and with an introduction by Karen E. Fields. New York: Free Press.

Eddy, Sherwood. 1950. *You Will Survive After Death*. New York: Rinehart.

Edwards, Emily. 1993. "Wondrous Events in a Small Group: A Field Study." (video). Greensboro, NC: University of North Carolina, Greensboro.

Emery, C. Eugene, Jr. 1987. "Catching Geller in the Act." *Skeptical Inquirer* 12 (1): 75-80.

Erasmus, Desiderius. 1941. *The Praise of Folly*, translated from the Latin with commentary by Hoyt Hopewell Hudson. New York: The Modern Library.

Fairley, John, and Simon Welfare. 1984. *Arthur C. Clarke's World of Strange Powers*. London: William Collins.

Festinger, Leon. 1957. *A Theory of Cognitive Dissonance*. Evanston: Row Peterson.

Festinger, Leon. 1974. *Conflict, Decision and Dissonance*. Stanford: Stanford University Press.

Festinger, Leon, Henry W. Riecken, and Stanley Schachter. 1956. *When Prophesy Fails: A Social and Psychological Study of a Modern Group That Predicted the Destruction of the World*. New York: Harper and Row.

Feilding, Everard. 1963. *Sittings with Eusapia Palladino and Other Studies*. Introduction by E. J. Dingwall. New Hyde Park, NY: University Books.

Finucane, Ronald C. 1984. *Appearances of the Dead: A Cultural History of Ghosts*. Buffalo, NY: Prometheus Books.

Fisher, Joe. 2001. *The Siren Call of Hungry Ghosts: A Riveting Investigation and Channeling and Spirit Guides*. New York: Paraview Press.

Fodor, Nandor. 1961. *Between Two Worlds*. West Nyack, NY: Parker Publishing Company.

Gallup, George. 1979. *The Gallup Poll. Public Opinion, 1978*. Wilmington, DE: Scholarly Research, Inc.

Gauld, Alan. 1968. *The Founders of Psychical Research*. New York: Schocket.

Gauld, Alan. 1977. "Discarnate Survival." In *The Handbook of Parapsychology*, edited by Benjamin B. Wolman. New York. Van Nostrand Reinhold Company.

Gauld, Alan. 1983. *Mediumship and Survival*. North Pomphrey, VT; David and Charles, Inc.

Gauld, Alan and Anthony D. Cornell. 1979. *Poltergeists*. London, Boston and Henley: Routledge and Regan Paul.

Glock, Charles Y. and Rodney Stark. 1965. *Religion and Society in Tension*. Chicago: Rand McNally.

Goffman, Erving. 1959. *The Presentation or Self in Everyday Life. New York*: Doubleday.

Goffman, Erving. 1963. *Stigma: Notes on the Management of Soiled Identity.* Englewood Cliffs, NJ: Prentice-Hall.

Gomez, Linda. 1987 (March). "8 Great Buried Treasures." *Life*, 29-38.

Goulet, Jean-Guy and David E. Young, eds. 1994. *Being Changed by Cross-Cultural Encounters: The Anthropology of Extraordinary Experience.* Toronto: University of Toronto Press.

Greeley, Andrew M. 1975. *Sociology of the Paranormal: A Reconnaissance.* Beverly Hills: Sage Publications.

Greeley, Andrew M. 1987. "Mysticism Goes Mainstream." *American Health*, Jan./ Feb.: 47-49.

Gregory, Anita. 1985. *The Strange Case of Rudi Schneider.* Metuchen, NJ: Scarecrow Press.

Grosso, Michael. 2016. *The Man Who Could Fly: St. Joseph of Copertino and the Mystery of Levitation.* Lanham, MD: Rowman and Littlefield.

Hallowell, A. Irving. 1934. "Some Empirical Aspects of Northern Salteaux Indians." *American Anthropologist* 36: 389-404.

Hallowell, A. Irving. 1942. *The Role of Conjuring in Salteaux Society.* Philadelphia: University of Pennsylvania Press.

Hansen, George P. 1982. "Review of *SORRAT: A History of the Neihardt Psychokinesis Experiments, 1961-1981* by John Thomas Richards." *Journal of Parapsychology* 46 (4): 373-376.

Hansen, George P. 1985. "A Critique of Mr. Cox's Mini-lab Experiments." *Archaeus* 3: 17-24.

Hansen, George P. 2001. *The Trickster and the Paranormal.* Philadelphia, PA: Xlibris.

Hansen, George P. and Richard S. Broughton. 1983. "An Investigation of Macro-PK: The SORRAT." In *Research in Parapsychology, 1982*, edited by W. G. Roll, J. Beloff, and R. A. White. Metuchen, NJ: Scarecrow Press.

Hansen, George P. and Richard S. Broughton. 1991. "Card-Sorting Tests with SORRAT." *Artifex* 9 (Summer): 19-26, 30.

Harrison, Vernon. 1988. "J'ACCUSE, An Examination of the Hodgson Report of l885." *Journal of the Society for Psychical Research* 53 (803): 236-310.

Healy, Tony and Paul Cooper. 2014. *Australian Poltergeist: The Stone-throwing Spook of Humpty Doo and Many Other Cases*. Sydney: Strange Nation.

Heider, Fritz. 1946. "Attitudes and Cognitive Organization." *Journal of Psychology* 21: 107-112.

Heider, Fritz. 1958. *The Psychology of Interpersonal Relations*. New York: Wiley.

Hitchings, Shirley and James Clark. 2014. *The Poltergeist Prince of London*, Stroud, Gloucestershire: The History Press.

Hobson, J. Allan. 1994. *The Chemistry of Conscious States: How the Brain Changes its Mind*. Boston: Little, Brown.

Hodgson, Richard. 1892. "Mr. Davey's Imitations by Conjuring of Phenomena Sometimes Attributed to Spirit Agency." *Proceedings of the Society for Psychical Research* 8: 253-310.

Hodgson, Richard and S. J. Davey. 1886-87. "The Possibilities of Mal-observation and Lapse of Memory from a Practical Point of View." *Proceedings of the Society for Psychical Research* 4: 381-495.

Houdini, Harry. 1953. *Houdini on Magic*. Edited by Walter B. Gibson and Morris N. Young. New York: Dover Publications.

Houran, James and Rense Lange, eds. 2001. *Hauntings and Poltergeists: Multidisciplinary Perspectives*. Jefferson, NC: McFarland & Company.

Huesmann M. and Friederike Schriever (1989). Steckbrief de Spuks. *Zeilschrift für Parapsychologie und Grenzgebiete der Psychologie* 31: 52-107.

Hufford, David J. 1982. *The Terror That Comes in the Night: An Experience-Centered Study of Supernatural Assault Traditions*. Philadelphia: University of Pennsylvania Press.

Hultkrantz, Ake. 1992. *Shamanic Healing and Ritual Drama: Health and Medicine in Native North American Religious Traditions*. New York: Crossroad Publishing Company.

Hunter, Jack. 2012. *Paranthropology: Anthropological Approaches to the Paranormal*. Bristol, UK: http://paranthropologyjournal.weebly.com.

Hunter, Jack and David Luke. 2014. *Talking with the Spirits: Ethnographies from Between the Worlds*. Brisbane, Australia: Daily Grail Publishing.

Huxley, Aldous, 1945. *The Perennial Philosophy*. New York: Harper and Row.

Hyman, Ray. 1994. "Anomaly or Artifact? Comments on Bem and Honorton." *Psychological Bulletin* 115: 19-24.

Jaher, David. 2015. *The Witch of Lime Street: Séance, Seduction, and Houdini in the Spirit World*. New York: Broadway Books.

James, William. 1909. "Report on Mrs. Piper's Hodgson Control." *Proceedings of the Society for Psychical Research* 21: 2-121.

James, William. 1961a. *The Varieties of Religious Experience: A Study in Human Nature*. London: Collier Books.

James, William. 1961b. *William James on Psychical Research*. Compiled and edited by Gardner Murphy and Robert O. Ballou. London: Chatto and Windus.

Jordan, David K. and Daniel L. Overmyer. 1986. *The Flying Phoenix: Aspects of Chinese Sectarianism in Taiwan*. Princeton, NJ: Princeton University Press.

Kalweit, Holger. 1992. *Shamans, Healers, and Medicine Men*, translated by Michael H. Kohn. Boston: Shambhala.

Keel, John A. 1975. *The Mothman Prophecies*. New York: Dublin and Company.

Keene, M. Lamar (as told to Allen Spraggett). 1976. *The Psychic Mafia*. New York: St. Martin's Press.

Keller, Matthew C. and Geoffrey Miller. 2006. "Resolving the Paradox of Common, Harmful, Heritable Mental Disorders: Which Evolutionary Genetic Models Work Best?" *Behavioral and Brain Sciences* 29: 385-404.

Kennedy, James E. 2003. "The Capricious, Activity Evasive, Unsustainable Nature of Psi: A Summary and Hypothesis." *Journal of Parapsychology* 67: 53-74.

Kennedy, James E. 2004. "The Roles of Religion, Spirituality, and Genetics in Paranormal Beliefs." *Skeptical Inquirer* 28: 39-42.

Kent, James L. 2010. *Psychedelic Information Theory: Shamanism in the Age of Reason*. PIT Press, Seattle, 2010.

Krauss, Herbert H. and Leslee L. Critchfield. 1975. "Contrasting Self-Esteem Theory and Consistency Theory in Predicting Interpersonal Attraction." *Sociometry* 33: 247-260.

Kripal, Jeffrey J. 2014. *Comparing Religions: Coming to Terms*. Malden, MA: John Wiley and Sons.

Landes, Ruth. 1968. *Ojibwa Religion and the Midéwiwin*. Madison: University of Wisconsin Press.

Laursen, Christopher. 2016. *Reimagining the Poltergeist in Twentieth-Century American and Britain*, Doctoral Thesis, University of British Columbia.

Lecky, Prescott. 2015. *Self-Consistency: A Theory of Personality*. New York: Long Island Press.

Lenzenweger, Mark F. 2010. *Schizotypy and Schizophrenia: The View from Experimental Psychology*. New York: Guilford Press.

Leo, Jonathan. 2016. "The Search for Schizophrenia Genes." *Issues in Science and Technology* 23 (2): http://issues.org/32-2/the-search-for-schizophrenia-genes/

Litvag, Irving. 1972. *Singer in the Shadows*. New York: Macmillan Company.

Lofland, John. 1966. *Doomsday Cult*. Englewood Cliffs, NJ; Prentice-Hall.

Lofland, John and Rodney Stark. 1965. "Becoming a World-Saver: A Theory of Conversion to a Deviant Perspective." *American Sociological Review* 30: 862-75.

Long, Joseph K. 1977. *Extrasensory Ecology: Parapsychology and Anthropology*. Metuchen, NJ: Scarecrow Press.

Lucadou, Walter von. 1995. "The Model of Pragmatic Information (MPI)." *European Journal of Parapsychology* 11: 58-75.

Lucadou, Walter von, 2015. "The Model of Pragmatic Information (MPI)." Pp. 221-242 in *Extrasensory Perception: Support, Skepticism and Science, Vol. 2: Theories and Future of the Field*, edited by Edwin C. May and Sonali Marwaha. Santa Barbara, CA: Prager.

Lucadou, Walter von, Hartmann Römer, and Harald Walach. 2007. "Synchronistic Phenomena as Entanglement Correlations in Generalized Quantum Theory." *Journal of Consciousness Studies* 14: 50-74.

Lucadou, Walter von and Franziska Wald. 2014. "Extraordinary Experiences in its Cultural and Theoretical Context." *International Review of Psychiatry* 26: 324-334.

Lucadou, Walter von and Frauke Zahradnik. 2004. "Predictions of the Model of Pragmatic Information about RSPK." Pp. 99-112 in *Proceedings of the 47 Annual Convention of the Parapsychological Association*, 2004, edited by S. Schmidt. Vienna: Parapsychological Association [abstracted in *Journal of Parapsychology* 69: 31-32). http://citeseerx.ist.psu.edu/viewdoc/download?doi=10.1.1.487.246&rep=rep1&type=pdf

Manning, Matthew. 1973. *The Link: The Extraordinary Gifts of a Teenage Psychic*. Gerrards Cross, England: Colin Smythe Ltd.

McClenon, James. 1981 (April). "Future Science: The Possibilities for Parapsychology." paper presented to the Southern Sociological Society, Louisville, KY.

McClenon, James. 1982. "A Survey of Elite Scientists: Their Attitudes Toward ESP and Parapsychology." *Journal of Parapsychology* 16: 127-152.

McClenon, James. 1984. *Deviant Science: The Case of Parapsychology*. Philadelphia: University of Pennsylvania Press.

McClenon, James. 1994. *Wondrous Events: Foundations of Religious Belief*. Philadelphia, PA: University of Pennsylvania Press.

McClenon, James. 1997. "Shamanic Healing, Human Evolution, and the Origin of Religion." *Journal for the Scientific Study of Religion* 36 (3): 345-354.

McClenon, James. 2000. "Content Analysis of an Anomalous Memorate Collection: Testing Hypotheses Regarding Universal Features." *Sociology of Religion* 61: 155-169.

McClenon, James. 2002a. *Wondrous Healing: Shamanism, Human Evolution, and the Origin of Religion*. DeKalb, IL: Northern Illinois University Press.

McClenon, James. 2002b. "Content Analysis of an Anomalous Experience Collection: Evaluating Evolutionary Perspectives." *Journal of Parapsychology* 66: 291-315.

McClenon, James. 2012. "A Community Survey of Psychological Symptoms: Evaluating Evolutionary Theories Regarding Shamanism and Schizophrenia." *Mental Health, Religion & Culture* 15: 799-816.

McClenon, James. 2013. "A Community Survey of Anomalous Experiences: Correlational Analysis of Evolutionary Hypotheses." *Journal of Parapsychology* 77: 55-78.

McCready, William C. and Andrew M. Greeley. 1976. *The Ultimate Values of the American Population*. Beverly Hills, CA: Sage Publications.

Miller, Brian. 1978. "The Observational Theories: A Primer." *European Journal of Parapsychology* 2: 304-332.

Mirowsky, John and Catherine E. Ross. 1989. *Social Causes of Psychological Distress*. New York: Aldine de Gruyter.

Moses, William Stainton. 1976. *Spirit Teachings*. New York: Arno Press.

Neihardt, John G. 1932. *Black Elk Speaks*. New York: William Morrow.

Nickell, Joe. 2001. *Real-Life X-Files: Investigating the Paranormal*. Lexington, KY: University Press of Kentucky.

Nicol, J. Fraser. 1977. "Historical Background." In *Handbook of Parapsychology*, edited by Benjamin B. Wolman. New York: Van Reinhold Company.

Ouellet, Eric. 2015. *Illuminations: The UFO Experience as a Parapsychological Event*. Charlottesville, VA: Anomalist Books.

Owen, Iris M. and Margaret Sparrow. 1979. *Conjuring Up Philip: An Adventure in Psychokinesis*. New York: Harper and Row.

Palmer, John. 1979. "A Community Mail Survey of Psychic Experiences." *Journal of the American Society for Psychical Research* 73: 221-251.

Phillips, Peter R. 1984. "A Note on the 'Sealed Bottle' Events." *Archaeus Newsletter* 3 (3/4): 9.

Phillips, Peter R. 2016. *Companion to the Project Alpha Papers*. Pari, Italy: Pari Publishing.

Phillips, Peter R. and Michael K. McBeath. 1983. "An Attempted Replication of the Cox Films of PK." In *Research in Parapsychology, 1982*, edited by W. G. Roll, J. Beloff and R. A. White. Metuchen, NJ: Scarecrow Press.

Prince, Walter Franklin. 1929. *The Case of Patience Worth*. Boston: Boston Society for Psychical Research.

Randi, James. 1982. *Flim-Flam! Psychics, ESP, Unicorns and Other Delusions*. Buffalo, NY; Prometheus Books.

Randi, James. 1983. "Project Alpha, Parts I and 2." *Skeptical Inquirer* 7 (4) and 8 (1): 24-33; 36-45.

Richards, John Thomas. 1982. *SORRAT: A History of the Neihardt's Psychokinesis Experiments, 1961-1981*. Metuchen, NJ: Scarecrow Press.

Richards, John Thomas. 1983. "The Incident of the Bottled Stickman." *Archaus Newsletter* 2: 9-11.

Richards, John Thomas. 1984 (Sept.). "The Question of Artifact Introduction." *Archaeus Newsletter* 3-7.

Rogo, D. Scott. 1975. *Parapsychology, A Century of Inquiry*. New York; Dell.

Rogo, D. Scott. 1976. *In Search of the Unknown: The Odyssey of a Psychical Researcher*. New York: Taplinger Publishing Company.

Rogo, D. Scott. 1982. *Miracles, A Parascientific Inquiry into Wondrous Phenomena*. New York: Dial Press.

Roll, William G. 1976. *The Poltergeist*. Metuchen, NJ: Scarecrow Press.

Roll, William G. 1977. "Poltergeists." Pp. 382-413 in *The Handbook of Parapsychology*, edited by Benjamin B. Wolman. New York; Van Nostrand. Reinhold.

Ruffin, C. Bernard. 1982. *Padre Pio: The True Story*. Huntington, IN: Our Sunday Visitor.

Schmidt, Helmut. 1978. "Can an Effect Precede Its Cause? A Model of a Non-Causal World." *Foundation of Physics* 8: 463-430.

Sheldrake, Rupert. 1981. *A New Science of Life*. Boston: Houghton Mifflin Company.

Sidgwick, Henry and Committee. 1894. "Report on the Census of Hallucinations." *Proceedings of the Society for Psychical Research* 13: 25-422.

Snow, David A., Louis A. Zurcher, Jr., and Sheldon Ekland-Olson. 1980. "Social Networks and Social Movements: A Microstructural Approach to Differential Recruitment." *American Sociological Review* 45: 787-801.

Solomon, Grant and Jane Solomon. 1999. *The Scole Experiment: Scientific Evidence for Life After Death*. London: Judy Piatkus Publishers.

Spencer, John and Anne. 1996. *The Poltergeist Phenomenon: An Investigation into Psychic Disturbance*. London: Headline Book Publishing.

Stark, Rodney and William Sims Bainbridge. 1980. "Networks of Faith: Interpersonal Bonds and Recruitment to Cults and Sects." *American Journal of Sociology* 85: 1376-1395.

Stevenson, Ian, Emily Williams Cook, Carolee A. Werner, Michael Dennis, H. H. J. Keil, Peter Phillips. 1985. "On Masuaki Kiyota." *Journal of the American Society for Psychical Research* 79 (2): 294-295.

Stillings, Dennis. 1985. "Two Unusual Cases of PKMB." *Artifex* 4 (6): 10-12.

Stillings, Dennis, ed. 1991. *Artifex*. Vol. 9 (Summer). St. Paul, MN: Archaeus Project (articles by Stillings, Hansen and Broughton, Müller, Duke and Hansen, and Richards).

Strieber, Whitley and Jeffrey J. Kripal. 2016. *The Super Natural: A New Vision of the Unexplained*. New York: Jeremy P. Tarcher/Penguin.

Stoller, Paul. 1989. *The Taste of Ethnographic Things: The Senses in Anthropology*. Philadelphia, PA: University of Pennsylvania Press.

Stoller, Paul and Cheryl Olkes. 1987. *In Sorcery's Shadow, A Memoir of Apprenticeship Among the Songhay of Niger*. Chicago: University of Chicago Press.

Tedlock, Barbara. 1991. "From Participant Observation to the Observation of Participation: The Emergence of Narrative Ethnography." *Journal of Anthropological Research* 47: 69-94.

Tietze, Thomas R. 1973. *Margery*. New York: Harper and Row.

Truzzi, Marcello. 1973. "The Problem of Relevance Between Orientations for Cognitive Dissonance Theory." *Journal for the Theory of Social Behavior* 3: 239-247.

Truzzi, Marcello. 1980. "Editorial." *Zetetic Scholar* 6: 3.

Truzzi, Marcello. 1987. "Reflections on Project Alpha: Scientific Experiment or Conjuror's Illusion?" *Zetetic Scholar* 12/13: 73-93.

Turner, Edith. 1992. *Experiencing Ritual: A New Interpretation of African Healing*. Philadelphia, PA: University of Pennsylvania Press.

Turner, Edith. 1993. "The Reality of Spirits: A Tabooed or Permitted Field of Study?" *Anthropology of Consciousness* 4: 9-12.

Uphoff, Walter H. "More on Masuaki Kiyota," *Journal of the American Society for Psychical Research* 81 (1): 87-90.

Walach, Harald, Walter von Lucadou, and Hartmann Römer. 2014. "Parapsychological Phenomena as Examples of Generalized Nonlocal Correlations - A Theoretical Framework." *Journal of Scientific Exploration* 28: 605-631.

Webster, Ken. 1989. *The Vertical Plane: The Mystery of the Dodleston Messages - A Bizarre Record of Communication Through Time*. London: Grafton Books.

Wiseman, Richard. 2011. *Paranormality: Why We See What Isn't There*. London, UK: Pan Macmillan.

Young, David E., and Jean-Guy Goulet. 1994. *Being Changed by Cross-Cultural Encounters: The Anthropology of Extraordinary Experience*. Toronto: University of Toronto Press.

Zukav, Gary, *The Dancing Wu Li Masters*. New York: Morrow, 1979.

INDEX

Lightning Source UK Ltd.
Milton Keynes UK
UKHW020642210819
348299UK00010B/2581/P